A UNIVERSAL APPEARANCE OF WAR

The Revolutionary War in Virginia, 1775–1781

Michael Cecere

HERITAGE BOOKS
2014

HERITAGE BOOKS
AN IMPRINT OF HERITAGE BOOKS, INC.

Books, CDs, and more—Worldwide

For our listing of thousands of titles see our website
at
www.HeritageBooks.com

Published 2014 by
HERITAGE BOOKS, INC.
Publishing Division
5810 Ruatan Street
Berwyn Heights, Md. 20740

Copyright © 2014 Michael Cecere

Heritage Books by the author:

A Universal Appearance of War: The Revolutionary War in Virginia, 1775–1781

An Officer of Very Extraordinary Merit: Charles Porterfield and the American War for Independence, 1775–1780

Captain Thomas Posey and the 7th Virginia Regiment

Cast Off the British Yoke: The Old Dominion and American Independence, 1763–1776

Great Things Are Expected from the Virginians: Virginia in the American Revolution

In This Time of Extreme Danger: Northern Virginia in the American Revolution

They Are Indeed a Very Useful Corps: American Riflemen in the Revolutionary War

They Behaved Like Soldiers: Captain John Chilton and the Third Virginia Regiment, 1775–1778

To Hazard Our Own Security: Maine's Role in the American Revolution

Wedded to My Sword: The Revolutionary War Service of Light Horse Harry Lee

All rights reserved. No part of this book may be reproduced or transmitted in any form or by any means, electronic or mechanical, including photocopying, recording or by any information storage and retrieval system without written permission from the author, except for the inclusion of brief quotations in a review.

International Standard Book Numbers
Paperbound: 978-0-7884-5594-0
Clothbound: 978-0-7884-6068-5

Contents

Ch. 1   "The People of Virginia
Manifest Open Rebellion."
April – October 1775..................1

Ch. 2   "Americans will Die, or be Free!"
October - November 1775 19

Ch. 3   "A Second Bunker Hill Affair,
in Miniature."
December 1775 43

Ch. 4   "Nothing less than Depriving [Dunmore]
of Life or Liberty will Secure Peace to
Virginia."
January - July 1776...............77

Ch. 5   "The Country was Entirely
a Wilderness."
1776 - 1779 109

Ch. 6   "Never was a State in such a
Confused Helpless Situation."
1779 - 1780......................141

Ch. 7	"The Spirit of Disaffection in the Southern Colonies had Received a Rude Shock." January 1781	177
Ch. 8	"We Attempt Everything and Sacrifice our own Blood for your Assumed Cause!" February – March 1781	233
Ch. 9	"The Militia Behaved with a Spirit and Resolution which would have done Honour to Veterans." April – May 1781	273
Ch. 10	"The Enemy's Intention has been to Destroy this Army!" May – July 1781	307
Ch. 11	"Should a Navy Superiority Come, Great Advantage Might be Obtained in this Quarter." July – September 1781	347
Ch. 12	"A Few Weeks Exertions and the Enemy Is Expelled from Our State Forever." September – October 1781	363

Bibliography..393

Index...........................…..........................407

Acknowledgements

I am indebted to a number of people for their assistance with this book, beginning with my friends and fellow re-enactors: Drummond and Gail Ball, Evan (Buzz) Deemer, Rob Friar, Norm Fuss, Jim Gallagher, and Jerry Majnich. Each provided advice, support and encouragement (and in some cases room and board and good company on frequent research trips. I am grateful to all of them for their generosity and friendship. Dr. Robert Selig kindly offered his insight (and research) on the battles of Spencer's Ordinary and Green Spring and Todd Braisted generously shared his knowledge of all things Loyalist with me.

As always, I found the Simpson Library at the University of Mary Washington and the Rockefeller Library at Colonial Williamsburg very valuable resources.

Lastly, I want to thank my wife, Sue, for indulging my passion (she says obsession) with the American Revolution. She has taken my numerous site visits and late nights at the computer in stride and supported me from the beginning. So thank you Sue for your patience and support.

About the Author

Michael Cecere Sr. teaches American history at Robert E. Lee High School in Fairfax County, Virginia, and was named the 2005 Outstanding Teacher of the Year by the Virginia Society of the Sons of the American Revolution. Mr. Cecere also teaches American history at Northern Virginia Community College. An avid Revolutionary War re-enactor, he currently is the commander of the 7th Virginia Regiment and participates in numerous living history events throughout the country. This is his tenth book.

Other books by Michael Cecere

They Behaved Like Soldiers: Captain John Chilton and the Third Virginia Regiment, 1776-1778 (2004)

An Officer of Very Extraordinary Merit: Charles Porterfield and the American War for Independence, 1775-1780 (2004)

Captain Thomas Posey and the 7th Virginia Regiment (2005)

They Are Indeed a Very Useful Corps: American Riflemen in the Revolutionary War (2006)

In This Time of Extreme Danger: Northern Virginia in the American Revolution (2006)

Great Things Are Expected from the Virginians: Virginia in the American Revolution (2008)

To Hazard Our Own Security: Maine's Role in the American Revolution (2010)

Wedded to My Sword: The Revolutionary War Service of Light Horse Harry Lee (2012)

Cast Off the British Yoke: The Old Dominion and American Independence, 1763 – 1776 (2014)

Chronology of Important Events in Virginia

1775

April 21	Williamsburg Gunpowder Seized
June 8	Dunmore flees Williamsburg
October 26-27	Battle of Hampton
November 14	Battle of Kemp's Landing
December 9	Battle of Great Bridge

1776

January 1	Norfolk is burned
May 15	Virginia votes for Independence
July 2	*Continental Congress votes for Independence*
July 9	Battle of Gwynn's Island
August 5	Dunmore leaves Virginia
Sept. – Oct.	Expedition against the Cherokee

1777

March-April	War on the Frontier Harrodsburg, Boonesborough, and St. Asaph are attacked.
August 31	Ft. Henry (Wheeling, WV) is attacked.

1778

July 4	George Rogers Clark captures Kaskaskia.
September 7	Siege of Boonesborough

1779

February 23	George Rogers Clark captures Vincenes.
May 8-24	Mathew-Collier Expedition

1780

May 12	*Virginia continental line is captured at Charleston, SC*
October 20 to November 22	Leslie Expedition

1781

January

1	Raid on Warwick
3-4	Arnold passes Hood's Point
5	Battle of Richmond
8	Raid on Charles City Courthouse
10-11	Ambush at Hood's Point
12	Raid on Cobham
16	Battle of Mackie's Mill
19	Portsmouth Occupied

February

10-14	Race to the Dan

March

19	Battle of Scott's Creek

April

1-14	Potomac River Raids
25	Battle of Petersburg
27	Battle of Osborne's Landing

May

20	Cornwallis Arrives in Virginia

June

4	Raid on Charlottesville
4	Raid on Point of Fork
26	Battle of Spencer's Ordinary

July

6	Battle of Green Spring

August

1	British occupy Yorktown and Gloucester Point

September

5	Battle of the Capes
14	General Washington Arrives in Williamsburg
28	Allied army marches to Yorktown

October

2	Battle of Gloucester Point
6	1st allied parallel (trench) is started
9	Allied bombardment commences
11	2nd allied parallel (trench) is started
14	Redoubts 9 & 10 are stormed
16	Abercrombie's Sortie
16	Cornwallis's escape is foiled
17	Truce
19	Surrender

Chapter One

"The People of Virginia Manifest Open Rebellion."

April – October 1775

In the pre-dawn hours of April 21, 1775, a detachment of British marines and sailors from the *H.M.S. Magdalen* (anchored four miles away in the James River) ventured into Williamsburg, Virginia and quietly removed 15 barrels of gunpowder from the powder magazine in the center of the city. This incident, which occurred two days after the opening engagement of the Revolutionary War at Lexington and Concord in Massachusetts, initiated a crisis in Virginia that led to open warfare in the Old Dominion six months later.

The removal of the gunpowder in Williamsburg sparked a wave of anger and suspicion against the Royal Governor, John Murray, Earl of Dunmore, whom most Virginians assumed had ordered the powder's removal. The seizure of the gunpowder, combined with the news about Lexington and Concord (which reached Virginia at the end of April) convinced many Virginians that a parliamentary plot to disarm the colonists existed and that Lord Dunmore was a willing participant.

Tensions increased in May when Dunmore (reacting to reports that hundreds of armed men, led by Patrick Henry, were marching on Williamsburg to demand the gunpowder's return) threatened to arm slaves and burn the capital to the ground. Henry was persuaded to halt and disband his force before he reached Williamsburg, but the situation remained volatile and by early June Lord Dunmore, concerned about the safety of his family, removed them from the capital and boarded the 24 gun *H.M.S. Fowey* anchored in the York River.

Members of the House of Burgesses assured Dunmore that he and his family were in no danger and they urged him to return to the capital so that the business of government could continue, but Dunmore refused and royal authority in Virginia essentially disappeared. Political authority in the colony shifted to a series of special conventions and a committee of safety comprised of "rebellious" burgesses.

Fearful that British troops might soon arrive and march on Williamsburg with Lord Dunmore at their head to punish those he deemed "rebels," Williamsburg's leaders requested help from neighboring counties. As a result, approximately 250 militia occupied the capital in late June and July.[1]

An annoyed Lord Dunmore, who was powerless to challenge this blatant affront to royal authority, described the tense situation in the capital to his superior, Lord Dartmouth in London:

> *A constant guard is kept in Williamsburg relieved every day from the adjacent Counties, and that place is become a Garrison, the pretence of which is the Security of the Person of their Speaker, who because he has been Chairman of the* [Continental] *Congress, it is reported, (in order to inflame), that* [the] *Government is anxious to Seize him.*[2]

---

[1] Purdie, *Virginia Gazette*, "30 June 1775," Supplement, 1
[2] William Clark, ed., "Dunmore to Dartmouth, 27 June, 1775," *Naval Documents of the American Revolution*, Vol. 1, (Washington D.C.: 1970), 764

Virginia in 1775

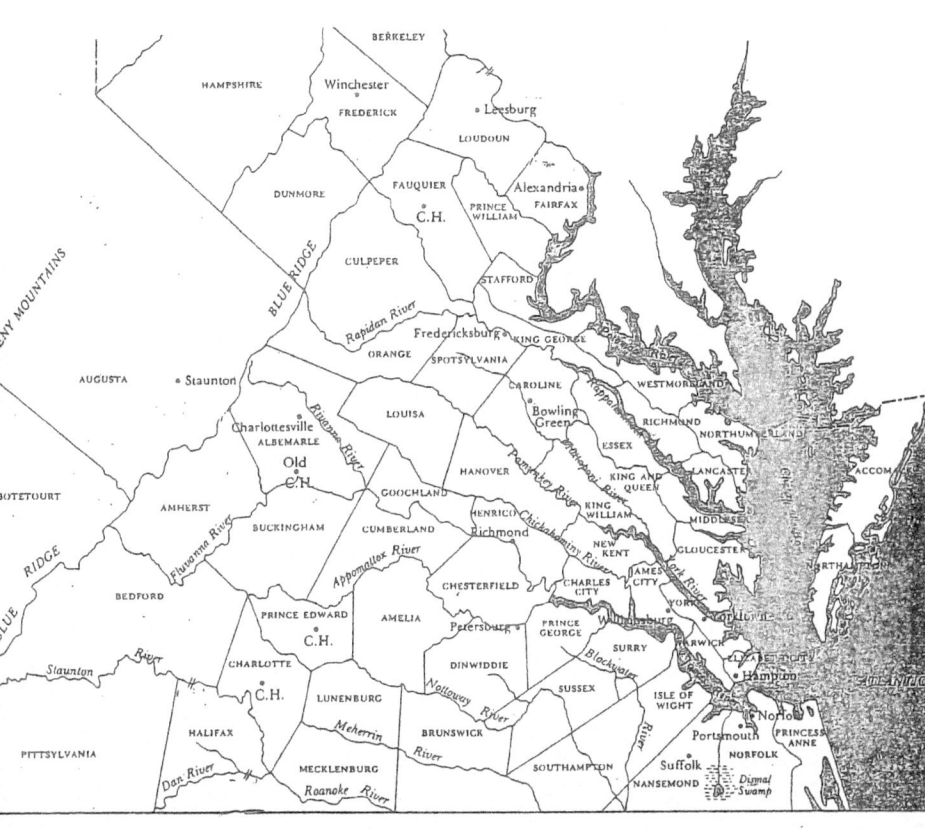

Counties of Virginia (1775)

The "constant guard" that Dunmore described in Williamsburg included the capital's independent militia company as well as volunteer detachments from nearby James City and New Kent counties. Dunmore also noted (no doubt with a great deal of frustration) that

> Guards likewise Continually mount at the Town of York opposite to which the Men of War [on which Dunmore was staying] lie, and thro' out the whole Country the greatest attention is paid to these Military preparations and a universal appearance of War is put on.[3]

Dunmore's expectation of hostilities with the "rebels" prompted him to send his wife and children back to England in late June aboard the *H.M.S. Magdalen*. The governor and a small number of loyalist supporters remained on the *H.M.S. Fowey*. Despite protests from Virginians that Dunmore's decision was another over-reaction from the volatile governor, the arrival in Williamsburg of militia troops from Goochland, Louisa, Spotsylvania, King George, Stafford and Albemarle counties in July added to the warlike atmosphere and suggested that Dunmore's concerns were valid. Alexander Purdie's *Virginia Gazette* announced that all of the volunteers were, "*ready to take a crack with any ministerial troops that may be sent to molest us.*"[4]

Lord Dunmore was also eager to take a crack at the "rebels", but he lacked sufficient force to act. Instead, he sat aboard the *H.M.S. Fowey*, anchored off of Yorktown, where

---

[3] Ibid.
[4] Purdie, *Virginia Gazette*, "14 July, 1775" Supplement, 2

he dutifully reported to Lord Dartmouth on the deteriorating (and increasingly militant) situation in the colony:

> *We have now a Camp of these People behind the Town of York, not half a Cannon-Shot from the Ships; and the men are Continually parading in arms along the Shore Close to us, and at night we hear them challenge every boat or person that approach them.*[5]

One reason the militia remained on alert were reports of British shore parties robbing local inhabitants of livestock and other provisions. The militia was determined to halt these raids. To demonstrate their resolve, a large detachment of militia at Yorktown forcibly detained a British shore party from the recently arrived *H.M.S. Otter* (14 guns). The detention of the sailors prompted Captain Matthew Squire to send a midshipman ashore to investigate. He reported that

> *I walked up to their camp, which consisted of a few pales* [fences] *covered with leaves, and found two hundred rebels round our men, whom they had been informed belonged to the Otter; and at my arrival vowed, that if they caught any belonging to the Fowey man of war, they would never let them go. I enquired into the reason why they detained the men, and was asked to whom they belonged; I answered to the King. The Captain of the Guard then asked me if I belonged to the Otter and* [whether] *any of the men or officers would venture on shore again. I told him, that both*

---

[5] Clark, ed., "Dunmore to Dartmouth, 12 July, 1775," *Naval Documents of the American Revolution,* Vol. 1, 873

officers and men would, if they were ordered, come on shore to [do their] *duty. They said they hoped they would behave themselves well, or they would get something they did not like. I replied that if saying they belonged to the King was impertinent, it was the answer they must always expect. Thus you see,* [concluded the midshipman] *that the people of York, in Virginia, are worse than at Boston.*[6]

Lord Dunmore reached a similar conclusion about the Virginia colonists, declaring in a letter to Lord Dartmouth in mid-July that the armed Virginians were "lawless ruffians" who displayed open rebellion:

The People of Virginia manifest open Rebellion by every means in their power, and they declare at the Same time that they are his Majesty's Most dutyfull Subjects...and that as designs have never been formed against my person, but that I may, whenever I please return to my usual Residence without the least danger; notwithstanding that my own Servants are prevented from passing with provisions which is thus cut off from me & denied to me, my people have been Carried off by the guard,; while my house has been a third time rifled, and is now entirely in the possession of these lawless Ruffians.[7]

---

[6] Clark, ed. "A Midshipman on Board the Otter to a Friend in London, 11 July, 1775," *Naval Documents of the American Revolution*, Vol. 1, 866

[7] Clark, ed., "Dunmore to Dartmouth, 12 July, 1775," *Naval Documents of the American Revolution*, Vol. 1, 873

Captain Charles Scott of Cumberland County, a veteran of the French and Indian War, may have actually agreed with Dunmore's characterization of the militia in Williamsburg as "*lawless ruffians*". Selected by the officers in the capital to command this mixed force of militia units, Scott faced the enormous challenge of instilling a degree of discipline among the largely untrained and untried troops – some 250 strong and encamped at Waller's Grove near the capitol building.[8]

The sudden departure of Dunmore and the British warships from the York River (they sailed to Norfolk on July 15th) actually made Captain Scott's task more difficult. With the threat to Williamsburg reduced, drill and guard duty in the capital seemed pointless to many. Men who knew little of military discipline chafed at the inactivity of camp life and some fell into mischief. A council of officers adopted a set of regulations to instill greater discipline, but verbal reprimands and brief confinements without food and drink had little effect on the troops and the misconduct continued.[9] Lieutenant George Gilmer of Albemarle County reluctantly blamed Captain Scott for the disorderly nature of the troops:

Capt. Scott, our Commander-in-chief, who's goodness and merit is great, fears to offend, and by that every member is rather disorderly. We appear rather invited to feast than fight.[10]

---

[8] R.A. Brock, ed., "George Gilmer to Thomas Jefferson in Papers, Military and Political, 1775-1778 of George Gilmer, M.D. of Pen Park, Albemarle Co., VA," *Miscellaneous Papers 1672-1865 Now First Printed from the Manuscripts in the Virginia Historical Society*, (Richmond, VA, 1937), 101

[9] Ibid.., "Resolutions Adopted by the Officers at Williamsburg, 18 July, 1775," *Gilmer Papers*, 92-93

[10] Ibid., "George Gilmer to Thomas Jefferson," *Gilmer Papers*, 101

Third Virginia Convention

The 3rd Virginia Convention, which met in Richmond in July as the de facto government of Virginia, offered a solution to Captain Scott's dilemma by restructuring Virginia's militia. The independent militia companies that had formed in many of Virginia's counties in 1774 and 1775 were disbanded and replaced by a three tiered military system that started with two regiments of regular (full time) soldiers raised for one year's service.

Twenty years had passed since Virginia raised such a military force (during the French and Indian War) so the formation of two such regiments marked a significant escalation in Virginia's military preparedness. Patrick Henry, of Hanover County, was selected to command the first regiment, which consisted of eight 68 man companies and totaled 544 men.[11] Colonel William Woodford, of Caroline County, was given command of the second regiment, which comprised 476 men in seven companies.[12]

To raise the troops for the two regiments, the Convention divided Virginia into sixteen districts and ordered each district (comprised of several counties) to recruit and send a company of regulars to Williamsburg as soon as possible.[13] The company of regulars from the eastern shore of Virginia remained there as a detached unit to help protect this isolated and vulnerable region of the colony.

The regular troops were not the only soldiers ordered to muster in Williamsburg; hundreds of minutemen were ordered

---

[11] William W. Henings, *The Statutes at Large Being a Collection of all the Laws of Virginia,* Vol. 9, (Richmond: J. & G. Cochran, 1821), 9
[12] Ibid., 10
[13] Ibid., 10, 16

to march to the capital as well. The minutemen comprised a second tier of Virginia's new military establishment. The Convention authorized sixteen battalions of minutemen. These men were drawn from the ranks of the militia and were *"more strictly trained to proper discipline"* than the ordinary militia.[14] Each of the sixteen districts was ordered to raise a 500 man battalion of minutemen *"from the age of sixteen to fifty, to be divided into ten companies of fifty men each."*[15] Like the regular troops, the minutemen were provided with proper arms as well as a hunting shirt and leggings.[16]

The last tier of Virginia's new military establishment was the traditional county militia. The Convention decreed that

> *All male persons, hired servants, and apprentices, above the age of sixteen, and under fifty years...shall be enlisted into the militia...and formed into companies....*[17]

Each member of the county militia had six months to furnish himself with

> *A good rifle...with a tomahawk,* [or a] *common firelock, bayonet, pouch, or cartouch box, three charges of powder and ball....* [Members of the militia] *shall constantly keep by him one pound of powder and four pounds of ball....*[18]

The militia companies were ordered to hold private musters every two weeks, except in the winter.

---

[14] Ibid., 16
[15] Ibid., 16-17
[16] Ibid., 20
[17] Ibid., 27-28
[18] Ibid.

While the convention spent much of July and most of August organizing the colony's new military force and establishing a set of regulations for the new troops (Articles of War), Lord Dunmore worked to strengthen his own force.

Dunmore Prepares for a Confrontation

Early in the morning of July 15th, two days before the 3rd Virginia Convention convened in Richmond, the *H.M.S. Otter*, with Lord Dunmore aboard, weighed anchor off of Yorktown and sailed for Norfolk. The *Otter* was joined by the 20 gun H.M.S. *Mercury*, which had arrived from New York to replace the Boston bound *H.M.S. Fowey*.[19]

While Lord Dunmore -- and the crews aboard the handful of warships and tenders that protected him – adjusted to their new anchorage in the Elizabeth River (between Norfolk and Portsmouth), reinforcements finally arrived. A 60 man detachment of British regulars from the 14th Regiment at St. Augustine arrived aboard the sloop *Betsy* on July 31st, and another 40 redcoats were expected momentarily. Purdie's *Virginia Gazette* reacted to the news with a declaration:

> *The good people of Virginia now consider Lord Dunmore as their mortal enemy, and will no longer brook the many insults they have received from him, which are daily repeated; and the "damn'd shirtmen," as they are emphatically called by some of his minions...will make* [them regret] *before long, their ill-timed, base, and ungenerous conduct.*[20]

---

[19] Clark, ed. "Journal of His Majesty's Sloop Otter," *Naval Documents of the American Revolution*, Vol. 1, 893
[20] Purdie, *Virginia Gazette,* "4 August, 1775," Postscript, 1

Although Dunmore acknowledged in a letter to Lord Dartmouth on August 2nd, that the newly arrived British troops were too few to restore order in this *"distracted colony"*, he confidently declared that

> [Were] *I speedily supplied with a few hundred more* [troops] *with Arms, Ammunition and the other requisites of War, and with full powers to act... I could in a few months reduce this Colony to perfect Submission.*[21]

Alas, the British Ministry had no troops to spare; the bulk of Britain's military force in North America was pinned down in Boston, where open warfare entered its fourth month.

Such was not the case in Virginia. Although the royal governor of Virginia had fled the capital and thousands of Virginians were preparing for war, the summer of 1775 passed without any gunfire or bloodshed in the Old Dominion.

Confrontation in Hampton

This changed in the fall when a dispute over a grounded British tender (which was pillaged and burned near Hampton) led to an armed confrontation and bloodshed in Hampton. The tender, with Captain Matthew Squire of the *H.M.S. Otter* aboard, was forced ashore in early September by a hurricane. Most of the crew, as well as two runaway slaves, were taken into custody and the tender's stores were seized before the vessel was burned, but Captain Squire eluded the militia and escaped into the woods. His sailors were eventually released but the two slaves were returned to their owners.

---

[21] Clark, ed., "Lord Dunmore to Lord Dartmouth, 2 Aug., 1775," *Naval Documents of the American Revolution*, Vol. 1, 1045

A few days later, Captain Squire (back aboard the *Otter* and unaware that the tender had been destroyed) sent a terse letter to the Hampton town committee threatening *"consequences"* if the seized vessel and stores were not immediately returned.[22] The Hampton Committee forwarded Captain Squire's threat to Williamsburg, along with a plea for assistance. One hundred volunteers marched to Hampton the next day to reinforce the local militia.[23]

The arrival of the reinforcements from Williamsburg bolstered the spirits of Hampton's inhabitants and prompted the town committee to belligerently respond to Captain Squire's letter on September 16th:

> *The sloop, we apprehended, was not in his majesty's service, as we are well assured that you were on a pillaging or pleasuring party.... Neither the vessel or stores were seized by the inhabitants of Hampton. The threats of a person whose conduct hath evinced that he were not only capable, but desirous, of doing us, in our then defensless state, the greatest injustice, we confess, were somewhat alarming; but, with the greatest pleasure, we can inform you, our apprehensions are now removed.*[24]

---

[22] Clark, ed., "Captain Squire to the Hampton Town Committee, 10 September, 1775," *Naval Documents of the American Revolution*, Vol. 2, 74

Note: The king's stores that Captain Squires demanded be returned included: 6 swivel guns, 5 muskets, 5 cutlasses, 2 powder horns, 2 cartouch boxes, swivel shot; seine and rope, and an anchor. (Ibid.)

[23] Robert L. Scribner and Brent Tarter, ed., *Revolutionary Virginia: The Road to Independence*, (University Press of Virginia, 1978), Vol. 4, 96

[24] Clark, ed., "Hampton Committee to Captain Squire, 16 September, 1775," *Naval Documents of the American Revolution*, Vol. 2, 123

Southeastern Virginia

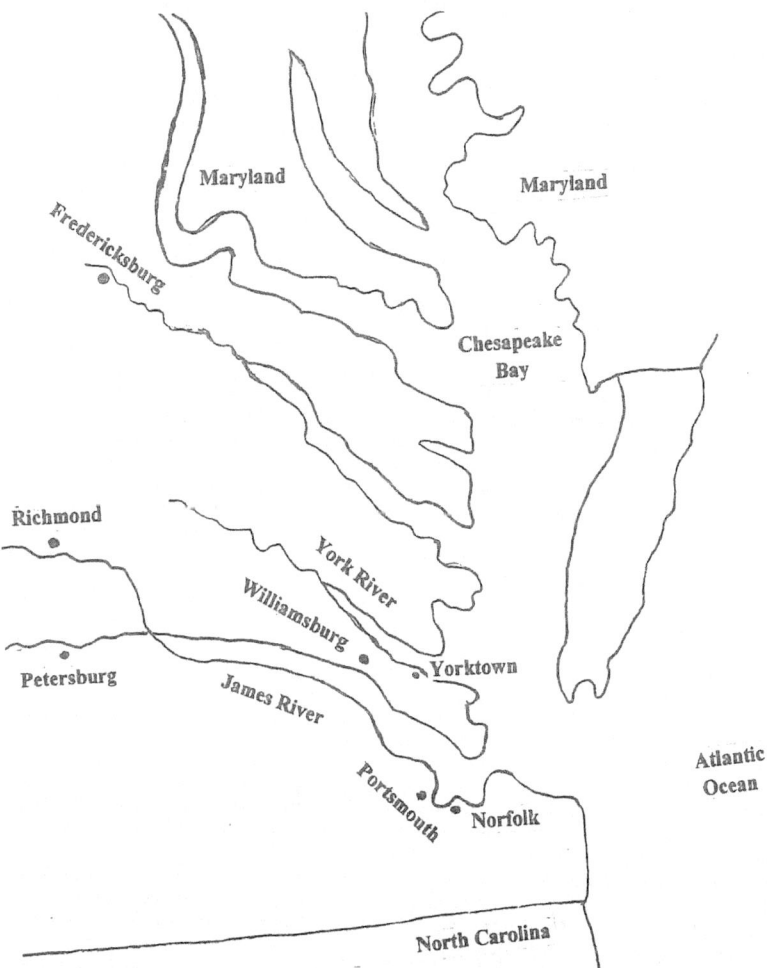

Captain Squire responded to the committee's defiant message with a blockade of Hampton, seizing ships that sailed to or from the town. Lord Dunmore described the situation to Lord Dartmouth:

> *We have demanded Satisfaction of the People at Hampton for the Sloop and desired that the King's Stores might be returned, to all which they have given us a positive refusal; their Port is now blocked up and we have taken two of their Boats and shall not permit a Vessell to pass or repass till they return the Stores etc, they have called to their assistance between two and three hundred of their Shirt men Alias Rebels.*[25]

Norfolk is Chastised

The boldness displayed by the inhabitants of Hampton was not replicated in Norfolk when Captain Squire suddenly seized John Holt's printing press in retaliation for unflattering accounts of Captain Squire in Holt's *Virginia Gazette*. A witness to the September 30th incident described the lack of resistance offered by Norfolk's residents to Captain Squire:

> *Yesterday came ashore about 15 of the King's soldiers, and marched up to the printing-office, out of which they took all the types and part of the press and carried them on board the new ship Eilbeck, in presence, I suppose, of between two and three hundred spectators, without meeting with the least molestation; and upon*

---

[25] Clark, ed., "Lord Dunmore to Lord Dartmouth, 5 October, 1775," *Naval Documents of the American Revolution*, Vol. 2, 317

> *the drums beating up and down the town, there were only about 35 men to arms....*[26]

The poor showing of the Norfolk militia embarrassed Virginia's leaders and gave great delight to Lord Dunmore and his supporters. Norfolk's committee tried to salvage the town's tarnished reputation by complaining to Lord Dunmore about the, *"illegal and riotous,"* actions of Captain Squire's landing party, but this only provoked derision from the governor who witnessed the entire affair from aboard his ship.

Dunmore's Raids

Emboldened by the lack of opposition in Norfolk, Lord Dunmore launched a series of raids in mid-October in Princess Ann and Norfolk County to seize arms and ammunition. Captain Samuel Leslie, the ranking officer of the 14th Regiment in Virginia, described the first raid on October 12th.

> *I landed the 12th of [October] at 11 o'Clock at night about three miles from hence with Lieut. Lawrie, two Serjeants, & forty rank and file of the 14th Regiment, and after marching three miles into the country in search of Artillery we found in a wood nineteen pieces of cannon, some of them twelve, others nine, six & three pounders; seventeen of which we destroyed, & brought off two, and then returning to our boats we reimbarked without the least opposition. Lord Dunmore accompanied us upon this expedition.*[27]

---

[26] Clark, ed., "Extract of a Letter from Norfolk, 1 October, 1775," *Naval Documents of the American Revolution*, Vol. 2, 267

[27] Clark, ed., "Captain Leslie to General Howe, 1 November, 1775," *Naval Documents of the American Revolution*, Vol. 2, 844-45

Lord Dunmore described the next raid:

> *On the 15th Instant, I landed with between 70 and 80 Men (which was all we could Spare to take with us) some little distance from [Norfolk] in the Night, and Marched about a Mile and a half up the Country, where we destroyed 17 pieces of Ordinance and brought off two more, that the Rebels had carried from...Norfolk, and concealed there.*[28]

Two days after this raid, Dunmore ordered another, led once again by Captain Leslie who recalled that

> *On the 17^h of October his Lordship was informed, that there was a great quantity of Artillery, small arms and all sorts of ammunition, concealed in different stores at a place called Kemp's landing, in consequence of which, I, with [a few officers] & seventy rank & file of the 14th Regiment, Lieut Allen, one sergeant and twenty marines, some young gentlemen of the Navy & ten of twelve seamen, embarked at 2 o' Clock in the Afternoon in boats & a Schooner in which some Guns were mounted to cover our landing, and proceeded seven or eight miles up the eastern branch of Elizabeth river to Newtown, where we landed without opposition notwithstanding above two hundred of the rebels were at exercise near that place the same evening, and marching three or four miles through the Country we arrived at Kemp's landing a little after it was dark, where we searched several stores and could discover*

---

[28] Clark, ed., "Lord Dunmore to Lord Dartmouth, 22 October, 1775," *Naval Documents of the American Revolution*, Vol. 2, 574-75

nothing but a good many small arms, which we either brought off or destroyed; and returning pretty near the same road we went we reimbarked about 2 o' clock the next morning without interruption. We likewise took several prisoners one of whom was a Captain of Minutemen and another a Delegate to the Convention at Richmond.[29]

More raids followed, prompting Dunmore to brag to General Howe in Boston on October 22nd that

I can assure your Lordship that landing in this manner has discouraged exceedingly the Rebels, and has raised the Spirits of the friends of Government so much that they are offering their Services from all quarters;[30]

Captain Leslie offered an equally optimistic assessment of the situation in Virginia to General William Howe in Boston:

Many great guns, small arms, & other implements of war have been taken since by small parties, so that there has been in all at least seventy seven pieces of ordinance taken & destroyed since my Detachment arrived here without the smallest opposition, which is a proof that it would not require a very large force to subdue this Colony.[31]

Events soon challenged Captain Leslie's brash assertion.

---

[29] Clark, ed., "Captain Leslie to General Howe, 1 November, 1775," *Naval Documents of the American Revolution*, Vol. 2, 844-45

[30] Clark, ed., "Lord Dunmore to Lord Dartmouth, 22 October, 1775," *Naval Documents of the American Revolution*, Vol. 2, 574-75

[31] Clark, ed., "Captain Leslie to General Howe, 1 November, 1775," *Naval Documents of the American Revolution*, Vol. 2, 844-45

Chapter Two

"Americans will Die, or be Free!"

October – November 1775

Battle of Hampton

On the morning of October 26th, 1775 Captain Matthew Squire anchored a small squadron of naval vessels consisting of a large schooner, two sloops and two pilot boats at the mouth of Hampton Harbor. He announced his intention to burn the town of Hampton in retaliation for the pillaging and destruction of one of his tenders that had washed ashore in a storm nearly two months earlier. Unlike their brethren in Norfolk, the inhabitants of Hampton were ready and willing to resist.

> *A company of regulars and a company of minutemen, who had been placed there in consequence of former threats...against* [Hampton] *made the best disposition to prevent their landing, aided by a body of militia, who were suddenly called together on the occasion.*[1]

As Captain Squire's flotilla entered the Hampton River, gunfire erupted from the rebels onshore. Governor Dunmore reported that

---

[1] Dixon and Hunter, *Virginia Gazette*, "28 October, 1775," 3

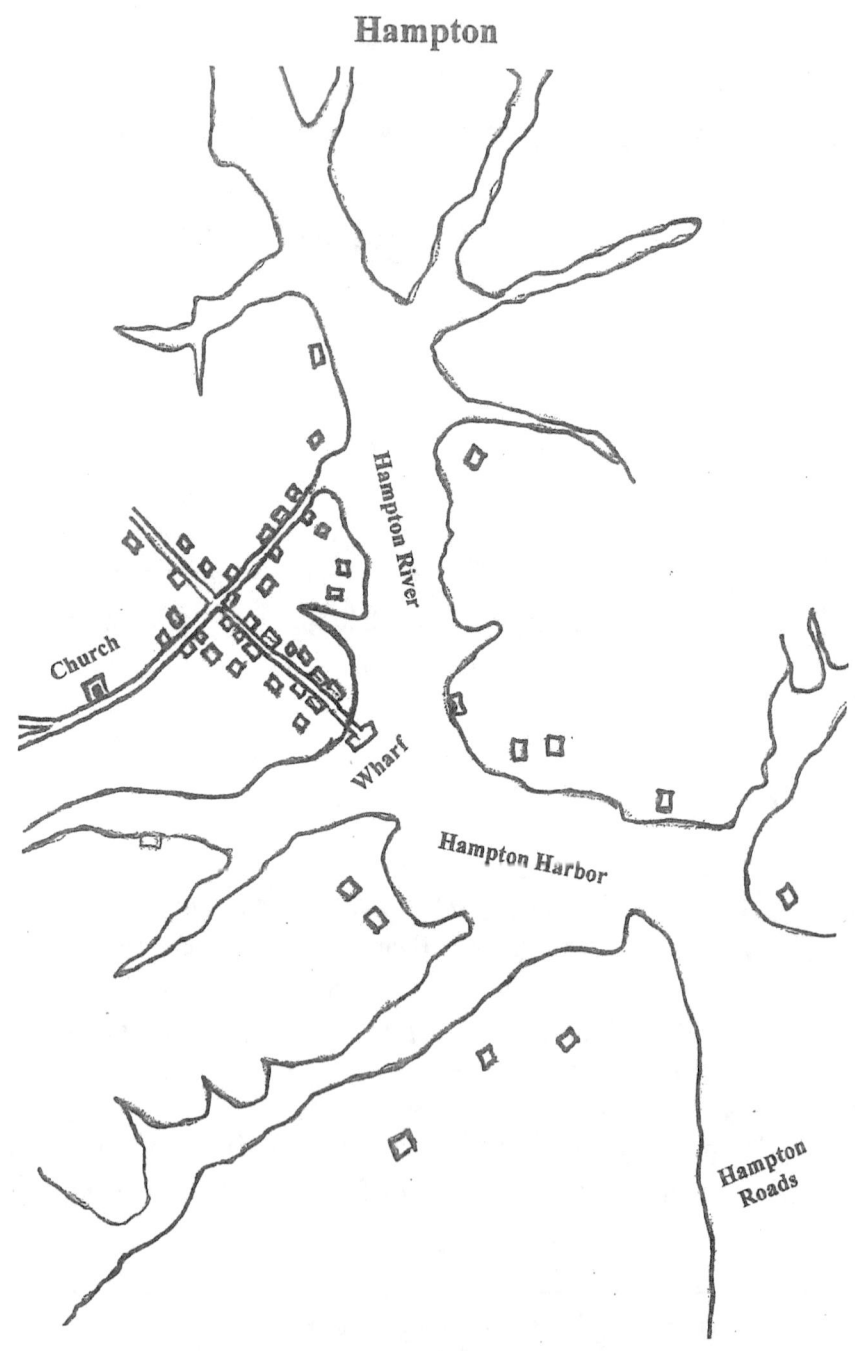

> *Some of the King's tenders went pretty close into Hampton Road. So soon as the rebels perceived them, they marched out against them and the moment they got within shot of our people, Mr. George Nicholas...who commanded a party of rebels at that time at Hampton, fired at one of the tenders, whose example was followed by his whole party. The tenders returned the fire but without the least effect.*[2]

Dunmore laid the blame for the first shot at Hampton (and thus the inauguration of war in Virginia) on Captain George Nicholas of the 2nd Virginia Regiment, but an American eyewitness saw the engagement differently. He reported that as the tenders approached Hampton

> *Two vollies of musquetry were discharged from the tenders, and answered by captain Lyne from his post by a rifle, which was answered by a four pounder from one of the tenders; then began a pretty warm fire from all the tenders. Captain Nicholas, observing this, soon joined about 25 of his men. The fire of our musquetry caused the tender nighest to us to sheer off some distance.*[3]

---

[2] K.G. Davis, ed., "Lord Dunmore to Lord Dartmouth, 6 December, 1775 through February, 1776," *Documents of the American Revolution*, Vol. 12, (Irish University Press, 1976), 58

[3] Clark, ed. "Pinkney, *Virginia Gazette*, 2 November, 1775," *Naval Documents of the American Revolution*, 842-43

Captain Lyne of the minute company was identified in a second account as the one, *"who fired the first gun in the attack at the mouth of the river,* [and] *killed a man by that very fire."*[4]

Whether this meant he fired the very first shot of the engagement is unclear. What is clear is that the two sides fired upon each other for over an hour with Squire's tenders getting the worst of it. Unable to maneuver past some sunken vessels obstructing the harbor, the tenders were raked with rifle and musket fire from shore. Their crews responded with cannon, swivel, and musket fire, but it apparently had little effect on the Virginians, who were well sheltered on shore. One rebel combatant recalled that

> *The fire* [from the tenders] *consisted of 4 pounders, grape shot etc. for about an hour. Not a man of our's was hurt. Whether our men did any damage is uncertain. They could not get nigher than 300 yards. Some say they saw men fall in one of the tenders.*[5]

Pinkney's *Virginia Gazette* boasted of the bravery the Virginians displayed against Captain Squire's squadron:

> *No troops could shew more intrepidity than the raw, new raised men, under the command of captain Nicholas, of the second regiment, and captain Lyne, of the minute men, together with some of the country militia. These brave young officers, at the head of their men, without the least cover or breast-work, on*

---

[4] Pinkney, *Virginia Gazette*, "26 October, 1775," 3
[5] Pinkney, *Virginia Gazette*, "2 November, 1775," 2

the open shore, stood a discharge of 4 pounders, and other cannon, from a large schooner commanded by captain Squire himself, and from a sloop and two tenders, which played on them with all their guns, swivels, and muskets. They stood cooly till the vessels were near enough for them to do execution, when they began a brisk and well directed fire, which forced the little squadron to retire.[6]

Battle of Hampton: Day Two

Although the fighting ended at nightfall, both sides remained active. Under cover of darkness and a driving rain the British returned to the sunken obstructions and worked to create a passage through the channel while the rebels strengthened their breastworks on the town wharf and anxiously waited for reinforcements from Williamsburg. Colonel William Woodford of the 2nd Virginia Regiment marched all night with a company of Culpeper Minutemen to reach Hampton by morning and assume command of the rebel forces. In a letter to his friend Thomas Jefferson, John Page, a prominent resident of nearby Gloucester County, provided a detailed account (probably supplied by Woodford) of the resumption of combat on October 27th:

Col. Woodford accompanied Captain Buford's rifle company through a heavy rain to Hampton and arrived about 7 a.m. When the Col. Entered the Town, having left the Rifle Men in the Church to dry themselves, he rode down to the River, took A view of

---

[6] Pinkney, *Virginia Gazette*, "26 October, 1775," 3

the Town, and then seeing the Six Tenders at Anchor in the River went to Col. Cary's to dry himself and eat his Breakfast. But before he could do either, the Tenders had cut their Way through the Vessel's Boltsprit which was sunk to impede their Passage and having a very fresh and fair Gale had anchored in the Creek and abreast of the Town.

The People were so astonished at their unexpected and sudden Arrival that they stood staring at them and omitted to give the Col. the least Notice of their approach. The first Intelligence he had of this Affair was from the Discharge of a 4 Pounder. He mounted his Horse and riding down to the Warf found that the People of the Town had abandoned their Houses and...the Militia had left the Breast Work which had been thrown up across the Wharf and street.[7]

Colonel Woodford deployed Captain Nicholas's company of 2nd Virginians, Captain Buford's Culpeper riflemen, and the local militia amongst the building overlooking the harbor and behind breastworks on the shore and at the wharf. John Page's account of the battle continued:

The Fire was now general and constant on both Sides. Cannon Balls Grape Shot and Musket Balls whistled over the Heads of our Men, Whilst our Muskets and Rifles poured Showers of Balls into their Vessels and they were so well directed that the Men on Board the Schooner in which Captain Squires himself commanded were unable to stand to their 4

---

[7] Clark, ed., "John Page to Thomas Jefferson, 11 November, 1775," *Naval Documents of the American Revolution*, Vol. 2, 991-92

Pounders which were not sheltered by a Netting and gave but one Round of them but kept up an incessant firing of smaller Guns and swivels, as did 2 Sloops and 3 Boats for more than an Hour and ¼ when they slipt their Cables and towed out except the Hawk Tender a Pilot Boat that had been taken some Time before from a Man of Hampton.....

In her they found 3 wounded Men 6 Sailors and 2 Negroes. Lieut. Wright who commanded her had been forced to jump over Board and was attended to the Shore by 2 Negroes and a white Man, one of the Negroes was shot by a Rifle Man across the Creek at 400 yds. distance. If Col. Woodford's Men whom he had ordered round to the Creeks Mouth could have got there soon enough they would undoubtedly have taken the little Squadron, for the Sailors could not possibly have towed them through their Fire. Although the nearest of the Tenders was 3 Hundred Yds, and the farthest about 450 from our Men, yet our Fire was so well directed that the Sailors were not able to stand to their Guns and serve them properly but fired them at Random at an Unaccountable Degree of Elevation.[8]

Lord Dunmore confirmed much of Page's account in his report of the battle to Lord Dartmouth:

---

[8] Ibid.

[On Oct. 27th] *the tenders returned again to the creek and ran up very near to the town. The rebels, being reinforced and taking possession of the houses, made a very heavy fire upon them but only killed one or two of the men and wounded several others, took a pilot boat that the gentlemen of the navy had made a tender of, and made seven men prisoners belonging to the Otter that were in her. The loss of the rebels must have been very inconsiderable if they suffered at all. The tenders were towed out of the creek by the boats with some difficulty.*[9]

Both of these second hand accounts were supported by accounts that appeared in the different Virginia Gazettes.

One account printed in Pinkney's Gazette a week after the engagement reported that

In the night they cut a passage through the vessels that were sunk, and the next morning, about 8 o' clock (which was about half an hour after colonel Woodford and captain Bluford arrived with a rifle company) 5 tenders, to wit, a large schooner, 2 sloops, and 2 pilot boats, passed the passage they had cleared, and drew up a-breast of the town; they then gave 3 cheers, and began a heavy fire.
Colonel Woodford immediately posted captain Nicholas with his company on one side of the main street, and captain Buford with his riflemen on the other, who were joined by the town company of

---

[9] Davis, ed., "Lord Dunmore to Lord Dartmouth, 6 December, 1775 through February, 1776," *Documents of the American Revolution*, Vol. 12, 58

> *militia; captain Lyne with his company was ordered to march to the cross roads just out of town to sustain any attack that might come from James or Back river. The colonel had been informed that men were landed from both these rivers. The musquet and rifle balls soon began to fly so thick that few men were seen upon the decks. The engagement continued very warm for some time.*
>
> *At length they began to cut and slip their cables, and all cleared themselves, except one, which was boarded and taken by some of our men. They took in her the gunner and 7 men, 3 of whom were wounded, 2 mortally (both since dead), 1 white woman, and 2 negro men lieutenant Wright, who commanded the prize, after receiving a ball, jumped overboard, and it is thought he was not able to reach the tenders. Several more jumped overboard; but it is not known what is become of them, or what damage is done on board of the other tenders. In those 2 different actions, Mr. Printer, officers and soldiers of the regular, minute, and militia acted with a spirit becoming freemen and Americans, and must evince that Americans will die, or be free!*[10]

Another account of the battle published the day of the engagement asserted that the defenders of Hampton were eager to face Dunmore's forces again:

> *The troops in town are in high spirits, and wish for* [another] *attack in this quarter; they are all excellent*

---

[10] Pinkney, *Virginia Gazette*, "2 November, 1775," 2

marksmen, and fine, bold fellows. After all the firing at the houses in Hampton, there were only a few windows broke, and a door panel. Lord Dunmore may now see he has not cowards to deal with.[11]

Both of these accounts included bold expressions of confidence from the Virginians, who clearly viewed the engagement as a victory. More importantly, the two day engagement marked the first spilling of blood in Virginia. A threshold was crossed at Hampton, one that was crossed in Massachusetts six months earlier, and there was no stepping back from it. The Revolutionary War had finally reached Virginia and in the weeks that followed it only intensified.

November: 1775

In retrospect, the outbreak of combat in Virginia seemed almost inevitable and in fact, long overdue. On the eve of the engagement at Hampton, the Virginia Committee of Safety, reacting to reports of the populace in Norfolk and Princess Anne County *"tamely"* submitting to Lord Dunmore, had ordered Colonel Woodford's 2nd Virginia Regiment and five companies of the Culpeper Minute Battalion to cross the James River and march to Norfolk to challenge him.[12]

Colonel Woodford's departure for Norfolk was delayed by events in Hampton and he did not rejoin his regiment in Williamsburg until early November. When he finally

---

[11] Pinkney *Virginia Gazette*, "26 October, 1775," 3

[12] Scribner and Tarter, ed., *Revolutionary Virginia: The Road to Independence,* Vol. 4, 294, 269

  Note: The Committee of Safety was created by the 3rd Virginia Convention and served as the de-facto government when the Virginia Convention was not in session.

returned, he set out with his unit to execute the Committee of Safety's instructions regarding Norfolk:

> *You are to use your best endeavors for protecting and defending the persons and properties of all friends to the cause of America, and to this end, to attack, kill, or captivate all such as you shall discover to be in arms for annoying of those persons, as far as you shall judge it prudent to engage them.*[13]

Colonel Woodford was also instructed to sever all communication and supplies between Norfolk and the countryside and to be especially watchful for slaves who attempted to join Dunmore. Lastly, the committee advised Colonel Woodford on how to treat the local population:

> *There may be many persons in those towns, or near them, who may be afraid in their present situation, exposed to the vengeance of the Navy, to declare their real sentiments. We think, therefore, that all those who will continue peaceable, giving no assistance or intelligence to our enemies, nor attempting to annoy your troops, or injure our friends, may for the present remain unmolested; those Tories and others who take an active part against us, must be considered as enemies.*[14]

---

[13] Scribner and Tarter, ed., "Orders for Colonel William Woodford," *Revolutionary Virginia: The Road to Independence,* Vol. 4, 271
[14] Ibid.

Skirmishes along the James River

Brimming with confidence after his victory at Hampton, Colonel Woodford was eager to cross the James River and lead his regiment and the minutemen, totaling over 650 men, to Norfolk.[15] A shortage of tents and the sudden arrival of a portion of Dunmore's flotilla off of Burwell's Landing and Jamestown Island (which threatened Williamsburg and obstructed the ferry crossing over the river) delayed Woodford's crossing. Numerous skirmishes between Dunmore's ships and rebel parties onshore occurred and although they resulted in little loss for either side, added to Colonel Woodford's delay.

Purdie's gazette included a detailed account of one of the engagements:

> "Yesterday, about one o' clock the King-Fisher sloop of war, and 3 tenders, came up to Burwell's ferry, and sent off a boat to board a small vessel lying near the shore, who were fired upon by the rifle guard stationed at that place; upon which they immediately tacked about, and made for the ship. The ship and tenders then began a heavy cannonading, and one six-pounder went through the storehouse at the water-side; many of the shot likewise hit the ferry-house, in which was a large family. Providentially, however, no person was hurt, either then, or about three hours afterwards, when they began a second cannonading, and fired three or four broadsides.

---

[15] Julian P. Boyd, ed., "Edmund Pendleton to Thomas Jefferson, 16 November, 1775," *The Papers of Thomas Jefferson*, Vol. 1, (Princeton, NJ: Princeton University Press, 1950), 260-61

> *They now lie before the ferry, and have not dared since to come near the vessel in shore.*[16]

Although the rebel troops guarding the shore lacked cannon to counteract Dunmore's naval guns, the accuracy of their rifles seemed an adequate alternative. John Page described the effectiveness of the riflemen against Dunmore's tenders in a letter to Thomas Jefferson:

> *I can assure you that about 20 Rifle Men have disputed with the Man of War and her Tenders for...2 Days and they have hitherto kept...the Ferry Boats safe, which it is supposed they wish to burn. It is incredible how much they dread a Rifle.*[17]

Edmund Pendleton, the President of the Committee of Safety, also acknowledged the crucial service of the riflemen:

> *The life and Soul of* [the troops guarding the shore] *is Capt. Green's Company of Riflemen from Culpeper, who in three Reliefs of about 22 at a time, scour the River, and have in various Attempts, prevented a landing of the enemy. Last week the King Fisher and four tenders full of men came up to Burwells Ferry and made several attempts to land during three days stay, but never came nearer than to receive a discharge of the Rifles, when they retired with great precipitation, and 'tis Supposed the loss of some men.*[18]

---

[16] Clark, ed., "Purdie, 10 November, 1775," *Naval Documents of the American Revolution,* Vol. 2, 973

[17] Clark, ed., "John Page to Thomas Jefferson, 11 November, 1775, *Naval Documents of the American Revolution,* Vol. 2, 991-92

[18] Boyd, "Edmund Pendleton to Thomas Jefferson, *The Papers of Thomas Jefferson,* Vol. 1, 260-61

Dunmore's attempt to prevent the passage of rebel troops across the James River was not the only factor behind Colonel Woodford's lack of progress southward. Woodford's force was also plagued by supply shortages that kept his troops in Williamsburg until mid-November. Once these shortages were adequately addressed, Woodford's troops crossed the James River further upriver out of the reach of Dunmore's ships and then proceeded south to Norfolk.[19]

Although concern remained about his supply situation, Colonel Woodford and his men marched towards Norfolk confident of success against Dunmore. The Committee of Safety estimated that Dunmore only had at his disposal

> *The Otter and* [Kingfisher] *– 20 guns & 170 men each;* in this number however are included those which man Occasionally the Following tenders Vizt*
>
> *4 Schooners*
> *3 Sloops*
> *3 Pilot Boats*
>
> *On board these Tenders are some 4 & 3 pounders, besides Swivels.*[20]

The Committee added that three other ships completed Dunmore's flotilla, the *William* mounted 14 guns, the *Eilbeck*, pierced for 22 guns but not equipped with them, and a brig that had just arrived from New York with 500 muskets.

---

[19] Clark, ed., "John Page to Congress, 17 Nov., 1775," *Naval Documents of the American Revolution*, Vol. 2, 1061
[20] Clark, ed., "Virginia Committee of Safety to Congress, 11 November, 1775," *Naval Documents of the American Revolution*, Vol. 2, 993-94
* Note: The *HMS Otter* and *HMS King Fisher* were 14 gun vessels with 110 man crews each.

In addition to this small flotilla, it was estimated that Dunmore's ground forces amounted to only 300 men, about half of which were British regulars from the 14th Regiment. The committee was unable to determine the number of Tories in Norfolk as, *"they are mixed with our Friends, who do not choose to declare until Our Army is there to protect them."*[21] The number of runaway slaves who had escaped to and now served under Dunmore was also difficult to determine; some accounts placed the number around a hundred, other accounts claimed it was less.[22]

The Virginia Committee of Safety also sheepishly acknowledged its inability to protect the inhabitants of Norfolk and the surrounding area from Dunmore and his Tory supporters.

> *We could not protect them, We had men enough, but were left to ransack every corner of the Country for Arms, tents & other necessarys. The few we collected were unavoidably retained here for the protection of our Magazine, Treasury & Records;*[23]

Many believed that the presence of Colonel Woodford and his troops south of the James River would intimidate the supporters of Dunmore and encourage greater resistance to him. Thus, it was urgent that Woodford reach Norfolk as soon as possible.

---

[21] Ibid.
[22] Ibid.
[23] Ibid.

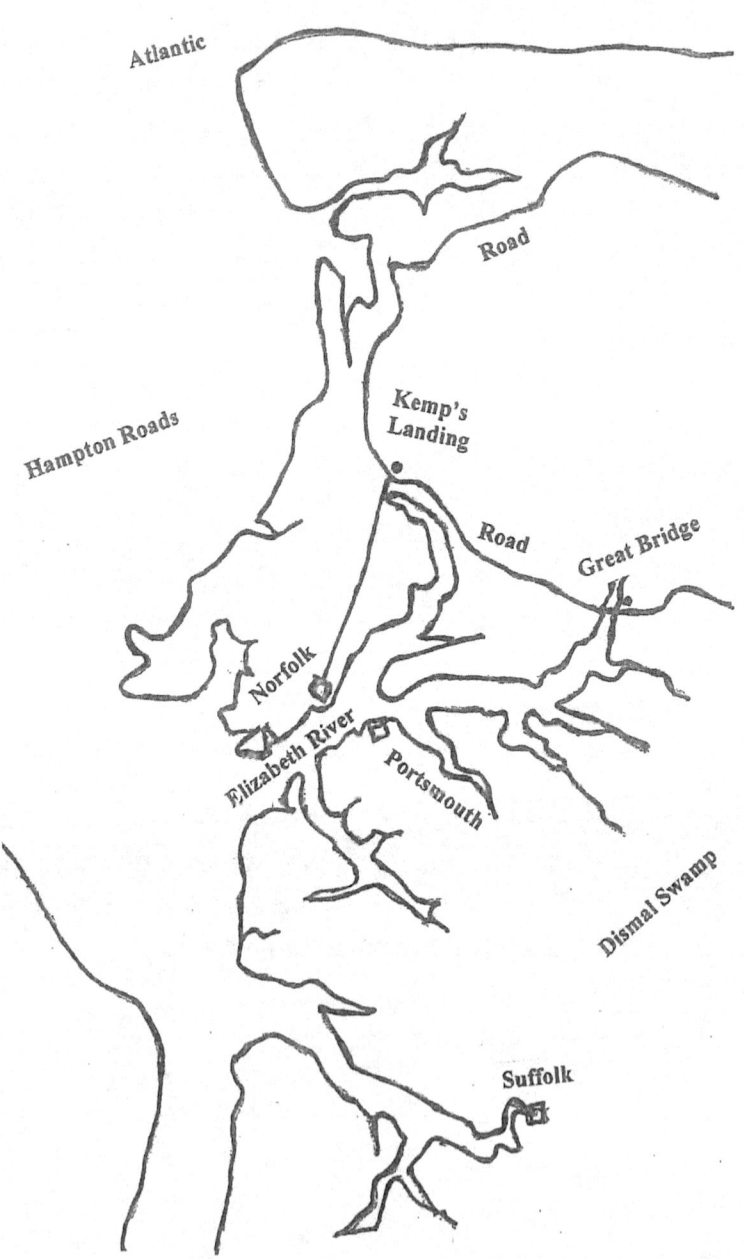

Kemp's Landing

Ever since the repulse of Captain Squire's squadron at Hampton, Governor Dunmore longed for a chance to strike back at the rebels. The efforts of his naval squadron off of Jamestown proved ineffectual, but on November 14th, Dunmore's forces routed a large party of rebels at Kemp's Landing in Princess Anne County. Dunmore described the engagement to Lord Dartmouth in a long letter in early December:

> *I was informed that a hundred and twenty or thirty North Carolina rebels had marched into this colony to a place called the Great Bridge, about ten miles from hence and a very strong post, in order to join some of ours assembled not far from thence. This I was determined not to suffer. I accordingly embarked in the night in boats with all of the 14th regiment that were able to do duty, to the amount of 109 rank and file, with 22 volunteers from Norfolk. The Carolina people had fled the evening before, but hearing at the Bridge that there were between three and four hundred of our rebels assembled at a place called Kemp's Landing nine or ten miles from the Bridge, I was then determined to disperse them if possible.*[24]

Captain Samuel Leslie, who commanded the British regulars with Dunmore, described what followed:

---

[24] Davies, ed., "Lord Dunmore to Lord Dartmouth, 6 December through 18 February, 1776," *Documents of the American Revolution*, Vol. 12, 58-59.

> *After directions had been given to erect a kind of wooden fort to secure the pass* [over the Great Bridge], *we proceeded nine or ten miles farther to Kemp's landing where we were informed there were three or four hundred of the rebels ready to receive us, under the command of a Colonel Lawson. When we arrived within sight of Kemps landing our advance guard was twice fired upon by the rebels, who had concealed themselves in very thick woods on the left of the road, but upon our rushing in among them they were very soon totally routed.*[25]

The inexperienced and undoubtedly nervous rebel militia had fired too soon, exposing their position without inflicting any damage to Dunmore's advance guard. Dunmore acknowledged that his troops were surprised by the ambush but recovered quickly and routed the rebels:

> *About a mile from* [Kemp's Landing] *our advanced party was fired upon by the rebels from a thicket before our people discovered them. I immediately ordered the main body, who were within two or three hundred paces, to advance and then detached a party with the volunteers to outflank them. At the same time the advanced guard with the grenadiers rushed into the woods. The rebels fled on all quarters; we pursued them above a mile, four of five were killed, a*

---

[25] Clark, ed., "Captain Samuel Leslie to General William Howe, 26 November, 1775," *Naval Documents of the American Revolution*, Vol. 2, 1148

> *good many wounded, and eighteen taken prisoners on that and the following day....*[26]

Captain Leslie credited the militia's precipitous flight through difficult terrain (which hampered pursuit) as the primary reason most of them escaped:

> *Their very precipitate flight and the closeness of the woods prevented our giving a much better account of them. It is said that some of them ran away even before the firing began. However, five of the rebels that we know of, were killed, two drowning in endeavouring to escape across a creek, and by all accounts a great many of them were wounded. We had only one Grenadier wounded in the knee. Colonel Hutchings and seven of the rebels were taken in the field, and Colonel Lawson & eight others were taken a day or two after.*[27]

Initial accounts from the rebel side described a much different engagement, one in which the militia stood bravely, inflicted losses on the enemy, but were eventually overwhelmed and forced to retreat. Reality set in among the rebels as more detailed accounts emerged from participants and witnesses. John Page, who neither participated in or witnessed the battle but likely received an eyewitness account from one of the militia officers involved, reported that

---

[26] Davies, ed., "Lord Dunmore to Lord Dartmouth, 6 December through 18 February, 1776," *Documents of the American Revolution*, Vol. 12, 59

[27] Clark, ed., "Captain Samuel Leslie to General William Howe, 26 November, 1775," *Naval Documents of the American Revolution*, Vol. 2, 1148

> *Two hundred of the Militia of Pr. Ann were as judiciously disposed of in Ambush as could be, and the Ministerial Tools fell into it very completely, but were so faintly attacked, that although the advanced Guards were thrown into Confusions, They with little or no Loss gained a compleat Victory. Not a tenth Part of the Militia fired. They fled in a most dastardly manner. Col. Hutchings, who served in the Ranks as a common Soldier, and several others stood bravely, but being shamefully deserted were taken Prisoners.*[28]

The Battle of Kemp's Landing was a humiliating defeat for the rebels and an important victory for Lord Dunmore. He seized upon his success to issue a bold proclamation that required, *"every Person capable of bearing Arms, to resort to His Majesty's STANDARD, or be looked upon as Traitors to His Majesty's Crown and Government."* This demand for Virginians to either support the King (and Dunmore) immediately or be viewed as a traitor was controversial in its own right, but it was overshadowed by Dunmore's declaration that, *"all indentured Servants, Negroes, or others (appertaining to Rebels,) [are] free that are able and willing to bear Arms."*[29]

In other words, Dunmore declared that any male slave or indentured servant of a rebel who ran away and agreed to take up arms under Dunmore would receive their freedom.

---

[28] Boyd, ed., "John Page to Thomas Jefferson, 24 November, 1775," *The Papers of Thomas Jefferson*, Vol. 1, 264-6

[29] Clark, ed., "Lord Dunmore's Proclamation," *Naval Documents of the American Revolution*, Vol. 2, 920

Dunmore's Force Grows

In the weeks that followed, hundreds of free Virginians (Tories) joined hundreds of runaway slaves and servants in Norfolk to comply with Dunmore's demand or accept his offer of freedom. A resident of Norfolk noted that

> *The day after* [Dunmore issued his proclamation] *the whole Country flocked to it, took the oath of allegiance...and declared their readiness to defend his Majesty's Crown & dignity.... I can assure you that L. Dunmore is so much admired in this part of the County that he might have 500 Volunteers to march with him to any part of Virginia.*"[30]

Lord Dunmore shared this optimism and confidently informed General Howe in Boston that

> *The inclosed Proclamation...has had a Wonderful effect as there are not less than three thousand that have already taken and signed the inclosed Oath.*
>
> *The Negroes are flocking in also from all quarters which I hope will oblige the Rebels to disperse to take care of their families, and property, and had I but a few more men here I would March immediately to Williamsburg my former place of residence by which I should soon compel the whole Colony to Submit.*[31]

---

[30] Scribner and Tarter, ed., "John Brown, Virginia, to Mr. William Brown, An Intercepted Letter, 21 November, 1775," *Revolutionary Virginia, The Road to Independence*, Vol. 4, 445

[31] Clark, ed., "Lord Dunmore to General William Howe, 30 November, 1775," *Naval Documents of the American Revolution*, Vol. 2, 1209-11

Dunmore emphasized his need for arms and supplies, (two items he hoped General Howe might assist him with), and detailed his efforts to organize the large number of runaway slaves and servants and loyal Virginians who had answered his call to arms:

> *We are in great want of small Arms, and if two or three light field pieces and their Carriages could be Spared they would be of great Service to us, also some Cartridge paper of which not a Sheet is to be got here, and all our Cartridges expended.*
>
> *I have...ordered a Regiment (Called the Queens own Loyal Virginia Regiment) of 500 men to be raised immediately consisting...Ten Companys each of which is to consist...50 Privates.*
>
> *You may observe by my Proclamation that I offer freedom to the Slaves, (of all Rebels) that join me, in consequence of which there are between two and three hundred already come in and these I form into a Corps as fast as they come in giving them white Officers and Non Commissioned Officers in proportion....*[32]

Governor Dunmore's optimism carried into early December, but in a report to Lord Dartmouth he included a cautionary note regarding the challenges he still faced:

> *Your lordship may observe that about three thousand have taken that oath, but of this number not above three or four hundred at most are in any degree capable of bearing arms, and the greatest part of these hardly ever made use of the gun; but I hope a short time (if they are*

---

[32] Ibid.

willing) will make them as good if not better than those who are come down to oppose them....

I am now endeavouring to raise two regiments, one of white people (called the Queen's Own Loyal Virginia Regiment), the other of Negroes called Lord Dunmore's Ethiopian Regiment. I wrote to your lordship in one of my former letters that I had taken ships into His Majesty's service, as also sloops and schooners as tenders, all of which I am now arming as well as I can; so your lordship sees I am equipping a fleet, raising an army, and all this without any order from your lordship or any other person....[33]

Dunmore's success was grudgingly acknowledged by his opponents. A week after the engagement at Kemp's Landing, John Page declared to Thomas Jefferson, that

[Dunmore's victory] *has made a compleat Conquest of Princess Ann and Norfolk and Numbers of Negroes, and Cowardly Scoundrels flock to his Standard.*[34]

However, Page was not completely discouraged by the turn of events. He remained hopeful that Colonel Woodford and his force would soon turn the situation around for the rebels:

---

[33] Davies, ed., "Lord Dunmore to Lord Dartmouth, 6 December through 18 February, 1776," *Documents of the American Revolution*, Vol. 12, 59

[34] Boyd, ed., "John Page to Thomas Jefferson, 24 November, 1775," *The Papers of Thomas Jefferson*, Vol. 1, 264-65

We hope soon to put a stop to his Career and recover all we have lost, for Col. Woodford after innumerable Delays for want of Arms &c. &c. is by this Time very near him with his Regiment and 250 Minute Men of the Culpeper Battalion and a Number of Volunteers....[35]

---

[35] Ibid.

Chapter Three

"A Second Bunker's Hill Affair, in Miniature."

December 1775

Colonel William Woodford's force of 2nd Virginia regulars and Culpeper minutemen reached Suffolk, 15 miles southwest of Portsmouth, on November 25th.[1] A day earlier, Woodford had sent Charles Scott, now a Lieutenant Colonel in the 2nd Virginia Regiment, ahead towards the Great Bridge with over 200 troops to observe the enemy. Ever the cautious officer, Woodford ordered Scott to, *"be safe kept 'till my arrival."*[2]

The Great Bridge was actually a long, narrow, manmade causeway with several wooden bridges spanning the southern branch of the Elizabeth River and its tributaries and marshland. Norfolk lay eleven miles north of the main bridge span and since most of the terrain south of Norfolk was marsh and swamp, the Great Bridge road was the primary southern land route to Norfolk.

Lieutenant Colonel Scott was eager to confront Dunmore's small force of *"Tories and Blacks"* (who had removed the planks from the main bridge and were posted in a small

---

[1] D.R. Anderson, ed., "Colonel Woodford to Edmund Pendleton, 26 November, 1775," in "The Letters of Colonel William Woodford, Colonel Robert Howe, and General Charles Lee to Edmund Pendleton," *Richmond College Historical Papers*, (June, 1915), 104

[2] Ibid.

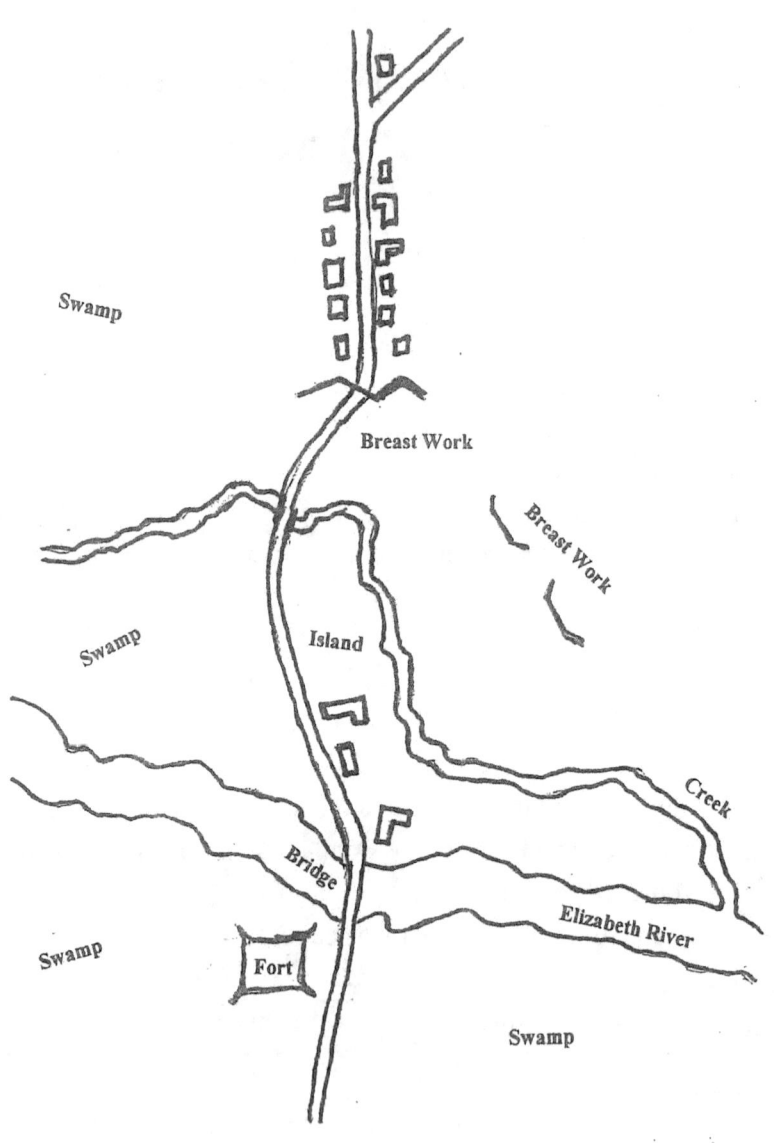

wooden stockade fort on the north bank of the river adjacent to the dismantled bridge) but Colonel Woodford cautioned against such a move.[3] Woodford informed Scott that a severe shortage of ammunition and arms made it impossible for him to march to the Great Bridge until, *"a number of Ball is run, cartridges made, arms Repair'd &ct. &ct."* [4] The best Woodford could do to support Scott was to send him two more companies of regulars under Major Alexander Spotswood.

In Norfolk, Lord Dunmore and his force of British regulars, runaway slaves, and Tory volunteers, braced for the arrival of Woodford's troops. Word of their approach in late November had prompted Dunmore to withdraw the troops of the 14th Regiment from their quarters in Gosport – a village next to Portsmouth where they had spent much of the fall sheltered in Andrew Sprowles shipyard buildings – and redeploy them across the Elizabeth River in Norfolk.[5] Captain Samuel Leslie, the ranking officer of the 14th Regiment, informed General William Howe in Boston of their move and pledged to do everything possible to prevent the destruction of Norfolk:

> *We took possession of this town the 23d Inst and are now busy intrenching ourselves in the best manner we can, as a large body of the Rebels consisting of eight or nine hundred men are within ten or twelve miles of us. They marched from Williamsburg about a fortnight ago with an intention to pillage and burn this town,*

---

[3] Ibid.
[4] Ibid.
[5] Clark, ed., "Captain Samuel Leslie to General William Howe, 26 November, 1775," *Naval Documents of the American Revolution*, Vol. 2, 1148

which however we shall do everything that is possible to prevent....[6]

Lord Dunmore realized that to maintain his base of operation at Norfolk he had to prevent the rebels from gaining control of the Great Bridge. He explained the bridge's importance, and his efforts to defend it, to General Howe:

Having heard that a thousand chosen Men belonging to the Rebels, a great part of which were Rifle men, were on their March to attack us here so to cut off our provisions, I determined to take possession of the pass at the great Bridge which Secures us the greatest part of two Counties to supply us with provisions. I accordingly ordered a Stockade Fort to be erected there, which was done in a few days, and I put an Officer and Twenty five men to Garrison it, with some Volunteers and Negroes.[7]

Bloodshed and Stalemate at the Great Bridge

While Colonel Woodford hurried to equip and supply his troops in Suffolk with functioning firearms and cartridges, Lieutenant Colonel Scott's advance guard entrenched just south of the Great Bridge and skirmished with Dunmore's forces. A few days after their first clash, Scott reported that, *"We have been well informed that we killed 16 negroes and 5 white men the first day we got to this place."*[8] Although

---

[6] Ibid.
[7] Clark, ed., "Lord Dunmore to General William Howe, 30 November, 1775," *Naval Documents of the American Revolution*, Vol. 2, 1209-11
[8] Clark, ed., "Lt. Col. Charles Scott to a Williamsburg Correspondent, 4 December, 1775," *Naval Documents of the American Revolution*, Vol. 2, 1274-75

Dunmore's losses were likely much lighter, (he claimed that after a week of skirmishes he had only suffered one or two slightly wounded soldiers while the "rebels" had 15-20 soldiers killed) the number of casualties that both sides claimed to have inflicted on the other suggests that the skirmish was heated.[9]

The bulk of Lieutenant Colonel Scott's force of nearly 200 men was posted behind hastily built breastworks on the southern edge of the causeway. Sentries were posted forward of the breastworks at night, on what was essentially an island, with the Elizabeth River to the north, a small creek to the south (fifty yards in front of the "rebel" breastworks), and marsh on either side of the causeway. Hidden amongst a few buildings and piles of debris close to the dismantled bridge and Dunmore's fort, Colonel Scott's sentries were positioned to alarm their comrades at the breastworks if the enemy approached at night. For their own safety, the sentinels were withdrawn back to the breastworks at dawn each day.

Scott also detached a party of about 40 troops five miles downriver to guard a crossing point and prevent a surprise attack from the enemy.[10] The day after they arrived this detachment was attacked by Dunmore's troops. Lieutenant Colonel Scott reported that

> *Lieutenant Tibbs, who had the command of the boat guard, about 5 miles from this place, was attacked by a party of the king's troops, and several negroes,*

---

[9] Clark, ed. "Lord Dunmore to Lord Dartmouth, 6 December through 18 February, 1776," *Documents of the American Revolution,* Vol. 12, 59

[10] Anderson, ed., "Colonel Woodford to Edmund Pendleton, 4 December, 1775," *Richmond College Historical Papers,* 106

> upon which some of our people gave ground; but mr. Tibbs, with 4 of his people, maintained his post until I reinforced him with 50 men under capt. [George] Nicholas, who were obliged to pass through a very heavy fire from the enemy. Before they got to the place, mr. Tibbs had beat off the enemy, and killed 7 of their men, amongst whom was the commander of the party.[11]

Although Lord Dunmore's account of the engagement suggests that Scott's casualty estimate was once again inflated, another heated engagement had obviously occurred between the two sides.

Colonel Woodford, with the main body of rebel troops, reached the Great Bridge soon after this skirmish, on December 2nd. Woodford informed Edmund Pendleton and the Committee of Safety of his arrival and reported that

> I...found the Enemy Posted on the opposite side of the Bridge, in a Stockade Fort, with two four pounders, some swivels & wall pieces, with which they keep up a constant Fire, have done no other damage than kill'd Corpl Davis with a cannon ball....[12]

Woodford estimated that Dunmore's fort was defended by 250 men, most of who were escaped slaves commanded by

---

[11] Clark, ed., "Lt. Col. Charles Scott to a Williamsburg Correspondent, 4 December, 1775," *Naval Documents of the American Revolution*, Vol. 2, 1274-75

[12] Anderson, ed., "Colonel Woodford to Edmund Pendleton, 4 December, 1775," *Richmond College Historical Papers*, 106

sergeants of the 14th Regiment.[13] A handful of Tories also manned the fort. Woodford speculated that it might be possible to capture it, but the presence of cannon meant that its conquest would come at a very high cost in lives:

> *The Enemys Fort, I think, might have been taken, but not without the loss of many of our Men, their Situation is very advantageous, & no way to attack them, but by exposing most of the Troops to their Fire upon a large open Marsh.*[14]

As for his own fortifications, Colonel Woodford reported that

> *We have raised a strong Breastwork upon the lower part of the street joining the Causeway, from which Centries are posted at some old Rubbish not far from the Bridge (which is mostly destroy'd).*[15]

Although he believed that he held a strong position, Woodford was concerned about his limited supply of gunpowder and the lack of blankets and shoes for his men.

> *Our small stock of Ammunition will be soon expended, & I must request another supply; an additional Blanket to each soldier* [will] *be very necessary, if to be had. The men are tolerably well at present, but the dampness of this Ground, without straw (which is not to be had) must soon lay many of*

---

[13] Ibid.
[14] Ibid., 107
[15] Ibid.

> them up, & Houses that are tolerably safe from the Enemy's Cannon, can only be procured for a few.[16]

One officer who likely found shelter in one of the "safe" houses out of range (but not earshot) of Dunmore's guns was Lieutenant Colonel Scott. It had been over a week since he had led his detachment ahead of Woodford's main body to the Great Bridge and now that reinforcements had arrived Scott allowed himself a well deserved rest. He wrote to a friend that

> *Last night was the first of my pulling off my clothes for 12 nights successively. Believe me, my good friend, I never was so fatigued with duty in my whole life;* [17]

Despite the large number of reinforcements, it is likely that Lieutenant Colonel Scott still found it difficult to rest:

> *We still keep up a pretty heavy fire between us, from light to light. We have only lost two men, and about half an hour ago one of our people was shot through the arm, which broke the bone near his hand.*[18]

The skirmishing continued downriver as well. Within days of his arrival, Colonel Woodford sent a large detachment of troops under Colonel Edward Stevens of the Culpeper Minutemen across the river to encircle and surprise Dunmore's guard at the crossing. Woodford reported that

---

[16] Ibid., 108-09
[17] Clark, ed., "Lt. Col. Charles Scott to a Williamsburg Correspondent, 4 December, 1775," *Naval Documents of the American Revolution*, Vol. 2, 1274-75
[18] Ibid.

> *They crossed about midnight, & got to the Enemy's centinals without being discover'd, one of them challenged & not being answer'd, Fired at our party, the fire was returned by our men, & an over Eagerness at first, & rather a backwardness afterwards, occasion'd some confusion, & prevented the Colo's plan from being so well executed as he intended, however, he* [burned] *their Fortification & House, in which one negro perished, killed one dead upon the spott, & took two others prisoners...this party (consisting of 26 Blacks & 9 Whites) escaped under the cover of night, he also took four new Muskets.*[19]

Lieutenant Colonel Scott confirmed Woodford's account and reported that Colonel Stevens's force of 100 men faced about 30 and, "*being too eager, began the fire...without orders, and kept it up very hot for near 15 minutes.*"[20]

Although the bulk of the enemy guard escaped, their post was destroyed. Discovered among the captured troops and abandoned equipment were altered musket balls designed to split into quarters upon impact. Colonel Woodford was outraged by the discovery and sent one to Williamsburg for the Committee of Safety and 4th Virginia Convention to see:

> *The bearer brings you one of the Balls taken out of the cartridges found upon the negro Prisoners, as they were extremely well made, & no doubt by some of the non comd. Officers of the Regulars, will submit it to*

---

[19] Anderson, ed., "Colonel Woodford to Edmund Pendleton, 5 December, 1775," *Richmond College Historical Papers*, 110

[20] Clark, ed., "Lt. Col. Charles Scott to a Williamsburg Correspondent, 5 December, 1775," *Naval Documents of the Am. Rev.* Vol. 2, 1299

the Convention, by who's orders this Horrid preparation was made for the Flesh of our Countrymen, the others are prepared in the same manner, likewise all that have been found in the Houses &ct; – I have never suffer'd a soldier of mine to do a thing of this kind – nor will I allow it to be done for the future, notwithstanding this provocation....[21]

Two nights later, the "rebels" struck again, attacking the same post – re-occupied and reinforced by Dunmore with 70 men. This time Lieutenant Colonel Scott led the attack with 150 men. Colonel Woodford described the engagement to Edmund Pendleton:

I have the pleasure to inform you...that my detachment last night under the Command of Lieut. Colo. Scott beat up the Quarters of the Enemys other party, who I inform'd you had again taken post opposite our Boat Guard, they killed one white man & three negro's, took three of the Latter Prisoners, two of which are wounded, one mortally, with six Muskets & 3 Bayonetts.[22]

Woodford explained that bad luck prevented his troops from surprising the enemy:

[Colonel Scott] *unluckily fell in with a cart coming from Norfolk, guarded by four men, some distance from the Enemy's post, who Fired upon our party &*

---

[21] Anderson, ed., "Colonel Woodford to Edmund Pendleton, 5 December, 1775," *Richmond College Historical Papers*, 112
[22] Anderson, ed., "Colonel Woodford to Edmund Pendleton, 7 December, 1775," *Richmond College Historical Papers*, 114

> *alarm'd them, otherways there is no doubt most of their men would have fallen into our Hands, their number 70, Scott's party, 150, who all escaped unhurt, one man only was grazed by a Ball in the Thumb.*[23]

Williamsburg Grows Anxious

Although Colonel Woodford's troops had successfully engaged Dunmore's forces in a number of skirmishes, apprehension grew among the leaders in Williamsburg that time was running out to drive Dunmore from Norfolk. Thomas Ludwell Lee of Stafford County summarized the concern of many in the 4th Virginia Convention and Committee of Safety:

> *Our Army has been for some time arrested in its march to Norfolk by a redoubt, or stockade, or hog pen, as they call it here, by way of derision, at the end of this bridge. Tho,' by the way, this hog pen seems filled with a parcel of wild-boars, which we appear not overfond to meddle with. My apprehension is that we shall be amused at this outpost, until Dunmore gets the lines at Norfolk finished; where he is now entrenching, & mounting cannon, some hundreds of negro's being employ'd in the work.*[24]

---

[23] Ibid.
[24] Clark, ed., "Thomas Ludwell Lee to Richard Henry Lee, 9 December, 1775," *Naval Documents of the American Revolution*, Vol. 3, 26-27

Another member of the Committee of Safety, John Page of Gloucester County, expressed a similar concern and declared that desperate measures might be necessary to dislodge Dunmore from Norfolk:

> *Col. Woodford with 600 Men has been hitherto prevented from passing the Great Bridge on his Way to Norfolk by a Body of Negroes headed by Scotch Men [Tories] & a few Regulars -- & I make no Doubt that before he can pass, Norfolk will be made impregnable by Land – it is capable of being strongly fortified on a small Neck of Land near the Church where it is said Ld D has for some Time past employd several hundred Negros – The only Way I conceive that Town can be taken without Cannon, must be, by taking Advantage of the Night & throwing into it by Water 3 or 400 resolute Fellows -- & make a bold push at the Sloops of War at the same Time.*[25]

Fortunately for the 'rebels", Page's dire assessment proved unnecessary; reinforcements from North Carolina, reportedly with cannon, were on the way.

Lieutenant Colonel Scott acknowledged as early as December 4th the arrival of a company of troops from North Carolina and reported that hundreds more (with artillery) were marching behind them:

---

[25] Clark, ed., "John Page to Richard Henry Lee, 9 December, 1775," *Naval Documents of the American Revolution*, Vol. 3, 25-26

> *The Carolina forces are joining us. One company came in yesterday, and we expect 8 or 900 of them by to-morrow, or next day at farthest, with several pieces of artillery, and plenty of ammunition and other warlike stores.*[26]

In expectation of the cannon, Colonel Woodford reported that his troops

> *Were now making the necessary preparations to raise Batterys for these Cannon upon the most advantageous Ground to play upon their Fort & send a large detachment at the same time to intercept their Retreat.*[27]

Even Lord Dunmore believed that a large reinforcement of rebel troops were on their way to the Great Bridge and this belief helped spur him to action:

> *The Rebels had procured some Cannon from North Carolina, [which were expected to arrive any day] and that they were also to be reinforced from Williamsburg, and knowing that our little Fort was not in a Condition to withstand anything heavier than Musquet Shot, I thought it advisable to risqué Something to save the Fort.*[28]

---

[26] Clark, ed., "Lt. Col. Charles Scott to a Williamsburg Correspondent, 4 December, 1775," *Naval Documents of the American Revolution*, Vol. 2, 1274-75

[27] Anderson, ed., "Colonel Woodford to Edmund Pendleton, 4 December, 1775," *Richmond College Historical Papers*, 108

[28] Clark, ed., "Lord Dunmore to Lord Dartmouth, 13 December, 1775," *Naval Documents of the American Revolution*, Vol. 3, 140-41

Dunmore Decides to Attack

A significant factor behind Lord Dunmore's ill fated decision to attack Colonel Woodford's breastworks on December 9th was inaccurate information he reportedly received from a deserter from the rebel camp. Colonel Woodford reported after the battle that

> *A servant belonging to major* [Thomas] *Marshal, who deserted the other night from col.* [Charles] *Scott's party, has completely taken his lordship in. Lieutenant* [John] *Batut...informs, that this fellow told them not more than 300 shirtmen were here; and that imprudent man* [Dunmore] *catched at the bait, dispatching capt. Leslie with all the regulars (about 200) who arrived at the bridge about 3 o' clock in the morning.*[29]

It remains uncertain whether the deserter purposefully or accidently misled Dunmore about Woodford's troop strength, but it appears likely that Dunmore viewed the news that such a small number of rebels were across the causeway as an opportunity that would soon disappear when the expected reinforcements arrived. As a result, on the evening of December 8th, Dunmore rushed his own reinforcements to the

---

[29] Clark, ed., "Colonel Woodford to Edmund Pendleton, 9 December, 1775," *Naval Documents of the American Revolution*, Vol. 3, 28

Note: Colonel Woodford repeated this account in a second letter to Edmund Pendleton the next day. A similar account was included in the *Annual Register for the Year 1776*, p. 29
"It has been said, that we were led into this unfortunate affair, through the designed false intelligence of a pretended deserter, who was tutored for the purpose."

fort, which included most of the regulars of the 14th Regiment (approximately 120 under Captain Leslie) 60 Tory volunteers, and a detachment of sailors (to help man the fort's cannon). A British midshipman from the *HMS Otter* was part of this force and recalled that

> *Our troops, with about sixty Townsmen from Norfolk, and a detachment of Sailors from the ships, among whom I had the honour to march, set out from Norfolk to attack once more the Rebels at the great bridge....We arrived at the Fort half an hour after three in the morning, and, after refreshing ourselves, prepared to attack the Rebels in their intrenchments.*[30]

These reinforcements joined the garrison of Tories, runaway slaves, and handful of regulars already at the fort early in the morning of December 9th.

Dunmore's Plan

Worried that his small wooden fort would not hold against an assault by the soon to be reinforced rebels, Lord Dunmore chose to strike preemptively. In his report to Lord Dartmouth after the battle, Dunmore explained that his plan called for

> *Two Companies of Negroes to make a detour,* [cross the river] *and fall in behind the Rebels a little before break of Day in the morning, and just as Day began to break, to fall upon the rear of the Rebels, which* [Dummore] *expected would draw their attention, and*

---

[30] Clark, ed., "Letter from a Midshipman on Board H.M. Sloop Otter, 9 December, 1775," *Naval Documents of the American Revolution*, Vol. 3, 29

> make them leave the breast work they had made near the Fort, [Captain Leslie] *was then with the Regulars, the Volunteers and some recruits to sally out of the Fort, and attack* [the rebel] *breast work....*[31]

Dunmore hoped that the distraction caused by his black troops would allow his main force under Captain Samuel Leslie to cross the dismantled bridge and narrow causeway and storm the rebel breastworks against limited opposition. Unfortunately for Dunmore, miscommunication, or perhaps a misunderstanding of orders, prevented the diversionary attack from occurring. Dunmore noted after the battle that

> *The Negroes by some mistake were sent out of the Fort to guard a pass, where it was thought the Rebels might attempt to pass, and where in fact some of them had Crossed a Night or two before, burnt a house or two, and returned; Captain Leslie not finding the Negroes there, imprudently Sallied out of the Fort at break of Day in the morning....*[32]

---

[31] Clark, ed., "Lord Dunmore to Lord Dartmouth, 6 December through 18 February, 1776," *Naval Documents of the American Revolution*, Vol. 3, 141

[32] Ibid.
   Note: Lord Dunmore claimed in this letter that he left the discretion of whether to actually launch the attack with Captain Leslie.

The Attack

Under cover of the dim light of dawn Captain Leslie's force of approximately 350 men advanced from their fort and hastily re-laid the bridge planks that had been removed weeks earlier.[33] If the handful of sleepy rebel pickets sheltered by the buildings on the island initially failed to notice the activity at the bridge, the discharge of the fort's cannon undoubtedly drew their attention that way. Startled at what they saw, the rebel sentries opened fire upon Dunmore's troops. One rebel account of the battle included high praise for the sentries:

> *The conduct of our sentinels I cannot pass over in silence. Before they quitted their stations they fired at least three rounds as the enemy were crossing the bridge, and one of them, who was posted behind some shingles, kept his ground till he had fired eight times, and after receiving a whole platoon, made his escape over the causeway into our breast works.*[34]

As the handful of sentinels scurried back to the rebel earthworks approximately 300 yards to the rear, their comrades behind the breastwork began to stir, realizing that the gunfire they heard was not the normal morning salute of the past few days.

---

[33] Clark, ed., "Letter to John Pinkney, 20 December, 1775," *Naval Documents of the American Revolution*, Vol. 3, 186-89
[34] Ibid.
   Note: The brave sentinel who stood his ground for so long was twenty year old Billy Flora, a free born black volunteer from Norfolk.

Four hundred yards south of the earthworks at the main rebel encampment, however, few of Colonel Woodford's troops (who had just awakened to reveille) took notice of the distant gunfire. Major Thomas Spotswood recalled

> *We were alarmed this morning by the firing of some guns after reveille beating, which, as the enemy had paid us this compliment several times before, we at first concluded to be nothing but a morning salute.*[35]

Colonel Woodford had a similar reaction:

> *After reveille beating, two or three great guns, and some musquetry were discharged from the enemy's fort, which, as it was not an unusual thing, was but little regarded.*[36]

The situation was much different at the rebel breastworks. Realizing that they were under attack, the commander of the guard, Lieutenant Edward Travis, ordered his small detachment of approximately sixty men, *"to reserve their fire till the enemy came within the distance of fifty yards."*[37] A small stream lay about 50 yards in front of the rebel breastworks and served as an excellent range marker for the rebels. To their front across the narrow 200 yard causeway were more than five times their number of enemy troops with

---

[35] Peter Force, ed., "Major Spotswood to a Friend in Williamsburgh, 9 December, 1775," *American Archives*, Vol. 4, 224
[36] Clark, ed., "Col. Woodford to Edmund Pendleton, 10 December, 1775," *Naval Documents of the American Revolution*, Vol. 3, 39-40
[37] Force, ed., "Major Spotswood to a Friend in Williamsburgh, 9 December, 1775," *American Archives*, Vol. 4, 224 and Clark, "Letter to Pinkney, 20 December, 1775", *Naval Documents of the American Revolution*, Vol. 3, 186-89

two cannon that one rebel recalled were, *"planted on the edge of the island, facing the left of our breast-work,* [and] *played briskly...upon us."*[38]

Joining the cannon at the edge of the island were the Tory and black soldiers of Dunmore, over 200 strong. Behind them rose the smoke of several buildings – formerly the outposts of the rebel sentries but now torched by Dunmore's troops. Captain Leslie remained on the island with the Tory and black troops while Captain Charles Fordyce led the British regulars of the 14th Regiment, 120 strong in a column six abreast, across the narrow causeway to storm the rebel earthworks.[39]

Back in the main "rebel" camp, the gravity of the situation had finally become apparent. Major Spotswood recalled

> *I heard Adjutant Blackburn call out, Boys! Stand to your arms! Colonel Woodford and myself immediately got equipped, and ran out; the Colonel pressed down to the breastwork in our front, and my alarm-post being two hundred and fifty yards in another quarter, I ran to it as fast as I could, and by the time I had made all ready for engaging, a very heavy fire ensued at the breastwork, in which were not more than sixty men;*[40]

The heavy fire that Major Spotswood heard came from Lieutenant Travis's guard detail and a few brave reinforcements who had rushed forward at the first alarm.

---

[38] Clark, "Letter to Pinkney, 20 December, 1775," *Naval Documents of the American Revolution*, Vol. 3, 186-89

[39] Clark, "Letter from a Midshipman on Board H.M. Sloop Otter, 9 December, 1775" *Naval Documents of the American Revolution*, Vol. 3, 29

[40] Force, ed., "Major Spotswood to a Friend in Williamsburgh, 9 December, 1775," *American Archives*, Vol. 4, 224

Lieutenant John Marshall of the Culpeper Minutemen (and future Chief Justice of the Supreme Court) was at Great Bridge and remembered

> *As is the practice with raw troops, the bravest rushed to the works, where, regardless of order, they kept up a heavy fire on the front of the British column.*[41]

The valor of some of the rebels was also acknowledged by Major Spotswood, who proudly noted in a letter immediately after the engagement that as the redcoats approached the breastworks with fixed bayonets, "*Our young troops received them with firmness, and behaved as well as it was possible for soldiers to do.*"[42] In his own letter after the battle, Colonel Woodford also commented on the rebel fire from the breastwork, writing that, "*perhaps a hotter fire never happened, or a greater carnage, for the number of troops.*"[43]

The hot fire delivered upon the British originated not only from the breastworks directly in front of them, but also from breastworks on some high ground west of the causeway. Riflemen from the Culpeper Minute Battalion manned this position and poured deadly enfilade fire into the British column's right flank.[44] According to one American account, the intense rebel small arms fire from both positions

---

[41] John Marshall, *The Life of George Washington,* Vol. 2, (Fredericksburg, VA: The Citizens Guild of Washington's Boyhood Home, 1926), 132
[42] Force, ed., "Major Spotswood to a Friend in Williamsburgh, 9 December, 1775," *American Archives,* Vol. 4, 224
[43] Clark, ed., "Col. Woodford to Edmund Pendleton, 10 December, 1775," *Naval Documents of the American Revolution,* Vol. 3, 39-49
[44] *The Annual Register for the Year 1776,* 4th ed. 29

> *Threw* [the advancing British regulars] *into some confusion, but they were instantly rallied by a Captain Fordyce, and advanced along the causeway with great resolution, keeping up a constant and heavy fire as they approached. The brave Fordyce exerted himself to keep up their spirits, reminded them of their ancient glory, and waving his hat over his head, encouragingly told them the day was their own. Thus pressing forward, he fell within fifteen steps to the breast-work. His wounds were many, and his death would have been that of a hero, had he met it in a better cause.*[45]

A British participant in the battle noted that

> [The rebel] *fire was so heavy, that, had we not retreated as we did, we should every one have been cut off. Figure to yourself a strong breast-work built across a causeway, on which six men only could advance a-breast; a large swamp almost surrounding them, at the back of which were two small breast-works to flank us in our attack on their intrenchments. Under these disadvantages it was impossible to succeed; yet our men were so enraged, that all the intreaties, and scarcely the threats of their Officers, could prevail on them to retreat; which at last they did.*[46]

---

[45] Clark, "Letter to Pinkney, 20 December, 1775", *Naval Documents of the American Revolution*, Vol. 3, 186-89

[46] Clark, "Letter from a Midshipman on Board *H.M. Sloop Otter*, 9 December, 1775," *Naval Documents of the American Revolution*, Vol. 3, 29

Captain Fordyce, riddled with over a dozen wounds, was one of many redcoats to fall before the American earthworks. Strewn about the ground just a few paces from the Virginians were over thirty British dead and wounded. One rebel officer described a scene of bloody carnage before the breastworks:

> *The scene, when the dead and wounded were bro't off, was too much; I then saw the horrors of war in perfection, worse than can be imagin'd; 10 and 12 bullets thro' many; limbs broke in 2 or 3 places; brains turning out. Good God, what a sight!*[47]

Captain Fordyce and twelve British privates lay dead in front of the breastworks and nearly a score of wounded redcoats, including Lieutenant John Batut, who led the British advance guard, were taken prisoner. An American observer noted that

> *The progress of the enemy was now at an end;* [the survivors] *retreated over the causeway with precipitation, and were dreadfully galled in their rear. Hitherto, on our side only the guard, consisting of twenty five, and some others, upon the whole, amounting to not more than ninety, had been engaged. Only the regulars of the 14th regiment, in number one hundred and twenty, had advanced upon the causeway, and about two hundred and thirty tories and negroes had, after crossing the bridge, continued upon the island.*[48]

---

[47] Charles Campbell, ed., "Richard Kidder Meade to Theodorick Bland Jr., 18 December, 1775" *The Bland Papers*, Vol. 1, (1840) 38-39
[48] Clark, "Letter to Pinkney, 20 December, 1775," *Naval Documents of the American Revolution*, Vol. 3, 186-89

Although the British assault had been repulsed, the battle was not over, for Captain Leslie rallied his men on the island:

> *The regulars, after retreating along the causeway, were again rallied by captain Leslie, and the two field pieces continued to play upon our men.*[49]

While Dunmore's troops re-grouped around their cannon, Colonel Woodford led troops from the main camp through heavy artillery fire to reinforce the breastworks:

> *It was at this time that colonel Woodford was advancing down the street to the breast-work with the main body, and against him was now directed the whole fire of the enemy. Never were cannon better served, but yet in the face of them and the musquetry, which kept up a continual blaze, our men marched on with the utmost intrepidity.*[50]

Major Spotswood also noted the severity of the enemy cannon fire:

> *The* [enemy] *field pieces raked the whole length of the street, and absolutely threw double-headed shot at far as the church, and afterwords, as our troops approached, cannonaded them heavily with grapeshot.*[51]

---

[49] Ibid.
[50] Ibid.
[51] Force, ed., "Major Spotswood to a Friend in Williamsburgh, 9 December, 1775," *American Archives*, Vol. 4, 224

Spotswood credited divine providence for protecting all but one man, who was wounded in the hand, from the intense artillery barrage.[52]

With Dunmore's battered troops stubbornly holding the island, Colonel Woodford sent Colonel Edward Stevens with the Culpeper minutemen to reinforce the riflemen on the left flank. The rebel militia poured more deadly enfilade fire from their rifles upon Captain Leslie's troops. The accurate American rifle fire finally prompted Captain Leslie, who was dismayed at his losses (especially that of his nephew, Lieutenant Peter Leslie) to withdraw to the fort. One "rebel" noted that

> *The enemy fled into their fort, leaving behind them the two field pieces, which, however, they took care to spike up with nails. Many were killed and wounded in the flight, but colonel Woodford very prudently restrained his troops from urging their pursuit too far. From the beginning of the attack till the repulse from the breast work might be about fourteen or fifteen minutes; till the total defeat upwards of half an hour. It is said that some of the enemy preferred death to captivity, from fear of being scalped, which lord Dunmore inhumanly told them would be their fate should they be taken alive. Thirty one, killed and wounded, fell into our hands, and the number borne off was much greater.*[53]

---

[52] Ibid.
[53] Clark, "Letter to Pinkney, 20 December, 1775," *Naval Documents of the American Revolution*, Vol. 3, 186-89

Aftermath

The Battle of Great Bridge was a decisive victory for the Virginians. Colonel Woodford proudly described it as, *"a second Bunker's Hill affair, in miniature; with this difference, that we kept our post, and had only one man wounded in the hand."*[54] More than one observer attributed the lack of rebel casualties to providence (divine intervention). The British 14th Regiment of Foot, on the other hand, was shattered in the attack. Their brave, bold assault on the rebel breastworks cost them half their men. Colonel Woodford initially estimated Dunmore's losses at 50 men, noting that some of their dead and wounded were taken back to the fort. He reported that

> *We buried 12, besides...*[Captain Fordyce] *(him with all the military honors due to his rank) and have prisoners lieutenant Batut, and 16 privates; all wounded; 35 stands of arms and accoutrements, 3 officers* [fusils], *powder, ball, and cartridges, with sundry other things, have likewise fallen into our hands.*[55]

Dunmore's report on the 14th Regiment's losses (which was presumably more accurate) claimed 3 officers and 17 men killed and 1 officer and 43 men wounded.[56] The number of casualties among Dunmore's Tory and black soldiers is unknown.

---

[54] Clark, ed., "Colonel Woodford to Edmund Pendleton, 10 December, 1775," *Naval Documents of the American Revolution*, Vol. 3, 39-40
[55] Ibid.
[56] Clark, ed., "Lord Dunmore to Lord Dartmouth, 13 December, 1775" *Naval Documents of the American Revolution*, Vol. 3, 141

Calm settled over the causeway after the battle as Colonel Woodford dispatched an officer under a flag of truce to allow Captain Leslie to collect his dead and wounded from the battlefield.[57] One observer reported that

> *The work of death being over, every one's attention was directed to the succor* [assistance] *of the unhappy sufferers, and it is an undoubted fact, that captain Leslie was so affected with the tenderness of our troops towards those who were yet capable of assistance, that he gave signs from the fort of his thankfulness for it.*[58]

With both sides secure behind their fortifications, the sun set with no more fighting. Captain Leslie abandoned the fort shortly after dark and marched the shaken garrison to Norfolk. Lord Dunmore explained Captain Leslie's decision to Lord Dartmouth:

> *This loss having so much weakened our before but very weak Corps, and Captain Leslie being much depressed by the loss of Lieutenant Leslie, his Nephew, and thinking that the Enemy elated with this little advantage they had gained over us, might force their way across the branch, either above, or below, and by that means, Cut off the Communication between us, determined to evacuate the Fort, and accordingly left it soon after it was dark, and*

---

[57] Clark, ed., "Colonel Woodford to Edmund Pendleton, 9 December, 1775," *Naval Documents of the American Revolution*, Vol. 3, 28

[58] Clark, "Letter to Pinkney, 20 December, 1775," *Naval Documents of the American Revolution*, Vol. 3, 186-89

> *returned with the whole to this place* [Norfolk]; *The Rebels however remained at the Bridge for a day or two.*[59]

Colonel Woodford's troops took possession of the abandoned fort in the morning and found it in disarray. Woodford reported that

> *We have taken possession of* [the fort] *this morning, and found therein the stores mentioned in the enclosed list, to wit, 7 guns, 4 of them sorry, 1 bayonet, 29 spades, 2 shovels, 6 cannon, a few shot, some bedding, a part of a hogshead of rum, two or more barrels, the contents unknown, but supposed to be rum, 2 barrels of bread, about 20 quarters of beef, half a box of candles, 4 or 5 dozen of quart bottles, 4 or 5 iron pots, a few axes and old lumber; the spikes, I find, cannot be got out of the cannon without drilling.*[60]

Woodford made another observation that led him to believe the enemy had suffered much greater than he realized:

> *From the vast effusion of blood on the bridge, and in the fort, from the accounts of the sentries, who saw many bodies carried out of the fort to be interred and other circumstances, I conceive their loss to be much greater than I thought it yesterday, and the victory to be complete.*[61]

---

[59] Clark, ed., "Lord Dunmore to Lord Dartmouth, 13 December, 1775," *Naval Documents of the American Revolution,* Vol. 3, 140-41

[60] Clark, ed., "Colonel Woodford to Edmund Pendleton, 10 December, 1775," *Naval Documents of the American Revolution*, Vol. 3, 40-41

[61] Ibid.

The 14th Regiment's heavy losses apparently had a strong impact on Captain Leslie. The Virginia Committee of Safety in Williamsburg gleefully reported a few days after the battle that

> *The Regulars, disgusted, refused to fight in junction with Blacks; and Captain Leslie, we are told, declared no more of his troops should be sacrificed to whims, and put them on board the ships, in consequence of which Norfolk is abandoned, and we expect is now occupied by our troops, who were on their march there when our last account was dispatched. Many Tories are come to us, and their cases now under consideration. More notorious ones are gone on board the vessels, which have in them very valuable cargoes.*[62]

Norfolk Abandoned

Whether Captain Leslie refused to cooperate further with Lord Dunmore (as the committee's account suggests) is unclear, but it does appear that Leslie had had enough of the land campaign. Upon his midnight arrival in Norfolk, he immediately placed his troops onboard two ships anchored off of the city.[63] The condition of his force, combined with the accounts of the battle, greatly unsettled the Tory and black troops who had worked so diligently constructing entrenchments on the edge of town. One Tory, who sought refuge aboard the H.M.S. *Kingfisher*, noted that

---

[62] Clark, ed., "Letter from the Virginia Committee of Safety, 16 December, 1775," *Naval Documents of the American Revolution*, Vol. 3, 132

[63] Clark, "Letter from a Midshipman on Board *H.M. Sloop Otter*, 9 December, 1775," *Naval Documents of the American Revolution*, Vol. 3, 29 and "Thomas Macknight to Rev. Macknight, 26 December, 1775," *Naval Documents of the American Revolution*, Vol. 3, 260-61

Norfolk and Portsmouth

A PLAN of PORTSMOUTH HARBOUR in the PROVINCE of VIRGINIA Showing the WORKS erected by the BRITISH FORCES for its DEFENCE 1781

> *This unfortunate attack* [at the Great Bridge] *which was made in the morning about sunrise dispirited most people.... All thoughts of defending the Town were given up. The Soldiers are gone on board two Transports and those who have dared to be active in supporting Government are under the necessity also of taking refuge in vessels. Such as had not that in their power are left to the mercy of the Rebels who have taken possession of the Town – a single regiment a few weeks ago would have reduced this colony to a sense of its duty. God only knows when it will be done, now....*[64]

Dunmore lamented the panic of his supporters and their abandonment of the trenches protecting the city, but speculated to Lord Dartmouth that they might be convinced to return if only reinforcements were sent to him:

> *This Town standing on a Neck of Land and by that means pretty easily made defensible against an undisciplined Army* [prompted] *the few remaining Inhabitants (most of whom are Natives of Great Britain) to throw up a breast work and to defend themselves, for which I had supplied them with the few Arms I had, but this work not being quite finished the News of this little advantage the Enemy had gained,* [at the Great Bridge] *threw them all into despair, and they at present give themselves up as lost, but their transitions from hope to despair are very quick, should any assistance (which God grant) they possibly may be*

---

[64] Clark, ed., "Thomas Macknight to Reverend Macknight, 26 December, 1775," *Naval Documents of the American Revolution*, Vol. 3, 260-61

> *induced to return to their Trenches, when they may soon put themselves in such a Situation as will make it very difficult for the Enemy to force them.*[65]

Dunmore's speculation proved to be wishful thinking for no assistance was coming, at least for him. Instead, Colonel Woodford's force was reinforced by hundreds of North Carolinians under Colonel Robert Howe. Together they led their troops northward from Great Bridge to Norfolk, occupying the abandoned city on December 14th. Offshore, the harbor was filled with desperate families fearful of retribution for their support of Dunmore. The governor described the bleak scene to Lord Dartmouth:

> *All who were friends of Government took refuge on board of the Ships, with their whole families, and their most valuable Effects, some in the Men of War, some in their own Vessels, others have chartered such as were here, so that our Fleet is at present Numerous tho' not very powerful. I do assure your Lordship it is a most melancholy sight to see the Numbers of Gentlemen of very large property with their Ladies and whole families obliged to betake themselves on board of Ships, at the Season of the year, hardly with the common necessarys of Life, and great numbers of poor people without even these, who must have perished had I not been able to supply them with some flour, which I purchased from His Majesty's service some time ago....*[66]

---

[65] Clark, ed., "Lord Dunmore to Lord Dartmouth, 13 December, 1775," *Naval Documents of the American Revolution*, Vol. 3, 141-42
[66] Ibid. 142

Onshore, the streets of Norfolk were full of "rebel" troops. With the arrival of Colonel Robert Howe and his North Carolina troops, the "rebel" force had swelled to well over a thousand men. While most encamped out of range of the naval cannon, guard detachments were posted along the shore to observe Dunmore's activities and warn of a possible attack. Some of the sentries succumbed to the temptation to take random shots at Dunmore's ships, especially the *Otter*, and frequent flags of truce went back and forth between the two sides concerning the issue of whether the sporadic gunfire from shore was authorized:

> *Norfolk Dec. 15, 1775*
> *Captain Squire's compliments to the commanding officer, informs him that several musquet balls were last night fired at the king's ship from some people at Norfolk. Captain Squire did not return the fire, from a supposition it was done out of wantonness. Captain Squire does not mean to fire on the town of Norfolk unless first fired at; must beg to know if any hostile intention was meant to his Otter sloop....*
>
> *The Virginia Officers' Reply*
> *Colonel Howe's and colonel Woodford's compliments to captain Squire, and assure him they gave no orders to fire upon the Otter, and conceive the musquet balls mentioned in captain Squire's message to have come from our guard, who fired by mistake upon one of our own parties.*[67]

---

[67] Clark, ed., "Captain Matthew Squire R.N., to the Officer Commanding at Norfolk, 15 December, 1775," *Naval Documents of the American Revolution*, Vol. 3, 119

In another message delivered by a midshipman aboard the *Otter*, Captain Squire threatened, " *that if another shot was fired at the Otter,* [the rebels] *must expect the town to be knocked about their ears.*"[68]

Oddly enough, despite all of the bloodshed and confrontation over the past month, both sides remained civil, to the point that Lord Dunmore had the audacity to ask rebel commanders (through Captain Squire) whether the navy and army would be allowed to obtain fresh provisions and water from shore.[69] Colonel Woodford shared with the Committee of Safety the reply that he and Colonel Howe (who was the ranking colonel) sent back:

Col. Howe and col. Woodford's compliments to capt. Squire, and return him for answer to his message, that as his majesty's troops and ships of war have long since committed hostilities upon the persons and property of the good people of this colony, and have actually taken and imprisoned several private gentlemen, and others, who did not bear arms at the time, our express orders are, to prevent, to the utmost of our power, any communication whatever between the said troops and ships of war and this town, or any part of this Colony.[70]

In other words, no shore parties were allowed to land.

---

[68] Clark, ed., "Letter from a Midshipman on board *H.M. Sloop Otter,* 14 December, 1775," *Naval Documents of the American Revolution,* Vol. 3, 103

[69] Clark, ed., "Lord Dunmore to Lord Dartmouth, 13 December, 1775," *Naval Documents of the American Revolution,* Vol. 3, 142

[70] Clark, ed., "Colonel Woodford to Edmund Pendleton, 17 December, 1775," *Naval Documents of the American Revolution,* Vol. 3, 140

Interestingly, when Captain Henry Bellew of the *H.M.S. Liverpool* (mounting 28 guns) arrived in Norfolk in mid-December and posed a similar request for fresh provisions, Colonel Howe referred the request to Edmund Pendleton and the Committee of Safety:

> *Yesterday, by a flag of truce, I received a letter from capt. Bellew.... Though col. Woodford and myself were sensible it was our duty to withhold from him...those supplies he wishes to obtain, yet the moderate conduct he has pursued, and the sentiments of humanity by which he seems to be actuated, induced us to delay an answer till to-day, and to couch it in terms which cannot but show him, that occasion, not inclination, had influence upon our conduct. Capt. Bellew's letter was brought to us by one of his lieutenants; he expressed for himself, and every officer on board, the reluctance they should feel, if compelled by necessity, they should be obliged by marauding parties to snatch from the indigent farmers of this colony those provisions they were so willing to purchase..... Col. Woodford and myself beg leave to submit it to the consideration of your Honourable Board, whether we are to show any indulgence to those people, and, if we are, to what bounds we are to extend it.*[71]

While Colonel Howe waited for a reply, news from across Hampton Roads bolstered the "rebels" already elevated spirits.

---

[71] Clark, ed., "Extract of a Letter from Col. Robert Howe to Edmund Pendleton, 25 December, 1775," *Naval Documents of the American Revolution*, Vol. 3, 244

Chapter Four

"Nothing less than Depriving [Dunmore] of Life or Liberty will Secure Peace to Virginia."

January – July 1776

Virginians were thrilled to learn in late December that their success against Dunmore extended beyond land engagements. In the days following the Battle of Great Bridge, Captain James Barron of Hampton scored a small naval victory over one of Dunmore's tenders near Hampton (capturing its crew of 17). Barron also seized two vessels loaded with salt, a commodity that was in desperately short supply in Virginia.[1]

The Committee of Safety was so impressed with Captain Barron that it announced that it had, *"strengthened his hands, by empowering him to fit out three armed vessels, to be employed in this way, and have great confidence in his prudence and valor."*[2]

Fostering a fledging navy was not the only thing Virginia's leaders in Williamsburg had done to strengthen their military capabilities. In mid-December, the 4th Virginia Convention, meeting in Williamsburg, expanded the colony's infantry from two regiments of regulars to eight and increased the length of

---

[1] Clark, ed., "Pinkney, Virginia Gazette, 23 December, 1775," *Naval Documents of the American Revolution*, Vol. 3, 220
[2] Ibid.

service for the 700 plus officers and men of each regiment to two years.[3]

The Convention also issued a stinging reply to Dunmore's November proclamation of martial law, declaring that he had assumed powers, *"which the king himself cannot exercise,"* had no real interest in reconciling with the colonies, and was, *"one of the principal causes of the misfortunes under which we now labour."*[4] The Convention indicted Dunmore as a, *"rigid executioner"* of *"that system of tyranny adopted by the ministry and parliament,"* and proclaimed that Dunmore, *"ever zealous in support of tyranny...hath broken the bonds of society, and trampled justice under his feet."*[5] In addition to the long standing charges against Dunmore of pillaging, plundering, and illegal seizure of property and slaves, was a new accusation. The Convention accused Dunmore of devising a scheme with his aide, Dr. John Connolly, to encourage the Indians in the west to enter the conflict as Dunmore's ally and sweep down upon northern Virginia in the upcoming spring to unite with Dunmore in Alexandria.[6] Connolly's capture by Maryland authorities in the fall of 1775 ended this scheme, but the fact that Dunmore was willing to employ Indians (on top of runaway slaves) against the colonists was one more reason many Virginians wished the governor harm.

---

[3] Scribner and Tarter, ed., *Revolutionary Virginia, The Road to Independence*, Vol. 5, 125-128
[4] Ibid.
[5] Ibid.
[6] Scribner and Tarter, ed., "Major John Connolly to General Thomas Gage: Captured Proposals," *Revolutionary Virginia, The Road to Independence* Vol. 4, 82-83
Printed in Purdie's *Virginia Gazette* on December 22, 1775

Even General Washington, stuck in the siege lines outside of Boston, recognized the danger of allowing Dunmore to continue to operate in Virginia. In a letter to Richard Henry Lee written the day after Christmas, Washington candidly shared his views on what should happen to Lord Dunmore:

> *If, my Dear Sir, that Man* [Dunmore] *is not crushed before Spring, he will become the most formidable Enemy America has – his strength will Increase as a Snow ball by Rolling; and faster, if some expedient cannot be hit upon to convince the Slaves and Servants of the Impotencey of His designs...I do not think that forcing his Lordship on Ship board is sufficient; nothing less than depriving him of life or liberty will secure peace to Virginia.*[7]

For the time being, Lord Dunmore was safe, protected in Norfolk harbor by the guns of the British navy, specifically, the 28 gun *Liverpool*, 14 gun *King Fisher*, 14 gun *Otter*, a sloop with 8 guns, the *Dunmore* (formerly Eilbeck, number of guns unknown) and 6 or 7 tenders armed with a few 3 and 4 pound cannon and swivel guns. Scores of other unarmed vessels were also anchored in the harbor, sheltering Tory refugees who had nowhere else to go.[8]

---

[7] Philander Chase, ed., "George Washington to Richard Henry Lee, 26 December, 1775," *The Papers of George Washington*, Vol. 2, 611

[8] Clark, ed., "Ships in Norfolk and Hampton Roads, 30 December, 1775," *Naval Documents of the American Revolution*, Vol. 3, 309-310

Destruction of Norfolk

Like Lord Dunmore and the miserable inhabitants of the floating Tory town in the harbor, Captain Bellew of the *Liverpool* and Captain Squire of the *Otter*, were increasingly annoyed by the daily harassment of the rebel "shirtmen" (who fired random shots at the ships and paraded about the Norfolk docks in full view of the harbor). Numerous warnings to curtail the provocations were sent ashore under flags of truce, but the conduct continued. Finally, in late December, Captain Bellew issued an ultimatum:

> *Captain Bellew to Colonel Howe, Dec. 30, 1775*
>
> *As I hold it incompatible with the Honor of my Commission to suffer Men in Arms against their Sovereign and the Laws, to appear before His Majesty's Ships I desire you will cause your Centinels in the Town of Norfolk to avoid being seen, that Women and Children may not feel the effects of their Audacity, and it would not be imprudent if both were to leave the Town.*[9]

Captain Bellew's request, and his threat, was clear. Rebel sentinels onshore had chided, insulted, and fired upon the ships in the harbor long enough. Either the harassment stopped, or Norfolk would be bombarded.

Colonel Howe replied immediately to Captain Bellew's ultimatum with an assurance that the sentinels had been instructed to avoid any insulting behavior and if any were guilty of such conduct, he agreed that they should be punished

---

[9] Clark, ed., "Captain Henry Bellow to Colonel Robert Howe, 30 December, 1775," *Naval Documents of the American Revolution*, Vol. 3, 310

for it. But, continued Colonel Howe, *"if...you feel it your duty to make your resentment extend farther than merely as to them, we should wish that the Inhabitants of this Town, who have nothing to do in this matter, may have time to remove with their Effects...."*[10]

The next day – the last of 1775 – passed incident free, but on New Year's Day rebel sentinels paraded before the harbor with their hats on their bayonets, taunting the British.[11] Captain Bellew, aboard the *Liverpool*, responded:

On the 1st Janry at 3 o'Clock in the Afternoon...their Centinels, came to the Wharf very near me, from their Guard House, which was close to it, and used every mark of insult; I then ordered three Guns to be fired into the House, it had its effect by setting them running; my Lord Dunmore sent (under those Guns) his Boats Arm'd to fetch off a Long boat they had taken from him, whose People set fire to some Store houses, which burnt a good number of Houses, the Rebels have since destroyed the greatest part of the Town.[12]

Lord Dunmore provided a similar account:

---

[10] Clark, ed., "Colonel Robert Howe to Captain Henry Bellew, 30 December, 1775," *Naval Documents of the American Revolution*, Vol. 3, 315

[11] Clark, ed., "A Letter from a Midshipman aboard the Liverpool, 4 January, 1776," *Naval Documents of the American Revolution*, Vol. 3, 621-22

[12] Clark, ed., "Captain Bellew to Philip Stephens, 11 January, 1776," *Naval Documents of the American Revolution*, Vol. 3, 737

Captain Bellow discovering the Rebels parading in the Streets, sent a few Cannon Shot amongst them, his example was immediately followed by all of us, and under Cover of the Cannon, I sent some boats on Shore to burn some detached Warehouses on the lower part of the Wharfs (from whence they used to annoy our boats as they passed) I, at the same time hailed Captain Bellew to beg he would send his boats to burn the Brig with the Salt, which he did immediately.[13]

Colonel Howe's account of the bombardment was similar to his adversaries, except he placed the blame for the destruction of the city upon the British:

The cannonade of the town began about a quarter after three yesterday, from upwards of one hundred pieces of cannon, and continued till near ten at night, without intermission; it then abated a little, and continued till two this morning. Under cover of their guns they landed and set fire to the town in several places near the water, though our men strove to prevent them all in their power; but the houses near the water being chiefly of wood, they took fire immediately, and the fire spread with amazing rapidity. It is now become general, and the whole town will, I doubt not, be consumed in a day or two.... The burning of the town has made several avenues, which yesterday they had [not], so that they now may fire with greater effect. The tide is now rising and we expect at high water another cannonade. I have only to wish it may be as ineffectual as the last; for we

---

[13] Clark, ed., "Lord Dunmore to Lord Dartmouth, 4 January, 1776," *Naval Documents of the American Revolution*, Vol. 3, 617-18

have not one man killed, and but a few wounded. I cannot enter into the melancholy consideration of the women and children running through a crowd of shot to get out of the town, some of them with children at their breasts, a few have, I hear, been killed.[14]

In Colonel Howe's account, the fire that destroyed Norfolk was set, "*in several places near the water,*" and spread rapidly because of all of the wooden structures. A number of other accounts from both sides of the engagement suggest that the fires set by Dunmore's men quickly spread throughout the city, but Lord Dunmore claimed that the wind, (which blew towards the water) prevented the fires set along the shore from spreading to the rest of the city. Dunmore placed the blame for the destruction of Norfolk upon the rebels:

The Vessels from the Fleet to shew their Zeal for His Majesty's Service, sent great Numbers of Boats on Shore, by which means the fire soon became general on the Wharfs, the wind rather blowing off Shore would have prevented the fire from reaching any farther than the Wharfs, but the Rebels so soon as the Men of War ceased firing, and our People came off, put the finishing Stroke to it, by Setting fire to every House, which has given them employment for these two days past, they have also burnt many houses on both sides of the River, the property of individuals who have never taken any part in this contest, in Short from every transaction they appear to me to have nothing more at heart, than the

---

[14] Clark, ed., "Colonel Howe to the Virginia Convention, 2 January, 1776," *Naval Documents of the American Revolution*, Vol. 3, 579-80

utter destruction of this once most flourishing Country, Conscious I suppose that they cannot long enjoy it themselves, they wish to make it of as little use as possible to others;[15]

Dunmore's claim that the "rebels" actually burned the bulk of Norfolk was dismissed by most Virginians as a lie, but an official inquiry of the incident in 1777 (which was not made public for over sixty years) concluded that Dunmore's claim was correct.[16]

Months of anger at the residents of Norfolk for their cooperation with and in many cases outright support for Dunmore erupted into a combustible fury, and although no one admitted it publicly, Norfolk was looted and burned to the ground by the soldiers under Colonel Howe and Woodford, some of who shouted, *"Keep up the Jigg! Keep up the Jigg!"* as they torched building after building.[17] Nearly 900 structures were destroyed over three days and the destruction spread across the river to Andrew Sprowles shipyard and warehouses in Gosport.[18] Colonel Woodford confirmed the extent of damage, declaring that nine tenths of Norfolk was destroyed.[19]

---

[15] Clark, ed., "Lord Dunmore to Lord Dartmouth, Aboard the Dunmore off Norfolk, 4 January, 1776," *Naval Documents of the American Revolution*, Vol. 3, 617-18

[16] *Journal of the House of Delegates,* 1835-36, Doc. No. 43, Richmond, 1835, Virginia State Library, 16

[17] Scribner and Tarter, *Revolutionary Virginia: Road to Independence*, Vol. 5, 16

[18] Ibid.

[19] Clark, ed., "Colonel William Woodford to Thomas Elliot, 4 January, 1776," *Naval Documents of the American Revolution*, Vol. 3, 617

Unfortunately for Lord Dunmore, the accounts of the devastation that appeared in the gazettes laid the blame upon the governor and his naval lackeys:

> *"It was a shocking scene to see the poor women and children, running about through the fire, and exposed to the guns from the ships, and some of them with children at their breasts. Let our countrymen view and contemplate the scene!...The cannonade had lasted twenty five hours when the express came away, and the flames were raging (it being impossible to extinguish them on account of the heavy fire from the ships) and had consumed two thirds of the town.... It is affirmed that one hundred cannon played on the town almost incessantly for twenty five hours....*[20]

The destruction of Norfolk did not mean an end to the fighting. The combatants remained where they were, Lord Dunmore's force onboard ships just offshore from the smoldering ruins of Norfolk, and Colonel Howe's troops on the outskirts and amongst the ruins of the city. Heated skirmishes occasionally erupted whenever Dunmore sent landing parties ashore and both sides suffered casualties, but for most of January the two sides shared the common misery of a winter encampment – wet, cold weather, and limited provisions and supplies.

---

[20] Clark, ed., "Pinkney Virginia Gazette, Account of the Burning of Norfolk, 6 January, 1776," *Naval Documents of the American Revolution*, Vol. 3, 661

Norfolk is Abandoned

It was no secret that Colonel Howe and Colonel Woodford wanted to abandon Norfolk and in doing so, burn what was left of the city to deny its use to Dunmore. Both officers argued (before and after Norfolk was burned) that it was dangerous for their force to remain at Norfolk; they ran the risk of being cut off by British reinforcements.[21] Colonel Howe went to Williamsburg in mid-January to report to the Convention and gain their approval to withdraw from Norfolk. On January 15th, the Virginia Convention relented, recommending that Norfolk be evacuated.[22] The rebels departed on February 6th, the bulk heading to Suffolk with detachments posted at Kemp's Landing and Great Bridge to block access and provisions from reaching Dunmore.[23] Before the troops left, they torched the remaining buildings of Norfolk, over 400 of them.[24]

Within a week, Lord Dunmore, covered by the 44 gun frigate *H.M.S. Roebuck* (which sailed into Norfolk harbor three days after the "shirtmen" marched to Suffolk), landed troops onto Tucker's Point (adjacent to Portsmouth and across the river from Norfolk). They immediately dug wells to

---

[21] Anderson, ed., "Colonel Robert Howe to Edmund Pendleton, 22 December, 1775," and 2 January, 1776, and Colonel William Woodford to Edmund Pendleton, 22 December, 1775," *Richmond College Historical Papers*, 136-39, 148

[22] Scribner and Tarter, eds., "Proceedings of the 4th Virginia Convention, 15 January, 1776," *Revolutionary Virginia, Road to Independence*, Vol. 5, 405

[23] Clark, ed., "Purdie Virginia Gazette, 9 February, 1776," and "Letter in London Chronicle," *Naval Documents of the American Revolution*, Vol. 3, 1187 and Vol. 4, 23

[24] *Journal of the House of Delegates*, 1835-36, Doc. No. 43, Richmond, 1835, Virginia State Library, 16

replenish their critically low supply of fresh water. A windmill and a few buildings stood on the point, damaged, but not destroyed in all of the conflict, and Dunmore converted some of them to barracks to house his growing number of smallpox patients.[25] Earthworks were also erected to, *"Secure the Watering Place from the Depredations of the Rebels,"* and ovens were built to supply bread.[26] It was clear that Lord Dunmore, the most despised man in Virginia, had no intention of leaving the colony.

In February it appeared that Dunmore might finally be able to take the offensive when British transport ships arrived in Hampton Roads with General Henry Clinton and 1,200 British soldiers. Lord Dunmore's optimism quickly turned to disappointment when he learned that General Clinton had orders to continue on to the Carolinas.

Dunmore was dumbfounded that troops he desperately needed to regain control of Virginia, the largest and most significant colony in North America, were instead ordered to the relatively insignificant colony of North Carolina. Try as he might to convince General Clinton to alter his plans, the British force that sailed into the Elizabeth River in mid-February, sailed south just two weeks later after repairs were completed to some of the ships.

To maintain royal authority in Virginia (and hold Tucker's Point) Dunmore was left with a force of runaway slaves, bolstered by a handful of Tories, British regulars, and British marines, and the cannon of a few British warships. To make

---

[25] John Selby, *The Revolution in Virginia: 1775-1783*, (Williamsburg, VA: The Colonial Williamsburg Foundation, 1988), 86

[26] Clark, ed., "Journal of HMS Liverpool, 13-14 February, 1776," *Naval Documents of the American Revolution*, Vol. 3, 1293 and Selby, 86

matters worse, illness swept through Dunmore's ranks, prompting a number of desertions and killing over 150 black soldiers.[27] The governor described his difficult situation to the new Secretary of State, Lord George Germain, in late March:

> *Your Lordship will observe...that I have been endeavouring to raise two Regiments here, one of White People, the other of Black. The former goes on very slowly, but the latter very well, and would have been in great forwardness, had not a fever crept in amongst them which carried off a great many very fine fellows.*[28]

In contrast to Dunmore's struggles, recruitment among the Virginia regiments of regulars went well. The Virginia Committee of Safety, recognizing that Virginia's many rivers left the colony vulnerable to Britain's naval forces, stationed the newly raised regiments near the James, York, Rappahannock, and Potomac Rivers. The 1st and 6th Regiments were stationed at Williamsburg, the 3rd Regiment was posted at Dumfries, the 5th Regiment at Richmond (county) Courthouse, and the 7th Regiment at Gloucester Courthouse. Colonel Woodford's 2nd Regiment remained at Suffolk, keeping a close watch on Dunmore and was reinforced by the 4th and 8th Regiments.[29]

Over the course of the spring, companies of recruits (68 men strong) were raised in their respective counties and when

---

[27] Purdie, *Virginia Gazette*, 8 March, 1776, 2-3
[28] Clark, ed., "Lord Dunmore to Lord Germain, 30 March, 1776," *Naval Documents of the American Revolution*, Vol. 4, 585
[29] Scribner and Tarter, ed. "Proceedings of the Virginia Committee of Safety, 10 February, 1776," *Revolutionary Virginia: Road to Independence*, Vol. 6, 85

complete, reported to their assigned regiments at their muster stations. Each regiment was allotted ten companies so when they reached full strength, each regiment numbered around 700 men. Of course, illness, desertion, and detached service typically decreased that number. Nonetheless, Virginia had successfully raised an impressive military force in the spring of 1776, one that appeared perfectly capable of subduing Lord Dunmore.

One of the biggest challenges that faced Virginia's military forces in 1776 was not attracting recruits, but rather equipping, training, and disciplining those that enlisted. Linen hunting shirts continued to serve as the uniform of Virginia's troops and they were relatively easy to supply, but firearms were another matter. Authorities scrambled to procure muskets and rifles for the regulars, often at the expense of the militia, many of who went without weapons.

As for training and drill, few Virginians had military experience beyond occasional militia service, and it showed in camp and on the parade ground. It was a daily struggle to maintain order and discipline among the ranks of newly recruited citizen-soldiers, and the resignation of Colonel Patrick Henry, the commander of Virginia's military forces in March 1776 only added to the challenge.

Colonel Henry's Resignation

Although Patrick Henry was the most popular public figure in Virginia in 1776, many political leaders questioned his selection and abilities as colonel of the 1st Virginia Regiment and commander-in-chief of Virginia's military forces. They believed that his lack of military experience and his well known political skills made him much better suited for politics than the military.

The Virginia Committee of Safety, headed by one of Henry's most frequent opponents, moderate Edmund Pendleton of Caroline County, held authority over the military when the Convention was not in session. When the Committee of Safety decided in November to send troops to Norfolk to limit Lord Dunmore's activities, it selected the 2nd Virginia Regiment and Colonel William Woodford to lead the force. The committee's slight to Henry was compounded by Colonel Woodford, who often communicated directly to the Committee of Safety instead of through Colonel Henry, the de facto commander-in-chief of Virginia and Woodford's superior officer.

Denied any chance of military glory in southern Virginia, Henry bristled further when three of his eight companies were detached from his regiment and sent to reinforce Colonel Woodford. The final insult for Henry occurred in late February when the Continental Congress appointed Andrew Lewis, the experienced commander of Lord Dunmore's expedition against the Shawnee Indians in 1774, as Brigadier General of Virginia's continental forces, making Henry, who remained colonel of the 1st Virginia Regiment, subordinate to Lewis. This blow to Henry's pride, which he believed occurred with the blessing of the Committee of Safety, was too much for Henry to accept, and he resigned his commission.

The news of Henry's resignation prompted a near mutiny in the ranks of the 1st Virginia; they went into, "*deep mourning*" and gathered under arms at Henry's lodging to address him.[30] Expressing their, *"sincere thanks,"* for his leadership and *"poignant sorrow"* at his resignation, the troops praised Henry's, *"spirited resentment to the most glaring indignity,"* of Congress.[31] Henry graciously thanked those assembled for their support and then attended a farewell dinner at the Raleigh Tavern in his honor. He was forced to postpone his departure from the capital, however, when word spread of, *"some uneasiness getting among the soldiery, who assembled in a tumultuous manner, and demanded their discharge, declaring their unwillingness to serve under any other commander."*[32] Henry spent most of the evening with the troops, *"visiting the several barracks, and* [using] *every argument in his power with the soldiery to lay aside their imprudent resolution, and continue in the service..."*[33] His efforts succeeded and the disgruntled troops eventually settled down.

General Charles Lee Arrives

The arrival of General Charles Lee in Williamsburg in late March offered a solution to the challenge of discipline among Virginia's troops. Lee, a former British officer with extensive military service in Europe, held the rank of Major-General in the Continental army and served with General Washington in Massachusetts in 1775. Although he was a native of Britain and had only arrived in the colonies in 1773, Lee had earned the trust and admiration of many in Congress and held the third highest rank in the continental army. He was the most

---

[30] Purdie, *Virginia Gazette*, 1 March, 1776, 3
[31] Ibid.
[32] Ibid.
[33] Ibid.

militarily experienced and knowledgeable officer in the army and was highly esteemed throughout the colonies.

Reports of planned British military operations in the southern colonies prompted Congress to send General Lee southward in March to oversee the region's defense. He arrived in Williamsburg on March 29th and informed General Washington of the situation in Virginia a week later:

> *The Regiments in general are very compleat in numbers, the Men (those that I have seen) fine – but a most horrid deficiency of Arms – no entrenching tools, no* [effective cannon] *(although the Province is pretty well stockd)...I have order'd...the Artificers to work night and day....*[34]

Lee criticized the scattered deployment of the colony's regiments, which he noted limited Virginia's ability to act offensively, and moved quickly to rectify the situation. He ordered the 5th Regiment and half of the 7th Regiment to march from their duty stations in Richmond Courthouse and Gloucester Courthouse to Williamsburg (to join the 1st and 6th regiments who were already in the capital).[35] He commenced work on fortifications for Jamestown, Burwell's Ferry, Yorktown, and Williamsburg and publically urged Virginia's young gentlemen (in the gazettes) to voluntarily form companies of light dragoons, something the convention had failed to do because of the expense.[36] When a shortage of muskets left many of the troops unarmed, Lee resorted to the

---

[34] Chase, ed., "General Charles Lee to General George Washington, 5 April, 1776," *The Papers of George Washington*, Vol. 4, 43

[35] Schribner and Tarter, ed. *Revolutionary Virginia, Road to Independence*, Vol. 6, 277

[36] Ibid., 278 and Purdie, *Virginia Gazette*, 26 April, 1776, 1

use of spears, arming two companies of the tallest and strongest men of each regiment with them:[37]

> *They were formed something like the Triarii of the Romans,* [reported Lee to Richard Henry Lee] *in the rear of the battalions, occasionally either to throw themselves into the intervals of the line, or to form a third, second, or front rank in close order. It has a fine effect to the eye, and the men in general seemed convinced of the utility of the arrangement.*[38]

As for the discipline and quality of the troops, General Lee informed Richard Henry Lee that

> *My opinion of your troops and officers is, thank God, so good, as to put me entirely at my ease with respect to action, corps to corps.*[39]

Virginia Approves Independence

While General Lee and the troops prepared for renewed fighting with Lord Dunmore (and possibly British reinforcements) in the spring of 1776, Virginia's political leaders approved a final break with Great Britain. A resolution urging the Continental Congress in Philadelphia to declare the American colonies free and independent from the crown and parliament of Great Britain unanimously passed the

---

[37] Chase, ed., "General Charles Lee to General George Washington, 10 May, 1776," *The Papers of George Washington*, Vol. 4, 258

[38] "General Charles Lee to Richard Henry Lee, 12 April, 1776, *The Lee Papers*, Vol. 1, (Collections of the New York Historical Society, 1871), 417

[39] Ibid., 416

5th Virginia Convention on May 15th, 1776. This vote was essentially a declaration of independence by Virginia and the main focus of every Virginian in mid-May. Within days of the passage of this historic resolution, however, the attention of Virginians swung to an island in the Chesapeake Bay.

Gwynn's Island

Governor Dunmore surprised many Virginians in late May when he suddenly abandoned Tucker's Point and the Elizabeth River and sailed his flotilla into Hampton Roads. Conditions on Tucker's Point and among the floating town in the river had become intolerably foul and unhealthy. In addition, reports that the rebels were about to deploy cannon in Norfolk and send fire rafts among his ships convinced the governor that it was time to leave.[40] The hope among most Virginians was that Dunmore and his flotilla of nearly 100 vessels would sail to New York or Nova Scotia, but his destination proved to be much closer, only thirty miles up the Chesapeake Bay at Gwynn's Island.

Gwynn's Island was a sparsely populated body of land just a few hundred yards off the coast of Gloucester County. A narrow, 200 yard wide channel separated the island from the mainland at its closest point and the flat, roughly four square mile island rose just a few feet about sea level.

Although it certainly was not an ideal location to establish a new base of operations, the island offered safe ground, free from rebel attack (or so Dunmore thought) on which his supporters and troops could recover from their long stay aboard their overcrowded, unhealthy ships. Gwynn's Island also possessed an abundant supply of livestock as well as plenty of fresh water (again, so Dunmore thought).

---

[40] William J. Morgan, ed. "Narrative of Captain Andrew Snape Hamond," *Naval Documents of the American Revolution*, Vol. 5, (Washington D.C.: 1970), 321

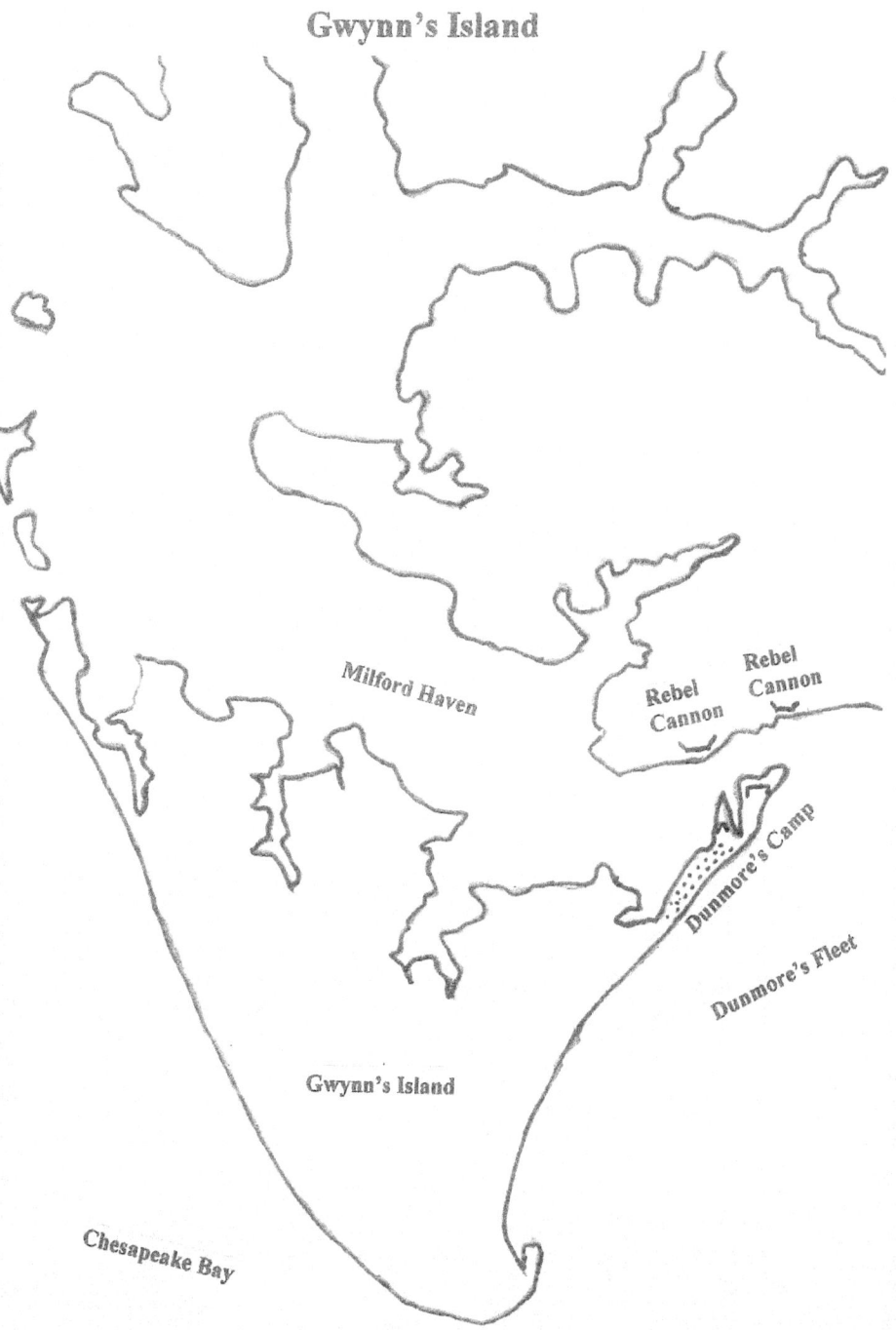

The island also allowed Lord Dunmore to maintain the royal standard (and the illusion of royal authority in Virginia) while he awaited reinforcements and assistance from Britain.

Dunmore's fleet arrived off Gwynn's Island on May 26th and anchored in Hills Bay at the mouth of the Piankatank River. A detachment from the 7th Virginia Regiment posted at Burton's Point (overlooking Hill's Bay) observed the ships and sent an express to Gloucester Courthouse. The 7th Regiment, under the command of Colonel William Daingerfield, had mustered at Gloucester Courthouse in early April and posted detachments throughout Gloucester County to watch for this very development. When the express arrived at the courthouse, at 3:00 p.m., the ranking officer at headquarters was Captain Thomas Posey. He immediately alerted Colonel Daingerfield (whose quarters were a few miles from town) and then prepared the troops at the courthouse to march to Gwynn's Island.[41]

Captain Posey, who was raised in Fairfax County (and was a neighbor to General Washington) did not march to Gwynn's Island with Colonel Daingerfield. Instead, he rushed to New Point Comfort to collect his company and then proceeded to Gwynn's Island.

The next day, while troops from the 7th Virginia Regiment and local militia converged on Gwynn's Island, Governor Dunmore secured the island at dawn by landing troops on its northern shore. British marines from the *Roebuck, Fowey and Otter* spearheaded the landing. Captain Andrew Hamond, the commander of the *Roebuck*, noted that

---

[41] Thomas Posey's Revolutionary War Journal, 27 May, 1776, *Thomas Posey Papers*, Indiana Historical Society Library, Indianapolis, IN (Referred to henceforth as Posey's Journal).

> *At day break we landed & took possession of the Island, with our whole force, which with the Marines of the Squadron, did not amount to more than 200 effective men, so great had been the mortality among the Negroes while at Tucker's Mills.*[42]

Dunmore's small force spread quickly across the island. Finding no opposition, the troops re-assembled on the narrow strip of land closest to the mainland. Separated by a channel of water only 200 yards wide, Lord Dunmore believed that this spot was most vulnerable to rebel attack, so he ordered the construction of earthworks and established his main camp behind them. The redoubt that protected the camp was dubbed Fort Hamond, after the captain of the *Roebuck*.

While Dunmore's troops searched the island and established a fort and camp on the narrow strip of land, Captain Posey and his company arrived on the scene, ahead of the rest of the 7th Regiment. They joined detachments of local militia who were perplexed on what they should do. Posey recorded in his diary that

> *I found a number of the militia assembled, which appear'd to be in the utmost consternation, some running one way, and some another, under no kind of control or regularity.*[43]

Colonel Daingerfield soon arrived with four more companies of his regiment (the other five companies were still in Williamsburg and would arrive a few days later). As the ranking officer on the scene, Daingerfield assumed command. He ordered all of the troops closer to shore to prevent Dunmore's troops from landing on the mainland. Captain Posey observed:

---

[42] Morgan, ed. "Narrative of Captain Andrew Snape Hamond," *Naval Documents of the American Revolution*, Vol. 5, 322
[43] Posey's Journal, May 27, 1776

> *The whole were put in motion, (though I must confess the militia were in very great motion before the orders were given). However, these orders served to put them in something grator; for as soon as we came neare enough for the grape[shot], and cannon shot to whistle over our heads, numbers of the militia put themselves in much quicker motion, and never stopped...to look behind them until they had made the best of their way home.*[44]

Captain Posey candidly admitted that it was not just the militia that was spooked by the enemy gun fire:

> *I cant say that our regulars deserved any great degree of credit for after two or three getting a little blood drawn, they began to skulk and fall flat upon there faces.*[45]

Despite their apprehension, Colonel Daingerfield's troops and most of the militia held their ground and endured enemy cannon fire and heavy rain into the evening. As the hours passed, they grew more determined to face the enemy. Posey recalled,

> *We began to grow very firm and only wish them to come into the bushes, where we are certain of beating them.*[46]

Rather than attack the mainland, however, Lord Dunmore was content to stay on the island and harass the Virginians with the navy's cannon. Captain Hamond seemed to agree with this strategy, noting that

---

[44] Ibid.
[45] Ibid.
[46] Ibid.

> *We have taken possession of this Island which is about three or four Miles in length and one in breadth. Seperated from the Main ½ a mile, except on one place (which is that where Lord Dunmore has his Camp) this is not above the reach of* [enemy] *Musquet Shot, However this part is defended by the Guns from the Ships.*[47]

As the days passed into June and Dunmore's hold on the island strengthened, General Andrew Lewis in Williamsburg, the commander of Virginia's continental troops during General Charles Lee's absence (he had proceeded to South Carolina in May) realized that without artillery of his own his troops were powerless to effectively challenge Dunmore. Lewis informed General Charles Lee on June 12th that he had

> *Ordered several Pieces of Cannon at Gloucester Town to be mounted which the workmen are about, in order to have them mounted opposite the Enemy and if possible, to prevent some small armed Vessels getting out which lie between the mainland and the island.* [He]...*sent under the Command of Col. Mercer three companies to reinforce Col. Dangerfield's Battalion....*[48]

Another month would pass before the Virginians were ready to attack Dunmore's force. In the interim, they contented themselves with sniping at Dunmore's camp and at several small vessels that had sailed into Milford Haven (the body of water that separated Gwynn's Island from the mainland). In one incident, the Virginians were able to seize a small sloop loaded with liquor that had run aground. General Lewis described the incident to General Lee:

---

[47] Morgan, ed. "Captain Hamond to Commodore Parker, 10 June, 1781," *Naval Documents of the American Revolution*, Vol. 5, 460

[48] "General Andrew Lewis to General Charles Lee, 12 June, 1776," *The Lee Papers*, Vol. 1, 63

> *Our men took a small sloop endeavouring to get out of the Narrows between the Island and our breastwork. She having run a Ground, a few men in two small Canoes boarded her, five men who were all her crew endeavoured to escape by swimming – three of which were shot from the shoar and sunk. Two hogsheads of Brandy, ½ Ditto of Rum, some tools and ropes...were taken out for the use of our Troops there, who were in need of the brandy and rum, as the water is very bad.*[49]

The loss of this sloop did not particularly concern Lord Dunmore; he was confident that his position on Gwynn's Island was secure. Of growing concern to Dunmore was his fresh water supply, which was inadequate for the hundreds of people who were with Dunmore on the island, and the rampant illness and death (largely to smallpox and fever) that ravaged his troops, particularly his black soldiers. A report in Dixon's *Virginia Gazette* attributed to a gentleman from Yorktown (who escaped Dunmore's custody) claimed that, "*there are not above 200 blacks now alive, 75 at least having died within six days after they left Norfolk, and that the number of whites on shore is very inconsiderable.*"[50]

Lord Dunmore privately acknowledged his losses to sickness to Lord Germain:

> *I am extreamly sorry to inform your Lordship that the Fever of which I informed you in my Letter No. 1, has proved a very Malignant one and has carried off an incredible Number of our People, especially the Blacks, had it not been for this horrid disorder, I am Satisfied I should have had two thousand Blacks, with whom I should have no doubt of penetrating into the heart of the Colony...There was not a ship in the fleet*

---

[49] "General Lewis to General Lee, 12 June, 1776", *Lee Papers*, Vol. 2, 64
[50] Dixon and Hunter, *Virginia Gazette*, June 15, 1776

that did not throw one, two, or three or more dead overboard every night.[51]

The Virginians were well aware of Dunmore's losses. General Lewis reported daily sightings of bodies washed ashore to General Lee. *"A Great Mortality among the Enemy, some both white and black, are discovered floating every day."*[52] Such daily discoveries bolstered rebel morale as it suggested the dire condition of the enemy on the island.

Despite all the suffering that was endured by Dunmore's troops and supporters on Gwynn's Island, they remained secure from attack, protected by the guns of Fort Hamond, several British warships, and additional land batteries placed along the western shore of the island.

Lord Dunmore's fortunes suffered a significant blow on June 19th, when the *Oxford,* a British transport ship with 217 Scottish Highland troops aboard, was captured by Captain James Barron in Hampton Roads. The ship, which was part of a large British reinforcement sent to America in the spring and meant for the British army in Boston, had altered its course to Halifax, Nova Scotia upon word that General Howe had evacuated Boston. Along the way the *Oxford* and another transport ship were seized by the Continental brig *Andrew Doria,* which disarmed the *Oxford*, removed most of the crew and officers, and placed an eight man prize crew aboard to sail the captured ship to port. A gale separated the *Oxford,* from the *Andrew Doria* and the Highland prisoners, led by a carpenter from the *Oxford*, overpowered the prize crew and retook the ship.[53] They decided to sail for Virginia and had entered Hampton Road when they unknowingly encountered two vessels from the fledgling Virginia state navy, the *Liberty*

---

[51] Morgan, ed., "Lord Dunmore to Lord Germain, 26 June, 1776", *Naval Documents of the American Revolution,* Vol. 5, 756
[52] "General Lewis to General Lee, 12 June, 1776", *Lee Papers,* Vol. 2, 64
[53] Morgan, ed., "Extract of a Letter from Williamsburg 22 June, 1776", *Naval Documents of the American Revolution,* Vol. 5, 687

and *Patriot*. Lieutenant John Trevett, one of the prize crew from the *Andrew Doria*, described how the captains of the two Virginia ships, who were brothers, (James and Richard Barron) used deception to capture the *Oxford*.

> *We got into Hampton roads about sunset, we immediately came along side 2 small pilot boats, and they informed us that the Fowey, ship of war, lay 40 miles up James River, and they must immediately get under way, after giving 3 cheers they weighed anchor and stood up the River.... After the Capt. of the Pilot boats had found out that we were all officers from on board the Andrew Doria, they called on me then having the Command to know how they should retake her.... At daylight I informed our new Capt. Canada that he had no more command, and that he must go forward, and all others but the women, and children, they might stay on the quarter deck; which was done, we stood up James River until we arrived at Jamestown, and there we landed 220 highlanders, which was escorted* [into Williamsburg] *by part of a regiment of riflemen, in their rifle frocks, I think the finest sight I ever saw.*[54]

The unarmed Highlanders had no choice but to submit to Captain Barron and the prize crew.

Lord Dunmore took the loss of the Highlanders hard, exclaiming to Lord George Germain in a letter, "*of what Service would they not have been to me here!*"[55] Captain Hamond confirmed the need for more troops to defend the island, noting that

---

[54] Morgan, ed., "Trevett's Journal," *Naval Documents of the American Revolution*, Vol. 5, 688

[55] Morgan, ed., "Lord Dunmore to Lord George Germain, 26 June, 1776," *Naval Documents of the American Revolution*, Vol. 5 757

> *The Negro Troops, which had been inoculated before they left Norfolk, got thro' the disorder with great success, but the Fever which had been so fatal to them there, followed them also to the Island; so that notwithstanding the Corps was recruited with Six or eight fresh Men every day, yet the mortality among them was so great, that they did not now amount to above 150 effective Men. The detachment of the 14th Regt also became very weak, and the few Men of the New raised Corps* [Queen's Own Loyal Virginians] *were all down with the small Pox: so that we were still under the necessity of keeping the Marines on Shore to do the Common duty.*[56]

Hamond added that it was necessary to strengthen the island's defenses because reports from rebel deserters revealed that General Lewis planned to attack as soon as several artillery batteries were completed. These reports proved to be correct.

The Attack

The morning of July 9th, 1776 dawned hot and humid, a typical summer day in Virginia. Six weeks had passed since Dunmore's arrival at Gwynn's Island and he and his supporters felt relatively secure, protected by the guns of the British navy and a series of artillery batteries along the southwestern shore of Gwynn's Island that could repulse any attempt of the rebels to land.

Unbeknownst to Dunmore, General Andrew Lewis had arrived in the rebel camp from Williamsburg to break the stalemate. A patriot battery of two 18 pound cannon, positioned directly across from Fort Hamond and within point blank range of Lord Dunmore's ship (the *Dunmore*) was finally finished and ready to commence fire. Four 9 pound

---

[56] Morgan, ed., "Narrative of Captain Andrew Snape Hamond, June 10, 1781," *Naval Documents of the American Revolution*, Vol. 5, 840

cannon formed another artillery battery a few hundred yards south of the 18 pounders. They were in range of the *Dunmore* as well, but their main focus was on Fort Hamond, Dunmore's encampment, and the three British tenders that were in Milford Haven to prevent the rebels from crossing to the island.

At some point in the morning (reports differ on the start of the bombardment) the 18 pound rebel cannon opened fire on the *Dunmore*, anchored close to the mainland. The first shot reportedly crashed through the stern of the ship, slightly wounding Governor Dunmore, who Purdie's *Virginia Gazette* reported received a splinter in his leg.[57] The other 18 pound gun quickly followed and also struck the *Dunmore*. The four 9 pound cannon joined the bombardment, directing their fire upon the camp and earthworks. Captain Hamond on the *Roebuck* reported that it was not long before the *Dunmore* realized it was overmatched.

> [The rebels] *directed their Fire principally upon Lord Dunmore's Ship.... The Dunmore returned the Fire, but seeing that her small Guns had no effect upon either of the Batterys, and that every shot from the Enemy struck the Ship she cut her Cable, and being Calm,* [was] *towed off out of reach of the Guns.*[58]

Lord Dunmore, who was aboard the *Dunmore*, provided a similar account of the start of the battle:

> *The Enemy brought down Ten Pieces of Ordnance, and on the 9th Instant began to play on my Ship from two Batteries; She was laid very near the Shore in order to prevent the Rebels from Landing on the Island. We were so near one of their Batteries*

---

[57] Purdie, *Virginia Gazette*" 12 July, 1776," 3
[58] Morgan, ed., "Narrative of Captain Snape Hamond, July 9, 1776", *Naval Documents of the American Revolution*, Vol. 5, 1078

(which consisted of an Eighteen and a Twenty four Pounder) that they Struck the Ship every Shott. I got our raw and weak Crew to fire a few Shott at them, but I soon perceived that our Six Pounders made no impression on their Batteries, our Boatswain being killed and several of the People Wounded, I found it impracticable to make them stand any longer to their Guns, we were therefore obliged to cut our Cable, tho' there was not a breath of Air Stirring, but the little Tide there was drifted us from the Shore;[59]

Claims in the Virginia gazettes after the engagement that the *Dunmore* was damaged beyond repair were contradicted by Captain Hamond, who reported that despite the many hits upon the ship, it actually did not suffer significant damage.[60] Whatever the case, the fire from the rebel batteries proved too hot for any of the ships anchored within range of the guns and they scrambled to move further away from the mainland. While the patriot 18 pounders focused their efforts against the *Dunmore*, the four patriot 9 pound cannon concentrated their fire on Fort Hamond and Dunmore's encampment. Dunmore's troops replied with cannon fire of their own, but the accuracy of the rebel 9 pounders quickly silenced Fort Hamond's cannon and raked the encampment, throwing Dunmore's troops into confusion.[61]

Captain Thomas Posey witnessed the barrage and reported that

---

[59] Morgan, ed., "Lord Dunmore to Lord George Germain, 31 July, 1776," *Naval Documents of the American Revolution,* Vol. 5, 1312

[60] Morgan, ed., "Narrative of Captain Snape Hamond, July 9, 1776," *Naval Documents of the American Revolution,* Vol. 5, 1078

[61] Morgan, ed., "Extract of a letter from Williamsburg, July 13, printed in the Pennsylvania Packet, July 22, 1776," *Naval Documents of the American Revolution,* Vol. 5, 1068

The fireing was kept up in a very regular manner from the whole of our works for near two hours; during which time [the enemy] *received great damage....Upon the enemies receiving this very unexpected* [bombardment], *they gave immediate orders to evacuate the Island.* [62]

The patriot fire came to an abrupt end when the commander of the two 18 pound cannon, Captain Dohickey Arundel, unwisely experimented with a wooden mortar that exploded on its first shot and killed Arundel instantly. This tragic episode was the one sour note to an otherwise immensely successful morning for the rebels. They had little to shoot at by noon, what with Dunmore's fleet drawn off deeper into the bay and many of his troops withdrawn from Fort Hamond and the camp.

Governor Dunmore and Captain Hamond agreed that the rebel artillery made Gwynn's Island untenable and they prepared to evacuate the island in the evening. Under cover of darkness, the cannon, tents and other military stores were loaded onto ships. Guards were posted along the shore to watch for a surprise rebel landing, but a shortage of boats prevented any such move by General Lewis.

During the evening of July 9th, Lewis's troops gathered a number of canoes and other small boats in anticipation of crossing Milford Haven and landing on Gwynn's Island in the morning. At dawn on July 10th, the patriot batteries opened fire on the three British tenders that had remained in Milford Haven. A rebel observer noted that

---

[62] Posey Journal, 9 July, 1776

> *There were three tenders in the haven, which attempted to prevent our passage. Their works were still manned as if they meant to dispute their ground, but as soon as our soldiers put off in a few canoes, they retreated precipitately to their ships. The tenders fell into our hands, one they set on fire, but our people boarded it and extinguished the flames.*[63]

With the tenders eliminated, a detachment of troops from the 7th Regiment embarked on canoes to cross over to the island. Captain Posey was one of the first to reach Gwynn's Island and described the landing in his diary:

> *Crossed into the Island but no fighting ensued except a few shot. By one o'clock the whole of the enemy had evacuated and embarked...I cannot help observing, that I never saw more distress in my life, than what I found among some of the poor deluded Negroes which they could not take time, or did not chuse to cary off with them, they being sick. Those that I saw, some were dying, and many calling out for help; and throughout the whole Island we found them strew'd about, many of them torn to pieces by wild beasts – great numbers of the bodies having never been buried.*[64]

British losses at Gwynn's Island are difficult to ascertain. Captain Posey estimated *"that at least 4 or 500 negroes lost their lives,"* during the six week occupation of the island.[65] Posey added that another 150 [white] soldiers were also lost. The vast majority of these deaths occurred prior to the attack

---

[63] Morgan, ed., "Extract of a letter from Williamsburg, July 13, printed in the Pennsylvania Packet, July 22, 1776," *Naval Documents of the American Revolution*, Vol. 5, 1068

[64] Posey Journal 10 July, 1777

[65] Ibid.

as a result of illness. Such losses significantly hampered the effectiveness of Dunmore's force and explained his feeble response to the attack.

The events at Gwynn's Island exasperated Lord Dunmore. His men were weak from disease and demoralized by defeat, and there was little hope of assistance from Britain. Dunmore made preparations to leave Virginia and join General William Howe's large invasion force off of New York. Ships were sent up the Potomac River to obtain badly needed fresh water. They sailed as far as Stafford County, where they engaged a party of local militia on the plantation of William Brent. Accounts of the skirmish vary, but the result was indisputable, the dispersal of the local militia and the destruction of Brent's home.

This small victory was not enough to change Dunmore's decision to leave. He abandoned Virginia in mid-August and sailed with half of his force to New York. The other half of Dunmore's flotilla sailed to St. Augustine, Florida.[66]

Dunmore's departure from Virginia was a significant development for it ushered in three years of relative peace in eastern and central Virginia and allowed thousands of Virginians to march north to reinforce General Washington's continental army in New York. Those Virginians played a crucial role in the battles to come, namely, Trenton and Princeton in the winter of 1776-77 as well at Brandywine, Germantown, Saratoga, and Monmouth in 1777 and 1778. Had they not been available to General Washington, it is possible that the outcome of the battles at Trenton and Princeton, as well as those that followed, could have ended quite differently.

---

[66] Selby, 126

Chapter Five

"The Country was Entirely a Wilderness."

1776-1779

The Virginia continentals that marched north in the summer and fall of 1776 were not the only Virginians to see bloodshed in the second half of that year. Tensions on Virginia's western frontier between settlers and Indians (which was briefly suppressed by Governor Dunmore's victory over the Shawnee at Point Pleasant in 1774) reignited in the summer of 1776. The expansion of settlements along the Holston and Watauga Rivers (in present day eastern Tennessee) angered the Cherokee. They viewed the settlers' presence as a threat to their hunting ground as well as a violation of the 1768 Treaty of Hard Labour and 1770 Treaty of Lochaber.

At the insistence of British Indian commissioners (who desired Cherokee support in Britain's conflict with the colonies but also wished to avoid an effusion of blood on the frontier) a letter was sent to the "trespassing" settlers giving them twenty days to abandon their illegal settlements and return east of the treaty line.[1] The settlers responded to this

---

[1] Nadia Dean, *A Demand of Blood: The Cherokee War of 1776*, (Cherokee, North Carolina: Valley River Press, 2012), 75-76

ultimatum with a request for more time to prepare for their departure.[2]

The Holston and Watauga settlers had no intention of leaving, however. They used the extra time (which stretched into six weeks) to fortify and better arm themselves and send for help. While the settlers prepared for an attack, the Cherokee debated amongst themselves what to do. Many of the older leaders counseled diplomacy, but younger leaders such as Dragging Canoe, son of Attakullakulla (known as the Little Carpenter to the English) insisted that the encroaching settlers be driven back across the treaty line.

By mid-summer it was evident that the settlers had no intention of leaving. Several forts had been hastily erected and an Indian trader reported that there was talk among the settlers of a large expedition against the Cherokee being formed.[3] This news convinced the Cherokee to attack all along the frontier. They were joined in Georgia and South Carolina by the Creek Indians.

Warfare exploded on the Virginia frontier in July with coordinated Cherokee attacks against the settlers on the Holston River (present day Kingsport, Tennessee) at Sycamore Shoals on the Watauga River (present day Elizabethton, Tennessee), and in southwestern Virginia all the way up to Wolf Hills (present day Abington, Virginia).

Warned by several white Indian traders that attacks were imminent, many settlers "forted up" (sought shelter in fortified locations). A few were caught outside the forts by the Cherokee and were captured or killed.

---

[2] Max Dixon, *The Wataugans: First "free and independent community on the continent...* (Johnson City, TN: Overmountain Press, 1976), 39
[3] Dean, 100

The Frontier

On July 20th, with scores of women and children sheltered inside Eaton's Station (a small fort near the Long Island on the Holston River) 170 militia gathered and marched from the fort in search of reported Cherokee war parties.[4] The troops soon encountered a party of 20 warriors who briefly skirmished with the militia before they fled. Worried that a much larger force of Indians was in the vicinity, the militia commanders decided to return to Eaton's Station. They recalled that

> *We had not marched more than a mile in good order when our rear was attacked by upwards of 100 of the enemy. Our men sustained the attack with great firmness, until a line was formed. The enemy endeavoured to surround us, but were prevented by the vigilance of Capt. James Shelby, who, with his division, took possession of an eminence, and bravely defended it, which prevented their design. Our line extended upwards of 600 yards, and after disputing the ground some time, we found 13 of them dead on the field.... Though the action was short, it is believed that the execution was great. The enemy attacked us with their usual fury, but our militia fought with a calmness and intrepidity that would have done honour to the veterans of any country.*[5]

The militia officers speculated that the Indians lost many more than the 13 dead they discovered on the field. Their own losses were light, with only four militiamen slightly wounded in the engagement.[6] The most significant casualty in the

---

[4] Dixon and Hunter, *Virginia Gazette*, August 3, 1776, 2
[5] Ibid.
[6] Ibid.

engagement was the leader of the Cherokee war party, Dragging Canoe, who was seriously wounded in the leg.

Twenty-five miles southeast of Eaton's Fort, near the southern bank of the Watauga River, sat Fort Watauga (also known as Fort Caswell). It was not originally constructed as a fort, but rather, a settler's farm. The farm's location on sloping ground near Sycamore Shoals made it an excellent defensive position, so upon receipt of the Cherokee ultimatum to leave the area, the settlers transformed the farm into a fort. A palisade was erected between the main cabin and several outbuildings (which were all incorporated in the walls of the fort) and several blockhouses were added to enclose an acre of land. Hundreds of settlers were crowded within Fort Watauga's walls on July 21st when

> *A large party of Indians attacked the fort at Watauga, in which were 150 men;* [the Indians] *fired on a number of women who went out at day-break to milk some cows, who providentially got safe into the fort; they fired briskly at the fort till 8 o' clock, without effect, and then retired, after sustaining considerable loss.* [7]

A handful of settlers caught outside the fort when the battle commenced were killed, (one unfortunate soul was captured, taken back to the Cherokee towns, and burned at the stake) but the garrison behind the walls of the fort stood firm and endured a loose, two week siege during which many in the fort lived off parched corn.[8] The Cherokee ended the siege before

---

[7] Purdie, *Virginia Gazette*, August 9, 1776, 3
  * Other sources put the number of defenders at Fort Watauga at 75.
[8] Dixon and Hunter, *Virginia Gazette*, August 17, 1776, 2

a relief force of 100 militia under Captain Evan Shelby arrived from Wolf Hills.[9]

North of Fort Caswell, in present day southwestern Virginia, Indian raids on isolated settlers spread fear throughout the region and prompted scores of settlers to abandon their homesteads and flee eastward. The situation was similar to the west in Kentucky, where many settlers fled the frontier. Others, however, resolved to stay and sought the safety of a handful of forts erected at Harrodsburg, Boonesborough and McClellan's Station. Luckily for these determined souls, help arrived in the form of a powerful offensive directed against the Cherokee.

Cherokee Expedition of 1776

In the late summer of 1776, Virginia's leaders joined those from North and South Carolina in authorizing a punitive expedition against the Cherokee. In September a force of 1,800 militia from South Carolina and Georgia marched against the Lower Towns of the Cherokee while an even larger force of 2,400 North Carolina militia attacked the Middle Towns of the Cherokee, destroying 36 towns with little loss.[10]

Virginia raised over 1,800 militia under Colonel William Christian of Fincastle County to march against the Overhill Cherokee (of present day Tennessee).[11] Colonel Christian informed his brother-in-law, Patrick Henry, Virginia's first state governor, that

---

[9] Dean, 109
[10] "Virginia Legislative Papers," *The Virginia Magazine of History and Biography*, Vol. 17, No. 1 (Jan. 1909), 52
[11] Dean, 231

I came to the Island [Kingsport] *on the 21 of September, since which time several parties of the Enemy have been about us, they killed one Soldier and one of the countrymen near the Island.... Several of the country people have been also fired upon and some wounded since I came to Holston. The Enemy generally fire from behind Logs and bushes, and seldom at a greater distance than eight or ten steps.*[12]

Colonel Christian spent the rest of September preparing to march over 100 miles westward to attack the towns of the Overhill Cherokee. He took with him a 30 day supply of flour and a 70 day supply of beef.[13] Christian departed the Long Island on the Holston in early October and slowly marched westward. One participant on the march recalled that

The country was entirely a wilderness unsettled and uninhabited except by savages. No road or path, not even a vistage of civilized man was to be seen. But forests almost impenetrable, canes, bushes, brambles and briers impeded them at every step.[14]

At one point in the long march it appeared that the Indians were going to contest Christian's crossing of the Tennessee

---

[12] "Colonel William Christian to Governor Patrick Henry, 6 October, 1776, "Virginia Legislative Papers…Reports of Colonels Christian and Lewis During the Cherokee Expedition, 1776," *The Virginia Magazine of History and Biography*, Vol. 17, No. 1, (Jan. 1909), 53-54

[13] Ibid., 54

[14] Sam'l C. Williams, "Col. Joseph Williams' Battalion in Christian's Campaign," *Tennessee Historical Magazine*, Vol. 9, No. 2, (July, 1925), 107

River, but he led 1,100 men a few miles downriver and crossed unopposed.[15] The Indians, *"overawed by Christian's superior numbers,"* fled and never offered serious resistance.[16] Colonel Christian marched on, noting that the abandoned Cherokee towns were full of, *"Horses, Cattle, Dogs, Hogs and Fowls,* [and] *the crops of Corn and sweet potatoes are very great."*[17]

Colonel Christian explained to Governor Henry his decision to exercise restraint against the Cherokee:

> *I am convinced that the Virg'a State would be better pleased to hear that I showed pity to the distressed and spared the suppliants; rather than that I should commit one act of Barbarity in destroying a whole nation of Enemies.*[18]

Christian identified one Cherokee leader, Dragging Canoe, as the primary instigator of the Cherokee raids, but he was unable to catch him. The Virginians settled for the destruction of six abandoned towns affiliated with Dragging Canoe as well as a pledge from the other Cherokee leaders to restrain their warriors and end the raids on the frontier. Satisfied that the Overhill Cherokee had been adequately chastised, Colonel Christian and his men returned east in November.

---

[15] "Charles Lewis to Governor Patrick Henry, 17 October, 1776, "Virginia Legislative Papers...Reports of Colonels Christian and Lewis During the Cherokee Expedition, 1776," *The Virginia Magazine of History and Biography*, Vol. 17, No. 1, 59

[16] Sam'l C. Williams, "Col. Joseph Williams' Battalion in Christian's Campaign," *Tennessee Historical Magazine*, Vol. 9, No. 2, 108

[17] "Colonel William Christian to Governor Patrick Henry, 23 October, 1776, "Virginia Legislative Papers...Reports of Colonels Christian and Lewis During the Cherokee Expedition, 1776," *The Virginia Magazine of History and Biography*, Vol. 17, No. 1, 61

[18] Ibid., 62

War in Kentucky 1777

Although the strong show of force by Virginia and the states to the south against the Cherokee succeeded in suppressing militant Cherokee activity on the frontier, it did little to prevent unrest in Kentucky and the upper Ohio River region where the Shawnee, Mingo, Delaware, and other Indians were encouraged by the British to act on their resentment towards the ever encroaching Americans.

In December of 1776, fifty Mingo warriors led by Chief Pluggy attacked a small fort at McClennan's Station (present day Georgetown, Kentucky (30 miles north of Harrodsburg).[19] The fort's defenders managed to ward off the attack, which ended when Chief Pluggy was killed, but within a month of the attack the settlers at McClennan's deemed the fort and surrounding area too isolated and vulnerable to further attack and abandoned it for the safety of Harrodsburg.

That left just two occupied settlements in Kentucky, Boonesborough and Harrodsburg. A third settlement, St. Asaph, about 20 miles south of Harrodsburg, had also been abandoned in the winter. Its inhabitants crowded into Harrod's Fort for protection. In February, six families and nine unmarried men, no doubt tired of the overcrowded conditions at Harrodsburg, re-occupied the fort at St. Asaph, (dubbed Logan's Fort).[20] They amounted to 17 armed defenders, including two women who were reportedly very proficient with rifles.[21] Luckily for the small garrison at

---

[19] Neal O. Hammon and Richard Taylor, *Virginia's Western War: 1775-1786*, (Stackpole Books, 2002), 48
[20] Ibid., 50
[21] Ibid., 50-51

Logan's Fort, the attention of the hostile Indians in the region centered on Harrodsburg and Boonesborough.

In early March of 1777 a party of 70 Shawnee Indians came upon a handful of men from Harrodsburg a few miles from the fort collecting sap to make sugar. One of the settlers was killed and scalped, another captured, a third managed to hide unseen from the Indians while a fourth fled back to Harrodsburg, chased the entire way.[22]

Approximately 80 men defended Harrod's Fort in the spring of 1777. The number of defenders increased to 100 when some of the women and older children were included in the ranks.[23] This force, protected by the walls and blockhouses of the fort, were enough to hold back the Indians when they arrived on March 7, 1777. A few unfortunate settlers caught outside of the fort by the Indians were killed or wounded, but the fort held firm and the Indians departed after two days. A party of around 30 Indians returned at the end of March and caught two settlers outside the fort (killing and scalping both).[24] Frequent alarms in April and May kept the settlers at Harrodsburg on edge, but little fighting actually occurred. The focus of the Indians had shifted 30 miles to the east to Boonesborough.

Boone's Fort held a much smaller garrison than Harrod's Fort, with only 22 armed defenders in April 1777.[25] Four of these were wounded and one killed on April 24th when half of the garrison (led by Captain Daniel Boone) unwisely left the fort to retrieve the body of a settler killed within sight of the

---

[22] Ibid., 51
[23] Ibid., 53
[24] Ibid., 56
[25] Ibid.

fort by a small party of Indians.[26] Ambushed sixty yards from the fort by 40 to 50 Indians hidden in the brush, Captain Boone and his small party fought desperately to escape the Indians (who had encircled them) and return to the safety of the fort.[27] In the melee that ensued, Boone and three others were wounded, but all managed to reach the fort (in Boone's case thanks to the assistance of Simon Kenton).

The Indians departed, but a month later approximately 100 warriors, led by a Shawnee chief named Black Fish, returned to Boonesborough and besieged the fort for three days. Multiple efforts to burn the walls of the fort failed, but the steady musket fire of the Indians upon Boone's Fort wounded three more settlers.[28]

Unable to breach the walls of Boone's Fort, approximately 50 Indians moved on to St. Asaph, whose inhabitants had "forted up" inside Logan's Fort upon word of their approach.[29] Fifteen defenders held off the Indians for several days without loss, but when it appeared the Indians had departed on May 30th, three women, escorted by four men, left the fort to milk several cows that were nearby.[30] The milking party was ambushed by waiting Indians who shot three of the four men. The women and unscathed man fled with one of the wounded men back into the fort and the siege resumed for another day.

---

[26] Ibid.
[27] William Dodd Brown, "Dangerous Situation, Delayed Response: Col. John Bowman and the Kentucky Expedition of 1777," *The Register of the Kentucky Historical* Society, Vol. 97 No. 2 (Spring 1999), 147-48 and George Rogers Clark Diary, April 24, 1777, 21
[28] James Alton James, ed., "George Rogers Clark Diary, May 23, 1777," *George Rogers Clark Papers: 1771-1781*, Virginia Series, Vol. 3, (Illinois State Historical Library : Springfield, Illinois, 1912), 22
[29] Hammon and Taylor, 59
[30] Ibid.

The besieged settlers watched helplessly as cabins and livestock outside of the fort were pillaged and destroyed by the Indians.[31]

In the more populated Virginia counties to the east, efforts to recruit militia troops to assist the threatened outposts in Kentucky went slowly over the summer of 1777. Colonel John Bowman was in charge of this effort and managed to raise two 50 man companies of militia in July.[32] They marched west and reached Boonesborough on August 1st. They moved to Harrodsburg at the end of the month and were replaced in mid-September at Boonesborough by another company of militia from the east under Captain William Bailey Smith.[33]

As it turned out, the need for militia reinforcements in Kentucky diminished considerably in the fall of 1777; the scene of conflict between settlers and Indians had shifted to the upper Ohio River.

Conflict on the Upper Ohio 1777-78

Lord Dunmore's successful expedition against the Shawnee Indians in 1774 resulted in a degree of relative peace for the settlers along the upper Ohio River (in present day West Virginia and Pennsylvania). The resulting treaty and a chain of forts that extended from Fort Pitt (Pittsburgh, PA) to Fort Randolph (Point Pleasant, WV) helped maintain the peace.

---

[31] Ibid., 60
[32] William Dodd Brown, "Dangerous Situation, Delayed Response: Col. John Bowman and the Kentucky Expedition of 1777," *The Register of the Kentucky Historical* Society, Vol. 97 No. 2, 156
[33] James, ed., "George Rogers Clark Diary, August 1 thru Sept. 2, 1777," *George Rogers Clark Papers: 1771-1781*, Virginia Series, Vol. 3, 23

Political unrest in Virginia and the rest of the colonies in 1775, however, prevented the implementation of Dunmore's treaty so by 1777 Shawnee disgruntlement and hostility towards the settlers (for what they viewed as repeated violations of the treaty) led to renewed Indian raids along the frontier. Settlers in the region, aware of the bloodshed in Kentucky, prepared for sustained Indian attacks upon their settlements.

Hundreds of militia assembled at Fort Henry (in present day Wheeling, WV) in the summer of 1777 to repulse an anticipated attack. As autumn approached with no sign of an attack, the militia at Fort Henry grew restless and company after company departed until by the end of August only two militia companies totaling around 60 men remained.[34]

On August 31st, a small party of settlers that had left the fort to retrieve some stray horses was ambushed by an equally small party of Indians. One of the settlers was killed, but the other three escaped and returned to warn Fort Henry of the presence of the Indians. Unaware that approximately 100 Indians were waiting in ambush, Captain Samuel Mason led 14 men out of the fort in pursuit of the offending party of Indians and was quickly overwhelmed.[35] A second militia detachment of only 12 men went to Mason's aid and met the same fate. Only three of the 26 men sent from the fort survived.[36]

---

[34] Hammon and Taylor, 63

[35] Reuben Gold Thwaites and Louise Phelps Kellogg, eds. "Col. John Gibson to General Hand, 4 September, 1777," *Frontier Defense on the Upper Ohio, 1777-1778,* (Madison : Wisconsin Historical Society, 1912), 73

[36] Hammon and Taylor, 64

The remaining defenders in the fort, assisted by a number of women, desperately repulsed numerous Indian assaults upon the weakened garrison. One participant remembered

> *Women ran bullets in frying pans, and two shot. Mrs. Drake cut bullet patches out of a...linen piece, like one cutting out shirts. And one Scotchman prayed all day.*[37]

When the Indians tried to burn the fort, "*the women brought up water in tubs, and scrubbed [drenched] the roofs.*"[38] Luckily for the inhabitants of Fort Henry, rain also started to fall, which hampered attempts to torch the fort. When they concluded that the fort would not fall, the Indians contented themselves with pillaging the cabins outside the walls and killing the livestock before departing at nightfall with a number of captured horses.[39]

Smaller Indian raids continued in the region through the fall of 1777, prompting an effort by General Edward Hand, the continental army commander at Fort Pitt (present day Pittsburg) to organize an expedition to strike the Indian settlements across the Ohio River. This expedition never materialized, however, and the plan was abandoned in early November.

---

[37] Reuben Gold Thwaites and Louise Phelps Kellogg, eds. "Recollections of Mrs. Joseph Stagg," *Frontier Defense on the Upper Ohio, 1777-1778*, 64

[38] Ibid., 64-65

[39] Reuben Gold Thwaites and Louise Phelps Kellogg, eds. "Portion of Reminiscences of Mrs. Lydia Cruger," *Frontier Defense on the Upper Ohio, 1777-1778*, 67

Murder of Cornstalk

Although much bloodshed had occurred throughout the western frontier in 1777, there remained some Indians who believed that peace with the Americans was the wisest policy. One Shawnee tribal leader, Cornstalk, had long advocated peace with the "Long Knives" (as the Virginians were known by the Indians) but his view had lost sway among most Shawnee by 1777. In November, Cornstalk, accompanied by his son and another Shawnee chief, went to Fort Randolph (Point Pleasant) under a flag of truce to explain why he could no longer remain peaceful and abide by the 1774 treaty that he had signed with Lord Dunmore.[40] Cornstalk and his party were detained at the fort for several days when suddenly a group of militia, enraged at reports of an Indian raid that killed several settlers nearby, burst into the room the Indians were held in and killed them all.[41]

Virginia authorities were shocked and appalled at Cornstalk's murder and they feared its repercussions on the frontier. A letter was sent to the Shawnee nation announcing that the culprits would be punished (they never were) and everyone braced for a very difficult winter, made even harder by a severe shortage of provisions due to the disruption and destruction all along the frontier of the previous spring, summer, and fall. With much of their livestock and crops destroyed and those that remained neglected in the fields, the food stores of the settlers for the winter was woefully small.

---

[40] Hammon and Taylor, 65
[41] Ibid.

Daniel Boone is Captured   1778

A shortage of desperately needed salt prompted Daniel Boone to lead a party of 30 men out of Boonesborough in early January 1778 to produce more salt at a salt lick many miles to the north. A month into this operation, Boone and his party were captured by a large band of Shawnee and marched all the way to Detroit where most were ransomed to the British Lieutenant Governor, Henry Hamilton.

Black Fish, a chief among the Shawnee, would not trade Boone, however, and instead, adopted him as a son. Boone returned to the Shawnee settlement of Chillicothe (in southern Ohio) and lived amongst the Indians for months, gaining their trust.[42]   When he discovered their plans to attack Boonesborough, Captain Boone resolved to escape. He recalled in his autobiography that

> *Alarmed to see four hundred and fifty Indians, of their choicest warriors, painted and armed in a fearful manner, ready to march against Boonesborough, I determined to escape [at] the first opportunity. On the 16th [of June] before sunrise, I departed in the most secret manner, and arrived at Boonesborough on the 20th, after a journey of one hundred and sixty miles during which I had but one meal.*[43]

---

[42] Hammon and Taylor, 67-69

[43] Cecil B. Hartley, *The Life and Times of Colonel Daniel Boone...to which is added Colonel Boone's Autobiography Complete, as dictated to John Filson, and published in 1784*, (Philadelphia : G. G. Evans Publisher, 1860), 342

Boone's wife and children (who had assumed that Boone was dead) had returned to North Carolina in the spring and were not at Boonesborough to greet him, but the garrison welcomed him back and upon his alarm set about to strengthen the fort's defenses.

Siege of Boonesborough 1778

As the days turned into weeks, it began to appear that Boone's warning of a large Indian attack was a false alarm. Numerous Indian raids continued throughout the summer, but no large force of Indians appeared at Boonesborough. This changed on September 7th, when hundreds of Shawnee, accompanied by several Frenchmen, arrived at Boonesborough to demand the settlement's surrender.[44] The settlers fled to the protection of their fort and Captain Boone recalled that

> *It was now a critical period with us. We were a small number in the garrison* [with] *a powerful army before our walls, whose appearance proclaimed inevitable death.*[45]

Captain Daniel Boone commanded the fort's 75 defenders and requested two days to consider the Shawnee's surrender demand, during which the garrison shored up its defenses and prepared to fight. When it was time to give an answer, Boone boldly proclaimed that, *"we* [are] *determined to defend the fort while a man was living.*[46] He then brashly added

---

[44] Ibid., 343
[45] Ibid.
[46] Ibid.

> *We laugh at your formidable preparations, but thank you for giving us notice and time to provide for our defense.*[47]

Whether such defiant language influenced the Shawnee to offer different terms is hard to say, but Boone recalled that the Indians' reaction was to offer a new scheme

> *To deceive us, declaring it was their orders from Governor* [Henry] *Hamilton* [in Detroit] *to take us captives, and not to destroy us, but if nine of us would come out and treat with them, they would immediately withdraw their forces from our walls, and return home peaceably.*[48]

Boone and the other officers agreed to the meeting. He recalled that

> *We held the treaty within sixty yards of the garrison...as we could not avoid suspicions of the savages. In this situation the articles were formerly agreed to, and signed; and the Indians told us it was customary with them on such occasions for two Indians to shake hands with every white man in the treaty, as an evidence of entire friendship. We agreed to this also, but were soon convinced their policy was to take us prisoners. They immediately grappled us; but, although surrounded by hundreds of savages, we extricated ourselves from them, and escaped all safe into the garrison, except one that*

---

[47] Ibid. 344
[48] Ibid.

was wounded, through a heavy fire from their army. They immediately attacked us on every side and a constant heavy fire ensued between us, day and night, for the space of nine days.[49]

Colonel John Bowman, who was actually 30 miles away at Harrodsburg, received detailed reports of the events at Boonesborough and provided a similar account of the meeting outside the fort. Bowman reported that 330 Indians with 8 Frenchmen surrounded Boone's Fort and upon their arrival on September 7th, demanded to meet with Captain Boone.[50] A meeting occurred two days later and the participants appeared to reach an agreement. Then, reported Bowman, the Shawnee chief,

Blackfish made a long Speech, then gave the word go, Instantly a Signal Gun fired, the Indians fastned on the eight men to take them off, the white People began to dispute the Matter, tho unarmd, and Broke Loose from the Indians, though there were two and three Indians to one White Man. In Running [back to the fort] *upwd of 200 Guns fired from Each Side and yet Every man Escaped But Squire Boone, who was Badley wounded though not Mortally...*[51]

For the next nine days Boone's Fort was besieged from all sides by a force of Indians more than four times the garrison's numbers. The musket and rifle fire was constant, but without

---

[49] Ibid., 344
[50] James, ed., "John Bowman to Clark, October 14, 1778," *George Rogers Clark Papers: 1771-1781*, Virginia Series, Vol. 3, 69
[51] Ibid., 70

cannon the Indians could do little against the fort's walls. They attempted to dig a tunnel into the fort from the riverbank but heavy rain caused it to collapse and it was abandoned.[52] Several attempts to rush the fort occurred, at least one after dark which was witnessed by William Patton, a settler of Boonesborough who was outside the fort when the siege began. Patton observed the siege from a distance for several days and witnessed what he thought was the fort's fall during a night assault. He made his way to Logan's Fort and described what he saw. Daniel Trabue, a settler at Logan's Fort, recalled in his journal that Patton claimed

> *The Indians made in the night a Dreadful attack on the Fort. A large number of them ran to the fort with great fire brands, or torches, and made the most Dreadful screams and hollowing that could be imagined.* [Patton claimed he heard] *the Indians killing the people in the fort. They took it by storm...& he heard the women, children and men also screaming when the Indians were killing them.*[53]

Patton was mistaken. He may have heard screams during the desperate fight, but the Indians failed to breach to walls so it was not the screams of dying settlers but only frightened ones and enraged combatants that he heard.

On the morning of September 20th, after nine days of fighting, the settlers inside the fort awoke to calm and quiet; the siege had been lifted and the Indians had vanished. The

---

[52] Hammon and Taylor, 87
[53] Lillie DuPuy VanCulin Harper, ed., *Colonial Men and Times: Containing the Journal of Col. Daniel Trabue,* (Innes & Sons : Philadelphia, PA, 1916), 34-35

loss of many warriors and the failure to breach the fort's walls broke the will of the Indians to continue the siege. Most re-crossed the Ohio River and returned to their towns, but some of the Indians went to Logan's Fort to stage a brief raid against St. Asaph. At Boonesborough, the relieved inhabitants, who had suffered enormous losses in livestock, crops, and property, emerged from their fort with few casualties.

Although violence and bloodshed remained a constant threat to the inhabitants of Kentucky and the frontier, events far to the west helped strengthen American control of the region over the British and their Indian allies.

Clark Captures the Northwest 1778-79

Twenty six year old Major George Rogers Clark saw the situation in the west clearly. If Virginia wished to secure Kentucky and much of the western frontier, the alliance between Britain and the many western Indian nations had to be disrupted, and the best way to do that was to strike at the British outposts in the Illinois County and ultimately, Detroit, the principle British outpost in the mid-west.

Henry Hamilton, the Lieutenant Governor of Canada, commanded the small British garrison at Detroit and had worked feverishly since 1776 to gain the support of the various Indian nations of the mid-west. Partly as a result of his efforts, the Shawnee, Delaware, Mingo and many other Indian tribes attacked American settlers with British supplied weapons and gunpowder, ransomed captured American prisoners to the British in Detroit and received payment for hundreds of American scalps taken by the Indians on the frontier. Enraged Virginians referred to Hamilton as "Hair

Buyer Harry" and few people were as reviled in Virginia as Hamilton was.

Clark's interest in capturing Detroit, as well as the British outposts in the Illinois Country near the Mississippi River, did not rest on a desire to capture and punish Hamilton but rather, his desire to undermine British relations with the western Indians. In a letter to Governor Patrick Henry in late 1777, Clark stressed the benefits that would occur if Kaskaskia (a town of approximately 100 families – mostly French – near the Mississippi River in Illinois Country that carried on an extensive trade with the Indians) was taken by the Virginians.

> [If Kaskaskia] *was in our possession it would distress the* [British] *garrison at Detroit for provisions, it would fling the command of the two great rivers* [the Mississippi and the Ohio] *into our hands, which would enable us to get supplies of goods from the Spaniards,* [in New Orleans] *and to carry on a trade with the Indians* [line obliterated] *then might perhaps with such small presents keep them our friends.*[54]

Clark added that scouts (which he had taken the liberty to send to Illinois in the summer of 1777) reported that Kaskaskia was very vulnerable to attack (especially a surprise attack) and the loyalty of its French inhabitants to Britain was weak.

Clark's bold proposal to Virginia's leaders for an expedition against the British outposts in the Illinois territory was approved in early January 1778. Clark was promoted to

---

[54] James, ed., "George Rogers Clark to Patrick Henry, 10 December, 1777", *George Rogers Clark Papers: 1771-1781*, Virginia Series, Vol. 3, 31-32.

Lieutenant Colonel and authorized to raise 350 men.[55] Secrecy and surprise were essential for the success of the expedition, so the recruitment of Clark's force was cloaked under the guise of recruiting more militia for Kentucky.

Recruitment of the authorized number of troops proved difficult; war fatigue was rampant in Virginia in 1778. Only 150 volunteers assembled at Fort Pitt in June for the expedition.[56] Hopeful that his recruiters in Kentucky and the Holston settlements had more success, (they did not) Clark and his small force embarked down the Ohio River. Clark's entire force of over 200 men assembled at the Falls of the Ohio River (Louisville, KY) where the troops learned that their true destination was Kaskaskia in Illinois Country. Many were displeased and approximately 50 deserted before Clark embarked further down the Ohio River on June 24th with what was left, approximately 175 men.[57]

They travelled downriver over 300 miles in four days, marched overland another 100 miles and reached Kaskaskia late in the day of July 4th. Crossing the Kaskaskia River above the settlement, the Virginians descended on the town under cover of darkness and captured it without a fight.

Initially the inhabitants of Kaskaskia were terrified by the Virginians, but Clark's restrained conduct towards them, combined with news of America's alliance with France, influenced nearly the entire town to cooperate with the Virginians. The inhabitants were so won over by Lieutenant Colonel Clark that a party of prominent citizens volunteered to

---

[55] James, ed., "Order of Council, 2 January, 1778", *George Rogers Clark Papers: 1771-1781*, Virginia Series, Vol. 3, 33
[56] James, ed., "Clark's Memoir: 1773-79," *George Rogers Clark Papers: 1771-1781*, Virginia Series, Vol. 3, 117
[57] Hammon and Taylor, 76

escort a detachment of Virginians to the French settlement of Cahokia, 60 miles up the Mississippi River, to persuade its inhabitants to also peaceably submit to the Virginians. Their efforts were a success, and on July 6th, 1778 another important British outpost fell to Clark without a fight. The French settlement of Vincennes, 240 miles to the northeast of Cahokia, submitted to the Virginians two weeks later under nearly identical circumstances.[58]

Lieutenant Colonel Clark, with the help of his new found French allies, had similar success dealing with the Indians of the region. Most had leaned towards the British side of the dispute with the Americans. However, Clark, through tense but firm negotiations, was able to sway nearly all of the tribes in the region to make peace with the Americans. This, along with the capture of the British outposts, was an enormous achievement for Clark, but when Lieutenant Governor Henry Hamilton in Detroit learned about Clark's success in early August, he immediately moved to regain the lost outposts.

Assembling the necessary supplies and troops for the 600 mile journey to Vincennes was a challenge for Hamilton. When he finally marched south in early October, Hamilton only had 40 British regulars from the 8th Regiment, 75 militia volunteers (mostly French), and 60 Indians with him.[59] He hoped to recruit more Indians along the way, but the lateness of the season forced him to march with what he had.

While Hamilton slowly advanced towards Vincennes (stopping frequently to confer with Indian tribes in a

---

[58] James, ed., "Clark's Memoir: 1773-79," *George Rogers Clark Papers: 1771-1781*, Virginia Series, Vol. 3, 227-24

[59] James, ed., "Report by Lieutenant-Governor Henry Hamilton....", *George Rogers Clark Papers: 1771-1781*, Virginia Series, Vol. 3, 177-78

successful effort to recruit their participation) Lieutenant Colonel Clark re-organized his small militia force and prepared for a probable attack from Hamilton. Clark's detachment was depleted by the departure of a number of men who refused to re-enlist when their terms expired in the fall. With so few men, Clark was forced to leave just a handful at Fort Sackville in Vincennes. These few men, commanded by Captain Leonard Helm, faced Hamilton's force, which had increased to nearly 500 with the addition of hundreds of Indians, in mid-December.[60] Outnumber 100 to 1, Captain Helm had no choice but to surrender; once again Vincennes fell without a shot being fired.

    Colonel Clark did not learn about the fall of Vincennes until late January and his first response was to prepare to defend Kaskaskia. While he busied himself with that, Clark discovered that Hamilton had significantly weakened his victorious force at Vincennes by sending the Indians home for the winter with instructions to return in the spring. Confident that the wet winter conditions (which flooded much of the area for miles around) would prevent the American rebels from threatening Vincennes, Hamilton kept only 80 British regulars and French militia with him to garrison Fort Sackville.[61]

    Lieutenant Colonel Clark correctly predicted Hamilton's plans. The British commander intended to use Vincennes as a staging area to assemble a powerful force (mostly of Indians) in the spring to retake Kaskaskia and then

---

[60] Ibid., 181
[61] Dixon and Hunter, *Virginia Gazette*, 26 June, 1779, "Extract of a letter from Col. George R. Clarke, to his Excellency the Governor, dated Kaskaskia (Illinois) April 29, 1779," 2

> *With this body he was to penetrate up the Ohio to Fort Pitt, sweeping Kentucky in his progress (having light brass cannon for the purpose) and as he was to be joined on the way by all the Indians that could be got to him, he was very sanguine it seems of forcing all West Augusta* [county].[62]

To prevent this impending disaster, Clark, *"came to the resolution of attacking* [Hamilton] *before he could have time to collect his Indians again."*[63] Lieutenant Colonel Clark led a force of 130 men (which included two companies of French militia volunteers) 240 miles overland from Kaskaskia in early February to surprise Hamilton at Vincennes.[64] A large batteau with two 4 pound cannon, 6 swivel guns and 40 additional militia floated down the Mississippi and approached Vincennes by the Wabash River.[65]

Lieutenant Colonel Clark and his men endured abysmal conditions on their 19 day march to Vincennes. Clark offered this description of the march to fellow Virginian George Mason.

---

[62] Ibid

[63] Ibid.

[64] Dixon and Hunter, *Virginia Gazette*, 26 June, 1779, "Extract of a letter from Col. George R. Clarke, to his Excellency the Governor, dated Kaskaskia (Illinois) April 29, 1779," 2 and
James, ed., "Journal of Joseph Bowman, 5 February, 1779," *George Rogers Clark Papers: 1771-1781*, Virginia Series, Vol. 3, 156

[65] James, ed., "George Rogers Clark to George Mason, 19 November, 1779", *George Rogers Clark Papers: 1771-1781*, Virginia Series, Vol. 3, 139

> *We had now a Rout before us of two hundred and Forty miles in length, through, I suppose one of the most beautiful Country in the world; but at this time in many parts flowing with water and exceeding bad marching.... The [flood] water...being at Least three feet deep, and in many places four.... This would have been enough to have stop'd any set of men that was not in the same temper.... It Rained nearly a third of our March; but we never halted for it.*[66]

Most nights Clark and his men camped in wet, miserable conditions then marched and waded all day through equally dreary conditions. Clark recalled to Governor Henry that

> *It took us 5 days to cross the drowned lands of the* [Wabash River] *being for upwards of* [six miles] *often up to our breasts in water. Had not the weather been warm, we must have perished.*[67]

Although the morale and strength of Clark's men wavered, it did not fail, and on February 23, 1779 they approached their destination, Vincennes. Captain Joseph Bowman described the final day of the march in his journal:

> *Set off to cross a plain...about 4 Miles long cover'd with Water breast high – here we expected Some of our brave men must certainly perish having froze in the Night and so long fasting and no other Recourse but wading this plain...we pushed into it with*

---

[66] Ibid.
[67] Dixon and Hunter, *Virginia Gazette*, 26 June, 1779, "Extract of a letter from Col. George R. Clarke, to his Excellency the Governor, dated Kaskaskia (Illinois) April 29, 1779," 2

> *Courage Col. Clark being the first.... Never were Men so animated with the thoughts of revenging the wrongs done to their back Settlements as this small Army was -- About one O Clock we came in sight of the Town.*[68]

The expedition had finally reached Vincennes. Clark halted outside of town and sent a message to the inhabitants warning them to stay in their homes. At sunset he advanced into Vincennes. Captain Bowman noted that

> *We began our March all in order with colors flying and drums* [beating] *after wading to the Edge of the Town in Water breast high we mounted the rising ground the town is built on about 8 o Clock* [Lieutenant Bailey] *with 14 Regulars was detached to fire on the fort, while we took possession of the Town.*[69]

Lieutenant Colonel Clark wished to avoid a prolonged siege of Fort Sackville out of concern that hostile Indians might appear in his rear to aid Hamilton. Clark decided to use deception and boldness to convince Hamilton to surrender the fort quickly. Hoping to give the impression that he commanded a much larger force that he actually had, Clark approached the town with a large number of flags flying. He was careful, however, *"to give* [the inhabitants] *no opportunity of seeing our Troops before dark."*[70] Clark recalled that

---

[68] James, ed., "Journal of Joseph Bowman, 23 February, 1779," *George Rogers Clark Papers: 1771-1781*, Virginia Series, Vol. 3, 159

[69] Ibid., 160

[70] James, ed., "George Rogers Clark to George Mason, 19 November, 1779", *George Rogers Clark Papers: 1771-1781*, Virginia Series, Vol. 3, 141

> *I detached Lieut. Bayley* [with] *a party to Attack the Fort at a certain Signal, and took possession of the strongest Posts of the Town with the main Body. The* [enemy] *Garrison had so little suspicion of what was to happen that they did not believe the Fireing was from an Enemy, until a Man was wounded through the Ports (which hapned the third or fourth shot) expecting it to be some drunk Indians.*[71]

Finally aware of the danger, Hamilton's troops in Fort Sackville commenced a warm, but ineffective fire on Clark's men. Clark described the engagement to George Mason

> *The Artillery from the Fort played briskly but did no execution. The Garrison was intirely surrounded within eighty and a hundred Yards behind Houses* [fences] *and Ditches...Never was a heavier fireing kept up on both sides for eighteen Hours with so little damage done.*[72]

Clark observed that the knowledge that "Hair Buyer Harry" was in Fort Sackville, "*inflamed our Troops with a Martial Spirit,*" so they needed no encouragement from the officers to fight.[73] The memory of family and friends "massacred" at the hands of Hamilton's Indian henchmen provided all the motivation Clark's troops needed to prevail.

Clark sent a flag to the fort on the morning of February 24th, demanding the unconditional surrender of the garrison. This was rejected by Lieutenant Governor Hamilton and the

---

[71] Ibid., 141-42
[72] Ibid., 142
[73] Ibid.

firing resumed. It ceased again in the afternoon when Clark agreed to meet Hamilton for a conference outside the fort. While this took place, a small party of Indians arrived in Vincennes unaware of the conflict. They were quickly seized by the Americans.

Once again Hamilton, dissatisfied with the surrender terms offered by Clark, (which was essentially unconditional surrender) returned to Fort Sackville determined to fight on, but Clark took the extreme measure of executing the captured Indians in full view of the fort in hopes of shocking the garrison into surrender. This brutal act so discouraged Hamilton's militia inside the fort (who concluded that they would meet the same fate if they continued to resist) that they abandoned Hamilton.[74]

Disgusted by this "treachery", Hamilton consulted with his officers and they agreed that, *"no advantage to His Majesty's service could result from our holding out in the present circumstances."*[75] Lieutenant Governor Hamilton and the garrison of 79 officers and men formally surrendered Fort Sackville the next day. At the cost of only one wounded man, Lieutenant Colonel George Rogers Clark and his intrepid men had recaptured Vincennes and eliminated the most notorious British villain on the frontier.

Clark's success at Vincennes did more than that; a new sense of optimism swept the American frontier. One Virginia newspaper reported that

---

[74] James, ed., "Report by Lieutenant-Governor Henry Hamilton....", *George Rogers Clark Papers: 1771-1781*, Virginia Series, Vol. 3, 191
[75] Ibid.

> *Colonel-Clark's success seems to have given such life and spirit of enterprize to all the troops and inhabitants of the back country, as has totally changed the face of affairs. All is despondency and terror on the part of our enemies, vigour and alacrity on our part.*[76]

When news of Colonel Clark's success in the west finally reached Williamsburg and the rest of Virginia in the summer of 1779 it helped offset some of the angst Virginians felt about a British raid upon Portsmouth in May. The sudden arrival of a British naval squadron with an expeditionary force of nearly 2,000 troops marked the first return of the British to Virginia since Dunmore's departure in 1776.

---

[76] Dixon and Nicolson, *Virginia Gazette*, "31 July, 1779," 2

Chapter Six

"Never was a State in such a Confused Helpless Situation."
1779-1780

In the spring of 1779, encouraging reports in the weekly gazettes that Spain had signed an alliance with America, Holland had publically recognized American independence, and Russia had refused all British overtures to send troops to fight America, gave Virginians hope that the long conflict with Britain might be drawing to a victorious conclusion.[1] One writer to the *Virginia Gazette* asked how Tories in America could possibly maintain hope for victory, "*When England cannot get an ally, and many nations* [are] *preparing to league themselves against her.*"[2] An unidentified member of Congress, upon receiving, "*intelligence of the most important and interesting nature to America*," reportedly declared that, "*the troubles of America are drawing fast to a conclusion* [in favor of] *the wishes of every friend to America.*"[3] By April, reports in the newspapers claimed that, "*the court of London, through...the Spanish Ambassador, has offered to Congress to acknowledge the independence of America.*"[4]

Although thousands of troops from Virginia had seen combat on battlefields outside the state, the vast majority of Virginia had largely been spared the destruction of war.

---

[1] Dixon and Nicolson, *Virginia Gazette*, 26 February and 19 March, 1779
[2] Dixon and Nicolson, *Virginia Gazette*, 12 March, 1779, 3
[3] Dixon and Nicolson, *Virginia Gazette*, 5 March, 1779, 3
[4] Dixon and Nicolson, *Virginia Gazette*, 24 April, 1779, 3

Almost three years had passed since the last British troops (attached to Lord Dunmore) had abandoned Gwynn's Island, and the fighting that raged on the frontier was distant and isolated to most Virginians.

By 1779 a combination of war fatigue and wishful thinking that the war was close to an end had generated a sense of military complacency in Virginia that left the state weak and vulnerable to attack. This weakness was exposed in May when a British naval force sailed into Chesapeake Bay.

Collier-Mathew Raid

The British flotilla that sailed into Chesapeake Bay on May 8, 1779 included 6 warships (the largest being the 64 gun *HMS Raisonable* and the 44 gun *HMS Rainbow*), a few privateers (armed loyalist ships), and 22 transport vessels carrying 1,800 troops.[5] The troops included the 42nd Highland Regiment, the Volunteers of Ireland (loyalists), the Hessian Regiment of Prince Charles, and the grenadiers and light companies of the Guards.[6] This combined land and naval force, commanded by General Edward Mathew and Commodore Sir George Collier, was sent from New York to Virginia by General Henry Clinton, the overall commander of British operations in America. He desired to disrupt Virginia's flow of reinforcements both northward, to General Washington's army in New York, and southward to General Benjamin Lincoln's army in South Carolina.[7] General Clinton also hoped his sudden raid on Virginia would draw the continent's attention away from New York and allow him to better prepare a much more significant movement against

---

[5] Selby, 204

[6] Davies, ed., "Sir George Collier to Lord George Germain, 22 May, 1779," *Documents of the American Revolution: 1770-83*, Vol. 17, 131

[7] William B. Willcox, ed., *The American Rebellion: Sir Henry Clinton's Narrative of His Campaigns, 1775-1782*, (New Haven: Yale University Press, 1954), 122

Portsmouth and Vicinity

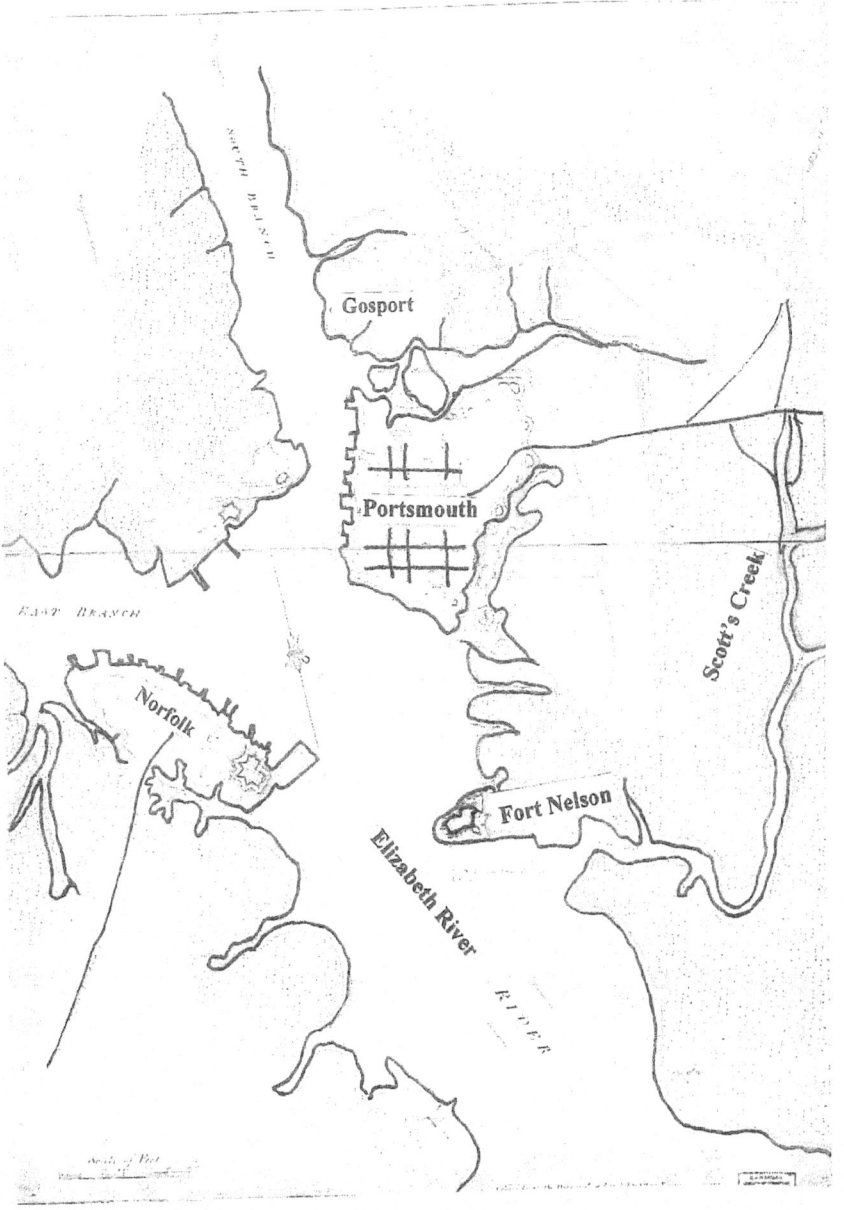

Washington's forces at West Point, a key strategic post on the Hudson River.[8]

The British fleet entered Hampton Roads on May 9th and most of the flotilla swung south into the Elizabeth River, leaving the *HMS Raisonable* anchored off of Hampton. Commodore Collier, concerned about the maneuverability of his largest warship in the narrow channel of the Elizabeth River, transferred to the *HMS Rainbow* to proceed up the river. The 14 gun *HMS Otter* and some of the privateers also broke off the fleet and sailed northward, up the Chesapeake Bay to harass whatever shipping they might encounter.[9]

Fall of Fort Nelson

The primary objective of the remaining British fleet was Portsmouth. The town, which sat across the river from the ruins of Norfolk, was principally defended by a strong fort on the north bank of the river about half a mile below Portsmouth. Located on the same point of land that Lord Dunmore had fortified in 1776 (Tucker's Point) Fort Nelson's 14 foot high wooden walls were 15 feet thick, filled with packed dirt and capable of absorbing almost any enemy broadside leveled against it.[10] Unfortunately for the Virginians, the fort was lightly manned with only 100 troops under Major Thomas Matthews and the rear of the fort, facing inland, was unfortified and open to assault.[11]

Such an attack was exactly what the British had in mind. On the afternoon of May 10th, with his ships anchored within sight of the fort but out of range of Fort Nelson's cannon,

---

[8] Ibid.
[9] Davies, ed. "Sir George Collier to Lord George Germain, 22 May, 1779," *Documents of the American Revolution: 1770-83*, Vol. 17, 131 and Charles Stedman, *The History of the Origin, Progress, and Termination of the American War*, Vol. 2, (London: 1794), 137
[10] Stedman, 137
[11] Selby, 205

Commodore Collier landed approximately 1,200 troops in two waves about three miles from the fort.[12] Collier described the operation to Lord George Germain.

The first division of troops embarked in the flatboats, and covered by the galley and two gunboats (each with two six pounders) the landing was made good without opposition at the Glebe.... A favourable breeze springing up soon after the flatboats advanced, the ships moved on immediately and the remainder of the troops joined the first division with great dispatch. Nothing hostile appeared from the rebels except firing a few shot at the Rainbow from the fort which did not reach her; they fled soon afterwards, leaving the rebel colours flying, and the fort was taken possession of by the King's troops the same evening together with the town of Portsmouth.[13]

According to Dixon and Nicolson's *Virginia Gazette*, when Major Matthews learned of the British landings,

He sent his ammunition up the Southern Branch to the Great Bridge, and immediately evacuated the fort, leaving his colours flying, and spiking up all his guns, except one...[brass cannon] *which he carried with him.*[14]

Abandoned in the fort were 22 spiked cannon on ship carriages (nine 24 pounders, two 9 pounders, and eleven 6 pounders) plus six additional cannon on field carriages (four 4 pounders and two 3 pounders).[15] The British also found

---

[12] Dixon and Nicolson, *Virginia Gazette*, 15 May, 1779, 2
[13] Davies, "Collier to Germain," *Documents of the American Revolution: 1770-83*, Vol. 17, 131
[14] Dixon and Nicolson, *Virginia Gazette*, 15 May, 1779, 2
[15] "Expedition to Portsmouth," *The William and Mary Quarterly*, 2nd Series, Vol. 12, No. 3, July 1932, 184

nearly 40 barrels of gunpowder and 1500 rounds of ordinance ranging from 24 pound solid shot (768 rounds) to grape and bar shot (58 and 56 rounds respectively).[16] American losses extended beyond the abandoned military stores; on his retreat southward, Major Matthews torched several ships in the stocks of the Gosport shipyard (adjacent to Portsmouth) as well as a newly built 24 gun continental warship and two large French merchant ships loaded with over 1000 hogsheads of tobacco anchored at Portsmouth.[17] The town of Portsmouth itself was spared much damage, and the British were able to take possession of it as well as Fort Nelson and Gosport by nightfall without the loss of a single man.

Major Matthews and his men were not the only Virginians to flee southward from the British. The approach of Commodore Collier's fleet prompted a number of merchant vessels at Portsmouth to sail up the South Branch of the Elizabeth River in an effort to avoid capture or destruction. Collier sent some ships in pursuit of the fugitive vessels the following day.

> *Apprehending that many rebel vessels had pushed up the river, I dispatched the Cornwallis galley, two gun boats, four flat boats manned and armed, together with four privateers...in pursuit of them. They were very successful in their enterprise, taking and burning a great number of the enemy's vessels.*[18]

---

[16] Ibid.

[17] Davies, ed. "Collier to Germain, *Documents of the American Revolution: 1770-83*, Vol. 17, 131

[18] Dixon and Nicolson, " Sir George Collier to General Henry Clinton, May 16, 1779," *Virginia Gazette*, 25 September, 1779, 2

One rebel ship, the 14 gun American privateer *Blacksnake*, put up a fight, exchanging cannon fire with British gunboats but eventually its crew was overpowered by a boarding party.[19]

Major Matthews and his troops fared little better; on word that the enemy was bearing down on his small force near Great Bridge, Matthews reportedly destroyed the gunpowder he had transported from Fort Nelson and continued his retreat south into North Carolina.[20]

With Portsmouth a secure base of operations (protected by a chain of picquets that extended in an arc from Gosport to Fort Nelson) General Mathew displayed his distain and disregard for Virginia's land forces by sending small detachments into the countryside to raid Suffolk, Great Bridge, and Kemp's Landing. All three sites held valuable military stores for the rebels and all were poorly defended, so the biggest challenge the British raiders faced was transporting the valuable stores they captured at each site back to Portsmouth. What goods could not be moved were destroyed and Suffolk, which lay 18 miles southwest of Portsmouth, was the first to experience the destruction.

Destruction of Suffolk

The town of Suffolk sat on the Nansemond River and had developed into an important supply center for Virginia with large quantities of salted provisions and naval stores. Nearly all of it went up in flames, along with the bulk of the town, on May 13th when a detachment of British Guards marched from Portsmouth under cover of darkness and arrived at sunrise. In

---

[19] Ibid.
[20] Dixon and Nicolson, *Virginia Gazette*, 15 May 1779, 2

a dispatch to General Clinton in New York, General Mathew noted that, *"The Town was hastily deserted; and some vessels, a very large Magazine of Provisions, Naval Stores, and Two Pieces of Cannon, were destroyed."*[21] General Mathew failed to mention that nearly the entire town was also burned to the ground by the British raiders.

Virginians were shocked at the degree of destruction inflicted on Suffolk. One witness described the stream of refugees fleeing from Suffolk.

> *On my way down (from Smithfield to Suffolk) I met numbers of the unfortunate and distressed inhabitants, flying from the rapid approach of the enemy, with such circumstances of distress as language cannot print.*[22]

The writer went on to report that, *"an express this moment arrived in town, bringing a positive account of the enemy's having burnt all Suffolk, except the civil and religious houses."*[23]

Colonel Robert Lawson, who was only a few miles northeast of Suffolk in Smithfield with a growing force of militia, described a similar scene of British destruction and misconduct to Governor Patrick Henry.

> *From accounts which I have received, the cruel and horrid depredations and rapine committed on the unfortunately and defenceless inhabitants who have*

---

[21] "Major General Mathew to General Sir Henry Clinton, 16 May, 1779," *William and Mary Quarterly*, 2nd Series, Vol. 12, No. 3, July 1932, 185

[22] Dixon and Nicolson, *Virginia Gazette*, 15 May 1779, 2

[23] Ibid.

> *fallen within their reach, exceed almost anything yet heard of with the circle of their tragick display of savage barbarity, household furniture, stocks of all kind, houses, and in short almost every species of perishable property are effectually destroyed, with unrelenting fury by those devils incarnate, murder, rape, rapine and violence fill up the dark catalogue of their detestable transactions.*[24]

A continental recruiting officer in Virginia provided similar details to General Washington, but attributed the destruction to a relatively small party of 70 to 80 enemy troops that, *"burned every house on the road without respect to Persons."*[25] A writer to Dixon and Nicolson's Virginia Gazette highlighted the *"barbarous and unmanly disposition,"* of the invaders and described a robbery committed by some of them.[26]

> *Four boys…who were on their way from Mr. Andrew's school near Suffolk, to their parents in Princess Anne county, were overtaken by three* [enemy] *light horse, and after striking one of* [the students] *with a cutlass, and the most abusive language, robbed them of their shoes and knee buckles, handkerchiefs, money, and all the clothes they had….*[27]

The writer lamented, *"how the laurels of British valor* [had] *fallen when women and boys are now become the target of*

---

[24] Dixon and Nicolson, *Virginia Gazette*, 15 May 1779, 2
[25] Edward Lengel, ed., "General Scott to General Washington, 18 May, 1779," *The Papers of George Washington*, Vol. 20, 530
[26] Dixon and Nicolson, *Virginia Gazette*, 22 May 1779, 2
[27] Ibid.

their vengeance."[28] Yet another writer to the gazette described how four British raiders had plundered a woman of her money, clothes, and valuable furniture, and then tore her fingers as they stole her rings off her hand.[29]

Virginia Responds

Virginia's government, led by Governor Patrick Henry, was initially slow to respond to the invasion, but once they sorted through the confusing reports they reacted forcefully. Governor Henry issued a proclamation on May 15th, that exclaimed,

> *Whereas a British fleet arrived...and landed troops who took the fort at Portsmouth, and also destroyed many vessels there, and have since marched and taken the town of Suffolk, and burnt a part thereof, committing on their way thither, horrid ravages and depredations, such as plundering and burning houses, killing and carrying away stock of all sorts, and exercising other abominable cruelties and barbarities...I issue this my proclamation requiring the county Lieutenants... to hold their respective militias in readiness to oppose the attempts of the enemy wherever they may be.*[30]

Militia troops gathered at the capital as well as in Hampton and Smithfield, all likely targets of the British. They fell

---

[28] Ibid.
[29] Dixon and Nicolson, *Virginia Gazette*, 15 May 1779, 2
[30] Ibid.

under the command of General Thomas Nelson Jr. of Yorktown.

The Virginia General Assembly had appointed Nelson brigadier general of the Virginia militia in 1777 but he had had little opportunity to exercise his command since. Described in the Virginia gazette at the time of his appointment as, *"universally beloved and esteemed for his zealous attachment to our sacred cause,"* Nelson scrambled to organize Virginia's citizen-soldiers. Major Robert Forsyth, a supernumerary continental officer in Williamsburg, observed on May 19th, that

> *Volunteer companys turn out from all quarters, and all hands appear to be full of fight.... We have about six hundred Troops mostly militia in* [Williamsburg] *and about that number at Hampton, under Colo.* [Thomas] *Marshall and six or seven hundred below Smithfield under Colo.* [Robert] *Lawson.*[31]

Although the militia appeared willing to confront the invaders, many were unarmed. Four years of war had drained Virginia of many of its military resources, most especially muskets and rifles. Major Forsyth lamented that,

> *Never was a State in such a confused helpless situation – no Arms nor accoutrements... The Arms in the hands of our Militia are very few and in general bad.*[32]

---

[31] Showman, ed. "Major Robert Forsyth to General Greene, 19 May, 1779," *The Papers of General Nathanael Greene*, Vol. 4, 48

[32] Ibid.

Not all the news from the militia was bad. Colonel Robert Lawson optimistically reported from Smithfield that,

> *The militia at this place on being informed that arms were coming down for them, are much spirited up, and profess the greatest desire of revenge and retaliation.*[33]

Edmund Pendleton credited the presence of the militia in Smithfield with saving the town from Suffolk's fate.

> *Colonel Lawson...collected some Militia in order to oppose the progress of the Enemy, which seems saved Smithfield, for the Freebooters having burned Suffolk were on their March for the other Village, when hearing of the Colonel's party, they changed their Route to Portsmouth.*[34]

Virginia's militia forces were not the only troops tapped to repulse the British invasion. Across the James River in Williamsburg, Brigadier General Charles Scott of the continental army responded to the General Assembly's request for assistance. General Scott, a native of Cumberland County, had risen from militia captain in 1775, to brigadier general in the continental army by 1777. A veteran of Trenton, Princeton, Brandywine, Germantown, Valley Forge, and Monmouth, Scott returned to Virginia on furlough in the winter of 1778-79 and proceeded to raise new continental recruits for General Washington's army in New York.

---

[33] Dixon and Nicolson, *Virginia Gazette*, 15 May 1779, 2
[34] John David Mays, ed., "Edmund Pendleton to William Woodford, 24 May, 1779," *The Letters and Papers of Edmund Pendleton*, Vol. 1, (Charlottesville: University Press of Virginia), 285

Granted special authority by the state legislature and governor during the invasion crisis to, *"do as he pleases and order matters as he thinks proper,"* General Scott apologetically informed General Washington on May 12th that he had ordered the continental levies in Fredericksburg and Alexandria (approximately 800 strong destined for New York) to march as quickly as possible to Williamsburg to protect the capital.[35]

> *There are now at Suffolk and Smithfield &ct. Vast Quantitys of public stores much exposed, this together with the earnest Request of the Assembly...has led me to Suppose it was proper for me to order down* [to Williamsburg] *the New Leavys that are collected at Fredericksburg & Alexandria.... I cannot but know that this is contrary to Your Excellencys Instructions to me, But as Circumstances Has so turned up...I thought It Best to employ them this way and Hope it will meet your... approbation.*[36]

A week later, with the continentals reportedly a day's march from the capital, General Scott updated Washington.

> *We have but few* [militia] *to oppose them and a large Proportion of them I am fearful panick Struck. However, if* [the enemy waits] *one day more we Shall have in from Fredericksburg a Considerable number of the* [continental] *recruits, whom together with*

---

[35] Showman, ed., "Major Robert Forsyth to General Nathanael Greene, 19 May, 1779," *The Papers of General Nathanael Greene*, Vol. 4, 49

[36] Lengel, ed., " General Scott to General Washington, 12 May, 1779," *The Papers of George Washington,* Vol. 20, 457

Note: GW gave his approval of Scott's action in his reply on May 25th.

what we now have, I have hopes of at least covering our most Valuable Stores.[37]

General Scott had taken the further initiative to order Colonel Theodorick Bland's 1st Continental Dragoons, who spent the winter in Winchester, to Williamsburg, another decision for which Scott apologized to General Washington for.

As things turned out, Williamsburg was never really threatened by the invaders. Their attention remained fixed on the south side of the James River.

British Raids on Great Bridge and Kemp's Landing

While General Scott impatiently waited for the continental levies and dragoons to reach Williamsburg, General Mathew's British troops moved through Princess Anne and Norfolk County with impunity. Mathew reported to General Clinton in New York that, *"We have continued to collect Stores of all Sorts to a very great Amount, Military, Naval, and Provisions."*[38] The general made a point of distributing much of the captured provisions to the local inhabitants in an effort to win them over.

On May 16th, a party of British troops marched to Great Bridge to surprise and disperse a small number of rebel militia that were, *"skulking about"*.[39] The following day, reports of public stores at Kemp's Landing, nine miles from Portsmouth, prompted General Mathew to send a strong detachment of the

---

[37] Lengel, ed., "General Scott to General Washington, 18 May, 1779," *The Papers of George Washington*, Vol. 20, 530-31

[38] Davies, ed., "Maj.-General Edward Mathew to General Sir Henry Clinton, 24 May, 1779," *Documents of the American Revolution*, Vol. 17, 133

[39] Ibid.

42nd Highland Regiment up the Eastern Branch of the Elizabeth River in flatboats (supported by a gunboat) to investigate. Meeting no resistance, the detachment seized two ships, eight cannon and assorted gear, and 164 barrels of tar for the navy.[40] Seven other vessels were burned. A few days later, another detachment of the 42nd Regiment in two flatboats rowed up Tanner's Creek and destroyed six additional vessels under construction upon stocks (one of 16 guns nearly complete).[41]

While British troops successfully plundered the countryside around Portsmouth, a large party of slaves worked to dismantle Fort Nelson. General Mathew reported to General Clinton that,

> *The Engineer has been employed for many Days, with near one Hundred Blacks, to destroy the Fort, which was so substantially constructed, as to give us a great Deal of Trouble in the Demolition.*[42]

There had been some disagreement between General Mathew and Commodore Collier on whether the fort should be destroyed at all. General Mathew never wavered from the view that the expedition was a temporary incursion into Virginia to disrupt and distract the rebels and he insisted on the fort's destruction. Commodore Collier, however, saw the situation differently. Impressed by the reception they had

---

[40] "Invoice of Stores found at Kemp's by the 42d or Royal Highland Regiment, May 17, 1779," *The William and Mary Quarterly*, 2nd Series, Vol. 12, No. 3 (July, 1930), 186

[41] Davies, ed., "Maj.-General Edward Mathew to General Sir Henry Clinton, 24 May, 1779," *Documents of the American Revolution*, Vol. 17, 133

[42] Ibid.

received from many of the inhabitants of southern Virginia, Collier asserted to General Clinton in New York that,

> *The most flattering Hopes of a Return to Obedience to their Sovereign may be expected from most of this Province; the People seem importunately desirous that the Royal Standard may be erected, and they give the most positive Assurances that all Ranks of Men will resort to it.*[43]

Collier also asserted that Portsmouth itself was an excellent port and the key to controlling the entire Chesapeake Bay.

> *I am firmly of Opinion…that this Port should remain in our Hands, since it appears to me of more real Consequence and Advantage than any other the Crown now possesses in America; for by securing this, the whole Trade of the Chesapeak is at an End, and consequently the Sinews of the Rebellion destroyed.*[44]

In a report to Lord George Germain, Collier expanded on all of the advantages Britain would derive by retaining control of Portsmouth.

> *Amongst other advantages resulting from our possessing this important post is putting an entire stop to the trade of the French and rebels in the Chesapeake from its vicinity…to the sea; our cruisers may clean and refit immediately upon the spot; it is so*

---

[43] "Sir George Collier to General Sir Henry Clinton, May 16, 1779," *The William and Mary Quarterly*, 2nd Series, Vol. 12, No. 3 (July, 1930), 182
[44] Ibid.

> *good an asylum for ships from its natural strength that a very small naval force will defend the harbor against almost any superiority; the adjoining counties produce all kinds of naval stores, and plenty of masts from 28 inches downwards can be procured without difficulty. This post cuts off the communication between the Carolinas and the Head of the Elk, by which trade has long been advantageously carried on with perfect security and the provisions for the rebel army under Washington was principally conveyed.*[45]

Collier reiterated to Lord Germain in dramatic language his view of

> *The favourable disposition the inhabitants show towards returning again to the obedience of His Majesty. The sacred flame of duty to their Sovereign seems ready to be reilluminated through this great continent. The people, tired of oppression, express their sentiments with much freedom against their present hard taskmasters.*[46]

The commodore concluded by declaring that, *"this invasion has been already attended with more advantages and success than could have been expected from the most sanguine expectations."*[47]

Alas, General Mathew insisted that the expedition not deviate from the original plan, which was to return to New

---

[45] Davies, ed., "Sir George Collier to Lord George Germain, 22 May, 1779," *Documents of the American Revolution*, Vol. 17, 131-32
[46] Ibid.
[47] Ibid.

York by June 1st in time to participate in an expedition up the Hudson River. To Commodore Collier's chagrin, General Mathew abandoned his outposts around Portsmouth on May 24th, and loaded his troops aboard the waiting transports.[48] The expedition was over; it was time to return to New York.

Major Thomas Matthews led approximately 130 men back into Portsmouth on May 25th.[49] Informed the night before by his scouts that the enemy had abandoned their outposts, Major Matthews acted quickly. He informed General Scott that,

> *I immediately began my march from the North West river bridge about 2 o' clock this morning, and by a forced march arrived* [at Portsmouth] *about 3 P.M.*[50]

Matthews found the town empty of enemy troops and Fort Nelson, as well as Gosport shipyard, destroyed. One enemy transport ship was grounded offshore within range of Matthews men. He reported that this, *"afforded us half an hours amusement, pretty smart, without any damage on our side, we hulled the ship once* [presumably with a cannonball] *and damaged her sails and rigging."*[51] The next high tide freed the stuck vessel and it sailed out of range.

Across the James River in Hampton, Colonel Thomas Marshall, the commander of Virginia's state artillery regiment and the ranking officer in Hampton, watched the British fleet

---

[48] Davies, ed., "Maj.-General Edward Mathew to General Sir Henry Clinton, 24 May, 1779," *Documents of the American Revolution*, Vol. 17, 133

[49] Dixon and Nicolson, "Extract of a letter from Major Matthews to Brigadier General Scott, dated Portsmouth, May 25, 1779, *Virginia Gazette*, 29 May, 1779, 3

[50] Ibid.

[51] Ibid.

sail out of the Elizabeth River and into Hampton Roads. Marshall was a veteran of the 1776 and 1777 campaign in the north and had fought at Harlem Heights, Trenton, Princeton, Brandywine and Germantown. He was also the father of Captain John Marshall, future chief justice of the Supreme Court. Colonel Marshall was unsure of the enemy's destination, but he assured General Nelson that he would march with the bulk of his troops at Hampton to join Nelson in Williamsburg if the enemy turned up the James River or Chesapeake Bay.

Colonel Marshall also took a moment to compliment the service of the general's brother, Captain Hugh Nelson, who commanded a detachment of state light horse (cavalry). Praise was also given to the volunteer soldiers of the college of William and Mary.

> *I cannot conclude this letter without mentioning the activity and zeal, with which the Gentlemen of the light horse under Capt. Nelson, have shewn on all occasions. They really are an exceeding useful corps.... No less applause is due to the college volunteers; they have submitted with the greatest cheerfulness to every duty of a soldier, and seem eagerly to wish for an opportunity to distinguish themselves.*[52]

The consensus among Virginia's leaders seemed to be that although it was unfortunate that the state had been caught off guard by the invasion, the militia responded well and their

---

[52] Dixon and Nicolson, "Extract of a letter from Col. Marshall to Brigadier General Nelson, dated Hampton, May 26, 1779, *Virginia Gazette*, 29 May, 1779, 3

strong turnout led to the withdrawal of the enemy force.[53] Of course, the British expedition's commanders paid little heed to the militia, their departure was all part of the original plan.

Impact of the Collier-Mathew Raid

General Clinton's main objectives for the Collier-Mathew expedition were to disrupt the flow of continental reinforcements to Washington's army in the north and simultaneously distract the attention of American leaders away from New York. The expedition succeeded on both counts, but ironically, a severe shortage of clothing for Virginia's continental recruits played as much a part in their delayed march out of the state as the expedition did.

Perhaps the biggest impact of the expedition was the material damage the raid inflicted on Virginia. General Clinton recalled in his memoir of the war that,

> *The loss which the enemy sustained* from [this expedition] *was prodigious – consisting chiefly of provision* [food] *magazines, gunpowder, and naval stores, about 150 vessels of different sizes (several being of force and richly laden), and a quantity of cannon and ordinance stores, together with some thousand hogsheads of tobacco, all of which were taken or destroyed in the short space of a fortnight.*[54]

Historian John Selby concluded that the value of the property stolen or destroyed by the forces under Collier and Mathew

---

[53] Selby, 207
[54] Willcox, ed., *The American Rebellion: Sir Henry Clinton's Narrative of His Campaigns, 1775-1782*, 123

exceeded two million pounds.[55] Scores of Tories and hundreds of slaves also fled with the British, who returned to New York with seventeen captured vessels loaded with tobacco and other plunder.[56]

Aftermath of the Raid

In Williamsburg, a committee of inquiry investigated the conduct of Major Thomas Matthews and concluded that his evacuation of Fort Nelson at the onset of the invasion was justified, *"and that Major Matthews in his retreat, and the removal of the publick stores, acquitted himself as a judicious, attentive and brave officer."*[57]

To improve Virginia's military preparedness, the General Assembly authorized the formation of four new battalions of state infantry (2,500 men total) and six troops of state cavalry.[58] Officials soon discovered, however, that the departure of the enemy significantly reduced the sense of urgency that had driven so many militia to turn out. Attracting recruits for the new battalions, not to mention the continental regiments that were still being raised to reinforce the southern army in Georgia (not Washington's army in New York as originally planned) was more difficult than anyone anticipated and recruiters came woefully short of their goal.

The General Assembly also responded to concerns that the capital in Williamsburg was too vulnerable to future enemy

---

[55] Selby, 208
[56] Ibid.
[57] Dixon and Nicolson, *Virginia Gazette*, 26 June, 1779, 3
[58] " Proceeding of 2 June, 1779," *Journal of the House of Delegates* (Richmond, 1827), 32

raids by transferring the state capital to Richmond, 45 miles up the James River.[59]

Luckily for Virginia, seventeen months passed before the state's defenses were tested by another invasion from the sea. Fighting on the frontier, however, which briefly subsided after Colonel George Rogers Clark's victory at Vincennes, resumed in the late spring of 1779 with an offensive launched by the Virginians against the Shawnee.

War on the Frontier : 1779-81

Colonel Clark's victory at Vincennes sparked a steady flow of settlers to the frontier in 1779 which in turn spurred a proliferation of settlements and forts in Kentucky. One such fort was constructed at the Falls of the Ohio and led to the establishment of Louisville, named in honor of the King of France.

The large increase in settlers in Kentucky also led to a more aggressive stance towards the Indians on the frontier. In May of 1779, Colonel John Bowman led 300 Kentucky militia across the Ohio River against the Shawnee.[60] They attacked the Shawnee town of Chillicothe on May 30th. Most of the town's inhabitants took shelter in a two story fortification that the militia was unable to breach, so Bowman's men pillaged what they could and eventually departed.[61]

The severe winter of 1779-80 limited activity on the frontier for both sides, but in the summer of 1780 Captain Henry Bird of the King's 8th Regiment of Foot led approximately 150 British, Canadian and Tory troops from

---

[59] " Proceeding of 2 June, 1779," *Journal of the House of Delegates*, 44
[60] Hammon and Taylor, 105
[61] Ibid., 106

Detroit, along with hundreds of Indians, into northern Kentucky.[62] Captain Bird also brought two cannon on the expedition, a 3 pounder and a 6 pounder. When his force reached Ruddle's Station, 35 miles north of Boonesborough, the mere presence of the 6 pound cannon convinced the settlers to surrender. Captain Bird reported to his superior, Major Arent DePeyster, that

> *The Three Pounder was not sufficient,* [but under cover of a thunderstorm] *our people raised a battery of rails and earth within 80 yards of the fort.... They stood two discharged of the little gun, which only cut down a spar and stuck the shot in the side of a house. When they saw the Six Pounder moving across the field, they immediately surrendered.*[63]

The fort's defenders realized their wooden walls could not stand against six pound cannon shot and offered to surrender, provided they were placed under the protection of the British. Captain Bird agreed, but he was unable to restrain the Indians, who, *"tore the poor children from their mothers breasts, killed a wounded man and every one of the cattle."*[64] The loss of the cattle was significant because they were needed to feed the prisoners. Bird recalled that, *"We had brought no pork with us*

---

[62] Maude Ward Lafferty, "Destruction of Ruddle's and Martin's Forts in the Revolutionary War," *The Register of the Kentucky Historical Society*, Vol. 54, No. 189, (October, 1956), 297

[63] Lafferty, Letter of Captain Bird to Major Arent S. Depeyster, 1 July, 1780," *The Register of the Kentucky Historical Society*, Vol. 54, No. 189, 297

[64] Ibid.

& were now reduced to great distress, & the poor prisoners [were] *in danger of being starved.*"⁶⁵

Five miles south of Ruddle's Station sat Martin's Station, and Captain Bird marched there next. The garrison at Martin's Station surrendered without a shot, placing themselves under Captain Bird's protection, but once again, despite promises from Indian leaders to restrain their warriors, *"the same promises...were broke in the same manner.*⁶⁶ News that Colonel Clark was, *"coming against them,"* combined with a severe shortage of provisions, and frustration with the undisciplined Indians, caused Captain Bird to end the expedition and head for Detroit.⁶⁷

Colonel Clark, who had assembled a militia force of nearly 1,000 men (with his own 6 pound cannon) followed in Bird's wake a few weeks later, crossing the Ohio River on August 1, 1780 to retaliate.⁶⁸ The Shawnee abandoned Chillicothe, which was destroyed, and fled to the Shawnee town of Piqua, pursued closely by Clark and his troops. Colonel Clark reported to Governor Thomas Jefferson that

> *At half past two in the evening of the 8ᵗʰ, we arrived in sight of the town and forts.... I had scarcely time to make those dispositions necessary, before the action commenced on our left wing, and in a few minutes became almost general, with a savage fierceness on both sides. The confidence the enemy had of their*

---

⁶⁵ Ibid.
⁶⁶ Ibid.
⁶⁷ Ibid.
⁶⁸ James, ed., "Clark to Governor Jefferson, 22 August, 1780," *George Rogers Clark Papers: 1771-1781*, Virginia Series, Vol. 3, 451

own strength and certain victory, or the want of generalship, occasioned several neglects, by which those advantages were taken that proved the ruin of their army, being flanked two or three different times, drove from hill to hill in a circuitous direction, for upwards of a mile and a half; at last took shelter in their strongholds and woods adjacent, when the firing ceased for about half an hour, until [the cannon was brought up]. *A heavy firing again commenced, and continued severe until dark, by which time the enemy were totally routed.*[69]

Colonel Clark noted that the effectiveness of the cannon left the Indians with no safe shelter and that their losses were triple the 14 killed and 13 wounded of his militia.[70] Clark's men pillaged and destroyed Piqua and the surrounding area and then returned to Kentucky, content that they had adequately chastised the Shawnee.

The War Escalates in the South

While the war effort on Virginia's frontier took a decided turn in favor of the Americans in 1780, the same could not be said for the situation to the east. British leaders had shifted much of their attention and military operations from the mid-Atlantic states to the southern states in 1779-80, and Virginia's war effort followed suit. The shift southward for Virginia had actually begun in the midst of the Collier-Mathew raid when General Washington instructed General Charles Scott in May 1779 to send the newly raised

---

[69] Ibid., 452
[70] Ibid.

continental recruits in Virginia to South Carolina to serve in the southern army rather than New York, where Washington's army was. Recruitment of the new Virginia continentals went poorly, however, and reinforcements were needed in the south, so at the end of 1779 General Washington sent the Virginia continentals that were still with his army in New York (which only numbered in the hundreds) to South Carolina as well.

They arrived in Charleston just in time to become trapped, and in May 1780, the bulk of Virginia's continental troops (only 700 strong) surrendered to the British with the rest of the American southern army at Charleston. With few continental recruits to send south to replace the losses and help rebuild the southern army, Virginian officials resorted to sending short term militia to the Carolinas. This proved disastrous in August when a brigade of Virginia militia fled the battlefield of Camden, South Carolina in panic without firing a shot. The American troops that held their ground at Camden were overwhelmed by the enemy and the American southern army was again defeated and dispersed.

Although American commanders, (first General Horatio Gates and then his replacement, General Nathanael Greene) still looked to Virginia for troops and supplies in 1780, the state struggled to send an adequate amount of either southward.

Leslie's Raid: Fall 1780

In New York, General Clinton was pleased with events in South Carolina; the state appeared firmly under British control. Clinton next expected General Cornwallis, who was in charge of British operations in the South, to march into North Carolina and extend British control there. To assist him, General Clinton sent 2,200 troops under General Alexander Leslie from New York to Virginia in order to *"make a diversion in favor of General Cornwallis, who by the time you arrive there will probably be acting in the back parts of North Carolina."*[71]

Clinton left it to Leslie as to how best to, *"make a diversion"*, but strongly suggested that Leslie

> *Proceed up* [the] *James River as high as possible, in order to seize or destroy any magazines the enemy may have at Petersburg, Richmond, or any of the places adjacent, and establish a post on the Elizabeth River.*[72]

Intercepting much needed supplies in Virginia that were destined for the weak American southern army in North Carolina would likely erode rebel resistance in North Carolina. Such resistance would further diminish if desperately needed Virginian reinforcements were detained in Virginia by Leslie's presence in the state. Both outcomes could hasten the fall of North Carolina to the British, but coordination between General Cornwallis and General Leslie was crucial for success

---

[71] Willcox, ed., " General Clinton to General Leslie, 12 October, 1780," *The American Rebellion: Sir Henry Clinton's Narrative of His Campaigns, 1775-1782*, 467

[72] Ibid.

so General Clinton instructed Leslie to establish communications with Cornwallis as quickly as possible.

With these instructions, (and 2,200 troops) General Leslie sailed for Virginia in mid-October, escorted by six British warships, the 40 gun *Romulus*, the 32 gun *Blonde*, the 16 gun *Delight*, a 20 gun privateer and two row gallies.[73] Leslie's infantry force included troops from the Brigade of Guards, the Hessian Regiment von Bose, the Provincial King's American Regiment, a battalion of light infantry drawn from several provincial (American loyalist) corps in New York, a detachment of German Jagers, a detachment of 17th Light Dragoons, and some British and German artillerists.[74]

The expedition sailed into Chesapeake Bay on October 20th, and General Leslie immediately sent detachments ashore to gain intelligence and obtain pilots to navigate the local waters.[75] The following day, Leslie landed a detachment of cavalry and infantry at Portsmouth and two days later, on October 23rd, another detachment landed across the James River at Newport News.

Thomas Jefferson, who replaced Patrick Henry as governor in June 1779, was informed that the enemy troops at Portsmouth numbered 800 and included a party of light horse which passed through Kemp's Landing on their way to Great Bridge.[76] Three hundred British troops (Jefferson was

---

[73] Boyd, "Thomas Jefferson to Samuel Huntington, 3 November, 1780," *The Papers of Thomas Jefferson*, Vol. 4, 92

[74] Willcox, ed., *The American Rebellion: Sir Henry Clinton's Narrative of His Campaigns, 1775-1782*, 231

[75] Davies, ed.,"General Leslie to Lord George Germain, 27 November, 1780," *Documents of the American Revolution*, Vol. 18, 235

[76] Boyd ed., "Thomas Nelson to Thomas Jefferson, 21 October, 1780," and "Thomas Jefferson to Samuel Huntington, 25 October, 1780," *The Papers of Thomas Jefferson*, Vol. 4, 54 and 67

incorrectly told 1,000) and a detachment of cavalry landed at Newport News; the cavalry moved northward midway up the road to Williamsburg while the infantry marched into Hampton unopposed and, according to Jefferson, committed "*horrid depredations.*"[77]

General Leslie, accompanied by Commodore George Gayton, the commander of the naval force, marched with the infantry into Hampton where he learned, through the local gazettes, about Major Patrick Ferguson's stunning defeat at King's Mountain in South Carolina in early October.

Approximately 1,000 frontiersmen from the Carolinas and Virginia had crushed an equal number of provincial troops under Major Ferguson and in doing so, disrupted General Cornwallis's plans. General Leslie informed Lord Germain that the news of the defeat at King's Mountain,

> *Made me determine to establish a post at Portsmouth until I could get certain intelligence of Lord Cornwallis's situation, for I knew he depended much on the support of the back settlers of N. Carolina and I concluded, if Major Ferguson was defeated, from my knowledge of the general disposition of the people that his lordship could not advance.*[78]

General Leslie explained to General Clinton – who years latter expressed disappointed in Leslie's decision to remain in Portsmouth and not attack Petersburg or Richmond – that the

---

[77] Boyd ed., "Thomas Jefferson to Samuel Huntington, 25 October, 1780," *The Papers of Thomas Jefferson*, Vol. 4, 67-68
[78] Davies, ed.,"Major-General Alexander Leslie to Lord George Germain, 27 November, 1780," *Documents of the American Revolution*, Vol. 18, 235

lack of pilots to navigate the difficult James River, combined with Leslie's uncertainty about Cornwallis's movements or wishes, and, *"the dissidence of the people of the country (who it was dangerous to leave behind us...) all led us to resolve unanimously that a post ought to be established at Portsmouth prior to our penetrating further into the country."*[79]

Leslie withdrew his troops from Hampton and the north side of the James River and focused all of his attention on Portsmouth, disembarking his entire force there and posting detachments in the surrounding countryside as far as Suffolk and Great Bridge. General Leslie defended his decision to forsake a movement up the James River to Petersburg and Richmond with the mistaken assertion that

> *The county was acquainted with our destination some weeks before our arrival, which had given them time to take measures to oppose us by erecting batteries on the banks of the narrow parts of the James River, fortifying Richmond, and collecting a formidable militia.*[80]

No such formidable militia or batteries waited for the British in Richmond or along the James River. General Leslie had been duped.

---

[79] Willcox, ed., " General Leslie, to General Clinton, 4 November, 1780," *The American Rebellion: Sir Henry Clinton's Narrative of His Campaigns, 1775-1782,* 472-73

[80] Ibid.

Virginia Responds

Once Governor Jefferson realized the magnitude of Leslie's invasion he acted quickly to organize Virginia's defense. General Gates, the soon to be replaced commander of the American southern army, was informed to expect a delay in reinforcements from Virginia as, *"We are taking Measures to collect a Body to oppose* [the invaders]; *for which purpose it seems necessary to retain such Regulars, Volunteers, and Militia as have not yet gone on to you."*[81] Jefferson instructed Colonel Robert Lawson, who was forming a legion of state cavalry and infantry that was supposed to join General Gates, to send his cavalry, *"into the neighborhood of the enemy,"* as soon as possible, and his infantry to Cabin Point, thirty miles north of Smithfield, to rendezvous with other militia units.[82]

The governor wrote to General George Weedon and General Peter Muhlenberg, two former continental generals who had left the American army and returned to civilian life in Virginia, and asked each to, *"aid in the command,"* of the militia. They would work with General Thomas Nelson, the ranking officer of the militia. Other furloughed continental army officers in Virginia, such as Colonel Josiah Parker, were also requested to serve. Jefferson explained to Parker that he was, *"very anxious as far as it can be done, to substitute in place of the militia officers, others who…*[possess] *experience in military duties."* In other words, Jefferson wanted as many experienced continental officers as possible to command the

---

[81] Boyd, ed., "Thomas Jefferson to Horatio Gates, 22 October, 1780," *The Papers of Thomas Jefferson*, Vol. 4, 57
[82] Boyd, ed., "Thomas Jefferson to Robert Lawson, 23 October, 1780," *The Papers of Thomas Jefferson*, Vol. 4, 64

militia. Realizing that such an arrangement might lead to disputes over rank and privileges, Jefferson asked potentially disgruntled officers to put aside their complaints until the crisis passed.[83]

Governor Jefferson initially called out 10,000 militia from the southeastern counties of the state, but that amount was reduced to 4,150 (plus approximately 1,500 levies and volunteers) once Jefferson better understood the strength of the enemy's force.[84] General Nelson commanded the militia that formed on the north side of the James River. General Muhlenberg took charge of the militia assembled on Pagan Creek near Smithfield on the south side of the James River.[85] Both forces were comprised of an assortment of troops. Governor Jefferson noted on November 10th that

> *The force called on to oppose the Enemy is as yet in a most Chaotic State, consisting of fragments of 3 Month Militia, 8 Month Men, 18 Month* [Continentals], *Volunteers, and new Militia.*[86]

A critical shortage of weapons and equipment left Virginia's forces with limited capabilities, and they remained at a safe distance from the enemy in Portsmouth. One militia commander informed Governor Jefferson on November 7th from Cabin Point that

---

[83] Boyd, ed., "Thomas Jefferson to Josiah Parker, 26 October, 1780," *The Papers of Thomas Jefferson*, Vol. 4, 71
[84] Boyd, ed., "Steps to be Taken to Repel General Leslie's Army, 22 October, 1780," *The Papers of Thomas Jefferson*, Vol. 4, 57 and "Thomas Jefferson to George Weedon, 2 November, 1780," 91
[85] Boyd, ed., "Governor Jefferson to Edward Stevens, 10 November, 1780, *The Papers of Thomas Jefferson*, Vol. 4, 111
[86] Ibid.

> *I am at this place with Two Hundred and Twenty five Men from Brunswick County and only fifteen Guns without any other accutryments. Should be glad you would please inform me in what manner We are to be accuterd as I do not think it prudent to March any lower without arms* [and] *shall remain here till Your Excellencys Orders and assistance Comes.*[87]

Governor Jefferson was well aware of the shortage of arms and urged General Weedon, who was in Richmond on November 3rd, to be strict in accounting for all public arms in possession of the militia.

> *The State of our Magazine renders it essential that we do not lose a single arm.... We have determined that no militia man who has received a public arm shall ever be discharged from duty till he has delivered such arm to the officer appointed to receive it...or until he shall give satisfactory proof that such arm has been lost by unavoidable accident.*[88]

Luckily for Virginia's poorly armed defenders, General Leslie remained inexplicably inactive at Portsmouth.

Leslie's inactivity did not prevent Governor Jefferson from ordering the removal of over 2,000 prisoners of war from Charlottesville to Fort Frederick in western Maryland. These were the convention prisoners from Saratoga and they had just begun their fourth year of captivity. Most of their captivity had been spent in Massachusetts, but in the winter of 1778-79

---

[87] Boyd, ed., "Richard Elliott to Thomas Jefferson, 7 November, 1780," *The Papers of Thomas Jefferson*, Vol. 4, 97-98

[88] Boyd, ed., "Thomas Jefferson to George Weedon, 3 November, 1780," *The Papers of Thomas Jefferson*, Vol. 4, 94

Congress decided to move them south, so Charlottesville became their new residence. They seemed to adjust nicely to their new surroundings and few exploited the loose supervision or restrictions on their conduct, content instead to sit out the war until they were exchanged.

Virginia officials, however, worried that the presence of a large enemy force in the state was too great of a temptation for many of the prisoners, so to prevent their escape or rescue, Governor Jefferson arranged to send them to Fort Frederick in western Maryland. When it was discovered that the Maryland fort could not accommodate all of the prisoners, it was decided to send only the 800 British captives, the assumption being that the 1,500 Hessians were less desirous to escape and rejoin the war.[89]

While Governor Jefferson arranged to secure the prisoners, he also grew more perplexed at the lack of activity by the enemy in Portsmouth. General Leslie seemed perfectly content to maintain the bulk of his force within the town, which he fortified. Outposts at Suffolk and Great Bridge were also manned to secure adequate provisions from the countryside. Governor Jefferson speculated to Samuel Huntington in Congress that,

> [The enemy's] *movements here had induced me to think they came in expectation of meeting with Lord Cornwallis in this country, that his precipitate retreat has left them without a concerted object, and that they were awaiting further orders.*[90]

---

[89] Boyd, ed., "Thomas Jefferson to Samuel Huntington, 3 November 1780," *The Papers of Thomas Jefferson*, Vol. 4, 92-93

[90] Boyd, ed., "Thomas Jefferson to Samuel Huntington, 1780," *The Papers of Thomas Jefferson*, Vol. 4, 71

This was indeed at least partly the case. As soon as General Leslie learned about Major Ferguson's defeat at King's Mountain, he realized that Cornwallis's advance into North Carolina was threatened. As a result, Leslie decided to wait in Portsmouth until her received instructions from General Cornwallis. He sent multiple dispatches southward, one of which was intercepted by the Virginians. Leslie's intercepted message confirmed to state officials that his movements were in coordination with Cornwallis, or at least supposed to be. The British defeat at King's Mountain had overturned Cornwallis's plans and left Leslie unsure on how to proceed.

The uncertainty was resolved on November 9th, when Leslie received instructions from Cornwallis to abandon Portsmouth and sail to the Cape Fear River in North Carolina to cooperate with his efforts in South Carolina. General Leslie, who had anticipated these orders, complied immediately. Forage was gathered for the horses (which took a few days) and the transport ships were loaded. By November 15th, Portsmouth was empty of British troops; hundreds of runaway slaves remained, however, abandoned by their "liberators" due to a shortage of space on the ships. Delayed by bad weather and contrary winds near the mouth of the Chesapeake, the expedition did not sail out to sea until November 22nd.

Virginians were pleased by both the turn of events, and the conduct of their forces during the crisis. Although the invasion exposed a severe shortage of arms with which to defend the state, an adequate number of militia answered the call and very little damage was inflicted on the state. Edmund Pendleton noted some, *"murmuring at the treatment* [the militia] *met...from forced Marches and too Strict Attention to Order,* [to] *not being allowed to break their Ranks...to avoid Deep Ponds or water or to drink.*[91] Such strict order was foreign to most of the militia, and Pendleton claimed that it brought on illnesses that cost eight lives.[92] He expressed his concern that such treatment would, *"have bad effects on the recruiting Service,"* in the future.[93] Little did he know that this claim would be tested within a month.

---

[91] Mays, ed., "Pendleton to James Madison, 4 December, 1780," *The Letters and Papers of Edmund Pendleton,* 325
[92] Ibid.
[93] Ibid.

Chapter Seven

"The Spirit of Disaffection in the Southern Colonies had Received a Rude Shock...."

January : 1781

General Henry Clinton in New York was very disappointed by the reversal of British fortunes in the south in October. Major Ferguson's defeat at King's Mountain caused General Cornwallis to temporarily abandon his operations in North Carolina which in turn led to General Leslie's departure from Virginia. Clinton lamented that,

> *The King's affairs before this misfortune were going on in the happiest train. The spirit of disaffection in the southern colonies had received a rude shock by Gates' defeat* [at Camden].[1]

General Clinton noted that the string of British victories in South Carolina prior to the defeat at King's Mountain had helped, "*cast a desponding gloom over* [the Americans]."[2]

The surprising outcome at King's Mountain, however, like American victories at Saratoga and Trenton before it, gave the rebels new hope and undermined British gains towards

---

[1] Willcox, ed., *The American Rebellion: Sir Henry Clinton's Narrative of His Campaigns, 1775-1782*, 430

[2] Ibid.

suppressing the rebellion in the South. Despite this disappointing setback, General Clinton remained supportive of further military operations in Virginia and was

> *Fully sensible of the great advantage likely to arise from our possessing a naval station* [in Virginia] *and from pursuing my original plan of striking at the enemy's depots at Petersburg and Richmond....* [3]

Clinton was determined to pursue these objectives and within days of learning about Leslie's departure from Virginia, he organized a new expedition to Virginia, to be led by a surprising British commander.

Benedict Arnold

For the first two years of the Revolutionary War, one American officer rose above all others for his bold deeds and accomplishments on the battlefield. Benedict Arnold of Connecticut first attracted notice as the commander of a party of militia that marched into New York to capture Fort Ticonderoga on Lake Champlain in May 1775. Four months later, Colonel Arnold led a 1,100 man detachment of continental troops on an epic march through the Maine and Canadian wilderness to strike Quebec. Although the attack on Quebec failed and Arnold was seriously wounded in the leg, he evaded capture, recovered, and played a pivotal role in defending Lake Champlain in 1776. Promoted to Brigadier-General by Congress, Arnold's fleet of gunboats, constructed under his supervision over the summer of 1776, challenged a British invasion force from Canada in October 1776. Although Arnold's fleet was destroyed, its presence on Lake

---

[3] Ibid., 234

Champlain delayed the British timetable and forced them to cancel further operations on the lake until 1777.

In 1777, General Arnold once again emerged as one of America's greatest military heroes, boldly leading troops in the battles of Saratoga, in New York. Grievously wounded in the same leg that was injured at Quebec -- a wound that affected him for the rest of his life – Arnold's leadership at Saratoga was instrumental in America's victory.

Arnold's wound prevented him from taking the field in 1778 and he found himself instead, appointed military commander of Philadelphia after the British abandoned the city in June 1778. It was during his tenure there that accusations of corruption surfaced, accusations that eventually led to a court martial. Although Arnold only received a mild reprimand for his questionable conduct, he felt wronged by the tribunal. Arnold's long held resentment of Congress over the issue of military rank now carried over to the army and contributed to his decision to betray the United States in 1780.

After an extended period of secret negotiations with the British, General Arnold agreed to help the British capture the key American post of West Point, on the Hudson River. His transfer to that post in 1779 placed Arnold, as commander, in the ideal position to hand the post over to the enemy without a fight. In late September 1780, Arnold delivered the defensive plans of West Point to a British officer, Major John Andre'; Andre' was subsequently apprehended by American militia on his way back to the British lines. The incriminating evidence on Major Andre' exposed Arnold, who successfully fled to the British for his safety before he could be arrested. Although he had failed to deliver West Point to the British, the revelation of Arnold's betrayal was a tremendous blow to the American cause. One of America's best generals had turned on the country, and it was only natural to ask who else might be working for the British.

General Henry Clinton honored his terms with Arnold and made him a Brigadier General in the British army. Expecting Arnold to do all he could to prove his worth to the British, and hoping that, *"the confidence I thus appeared to place in an officer who had acted against us might be a strong incitement to other able leaders of the rebel army to desert their cause and seek employment in that of the King,"* Clinton placed Arnold in command of a 1,800 man expedition to Virginia in December, 1780.[4]

Arnold's Expedition Departs for Virginia

On December 20th, 1780 over twenty transport ships, escorted by the 44 gun *HMS Charon*, the 24 gun *HMS Amphitrite*, the 20 gun *HMS Fowey*, the 18 gun *HMS Hope*, and the 16 gun *HMS Bonetta*, plus several smaller British warships and privateers, all under the command of Commodore Thomas Symonds, sailed out of New York harbor for Virginia.[5] Onboard the transports were over 750 soldiers from Lieutenant Colonel Thomas Dundas's 80th Edinburgh Royal Volunteers Regiment, a detachment of 110 German Jagers (riflemen) under Captain Johann Ewald, three loyalist American units, the Queen's Rangers with over 500 men, commanded by Lieutenant Colonel John Simcoe of the British

---

[4] Ibid., 235

[5] Joseph Tustin, ed. *Diary of the American War: A Hessian Journal*, (New Haven: Yale University Press, 1979), 258
   Henceforth referred to as Ewald   and
Davies, ed., "Disposition of H.M. Ships, 4 July, 1781",
Documents of the American Revolution, Vol. 20, 173

army, the Loyal American Regiment, over 200 strong, commanded by Colonel Beverly Robinson Jr., a loyalist from New York, and Arnold's own newly formed American Legion, with only 30 men.[6] A 30 man detachment of pioneers, a 45 man company of loyalist New York riflemen under Captain John Althouse and a 70 man detachment of Royal Artillerists completed the expedition.[7]

Severe weather struck Arnold's expedition two days into the voyage and scattered his fleet. Their destination had been a secret, even to many of the ship captains, but each had a letter to be opened if they became separated instructing them of their destination. Three transport ships with 400 of Arnold's troops and an armed escort ship were driven so far off course it took them a week to catch up to the fleet. By the time they did, Arnold was well on his way to fulfilling General Clinton's objectives for the expedition.

In his recollections of the war, Clinton asserted that,

My chief objects in sending expeditions to the Chesapeake were…to endeavor to destroy the stores collected at the head of James River for the supply of Gates' army, and to lay hold of some convenient post at its mouth for covering frigates – from whence we might obstruct the enemy's trade in those waters and, by commanding that noble river, prevent their forming depots on its banks for the service of Carolina.[8]

---

[6] "Embarkation Return for the Following Corps, 11 December, 1780, New York," *Sir Henry Clinton Papers*, Vol. 113, item 15, University of Michigan, William L. Clements Library

[7] Ibid.

[8] Willcox, ed., *The American Rebellion: Sir Henry Clinton's Narrative of His Campaigns, 1775-1782*, 234

Although General Clinton's instructions allowed Arnold to strike at the rebel supply depots provided there was little risk to the expedition, Clinton's primary objective was to secure a post at Portsmouth from which to encourage loyalist Virginians to, "*assemble and arm*" themselves.[9] Arnold's expedition was not to be just another quick raid on Virginia, but rather, a permanent occupation of the southeastern section of the state and a rallying point for loyalists throughout the region. If Arnold was also able to disrupt aid to the American southern army by destroying key supply depots so much the better for the British.

The Expedition Arrives

Commodore James Barron onboard the Virginia State Navy brig *Liberty* in Hampton Roads, witnessed a surprising site on December 30th, a fleet of nearly 30 vessels entered Chesapeake Bay. Other Virginians along the shore of Princess Anne County (present day Virginia Beach) likely spotted Arnold's ships a day earlier when the fleet reached the Virginia capes (entrance to Chesapeake Bay) and anchored in Lynnhaven Bay, but it was Commodore Baron who first sounded the alarm, sailing into Hampton where he encountered a local merchant named Jacob Wray and instructed him to get word to General Thomas Nelson in Yorktown about the unidentified fleet's arrival. General Nelson received the news by horseman and immediately forwarded it to Governor Jefferson in Richmond, who received the news the next morning (Dec. 31st).

---

[9] Davies, ed., "General Henry Clinton to General Arnold, 14 December, 1780," *Documents of the American Revolution*, Vol. 18, 256

Unsure of the identity of the fleet and unwilling to call out the militia for a possible false alarm (the ships might have been French), Jefferson waited for additional information and passed the report on to General Friedrich von Steuben at Wilton Plantation, a few miles downriver from Richmond. Steuben, a foreign volunteer from Prussia who was instrumental in developing a uniform system of military drill for the American army at Valley Forge during the winter of 1777-78, arrived in Virginia in the fall of 1780 on his way to join the American southern army in the Carolinas. General Nathanael Greene, the newly appointed commander of America's southern forces, revised Steuben's instructions and ordered him to remain in Virginia to oversee the recruitment of continental troops as well as the flow of supplies southward. Steuben was the ranking continental officer in Virginia and thus, the de facto military commander of the state. It was only natural then for Governor Jefferson to turn to Steuben upon notice of the ships, informing him on December 31st that,

> *I have this moment received information that 27 sail of vessels, 18 of which were square rigged, were yesterday morning just below Willoughby's point. No other circumstance being given to conjecture their force or destination, I am only able to dispatch Genl. Nelson into the lower country to take such measures as exigencies may require for the instant, until further information is received here. Then or in the meantime your aid and counsel will be deemed valuable.*[10]

---

[10] Boyd, ed., "Governor Jefferson to General Steuben, 31 December, 1781," *The Papers of Thomas Jefferson*, Vol. 4, 254

While Virginia's authorities struggled to determine the threat level of the mysterious ships, General Arnold moved quickly to exploit the confusion and surprise caused by his arrival.

Raid on Hampton

Arnold's fleet anchored off Newport News on the evening of December 30th and the next day he transferred his infantry onto smaller vessels (some of which had been captured from the Virginians the day before) in order to better navigate the broad, shallow James River. Securing pilots to help navigate the tricky river channel was a priority for Arnold, so on the evening of December 31st he sent a 300 man detachment ashore to reconnoiter and obtain the necessary river pilots.[11]

Lieutenant Bartholomew James of the *HMS Charon*, along with 100 seamen, was part of the detachment that also included troops from the Queen's Rangers and the 80th Regiment (under the command of Captain Hawthorne of the 80th Regiment).[12] They landed at Newport News around 7 p.m. and marched to Hampton, a few miles away. Guided by a local resident who was pressed into service at one of the houses they passed, the detachment reached Hampton at midnight and commenced a search of the town. Lieutenant James recalled that

---

[11] John K. Laughton, ed., *The Journal of Rear-Admiral Bartholomew James*, (1896), 94

Henceforth referred to as: Bartholomew James Journal

[12] Ibid.

We entered the town of Hampton, dividing ourselves in three divisions, and surrounding with a profound silence the chief streets and houses, and taking out of their beds the principal inhabitants.[13]

Pains were taken by British commanders to restrain the troops from plundering the inhabitants. Lieutenant James spent an hour with one family, assuring them that no harm would come to their persons or property. He admitted later, however, that "*outrages* [that were] *unavoidable with such a body of men, in the enemy's town in the dead of night*," did occur.[14]

By 2 a.m. Captain Hawthorne and Lieutenant James, concerned that the countryside (and local militia) would soon learn about the raid and try to cut the detachment off from their boats, reassembled their men, along with a handful of river pilots pressed into service, and proceeded back to shore.[15]

The officers' concerns about the local militia were justified for rebel troops did assemble, but due to either the lack of men or lack of spirit, they only harassed the rear of the British column on its march back to shore.

Only two of the Queen's Rangers were wounded in these skirmishes. However, when the fatigued British troops reached their boats at 7 a.m., they discovered that seven fellow soldiers, including one of Lieutenant James's seamen, were

---

[13] Ibid.
[14] Ibid., 95
[15] "Extract of a letter from a Gentleman in Portsmouth, Virginia, to his Friend in this city, dated, January 24, 1781" *New York Gazette and Weekly Mercury,* February 5, 1781

missing. They had likely deserted but were possibly killed or captured on the march.[16]

Skirmish at Warwick

Hampton was not the only town to host British troops on New Year's Eve. General Arnold sent a second detachment ashore near the village of Warwick, just north of Newport News. A party of militia had been spotted at nightfall along the shore and General Arnold wanted to investigate. Arnold ordered Captain Johann Ewald of the Jaegers to, "*approach these people to reconnoiter them*," and capture some prisoners to gain intelligence on the enemy.[17]

Ewald was a bold German commander and veteran of numerous battles in New York, New Jersey, and Pennsylvania, as well as the more recent campaign that captured Charleston, South Carolina in 1780. He and his jaegers (German riflemen) were well suited to fight the Virginia militia with their open order style of combat. Maneuverability on the battlefield was essential when fighting an elusive enemy like the American militia, and Ewald's jaegers were possibly the most maneuverable infantry force Britain had in America.

Captain Ewald and his jaegers, joined by Captain Althouse's loyalist riflemen from New York, rowed ashore in four boats. They were supported by a detachment of the Queen's Rangers who followed in their own boats. Captain Ewald described his landing.

---

[16] Bartholomew James Journal, 96
[17] Ewald, 259

> *I approached within rifle shot, the shore was high. I ordered several shots fired at them, which they answered with small-arms fire, where upon I concluded that they did not have any cannon with them. They were posted behind fences and appeared to number several hundred men.*[18]

When he realized that the water beneath the boats was only waist deep, Ewald,

> *Called to my men to fire a volley, draw their hunting swords, plunge into the water, and swiftly attack the foe.*[19]

The bold German captain proudly recalled that,

> *Everyone obeyed. The enemy fired a volley when we jumped into the water and three men were wounded. But the enemy was startled by the unexpected attack and withdrew.*[20]

Ewald and his men scrambled up the steep bank of the river in pursuit. "*I formed my men as well as I could,*" he recalled, "*and took fifty men with me to pursue the enemy.*"[21] The Virginians, reportedly 230 strong, halted to make a stand at a nearby plantation.[22] Undeterred by their numbers, Captain Ewald ordered his men forward, but the militia held their ground. The Queen's Rangers soon arrived to tip the balance

---

[18] Ewald, 259
[19] Ibid.
[20] Ibid.
[21] Ibid.
[22] Ibid.

and the militia withdrew under cover of darkness. Ewald cautiously pushed on into Warwick where he collected fresh provisions and spent a restless night, *"alarmed three times by the enemy."*[23]

At some point in the operation General Arnold came ashore to congratulate Captain Ewald on his success. Arnold, *"admired the bravery of the men and expressed his heartfelt thanks for my good will,"* recalled Ewald.[24] Captain Ewald was dis-interested in Arnold's praise; he viewed Arnold's order to attack the militia as reckless.

> *I do not deny that this little trick left me with no great opinion of General Arnold's judgment, ordering men without bayonets to land and attack an enemy equipped with bayonets since the light infantry was just as close to them as I was. That the enemy lost his nerve and left – that was luck! But had they taken a stand, and thrown themselves upon the jagers and* [riflemen] *when I climbed up the steep bank with my men, which could not be done in the best order, all would have been lost.*[25]

Skirmishes resumed at daybreak as the Virginia militia returned and probed Ewald's force. Ewald received orders to return to the fleet at 9 a.m., but when he reached the shore, he found that low tide had forced the boats to remain far offshore, so the tired captain and his men had to wade through the chilly water that eventually rose to their waists. It took the wet and exhausted troops, *"a good quarter of an hour"* to reach the

---

[23] Ibid.
[24] Ibid., 260
[25] Ibid., 259-260

boats, which then transported them to the fleet, still anchored in the river channel.[26]

General Arnold proceeded upriver with his transports and several warships, sailing on the flood tide to Hog Island. Along the way they chased and seized several merchant ships loaded with tobacco. One of these ships became grounded in low water along the north bank of the James. When Arnold sent a party to free the vessel, they were fired upon by militia onshore. Arnold sent a flag with a message to the rebels to cease their actions or face the destruction of their town (Warwick).

> *I have to* [tell] *you that however disagreeable It may be to me, unless you immediately desist firing, and suffer the Prize* [grounded ship] *to be taken away with all Her Materials, I shall be under the Necessity of landing and burning the Village, which I wish to avoid.*[27]

The militia apparently believed Arnold's threat and withdrew, trading the stuck ship for the safety of their town.

Activity off Hampton Roads

Not all of Arnold's ships sailed upriver on New Year's Day. In fact, most of Arnold's warships, including his largest, *the H.M.S. Charon*, remained anchored off Newport News awaiting the arrival of the missing transport ships and guarding against the sudden appearance of the French navy.

---

[26] Ewald, 260
[27] Michael Kranish, *Flight from Monticello: Thomas Jefferson at War*, (Oxford University Press, 2010), 172

While the squadron sat anchored in Hampton Roads, a reconnaissance party of five longboats under Lieutenant James of the *HMS Charon* rowed up the Nansemond River, which lay across the James River from Newport News, to reconnoiter. This 25 mile long tidal river connected the town of Suffolk with the James River. It was half a mile wide in some stretches and only 50 yards wide in other spots. Concerned about the possibility of ambush from shore along some of the narrower stretches, the boats moved as quietly as possible upriver. James reported that,

> *With my oars all muffled and with a profound silence we entered the river at 10 p.m., landing frequently* [in search of houses] *to gain intelligence.... After many fruitless searches we discovered a house of some consequence in appearance; on entering we found a most lovely young lady alone, sitting by the fire, weeping immoderately.*[28]

Lieutenant James comforted the young lady, assuring her that she was in no danger and had nothing to fear. After a few minutes, the relieved girl delivered some disturbing news to Lieutenant James.[29]

> *You are much mistaken...if you think your being in this river is a secret, for know, sir, it has been discovered ever since you entered it, and the country some hours alarmed.*[30]

---

[28] Bartholomew James Journal, 96
[29] Ibid., 97
[30] Ibid.

The young girl claimed that several militia detachments under her father, who was a colonel in the militia, had gathered downriver to confront the British on their return.

Realizing the danger, Lieutenant James ordered, "*a precipitate retreat*," downriver.[31] As predicted by the young lady, the British were, "*warmly attacked*" and endured heavy but ineffective fire from the shore that wounded just one of their men.[32] Lieutenant James attributed their escape to

> *The rapidity of the ebb tide and extreme darkness of the night* [which] *prevented the execution of the enemy's fire....we passed the whole river* [and] *the town of Nansemond with no other accident than one man wounded and several shots through the boats.*[33]

Safely aboard the *Charon* by 10 a.m., Lieutenant James was next sent to Hampton under a flag of truce. He was well received by the inhabitants, many of whom appreciated his earlier restraint on New Year's Eve, and spent the bulk of the day with the Jones family – the same family he had spent an hour with on New Year's Eve. When it was time to leave, he departed, "*loaded with presents from Mrs. Jones and her amiable daughters.*"[34]

The following day Lieutenant James was directed to, "*take command of a hundred seamen and marines from the different ships of war, and land and forage for the squadron.*" James recalled that

---

[31] Ibid.
[32] Ibid., 98
[33] Ibid.
[34] Ibid.

> *At* [8:00 a.m.] *we began our march from Newport News into Elizabeth county, and advanced ten miles, in the course of which time I had collected 57 head of cattle, 42 sheep, some hogs, poultry, etc. and at* [3 p.m.] *began our retreat* [to the ships].[35]

At some point in the day they encountered rebel militia; Lieutenant James included a curious reference in his journal regarding the return march to the ships. He led the column

> *Mounted on a horse, having been wounded in my foot with a bayonet when in pursuit of a rebel; six butchers with their professional instruments* [formed a kind of] *advanced guard; the cattle drove by thirty negroes; two carts with dead hogs, and one with poultry; the seamen in the centre, and the marines in the rear to cover our retreat; with four marines on each flank, occasionally relieved from the rear.*[36]

Lieutenant James gave no further details of his wound or encounter with the rebels and it appears that his detachment suffered no further casualties. He did, however, lament the loss of some of the cattle on the return trip; they apparently strayed off into the woods (which covered most of the route).

Another foraging party was sent ashore the next day. Its commander, Lieutenant Tulloch, confident that the rebel militia posed no serious threat, took only 40 marines with him. They followed the same route that Lieutenant James's party took the day before and gathered a considerable amount of forage when, on their return, they were attacked by a party of

---

[35] Ibid.
[36] Ibid., 98-99

rebel horsemen and infantry. The engagement was fierce and half of the British detachment fell into rebel hands (half of those captured also being wounded). Lieutenant Tulloch and his remaining troops fought their way back to shore and the safety of the warships, expending nearly all of their ammunition and abandoning their forage.[37]

Arnold Sails Upriver

While most of General Arnold's ships of war remained in Hampton Roads, his transport ships, escorted by the 24 gun *HMS Hope*, the 14 gun *HMS Swift* and the 12 gun privateer *Cornwallis*, slowly made their way up the James River.[38] By January 2nd, Arnold had reached Burwell's Ferry which lay on the north bank of the river about four miles from Williamsburg.

The former capital was in a state of panic. William Tatham, a messenger from Richmond, recalled years later that when he arrived in Williamsburg with a dispatch for General Nelson from General Steuben, *"he found the Town in confusion, and the inhabitants alarmed by the expectation of an immediate engagement at Kings Mills."*[39] Tatham was informed that he would find General Nelson at Kings Mill.

> *On my arrival I found...General Nelson, and...Colonel Innis at the head of about fifty five men, under the more immediate command of a Major Harrod, waiting to give the enemy battle as they*

---

[37] Ibid., 100

[38] Davies, ed., "General Arnold to General Clinton, 21 January, 1781," *Documents of the American Revolution,* Vol. 20, 40

[39] Boyd, ed., "William Tatham to William Armistead Burwell, 13 June, 1805," *The Papers of Thomas Jefferson,* Vol. 4, 274

> *landed; and most of the Enemy's Ships were come to an anchor off the Place....*[40]

In truth, there were closer to 200 militia formed at Kings Mill and Burwell's Ferry, but even that number was far too few to offer any effective opposition to Arnold's force.[41]

Nathanael Burwell was with the militia at his ferry landing on the James River and described a bleak situation to Governor Jefferson in Richmond.

> *The Enemy's Fleet have just now* [arrived] *off this Place; they consist of 23 Sail, including two Men of war; a number of Flat bottom'd Boats are a-Stern of the Ships full of men. We have near 200 men under the Command of Colo. Innis and myself a number very insufficient for the present Purpose: however nothing shall be wanting as far as we're able to oppose the Enemy if they attempt to land. A Small Party of Foot and Horse are now engag'd with a Boat detachd from the Fleet.* [42]

From General Arnold's vantage point on the river, it was difficult to judge the size of the militia force gathered onshore. Captain Ewald described it as, *"several battalions"* strong. Arnold hoped he could once again intimidate the militia and inhabitants into submission with a stern warning and sent a flag ashore.

---

[40] Ibid.
[41] Boyd, ed., "Nathaniel Burwell to Governor Jefferson, 2 January, 1781," *The Papers of Thomas Jefferson*, Vol. 4, 294
[42] Ibid.

> *Having the honor to command a Body of His Majesty's Troops, sent for the protection of his Loyal Subjects in this country, I am surprised to observe the hostile appearance of the Inhabitants under Arms on the Shore. I have therefore sent Lieut. White, with a Flagg of Truce, to be informed of their intentions. If they are to offer a vain opposition to the Troops under my command, in their landing, they must be answerable for the consequences.*[43]

Asserting that he had, *"not the least intention to injure the peaceable Inhabitants in their persons or property,"* Arnold pledged that whatever provisions the inhabitants willingly supplied his force, *"shall be punctually paid for."*[44]

General Nelson, the ranking Virginia commander at Burwell's Ferry, was not interested in any deal with Arnold. Nelson replied that he, *"would not and could not give up to a traitor."* Furthermore, continued the militia general, *"If he were to get hold of Arnold, he would hang him up by the heels, according to the orders of the Congress."*[45] Captain Ewald was with Arnold when he received Nelson's reply and noted with some satisfaction Arnold's displeasure. General Arnold, *"was obliged to make a very wry face,"* recalled Ewald.[46]

Arnold chose to ignore Nelson's bravado and continued upriver, anchoring off Jamestown Island at nightfall. He apparently intended to send troops ashore the next day, but reversed himself before they landed when he learned that, *"a*

---

[43] Kranish, "General Arnold to the Officer Commanding the Party on Shore, 2 January, 1781," 173
[44] Ibid.
[45] Ewald, 260-61
[46] Ibid., 261

strong corps of Virginia militia had assembled...."[47] With his troops back onboard the transports, Arnold headed further upriver.

Virginia's Government Finally Reacts

On the same day that General Nelson rebuffed Benedict Arnold at Burwell's Ferry, Governor Jefferson in Richmond finally learned the extent of the invasion and danger the mystery fleet (now confirmed to be a British expedition) posed for Virginia. Jefferson sent letters to the county lieutenants of over 20 counties in central Virginia instructing them to muster one quarter of their militia and rendezvous as quickly as possible at Petersburg. The governor also sent letters to the frontier counties of Shenandoah, Rockingham, Augusta, and Rockbridge, instructing a portion of their militia to march with their weapons (preferably rifles) to Richmond.

To General Thomas Nelson in Williamsburg, Jefferson offered a weak explanation for his delay in summoning the militia.

> *It happened unfortunately that from the Tenor of Mr. Wrays Letter*, [of December 31st, which gave Jefferson the first news of a fleet's arrival] *we had reason to expect more precise information within a few hours.*[48]

Instead of a few hours, however, it took two days for Jefferson to learn that the unidentified ships were British. Why he was

---

[47] Ibid.
[48] Boyd, ed., "Governor Jefferson to General Nelson, 2 January, 1781," *The Papers of Thomas Jefferson*, Vol. 4, 297

not more proactive in discovering this was never explained by the governor, but upon his discovery that the fleet belonged to the enemy, Jefferson acted decisively, assuring General Nelson that, "*we mean to have four thousand six hundred Militia in the Field*," as soon as possible.[49]

Governor Jefferson also turned to General Steuben at Wilton, updating the continental officer about the fleet. The governor declared to Steuben in a letter that, "*We shall be very glad of the aid or your counsel....*" and requested that Steuben immediately appear before the executive council in Richmond.[50] General Steuben, concerned that the large cache of continental military stores at Petersburg was the enemy's real target, rushed 150 continental levies there from Chesterfield Courthouse to protect and help remove the supplies to a more secure location.

Before January 2nd ended, Jefferson also took measures to transfer the Hessian prisoners in Charlottesville (some 1,500) to Fort Frederick, Maryland and remove the military stores and government records in Richmond to a safe location across the James River.[51] Despite all of the activity in and around the capital, a sense of urgency had yet to develop. Jefferson was not even certain that Richmond was a target of the enemy, and even if it was, the British still had to overcome a defensive battery that overlooked the river at one of its narrowest spots, Hood's Point.

---

[49] Ibid.
[50] Boyd, ed., "Governor Jefferson to General Steuben, 2 January, 1781," *The Papers of Thomas Jefferson*, Vol. 4, 298
[51] Boyd, ed., "Jefferson Diary, 2 January, 1781," 258 and "Governor Jefferson to Francis Taylor, 2 January, 1781," *The Papers of Thomas Jefferson*, Vol. 4, 299

Hood's Point

About thirty miles downriver from Richmond, high on a one hundred foot bluff on the southern bank of the James River at a point where the flow of the river curved sharply from south to north, was Hood's Point. It was the strongest defensible position along the entire river, the ideal place to challenge enemy ships struggling upriver against the current. Cannon positioned on the bluff could pound vessels mercilessly as they approached the curve and maintain a deadly and accurate barrage as ships slowed to make the turn and continue upriver (assuming the ships were still afloat). A hastily constructed fort with a battery of three 18 pound and one 24 pound iron cannon, plus an eight inch brass howitzer, was erected on the bluff in the fall of 1780, but the fort was significantly undermanned (only fifty troops held the works) and the fortifications were incomplete and open in the rear.[52]

Early in the evening of January 3rd, General Arnold, whose fleet had made excellent progress that day sailing up the river from Jamestown, ordered his transports and warships to anchor in a thick haze about half a mile downriver from Hood's Point. One transport mistakenly continued on and sailed within range of the rebel battery, which promptly opened fire on the vessel. Lieutenant Colonel Simcoe described what happened next.

---

[52] Boyd, ed., "Arnold's Invasion as Reported by Jefferson in the *Virginia Gazette*, 13 January, 1781," *The Papers of Thomas Jefferson*, Vol. 4, 269

> *Upon the first shot the skipper and his people left the deck; when Capt. Murray [of the Queen's Rangers] seized the helm, and the soldiers assisting him, he passed by the fort without any damage from its fire, and anchored above it.*[53]

The haze that hung over the river obscured Arnold's fleet and prompted the militia commander of Hood's Point, Colonel James Cocke, to hold his fire on them. Around 10 p.m., however, the wind picked up and the haze cleared away. Cocke reported that,

> *We could see their Hulls very plain, at which time we began a Fire of Twice every half hour from One of the Three Guns that we could make Bare on them, which Fire, I intended to keep up, during the night, as I had not the least thought of their attempting to land till near the morning, as the Wind Blew very fresh and made* [large waves], *which must make it very troublesome for them to Land.*[54]

Colonel Cocke sent 25 men from the garrison down to the mouth of Ward's Creek, which flowed into the James River about a quarter of a mile downriver from the fortification. They were ordered to, "*keep a lookout, should the Enemy attempt to Land.*"[55]

---

[53] John G. Simcoe, *Simcoe's Military Journal: A History of the Operations of a Partisan Corps Called the Queen's Rangers...* (New York: Bartlett & Weldord, 1844), 159
    Henceforth referred to as Simcoe
[54] Wm. Palmer, ed., " James Cocke to Col. George Muter, 18 January, 1781," *Calendar of Virginia State Papers*, Vol. 1, (1875), 442
[55] Ibid.

A shore landing was exactly what General Arnold intended to do. In spite of the ease in which his stray ship had passed Hood's Point, (revealing the battery as an ineffective obstacle to the navigation of the river) Arnold decided to neutralize the enemy fort with a ground assault upon its rear. He ordered the *Hope* and *Cornwallis* to bombard the fort while troops landed up Ward's Creek and circled around to attack Hood's Point in its open rear. Captain Ewald recalled that a detachment of jagers along with Captain Althouse's New York loyalists and two companies of Queen's Rangers, all under Lieutenant Colonel Simcoe, boarded boats and rowed to Ward's Creek.[56] Simcoe remembered the attack differently, crediting 130 of his Rangers along with the flank companies (light and grenadier) of the 80th Regiment with capturing the fort.[57] Simcoe noted that

> *The landing was effected silently and apparently with secrecy about a mile from the battery, and a circuit was made to surprise its garrison: in the meantime the fleet was fired upon, but ineffectually on account of its distance.*[58]

Colonel Cocke's detachment at Ward's Creek spotted the enemy boats making their way up the creek and immediately warned the garrison inside the fort.[59] Colonel Cocke speculated that

---

[56] Ewald, 261
[57] Simcoe, 160
[58] Ibid.
[59] Palmer, ed., " James Cocke to Col. George Muter, 18 January, 1781," *Calendar of Virginia State Papers*, Vol. 1, 442

> By their place of landing I was confident that their Intention was to come Round on our Backs and cut off our Retreat. As we then had but about 40 men in the Fort, we thought it was in Vain for us to continue, as we had not the least hopes of defending ourselves, therefore I gave orders for every man to take his arms, and march out of the Fort.[60]

When Simcoe's detachment reached the fort, they found it deserted. After spiking the iron cannon, Simcoe returned to the shore with the howitzer.[61]

At the loss of one man aboard ship, who was killed by the fort's, *"brisk"* cannon fire during Simcoe's landing (reportedly 20 shots total) Arnold had neutralized the strongest rebel defensive position on the James River.[62]

Westover

Arnold's fleet remained anchored below Hood's Point until dawn, at which time it resumed its movement upriver, reaching Westover Planation, six miles from Hood's Point around 10:00 a.m. Westover was the seat of the late William Byrd, the patriarch of one of Virginia's most prominent families. Heavy debt (much of it gambling related) and Tory sympathies caused much angst for Colonel Byrd on the eve of the Revolution, and he escaped from his many pressures in 1776 by committing suicide. His wife, Mary Willing Byrd, a cousin of Benedict Arnold's wife, Peggy Shippen, assumed

---

[60] Ibid.
[61] Davies, "General Arnold to General Clinton, 21 January, 1781," *Documents of the American Revolution*, Vol. 20, 40
[62] Ibid. and Ewald, 261

responsibility of the estate and managed, with the help of dozens of slaves, to stave off bankruptcy. Mrs. Byrd's political sentiments were a mystery to most people. It was probable that she was a Tory, but if so, she was wise enough to keep such sentiments to herself.

When Arnold's fleet anchored directly offshore from her mansion house, Mrs. Byrd found herself with little choice but to play the role of hostess to the British. Her plantation, with its numerous outbuildings, as well as the mansion, became Arnold's base of operation for the next week.

While General Arnold and his officers enjoyed a late breakfast, compliments of Mrs. Byrd, the British transports emptied their holds of troops, horses, artillery, and supplies. A meeting between Arnold and his officers resulted in an agreement to march on Richmond, a town of some 600 inhabitants and the new capital of Virginia, 25 miles northwest of Westover.[63]

The march commenced late in the afternoon of January 4th, under a heavy winter rain. Lieutenant Colonel Simcoe estimated that the column was 800 strong, meaning that 300 to 400 men were left behind at Westover.[64] Captain Ewald was placed in charge of the advance guard, made up of his jagers and Captain Althouse's New York loyalist riflemen as well as the light infantry of the Queen's Rangers and 30 mounted Rangers.

Lieutenant Colonel Simcoe, with the rest of his cavalry, followed by Lieutenant Colonel Dundas with the 80th Regiment, Colonel Robinson and his Loyal American corps, and 4 six pound cannon, comprised the main body. The rear

---

[63] Kranish, 122
[64] Simcoe, 161

guard trailed behind with an officer and ten mounted Queen's Rangers.[65] The night was very dark due to the heavy rain and Ewald's advanced guard moved cautiously out of concern of an ambush. He observed in his diary that there were many excellent spots on which the rebels could have ambushed Arnold's column, but they failed to take advantage of any of them.

One reason for this was that Arnold's sudden appearance at Westover and subsequent march towards Richmond caught Virginia's authorities by surprise. Although the militia had been ordered to muster two days earlier and indeed did so throughout the state, Virginia's leaders were still uncertain of Arnold's destination. In fact, many, including General Steuben, assumed that Arnold intended to march on Petersburg. Thus, Arnold's rapid evening march from Westover towards Richmond gave the Virginians little time to react.

Another reason few militia opposed Arnold's march was that the local forces in the area, namely the Henrico, Charles City and New Kent County militia, were poorly armed and supplied. Benjamin Harrison, a neighbor of Mrs. Byrd at Berkeley Plantation and the County Lieutenant of Henrico County, (not to mention signer of the Declaration of Independence), reported to Governor Jefferson on the afternoon of January 4th that the militia

> *Are assembling fast...but many of them are quite without arms of any kind, what they have are mostly unfit for service, to add to this dismal account I must*

---

[65] Ewald, 266

inform you that we have no ammunition of any kind, or so small a quantity that it is scarcely worth naming.[66]

Although they lacked arms and ammunition, Virginia's defenders were not completely helpless and inactive. A small party of rebel militia officers reconnoitering the road to Richmond stumbled upon Ewald's advance guard around midnight. Captain Ewald described what happened:

The [rebel] *major had gone out to observe exactly where we were in our march. I had marched so quietly that he was quite astonished when several men grabbed his horse by the bridle and knocked him off.*[67]

Lieutenant Colonel Simcoe had similar good fortune early on the second day of the march. After a brief rest at Four Mile Creek (14 miles from Westover and 11 miles from Richmond) Arnold's column resumed its march at dawn. They soon arrived at a dismantled bridge. Simcoe, with his mounted rangers of the advance guard, managed to cross the stream, but the bridge had to be repaired for the cannon to cross, so the column halted. During this halt, a party of Virginia militia appeared on the other side of the creek near Arnold's advanced guard. Lieutenant Colonel Simcoe described what happened:

Some of the enemy's militia, who had destroyed [the bridge] *the evening before, and were to assemble with others to defend it, were deceived by the dress of*

---

[66] Boyd, ed., "Benjamin Harrison to Governor Jefferson, 4 January, 1781," *The Papers of Thomas Jefferson,* Vol. 4, 304
[67] Ewald, 266-67

> the Rangers, and came to Lt. Col. Simcoe, who immediately reprimanded them for not coming sooner, held conversation with them, and then sent them prisoners to General Arnold.[68]

The green coats of the Queen's Rangers had confused the militia; they assumed the rangers were fellow rebels and were much chagrined to discover otherwise when Simcoe announced that they were now prisoners of His Majesty's forces.

Richmond

Arnold's troops continued their march to Richmond, arriving early in the afternoon of January 5th. General Arnold wished to make a strong impression upon both the inhabitants and the militia that had assembled in Richmond, so he formed his column in open order (which extended the column and gave it the appearance of being larger than it was).

The small town of Richmond, which had been established in the 1730's near the rapids of the James River, was ringed by a series of very steep hills. When Arnold's column reached the outskirts of Richmond, one such steep, 100 foot high hill loomed before them. Upon it, staring down at Arnold's column, were two to three hundred Virginia militia.[69]

Known today as Church Hill (because the church in which Patrick Henry declared, "Give Me Liberty, or Give Me Death," sits upon it) it was a strong defensible position that commanded the road to Richmond. Arnold and his column had to pass directly under the hill, well within musket range of

---

[68] Simcoe, 161
[69] Simcoe, 162

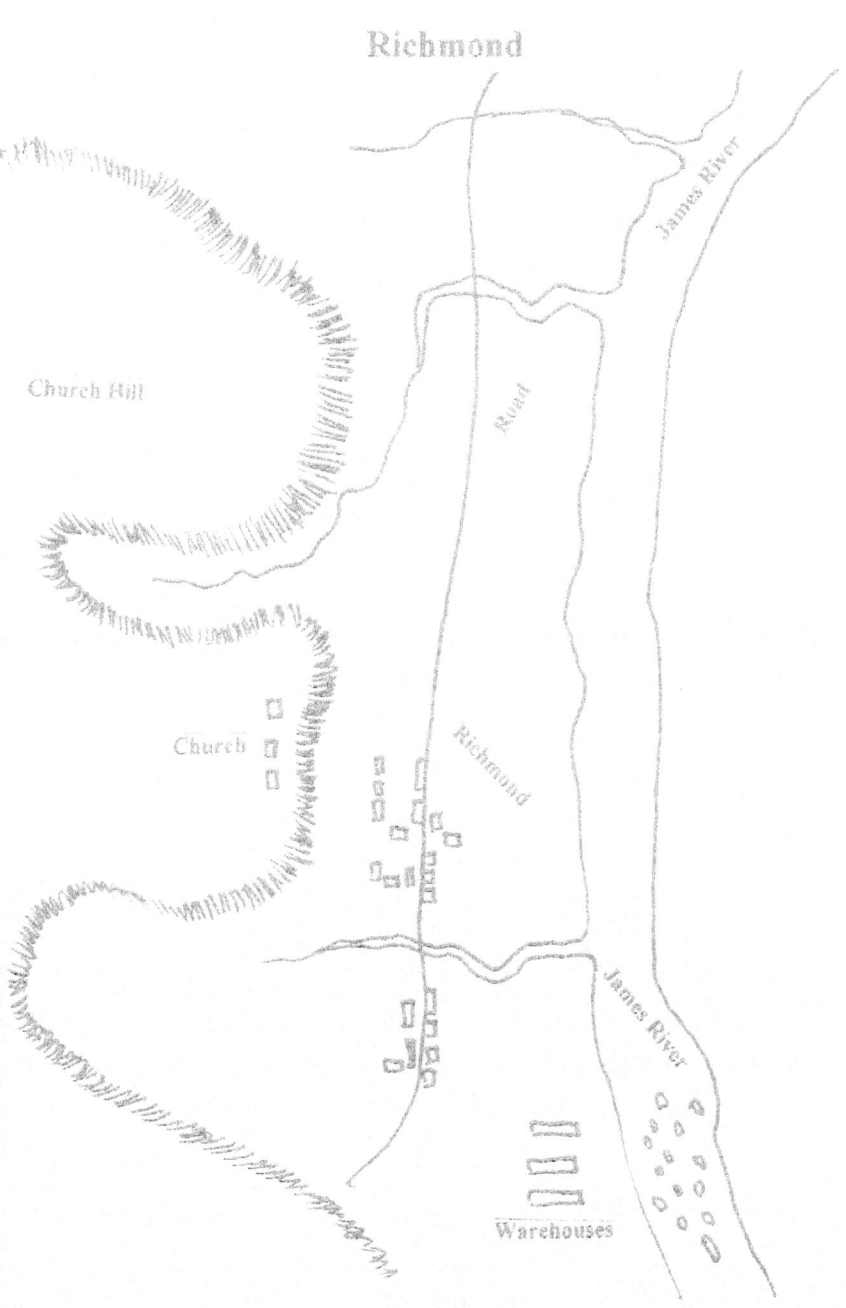

the rebel militia. Arnold was particularly concerned about the possibility of rebel riflemen hidden in the brush on the hill. He pointed to the overgrown brush and declared to Captain Ewald, "*That's a task made for you!*"[70] Ewald recalled,

> *I deployed at once, formed two ranks well dispersed, and climbed up the hill. The enemy left after firing a volley which wounded one jager, but three others who had gone too far to the right were captured.*[71]

Captain Ewald and his jagers inclined to their right on their ascent up the steep hill in an effort to swing around the militia's left flank. A portion of the rebel militia responded by filing to their left to extend their flank, but they were too few, too inexperienced, and too scared to stop Ewald's advance. The frightened militia also faced Simcoe's mounted rangers, who struggled up the hill to the left of Ewald.

The militia on top of the hill withdrew rearward before Ewald's riflemen reached the crest. Many of the Virginians fled into nearby woods "*in great confusion*," their fight finished for the day.[72] Others crossed a deep ravine in their rear (that cut into Church Hill) and scrambled up the steep embankment to join other militia already posted there.[73] This location, known today as Libby Hill, was essentially a knoll of Church Hill that jutted out towards the river. It overlooked both the road that Arnold's column was on and the flat plateau of Church Hill that Ewald's jagers had just captured.

---

[70] Ewald, 267
[71] Ibid.
[72] Simcoe, 162
[73] Ewald, 267

Captain Ewald was initially hesitant to charge across the flat, open plateau that stood between the ravine and his position on the eastern edge of Church Hill (known today as Chimborazo Park) *"On the whole,"* Ewald declared in his diary years later, *"it was a crucial moment for me. I was on barren, level ground and the enemy could count my men."*[74] To make matters worse, Ewald continued, *"My men appeared to be so tired and worn out that I no longer dared to rely on their legs for a hurried flight."* Ewald opted to *"try to detain* [the enemy militia] *by skirmishing until more troops came up for my support."*[75]

Luckily for Captain Ewald and his tired jagers, Lieutenant Colonel Simcoe and his mounted rangers soon appeared on the hill and supported Ewald's left flank. It had been a difficult ascent for Simcoe's horses and their riders, so difficult that the cavalrymen had to lead their horses up the slope by the bit. *"Luckily,"* remembered Simcoe, *"the enemy made no resistance, nor did they fire, but on the cavalry's arrival on the summit* [they] *retreated to the woods in great confusion."*[76]

Simcoe's horsemen benefited from Ewald's aggressive charge up the hill on the right flank minutes earlier, a charge that drove most of the militia from the plateau. Confronted by both Ewald's jagers and Simcoe's mounted rangers, (who at any moment might swing behind Ewald and charge upon the Virginians vulnerable left flank, a flank that was not protected by the ravine) the Virginians hastily withdrew from Libby Hill and fled westward.

---

[74] Ibid.
[75] Ibid.
[76] Simcoe, 162

Captain Ewald led his men down Church Hill and re-joined Arnold's main column on the road while Simcoe and his cavalry trailed the fleeing militia westward. When he reached the western edge of Church Hill, Simcoe's attention was drawn to a party of militia horsemen in the valley below (known today as Shockoe Bottom). The rebel horsemen were focused on Arnold's advancing column, which was marching straight at them on the road into town. Simcoe attempted to swing his cavalry behind the mounted rebels, but a creek blocked his way and the rebel horsemen spotted Simcoe's movement and withdrew westward up Shockoe Hill, (yet another steep hill that lay across the valley from Church Hill.[77]

Undeterred, Simcoe tried a little deception, presenting himself and his men as fellow militia. Simcoe recalled that,

> *Having crossed* [the creek] *lower down,* [I] *ascended the hill, using such conversation and words towards* [the militia] *as might prevent their inclination to retreat; however, when the Rangers were arrived within twenty yards of the summit, the enemy greatly superior in numbers, but made up of militia, spectators, some with and some without arms, galloped off.*[78]

The militia horsemen were not fooled by Simcoe's ruse and withdrew westward. Simcoe's cavalry pursued, but most rode upon horses still weak from the voyage from New York, so only a handful of rebels were captured.

---

[77] Ibid.
[78] Ibid.

Destruction of Westham Foundry and Richmond

Upon his return from the pursuit, Lieutenant-Colonel Simcoe was ordered by General Arnold to lead a detachment a few miles west of Richmond to destroy a foundry near the village of Westham on the James River. Westham was the site that Governor Jefferson had sent much of Richmond's military stores and government papers to. More importantly, the foundry at Westham was one of the few places in Virginia capable of casting cannon and producing gunpowder. Hundreds of barrels of powder were stored there as were nearly thirty cannon. The destruction of the foundry and supplies would be a big blow to the rebels.

General Arnold sent Lieutenant Colonel Simcoe with his corps of Rangers as well as the flank companies of the 80th Regiment and a detachment of Ewald's Jagers and Althouse's loyalists to the foundry while he remained in Richmond with the remainder of his force (essentially the 80th Regiment, Robinson's Loyal American Corps, and those soldiers unable to make the march due to fatigue). Simcoe and his force met no opposition on their march west. When they reached the foundry, about six miles from Richmond, Simcoe tasked Captain Ewald with destroying what he could while he led 100 men another mile west to the village of Westham. The ever efficient Ewald recalled that,

> *I...tried to attack the* [foundry], *which lay in a valley close to the left bank of the James River, from all sides. All the people of the foundry fell into my hands.... I had left half of the men under arms in the hills, and with the other half I damaged and made*

unserviceable as much of the machinery and tools found at the smelter as was possible.[79]

Lieutenant Colonel Simcoe, who apparently was not present for most of the damage but was informed by subordinates what was accomplished, noted in his memoirs that,

> *Upon consultation with the artillery officer* [that accompanied Simcoe's detachment] *it was thought better to destroy the magazine than to blow it up, this fatiguing business was effected by carrying the powder down the cliffs, and pouring it into the water; the warehouses and mills were then set on fire, and many explosions happened in different parts of the buildings...and the foundry, which was a very complete one, was totally destroyed.*[80]

General Arnold was very pleased with the raid, reporting to General Clinton that 310 barrels of powder and a large supply of oats were destroyed (mostly by dumping it in the James River), as well as the cannon foundry and 26 cannon.[81]

Although the Virginia militia had thus far offered little opposition to Arnold's troops, Lieutenant Colonel Simcoe and Captain Ewald were both very eager to return to Richmond as soon as possible. Both officers worried that every hour that passed increased the possibility of enemy reinforcements cutting their detachment off from Richmond, so they commenced their march back to the rebel capital at 10 p.m.

---

[79] Ewald, 267-68
[80] Simcoe, 163
[81] Davies, ed.," General Arnold to General Clinton, 21 January, 1781," *Documents of the American Revolution*, Vol. 20, 40

Captain Ewald's troops were apparently not as concerned about the enemy as their commander was, for Ewald complained that many of his men marched back to Richmond drunk, having found a large supply of wine and beer near the foundry.

> *I assembled my men at once, of whom two thirds were drunk because large stores of wine and beer had been found in the houses. They were now so noisy that one could hear us two hours away.*[82]

The entire detachment reached Richmond incident free well after midnight where many of the men literally collapsed from fatigue and slept in the numerous abandoned buildings of the city.

Virginians React

Arnold's men were not the only ones fatigued by the day's activities. Governor Jefferson spent much of January 5th on horseback, riding from Tuckahoe, his boyhood home located about ten miles west of Richmond, where he had sent his wife and three daughters, to Westham to superintend the removal of arms and supplies across the river, and then to Manchester, a town directly across from Richmond, where Jefferson observed Arnold's troops enter the city. The governor did not stay long in Manchester, he wished to confer with General Steuben, so he rode along the south side of the James River in search of the general, but could not locate him. Late in the day a messenger from Richmond reached Jefferson with a proposal from General Arnold to spare much of the capital

---

[82] Ewald, 268

from destruction. Arnold described his offer to his superior, General Clinton.

> On my arrival at Richmond I was informed there was in stores a large quantity of tobacco, West India goods, wines, sailcloth, etc. There were between 30 and 40 sail of vessels loaded with tobacco between Westover and Richmond. As the navigation of the river above Westover was intricate, the season critical, and many difficulties attending the removal of the goods, a proposal was made to the merchants who remained at Richmond to prevent the destruction of private property...that upon their delivering the whole of the enumerated goods on board *His Majesty's fleet in the James River*, that one-half the value should be paid to them.[83]

It was an audacious proposal, especially coming from the infamous American traitor. If Richmond's merchants delivered their goods as well as the ships loaded with tobacco in the James River to Arnold by the following morning, he would pay them half of the value of the goods and spare the town.

Many of the merchants were tempted by this offer, no doubt concluding that something was better than nothing for their property; they forwarded Arnold's proposal to Governor Jefferson for his approval. Jefferson refused to ransom the safety of Richmond and flatly rejected Arnold's offer.[84] The

---

[83] Davies, ed., "General Arnold to General Clinton, 21 January, 1781," *Documents of the American Revolution*, Vol. 20, 41

[84] Boyd, ed., "Jefferson Diary, 5 January, 1781," *The Papers of Thomas Jefferson*, Vol. 4, 259

thought of cooperating with the infamous traitor Arnold was unacceptable.

Although resistance to Arnold in Virginia had thus far been weak and ineffective, Governor Jefferson was informed on January 5th in a letter from General Steuben that nearly 1,000 militia had assembled in Petersburg. Only 400 carried arms, but more weapons were being sent to them on the assumption that Petersburg would be Arnold's next target. Steuben also reported that he had ordered approximately 150 newly raised Virginia continentals meant for General Greene's army in the Carolinas to join the militia in Petersburg.[85]

The shortage of weapons among the militia at Petersburg also existed on the north side of the James River. Large bodies of militia gathered near Westham and southeast of Richmond in New Kent County under General Nelson, but in both cases, gun and powder shortages significantly limited their effectiveness. Jefferson, Steuben, Nelson, and others did all they could to find weapons for the men, but the confusion caused by Arnold's rapid march to Richmond and the destruction of the supplies at the Westham foundry and in Richmond significantly hampered these efforts.

---

[85] Boyd, ed. "General Steuben to Governor Jefferson, 6 January, 1781," *The Papers of Thomas Jefferson*, Vol. 4, 312

Arnold Departs

Benedict Arnold reacted to Jefferson's rejection of his offer to spare Richmond by unleashing his troops on the capital. Arnold recalled that,

> *I found myself under the disagreeable necessity of ordering a large quantity of rum to be stove, several warehouses of salt to be destroyed; several public storehouses and smith's shops with their contents were consumed by the flames; a very fine ropewalk full of materials, private property, was burnt without my orders by an officer who was informed it was public property; a large magazine with quartermaster's stores, sailcloath was burnt; a printing press and types were also purified by the flames.*[86]

A return of the public property destroyed or taken by Arnold's troops in Richmond and Westham included 2,200 small arms, 4,000 French musket locks in two casks, and nearly forty cannon, ranging from 32 to 4 pounders – all destroyed or damaged, and five 6 pound French brass cannon taken. Over 7,000 solid shot cannon rounds and 20,000 grape shot rounds were tossed in the river, 503 hogsheads of rum stove in on the capital streets, and two warehouses full of salt were burned to the ground.[87]

---

[86] Davies, ed. "General Arnold to General Clinton, 21 January, 1781," *Documents of the American Revolution*, Vol. 20, 41

[87] "Return of Ordinance, Ammunition, Stores, Small Arms, taken and destroyed at Richmond and Westham in Virginia," *Royal Georgia Gazette*, 8 March, 1781, 2

Private property was apparently not immune to seizure either. Captain Ewald claimed that, *"forty-two vessels were loaded with all kinds of merchandise for the corps' booty and sailed down the James River."*[88] Some of the merchandise loaded aboard the ships was undoubtedly the plunder that Arnold's troops took from the many abandoned homes and buildings in Richmond.[89] Much of it was also seized tobacco.

By noon of January 6th, General Arnold was ready to depart Richmond and return to Westover. Trudging through driving rain that turned the road into a quagmire, Arnold's men had great trouble on the march. Lieutenant Colonel Simcoe recalled

> *The roads were rendered by the rain slippery and difficult, and in most places were narrow and overhung by bushes, so that the troops were frequently oblige to march by files, which made it impossible for the officers, who were on foot, to see far before them, and to take their customary precautions.*[90]

Simcoe claimed that nine of his Rangers, either overcome by fatigue or the desire to desert, were taken by the rebels on the march back. Captain Ewald claimed that, *"Since the march back took place rather hastily, some sixty men – too fatigued to keep up – fell into the hands of the [rebels]."*[91]

The expedition halted in the early evening at Four Mile Creek, only eleven miles outside of Richmond. Most of

---

[88] Ewald, 268
[89] Ibid.
[90] Simcoe, 164
[91] Ewald, 268

Arnold's men were exhausted and all were wet and miserable as they camped without any cover from the cold, driving, rain. They endured the night and resumed their march to Westover at sunrise.

Parties of militia hovered on their rear, but none attacked Arnold's force. Interestingly, the very storm that tormented Arnold's men prevented General Thomas Nelson from striking Arnold. Nelson explained to Governor Jefferson how Arnold escaped a blow from the militia troops under his command:

> *Even the Elements have conspired to favour* [the enemy]. *On Saturday Night* [Jan. 6th] *I intended a Blow at their Rear, when the Gates of Heaven were opened, and such a Flood of Rain poured down as rendered my Plan abortive by almost drowning the Troops, who were in Bush Tents, and by injuring their Arms and Ammunition so much that they were quite unfit for Service.*[92]

Had Nelson been able to attack, it is unlikely he would have inflicted much damage on Arnold's force. The militia commander had at most 400 poorly armed troops, less than half of Arnold's force. In fact, the total number of militia hovering around Arnold's expedition (divided amongst three separate detachments) came to only 900 men.[93] As a result, there was little, besides poor weather, to stop Arnold and his men from reaching Westover unscathed on January 7th.

---

[92] Boyd, ed., "General Nelson to Governor Jefferson, 8 January, 1781," *The Papers of Thomas Jefferson*, Vol. 4, 321

[93] Boyd, ed., "Governor Jefferson to General Washington, 10 January, 1781," *The Papers of Thomas Jefferson*, Vol. 4, 334

Charles City Court House Raid

A day after Arnold's return to Westover, a party of militia was observed on the heights east of Westover, overlooking Herring Creek. General Arnold, uncertain of the size and proximity of the rebel militia, ordered Lieutenant Colonel Simcoe to patrol towards Long Bridge, north of Westover, to investigate.

Simcoe led forty mounted Rangers, supported by two companies of his infantry under Captain Ewald, northward after dark.[94] They had only gone a couple of miles when Simcoe's lead rider, Sergeant Kelly, was challenged by rebel horsemen on the road. The quick witted sergeant approached the rebels in as friendly a manner as he could, then rushed at them, grabbing one rebel and scaring the other off his horse and into the bushes.[95] A runaway slave that the two rebels had intercepted earlier in the evening was freed and he readily cooperated with Simcoe. From the liberated slave and the captured rebel, Simcoe learned that a large party of militia had gathered at Charles City Court House, about nine miles from Westover.

In his memoirs, Simcoe estimated that close to 800 rebels were mustered in the vicinity in Charles City Court House. This was greatly exaggerated; other contemporary accounts of Simcoe's raid on Charles City Court House placed the number of militia at 125 to 200. Whatever their number, Simcoe's 40 cavalry and two companies of Rangers were outnumbered by the militia at Charles City Court House.

---

[94] Simcoe, 165
[95] Ibid. 166

Led by the grateful runaway slave who directed Simcoe along a little used path to Charles City, Simcoe's detachment approached the outskirts of the village undetected. Lieutenant Holland, who was similar in size to the captured rebel horseman, led Simcoe's force and was challenged by a mounted rebel sentry near the village. Simcoe described what happened:

> *The patrole passed through a wood, where it halted to collect, and had scarcely got into the road when the advance was challenged; Lt. Holland answered, "A friend," gave the countersign procured from the prisoner, "It is I, me, Charles," the name of the person he personated:* [96]

The ruse worked and the rebel horseman allowed Lieutenant. Holland, accompanied by Sergeant Kelly, to pass. Before the lone militiaman realized his mistake, Sergeant Kelly drew his weapon upon him and announced that he was a prisoner. They continued forward and encountered another rebel vidette (mounted sentry), who Lieutenant Holland attempted to seize himself. Lieutenant Colonel Simcoe recounted what happened next:

> [Lieutenant Holland] *caught hold of another* [rebel], *who in a struggle proved too strong for him, got free, presented* [his weapon] *and snapped his carbine at his breast; luckily it did not go off, but the man galloped away, and at some distance fired, the signal of alarm; the advance division immediately rushed*

---

[96] Ibid.

on, and soon arrived at the Court-house; a confused and scattered firing began on all sides.[97]

The shock of the sudden attack, combined with the darkness of the evening, which only heightened the fear of the militia, prevented the militia from organizing an effective defense, and instead, they fled in all directions. Simcoe was satisfied to let them flee, not wishing to reveal his true strength by staying at the courthouse too long. The Rangers gathered up their prisoners and headed back to Westover. Simcoe reported one ranger killed and three wounded. British estimates of the militia losses were twenty to thirty killed and wounded, in addition to nearly twenty prisoners taken.[98] American accounts claimed just a handful of losses and downplayed the incident.[99] Whatever the true American casualties were, the fact remained that a small British patrol surprised and routed a larger militia force at Charles City Court House.

The good news continued for General Arnold the following day with the arrival of his missing transport ships with 400 reinforcements. Separated by a gale in December, the ships had finally caught up with the expedition. Their stay at Westover was brief, however, for General Arnold decided on January 10th, to embark for Portsmouth.

---

[97] Ibid.
[98] Ewald, 269 and New *York Royal Gazette*, 7 February, 1781
[99] *Connecticut Journal*, 15 February, 1781, 2

Ambush Near Hood's Point

Arnold's preparations to depart were observed across the river by General Steuben, who moved his force of approximately 800 militia from Petersburg further south to Prince George Courthouse in anticipation of Arnold's departure. Steuben concluded that re-fortifying Hood Point was impracticable, but he speculated that since General Arnold could not be certain of this, the British commander would send troops ashore to investigate before his fleet passed the point. Steuben decided to lay an ambush for the expected landing party. He explained his actions to General Greene in the Carolinas:

> *Thinking it very* probable [that Arnold] *would land a party to examine* [the] *works* [at Hood's] *before they attempted to pass, I ordered 300 Infantry & about 30 Horse under Col. Clark to lay in Ambush to receive them.*[100]

Accounts of what happened next vary. Steuben, who was not actually present at the ambush, claimed that Arnold's troops began landing near Hood's Point at dusk. Arnold reported that he sent 350 troops ashore under Lieutenant Colonel Simcoe at 7 p.m. with orders to march to a crossroad two miles inland and attack the enemy that was reportedly

---

[100] Showman, ed., "General Steuben to General Greene, 11 January, 1781," *The Papers of Nathanael Greene,* Vol. 7, 98
  Note: Col. Clark was George Rogers Clark, of Vincennes fame. He happened to be in Richmond when Arnold arrived in Virginia and offered his services to Governor Jefferson, who accepted and sent Clark to General Steuben.

there.[101] Simcoe claimed his troops landed at night and that General Arnold wanted Simcoe to surprise a detachment of rebels at Bland's Mill, a few miles inland.[102] The person that actually led the advance of Simcoe's detachment, at least initially, Captain Johann Ewald, reported that they landed at 10 p.m. on Hood's Point with no opposition.[103] Ewald recalled in his diary

> *I was the first to go ashore. Since the thunderstorm had subsided and a beautiful, clear evening with moonlight followed, by which one could see far around, I took four men, a horn blower, and Captain Murray of the rangers to reconnoiter and patrol a short distance into the country. I ordered two men to proceed in front of me at a distance of fifty paces, and I followed with the people mentioned.*[104]

About five hundred paces up the wide, sandy road, Captain Ewald suddenly heard horses trotting through water and getting closer. Ewald recalled,

> *I had no desire to run back, since I thought that it would be several men whom I could seize. To the right on this side of [a] fence, or railing, I found three or four trees, behind which I concealed myself and the other four men. A moment later, a body of twenty or thirty horse appeared. I had in mind to let them*

---

[101] Davies, ed., "General Arnold to General Clinton, 21 January, 1781," *Documents of the American Revolution*, Vol. 20, 41
[102] Simcoe, 168
[103] Ewald, 269
[104] Ibid.

> *pass and fire upon them from the rear. But the officer, who looked my way just as he approached me, ordered a halt and called to me, "Who's there?" I kept still; he called again, "Who's there?" Since the game was now too serious for me, I jumped out from behind the tree and shouted to him, "Friend of the watch!" At that moment I called for fire. The two jagers who were with me, and the horn blower, who was armed with one of my double pistols, gave fire and the entire troop fled. The two jagers whom I had sent ahead* [had] *dropped to the ground at* [the enemy's] *approach and contributed their fire.*[105]

Frustrated that he had not taken more troops with him (which, he insisted, would have enabled him to capture the enemy horsemen) Ewald returned to the shore to report to General Arnold. He found the rest of the landing party, about 200 troops of the 80th Regiment, ashore and the whole detachment, 550 strong, ready to march.

Lieutenant Colonel Simcoe pulled Captain Ewald aside and informed him that Colonel Robinson's Loyal American Corps, instead of Ewald and his jagers, would be the advance guard. Simcoe, *"begged me not to take offense,"* Ewald recalled, and the German officer attributed the decision to Arnold's desire to give Robinson, *"an opportunity to get his name in the Gazette."*[106] Captain Ewald's 50 jagers trailed behind Robinson's advance guard, which was 170 strong. Behind the

---

[105] Ibid., 270
[106] Ibid.

jagers came Simcoe's rangers, (120 strong) and finally, 200 troops from the 80th Regiment.[107]

Ewald noted that the detachment had marched along the road for about a half hour when approximately twenty musket shots were fired towards the head of the column. No one was injured and the column soon resumed its march. Captain Ewald provided a detailed description of what happened next:

> *After...about a half an hour, we heard two extraordinary loud voices challenge the head with a very clear "Who – is—there?" The good* [Colonel] *ordered, "Forward!" At that instant, a terrible fire fell out of the woods from the front and left among Robinson's honorable Americans. Weeping, wailing, and gnashing of teeth arose, and one captain, two officers, and some forty men were either killed or seriously wounded. I ran to the head and found a deplorable situation: the honorable fellows were so disconcerted by their bad luck that if the enemy party had suddenly attacked them with the bayonet, the entire column certainly would have been thrown back to Hood's Point.*[108]

Although the ambush was clearly devastating to Robinson's corps, other accounts described a less chaotic situation. General Arnold reported that after the heavy fire of the militia, Robinson's men, *"charged the enemy with such firmness and resolution that* [the enemy] *instantly fled on all*

---

[107] Davies, ed., "General Arnold to General Clinton, 21 January,1781," *Documents of the American Revolution*, Vol. 20, 42
[108] Ewald, 270-71

sides....,"[109] Simcoe gave a similar account, and a report in one loyalist gazette claimed that after the militia fired their volley they, *"ran away, leaving hats, wigs, &c. &c. behind them."*[110]

Captain Ewald, frustrated at what he viewed as unnecessary losses due to incompetence, snapped at General Arnold when he appeared at the head of the column to survey the damage. *"So it goes when a person wants to do something that he doesn't understand!"* announced Ewald.[111] Arnold ignored Ewald's biting comment and "courteously" requested the German captain take command of the advance guard. The 80th Regiment remained behind to tend to the wounded while the rest of the column resumed its march, but after another thirty minutes, General Arnold reversed direction and the column marched back to the river, throwing the damaged rebel cannon from their previous attack on Hood Point into the river in frustration and re-boarding their ships.

The next day was rather uneventful. Arnold's fleet slowly made its way downriver, stopping at Cobham (across from Jamestown) on January 12th. Approximately 100 Surry County militia vainly attempted to repel a landing party under Colonel Dundas of the 80th Regiment that was four times their size, but the militia only managed to wound three men before they were forced to withdraw.[112] Dundas burned a warehouse full of flour and seized 60 hogsheads of tobacco. After another uneventful day on the river, General Arnold anchored off of Isle of Wight County on January 14th and disembarked

---

[109] Davies, ed., "General Arnold to General Clinton, 21 January,1781," *Documents of the American Revolution*, Vol. 20, 41

[110] *Royal Gazette*, New York, 3 February, 1781, 2

[111] Ewald, 271

[112] Ibid., 272

his entire army about 12 miles northwest of Smithfield. Arnold's ultimate destination was Portsmouth, some 30 miles away.

Virginia's military leaders, led by General Steuben, struggled to keep up with Arnold's movements. Their efforts were hampered by the scattered nature of the militia, (deployed on both sides of the James River), and the severe shortage of weapons and equipment for the troops. General Steuben was actually pleased by the strong turnout of militia, but discouraged by their lack of arms and gear. *"Large Numbers of Men are hourly Crowding to this place destitute of Arms,"* Steuben wrote to Jefferson on January 12th. [113] Many of the unarmed men looked to Steuben for weapons and orders, but he declined to take responsibility for them until they were properly armed by the state.

The approximately 700 militia troops that were armed and under Steuben's command south of the James River were ordered to march from Hood's Point to Cabin Point, just a few miles further south, on January 13th. This force no longer included the 150 continental levies that Steuben had ordered into the field at the start of the invasion. The general reported with regret that, *"The Continental troops being too naked to keep the field, were sent back to Chesterfield Court-house."* [114]

When Steuben learned that Arnold had landed above Smithfield on January 14th, he sent Major Willis and 350 infantry with 50 cavalry southward to harass Arnold's rear. Unfortunately, Steuben reported later that his orders were

---

[113] Boyd, ed., "General Steuben to Governor Jefferson, 12 January, 1781," *The Papers of Thomas Jefferson*, Vol. 4, 345

[114] Friedrich Kapp, *The Life of Frederick William Von Steuben*, (1999), 378 (Originally published in 1856)

Battle of Mackie's Mill

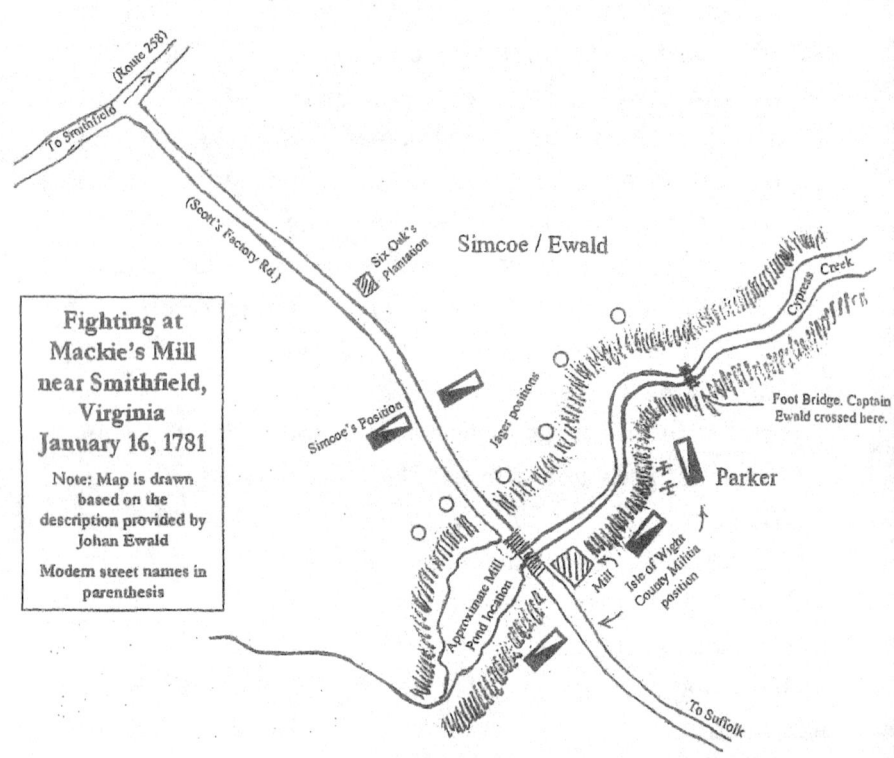

poorly executed, so opposition to Arnold fell to Colonel Josiah Parker and the militia of the lower counties.

Colonel Parker was an experienced commander who led militia troops in 1775 at Great Bridge and continental troops from 1776 to 1778 as colonel of the 4th Virginia Regiment. A veteran of the battles of Trenton, Princeton, Brandywine, and Germantown, Parker was an outstanding leader that General Steuben confidently tapped to command the militia in Isle of Wight, Nansemond, Princess Anne, and Norfolk counties. Although Colonel Parker was unable to challenge Arnold's advance into Smithfield, he established a defensive position with approximately 200 militia and two cannon a few miles south of town on the road to Portsmouth.[115]

Battle of Mackie's Mill

Colonel Parker's position was a strong one. His men defended a dismantled bridge that crossed Cypress Creek, a narrow, but deep obstacle on the road to Portsmouth. The banks of both sides of the creek were steep and access to the bridge passed through a narrow defile that Colonel Parker covered with two cannon. The dismantled bridge also served as a dam which formed an impassible mill pond on the left side of the bridge. This allowed Colonel Parker to concentrate most of his force and cannon upon high ground to the right of the bridge. The mill, which sat just to the right of the bridge, was also used by the militia for cover.

On the morning of January 16th, Lieutenant Colonel Simcoe and his cavalry rode out of Smithfield, discovered

---

[115] Rob Friar, *The Militia Are Coming in from All Quarters; The Revolution in Virginia's Lower Counties, 1781*, (2010), 21

Parker's position at Mackie's Mil and sent word back to General Arnold, who ordered Captain Ewald and his jagers, along with three companies of Simcoe's rangers to reinforce Simcoe. As the task of dislodging the rebels was better suited for the infantry than cavalry, it appears that Lieutenant Colonel Simcoe gave Captain Ewald the responsibility of driving the rebels out. Ewald recalled in his diary that

> *The enemy had placed his infantry and two* [cannon] *in the gardens in such a way that they could enfilade the bridge and a great distance on our side. There was much to reconnoiter, but no time for it; we saw the enemy right before our eyes. He had to be driven out, and we immediately proceeded quickly to the task.*[117]

Ewald posted 30 jagers on the high ground near the road behind trees. Half were ordered to keep a constant fire on the cannon crews, the other half, on the militia in the gardens. "*I distributed the remaining jagers* [among Simcoe's Rangers] *along the creek and ordered them to fire continuously at anyone who showed himself,*" recalled Ewald.[118] The rifle fire of the jagers quickly took effect on the rebels and after only four cannon shots, (two of solid ball and two of grape) the rebel guns were withdrawn.[119] Captain Ewald smugly speculated that the reason the cannon were pulled back from the fight so quickly was that the crews serving them had no more desire to load them in the face of the heavy rifle fire of the jagers.

---

[117] Ewald, 273
[118] Ibid.
[119] Ibid.

In the midst of this firefight, Captain Ewald learned about the existence of a foot bridge over the creek about 1000 paces to his left. He hurried to investigate and upon confirmation, ordered ten or twelve men to cross over. Ewald claimed:

> *This had the effect of causing the enemy to abandon the gardens and hedges, and it looked as though he intended to withdraw to the wood lying behind him. To my astonishment, however, all the jagers and rangers left their posts* [near the dismantled bridge] *rushed to the footbridge and crossed it, without my being able to prevent it.*[120]

Ewald managed to restore some order to his troops, but no further advantage was gained because the militia, *"was so surprised by the spirit of the men that* [they] *ran head over heels to the woods."*[121] Ewald claimed the rebels left 11 dead and 8 wounded men who joined 8 other unscathed prisoners. Two jagers and a Queen's Ranger were also killed in the fight and five other crown force soldiers were wounded.[122]

With the crossing point secured and the bridge soon repaired, General Arnold and the rest of his corps crossed Cypress Creek the next day. The remainder of their march to Portsmouth was incident free and early in the morning of January 19th, Simcoe's cavalry entered the largely deserted town.

It had been an extremely arduous as well as profitable three weeks for General Arnold and his expedition. At the loss of less than 100 men, Arnold's force had wreaked havoc and

---

[120] Ibid.
[121] Ibid.
[122] Ibid.

destruction all along the James River. Virginia's inability to mount an adequate defense against such a relatively small enemy force exposed the state to ridicule and Virginia's leaders chafed at the thought that the traitor Arnold, was the cause of this. As Arnold fortified Portsmouth for what looked like a long stay, Jefferson, Steuben, Nelson and the rest of Virginia's patriots, hoped for a chance at revenge.

Chapter Eight

"We Attempt Everything, and Sacrifice our own Blood for Your Assumed Cause!"

February – March 1781

Despite the overwhelming success of Benedict Arnold's raid on Richmond, his primary objective -- to establish a secure base of operations for the British at Portsmouth – had yet to be achieved. This changed on January 20th when General Arnold and his troops marched into Portsmouth.

Although Virginia had thus far offered little opposition to General Arnold, he knew that his raid had awakened the state from its lethargy and he prepared accordingly. Arnold ordered the construction of earthworks, redoubts, and abatis (sharpened piles of branches that served as 18th century barbed wire) along the land approaches to Portsmouth, (mostly on the western edge of town), employing both slaves and his troops in the task. The fleet of warships and transports that had reunited with Arnold on his return from Richmond defended the water approach to Portsmouth.

General Steuben still commanded Virginia's military forces, a task that grew somewhat more promising due to the influx of militia troops from throughout the state in late January. Thousands turned out and were deployed on both sides of the James River. Despite their large numbers,

Virginia's defenders faced significant challenges thanks to a shortage of arms and equipment, particularly tents, kettles, and axes. The last item was needed to construct winter huts for the troops, many who grew sick from prolonged exposure to the elements. Further complicating matters for the Virginians was the desperate need of General Greene and his southern army for reinforcements and supplies from Virginia.

Although the light corps of Greene's southern army (commanded by General Daniel Morgan of Virginia) scored a decisive victory over the British at the Battle of Cowpens in mid-January, Greene's southern army was still significantly outnumbered in the Carolinas and the British commander in the South, Lord Charles Cornwallis, was determined to gain revenge for Cowpens. Thus, General Greene needed every soldier and all the supplies that he could get from Virginia.

It proved to be a difficult, if not impossible, balancing act for General Steuben to attempt; to supply enough men and equipment to defend Virginia, while at the same time adequately reinforce General Greene's army. For the time being, General Greene had to go without reinforcement. Virginia's militia was needed to deal with Arnold, and the 400 continental levies assembled at Chesterfield Courthouse were inadequately clothed or supplied, so a march south was out of the question.[1] The continentals remained in their barracks in the center of the state waiting for promised supplies from Congress to arrive.

Many of the militia troops posted in southern Virginia suffered similar hardships, yet few were exempted from service in the field. General Robert Lawson, a veteran of the

---

[1] Showman, ed., "General Greene to General Washington, 28 February, 1781," *The Papers of General Nathanael Greene*, Vol. 7, 370

Continental army in command of the militia at Mackie's Mill, reported to Governor Jefferson on January 28th that

> *We have no Tents; and are posted where we cannot have the benefit of Houses. The severity of the Season coming on daily, the Baron ordered us to build Hutts; but this cannot be done without proper Tools, and those we have not as yet been able to procure.... Indeed it is a lamentable fact that we have* [not enough axes] *for the purpose of cutting wood to make fires for the Men, who are decreasing my strength daily by sickness, occasion'd I am confident from their expos'd state to the severity of the excessive bad weather we have had in this quarter. We want exceedingly ammunition Waggons, with proper military Chests, Cartridges, and almost every article of Camp Equipment.*[2]

General Peter Muhlenberg, a former continental army general who upon Steuben's return to Richmond in late January assumed field command of the militia south of the James River and was at Cabin Point with 800 militia, described a similar situation to General Steuben:

General Lawson complains heavily of the wretched situation of the sick in his camp, who are without medicine, physicians, and necessaries. We are here [at Cabin Point] *in the same situation, and no other alternative is left us than to disperse the sick in the neighboring houses.*[3]

---

[2] Boyd, ed., "Colonel Robert Lawson to Governor Jefferson, 28 January, 1781," *The Papers of Thomas Jefferson*, Vol. 4, 461

[3] Henry A. Muhlenberg, " General Muhlenberg to General Steuben, 31 January, 1781," *The Life of Major-General Peter Muhlenberg*, (Philadelphia: Cary and Hart, 1849), 381-82

The shortage of supplies, particularly arms, was likely one important factor behind the decision of General Steuben and his subordinate officers to forego an assault on Portsmouth and instead, attempt only to confine Arnold's movements to the vicinity of Portsmouth. Steuben posted detachments outside of Portsmouth accordingly.

Colonel Josiah Parker, a seasoned former regimental commander in the continental army, commanded 500 troops (along with 300 cavalry under Major Willis) near Suffolk, while General Robert Lawson, commanded 900 troops at Mackie's Mills, just outside of Smithfield. General Muhlenberg was encamped, further up the James River at Cabin Point with 800 troops plus continental cavalry under a French volunteer, Colonel Charles Armand.[4] Strong picket detachments were posted at Sleepy Hole (the ferry crossing of the Nansemond River), as well as at the mouth of the Nansemond.

Across the James River, in Williamsburg, General Thomas Nelson protected the former capital with 1,000 troops and a detachment of volunteer cavalry, while former continental brigadier-general George Weedon commanded hundreds of additional militia in the vicinity of Fredericksburg.[5] Weedon's primary responsibility was to defend Hunter's Foundry, the all important foundry and arms manufactory along the Rappahannock River at Fredericksburg.

Virginia's forces were not the only ones scattered about, General Arnold established two key British outposts south and east of Portsmouth in Norfolk and Princess Anne County to help secure forage and provisions for his troops.

---

[4] Kapp, 379
[5] Ibid.

Princess Ann and Norfolk Counties

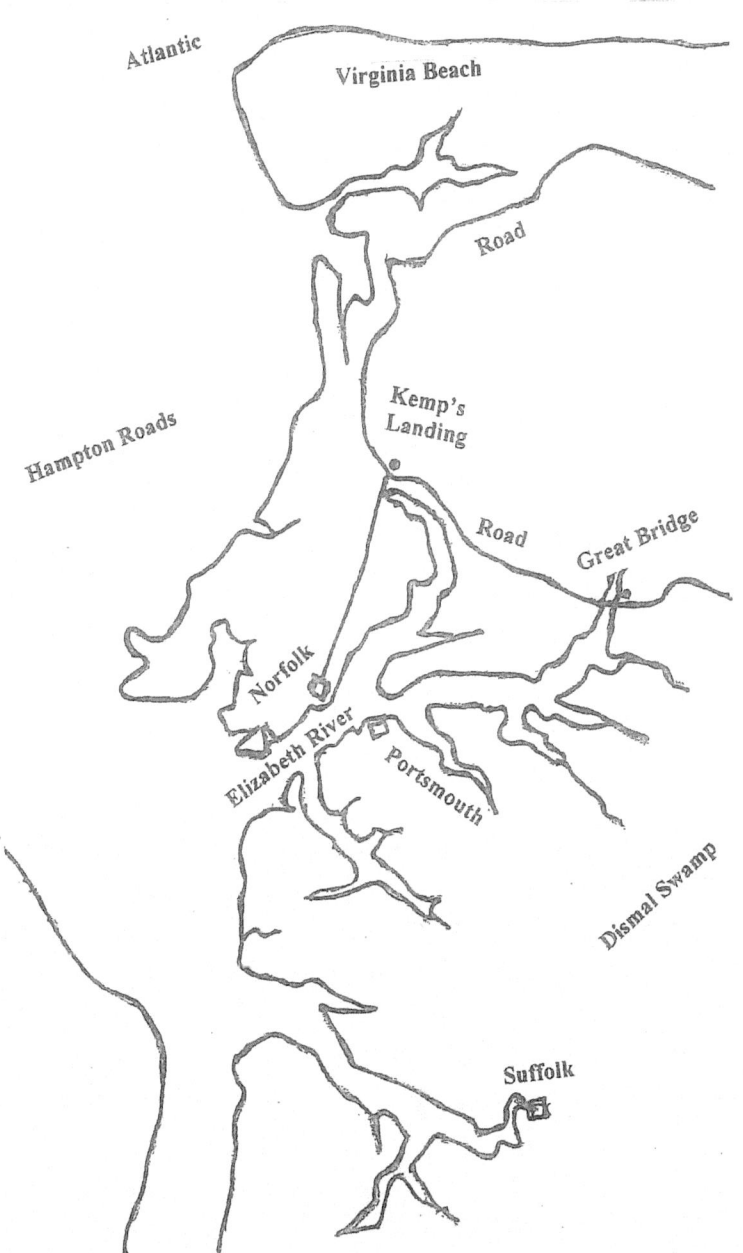

British Outposts

As it was in 1775, the Great Bridge over the southern branch of the Elizabeth River, about nine miles south of Norfolk, remained the key access point into Norfolk and Princess Anne County from the south. Control of this crossing point, and a smaller bridge a few miles further south, secured much of the area around Portsmouth and Norfolk from attack or encroachment. Within days of his occupation of Portsmouth, Arnold sent a strong detachment to Great Bridge to secure the bridge and erect a redoubt to be garrisoned by 100 men and two cannon. Captain Ewald, who accompanied the detachment to Great Bridge described the location in his diary:

> *Great Bridge is an important position in Virginia if Portsmouth is to be designated and maintained as a fortified post. It consists of a village of twenty-five fine buildings and is inhabited by tradespeople, who had...all flown* [away].[6]

Ewald noted that several small creeks flowed into the Southern Branch of the Elizabeth River at Great Bridge and created, *"an impenetrable marsh of fifteen or sixteen hundred paces."*[7] The marsh was overcome by, *"a single causeway* [which] *passes over this swampland, and there is a wooden bridge in the middle which rests on trestles and piers."*[8] The wooden bridge was over 200 paces in length and was the primary crossing point for nearly all travelers to and from

---
[6] Ewald, 277
[7] Ibid.
[8] Ibid.

northeastern North Carolina and southeastern Virginia. Thus, control of the Great Bridge was essential for the security of General Arnold and his men in Portsmouth.

The other important outpost that Arnold fortified outside of Portsmouth was a few miles to the northeast of Great Bridge. Three roads converged on the village of Kemp's Landing, which was located at the headwater of the Eastern Branch of the Elizabeth River. From Kemp's Landing, one could travel straight to Norfolk, just seven miles to the west. The village of Kemp's Landing was three times the size of Great Bridge, yet, the British garrison left to defend this important intersection in Princess Anne County numbered only 60 men, just over half of the force guarding the Great Bridge.[9]

Major Amos Weeks

General Arnold undoubtedly would have preferred to leave more troops at these outposts, but with so many men needed to build and defend the lines of the western edge of Portsmouth, he had few to spare, especially since he sent regular patrols into the countryside to reconnoiter and forage. One such foraging party was ambushed in late January on the road to Great Bridge. Captain Ewald observed that

> [The culprits were] *said to have been from a light corps commanded by a certain Major Weeks, to whom the country people are greatly devoted, partly from inclination and partly from fear. In the countryside he is considered an excellent officer and a good partisan. There was much talk about him at*

---

[9] Ibid.

> *Kemp's Landing, but we laughed because we had neither seen nor heard anyone. Afterward, we were astonished over the trick [ambush] that he had played in our rear.*[10]

Major Amos Weeks was an experienced militia commander who had led Princess Anne County troops since the beginning of the war. For a brief period in February 1781, Major Weeks represented the only active opposition to General Arnold in Portsmouth. His troops staged a series of daring ambushes and raids throughout Princess Anne County upon both Arnold's troops and the loyalists who looked to Arnold for protection. The actions of Major Weeks eventually prompted General Arnold to send two strong detachments under Captain Ewald and Lieutenant Colonel Simcoe to subdue the aggressive militia commander. Captain Ewald recalled that on February 12th,

> *The news came in from Princess Anne County that Major Weeks was spreading ruin in the area and severely harassing the few good loyalists. The communication between Portsmouth and Great Bridge was made unsafe. Therefore, General Arnold decided to send two parties there, one under Colonel Simcoe and the other under myself, in order to drive away the honorable gentleman.*[11]

Colonel Simcoe commanded 200 infantry and 40 cavalry and Captain Ewald the same number with ten fewer cavalry. Simcoe headed for Kemp's Landing while Ewald marched to

---
[10] Ewald, 278
[11] Ibid., 279

Great Bridge. The plan called for Simcoe to occupy Major Weeks's attention by marching straight at his reported location east of Kemp's Landing, while Captain Ewald circled around to the rear of the militia by crossing Devil's Elbow Swamp (which lay between Great Bridge and Kemp's Landing) to strike Major Weeks from behind. Ewald recorded in his diary that

> *I departed at once from the vicinity of Great Bridge, crossed the Devil's Elbow Swamp – two good hours wide – and about nine o' clock in the morning arrived on the other side at a plantation which belonged to a loyalist and a relative of my guide. This swampy wood was crossed on a very dark night.... The men had to march in single file, constantly going up to their knees in the swamp. We had to climb over countless trees which the wind had blown down and that often lay crosswise, over which the horses could scarcely go. They had to be whistled at continually to prevent them from going astray. Men and horses were so worn out that they could hardly go on when I happily left this abominable region behind.*[12]

A coded message from Lieutenant Colonel Simcoe instructing Ewald to continue on through Dauge's swamp awaited Ewald at the plantation. The German captain obediently led his detachment onward and recalled

---

[12] Ibid., 280

Although I had crossed the first swamp with great difficulty during the night, this last passage surpassed the first one very much with respect to all hardships. The men had to wade constantly over their knees in the swampy water and climb over the most dangerous spots with the help of fallen and rotted trees. At times there were places such that if a foothold were missed, a man could have suffocated in the swamp. I had to cross a flooded, swampy cypress wood with the cavalry, a quarter of an hour further to the right, where one had to ride continually in water over the saddle. At the end of the swamp, wither our two guides led us safely at the same time, there was a log causeway – a good quarter hour long – which because of its great holes was just as difficult for the horses and men to cross as the swamp had been.[13]

Ewald and his men surprised the occupants of a small house and learned from them that Major Weeks had just burned Dauge's Bridge, southeast of Kemp's Landing, and withdrawn. Through a combination of persuasion (in the form of monetary reward) and threat (to hang the occupants if they didn't cooperate) Ewald learned that Major Weeks was seen just a few hours earlier with 600 to 800 troops at a nearby plantation. [The actual number of militia with Major Weeks was 520][14]

Despite being significantly outnumbered, Ewald was determined to attack. He sent Captain Shank with the cavalry (thirty strong) and twenty jagers straight down the road to the

---

[13] Ibid., 281
[14] Ibid., 281, 284

plantation that Weeks was reportedly encamped at to open the attack while Ewald circled through the woods with the rest of his detachment (180 strong) to strike the rebels on their flank. Ewald recalled that, *"I had marched scarcely eight hundred to a thousand paces when I heard strong rifle fire."*[15] His guide speculated that Major Weeks was actually camped at a closer plantation so Ewald had to adjust his attack on the fly:

> *I quickly formed a front on the flank and directed my men to fire a volley as soon as they caught sight of the enemy and then boldly attack the foe with the bayonet and hunting sword. I ordered the jagers to disperse on both flanks and kept the rangers in close formation. We had not passed five to six hundred paces through the wood when we saw the enemy in a line facing the side of the highway to London Bridge, firing freely against Captain Shank's advance. In doing so, they carelessly showed us their left flank. I got over a fence safely without being discovered by the enemy. Here I had a volley fired, blew the half-moon, and shouted, 'Hurrah!' I scrambled over a second fence and threw myself at the enemy, who was so surprised that he impulsively fled in the greatest disorder into the wood lying behind him. At this moment the gallant Captain Shank advanced with his cavalry, ably supported by Lieutenant Bickell with his twenty jagers. Some sixty men were either cut down or bayoneted by the infantry. We captured one captain, one lieutenant, four noncommissioned officers, and forty-five men, some sound and some wounded. All the baggage, along with a powder cart and a wagon loaded*

---

[15] Ibid.

> with weapons, was taken as booty by the men. I ordered Lieutenant Bickell with all the foot jagers to quickly follow the enemy into the wood. He followed him until night fell and brought back seven more prisoners. On my side, I had three jagers and two rangers wounded and one horse killed.[16]

Ewald's efforts had resulted in a decisive victory and he sent word of the engagement to Simcoe who was a few miles north of Ewald at London Bridge. Ewald and his detachment rested at James's Plantation until the morning during which Ewald attempted to convince some of the militia prisoners to join the crown side

> I learned from the prisoners that Major Weeks designated daily a rallying point where they were to reassemble after a reverse. He seldom remained in one place for twenty-four hours, and toward evening they were on the march again. Their present rendezvous was Northwest Landing. The enemy strength had been 520 men, and his people were so devoted to him that none of them were willing to enlist in our service.[17]

Lieutenant Colonel Simcoe and his detachment joined Ewald in the morning and both detachments marched southward to Pungo Church on the assumption that Major Weeks would pass there on his way to Northwest Landing. Simcoe and Ewald reached the church before noon, searched the area and set up an ambush. Simcoe then took his cavalry

---

[16] Ibid.
[17] Ibid., 284

to a nearby plantation and suggested that Ewald march to another plantation east of Pungo with the rest of his detachment. On his march there, one of Ewald's men spotted, *"several sentries in blue coats at a distance of several hundred yards."*[18] Worried that the enemy had discovered him, Ewald divided his jagers into two groups and ordered them off the road to approach the plantation from the right and left. Ewald led the rangers that were with him straight up the road towards the plantation. Fighting erupted to the right of the road and Ewald's detachments converged on the sound of battle. He recalled

> *I found the enemy in full flight, running through a marshy meadow to a wood. Two of their men were killed and a lieutenant with five men captured. Had Lieutenant Bickell seized another officer who stood a few paces away instead of the lieutenant, the commander of the party – Major Weeks himself— would have been captured. But since he was not as well dressed as the lieutenant, he was not taken for an officer. Just before, a jager had killed his horse. This man, whom I had the good luck to chase all around, knew the countryside better than I could ever know it. That was evident from the positions he took, for a retreat always remained open to him in the impassable woods which he alone knew. But on this occasion, my spies were better than his; and luck, on which everything depends in war, was on my side.*[19]

---

[18] Ibid., 285
[19] Ibid.

Close Call for Arnold

Although the efforts of Captain Ewald and Lieutenant Colonel Simcoe handed Major Weeks a series of defeats in mid-February, the Virginians were able to score a small victory of their own on the outskirts of Portsmouth. On February 17th, General Muhlenberg, encouraged by the arrival of three powerful French warships, decided to increase the pressure on General Arnold in Portsmouth by marching 1,100 troops to within a mile and a half of Arnold's lines. Muhlenberg recounted to General Greene that

> *I marched...with six hundred riflemen and five hundred musketry, with which we formed an ambuscade about one mile and a half from Portsmouth and on the morning of the 18th, a party of horse was ordered to charge the* [enemy] *picket, which was posted within shot of their redoubts. The horse charged and took the picket, consisting of a sergeant, corporal, and twelve men without having a shot fired at them.*[20]

General Muhlenberg added that two jagers and three pioneers were killed in the charge, and a wagon and six horses were seized. General Muhlenberg apparently had more in mind than just capturing the enemy's picket, for a Virginia soldier who participated in the engagement recalled that

> *A detachment of horse was sent forward to skirmish with the pickets of the enemy.... They were ordered to retreat in haste and draw the enemy on to Hall's Mill dam, they*

---

[20] Muhlenberg, "General Muhlenberg to General Greene, 24 February, 1781," *The Life of Major-General Peter Muhlenberg*, 388-89

were then to wheel and attack in front while the Militia took them in flank and rear. It was hoped that they might easily be taken. The Militia passed the night under arms. It was a dreadful night, thundering and lightening, though in the depths of winter and clearing off so piercingly cold that the ponds were covered with ice before morning. The enemy did not follow.[21]

Had General Muhlenberg realized at the time that Arnold only had 300 effective troops to man the lines in Portsmouth, the rest of his army being sick, away from Portsmouth on the hunt for Major Weeks, or posted at Great Bridge and Kemp's Landing, he may have risked a direct assault on Arnold's lines.[22] Alas, the opportunity passed, and the departure of the French ships on February 19th, (surprisingly after a successful engagement with Arnold's fleet in which they captured the 44 gun *Romulus* and two privateers), coupled with the return of Simcoe and Ewald (with nearly 500 men) secured Portsmouth for the time being.

Race to the Dan

While events in southeastern Virginia developed into a standoff at Portsmouth, a new crisis involving troops from Virginia unfolded in the Carolinas and spilled into Virginia. The surprising American victory in mid-January at Cowpens in South Carolina had gone far to boost American morale.

---

[21] Friar, 40
Note: This is an account of the incident from a participant, William McLaurine of the Powhatan County militia. The full account is found in the *Virginia Magazine of History and Biography*, Vol. 14, 198
[22] Muhlenberg, "General Isaac Gregory to General Muhlenberg, 23 February, 1781," *The Life of Major-General Peter Muhlenberg*, 386

Race to the Dan

After a seemingly endless series of defeats in the Carolinas in 1780, General Morgan's decisive victory over Banastre Tarleton and his British Legion fostered new hope for the Americans. General Cornwallis was determined, however, to reverse this, and he pursued General Morgan deep into North Carolina.

Morgan's corps reunited with the rest of General Greene's southern army at Guilford Courthouse on February 9th, and Greene immediately called a council of war to determine how to proceed. Greene's army consisted of only 1426 ill-clad and poorly armed continentals along with 600 poorly armed militia.[23] Approximately 25 miles west of Guilford Court House was General Cornwallis and 2,500 troops eager to catch the Americans and avenge Cowpens. General Greene and his officers agreed that it would be best to avoid an engagement with Cornwallis until they were reinforced by more militia, and the most likely place to find more militia was in Virginia, so Greene ordered a retreat northward to the Dan River, some 70 miles to the northeast. Before he departed, General Greene wrote to General Washington and explained his decision:

> *We have no provisions but what we receive from our daily collections. Under these circumstances I called a council who unanimously advised to avoid an action and to retire beyond the* [Dan River] *immediately.... I have formed a light army composed of the cavalry...and the Legion* [Lee's] *amounting to 240, a detachment of 280 Infantry under Lt. Col. Howard, the Infantry of Lt. Col. Lee's legion and 60*

---

[23] Showman, ed., "War Council 9 February, 1781," *The Papers of General Nathanael Greene*, Vol. 7, 261

> *Virginia Rifle Men making in their whole 700 Men which will be ordered with the Militia to harass the enemy in their advance, check their progress and if possible give us an opportunity to retire without a general action.*[24]

To save the bulk of his army, General Greene had to risk his light infantry corps. With General Morgan too ill to continue in the field, command of the light corps fell to Colonel Otho Williams of Maryland. He was instructed by General Greene to screen the main army's retreat northward. Williams began his mission with deception, leading his light corps northwest to give the appearance that he was heading for the upper fords of the Dan River. This fed into General Cornwallis's assumption that the American army had no choice but to cross the Dan River at the upper fords (where the water was shallow) rather than further down river where ferry boats were required to cross.

Unbeknownst to Cornwallis, who took the bait and moved to intercept Williams, General Greene had made arrangements to gather boats in the vicinity of Irwin's and Boyd's ferries on the Dan River in Halifax County Virginia. Greene just needed time to reach the river and transport his army and its baggage across, and time was what Colonel Williams was trying to provide Greene. Thus, while Williams lured Cornwallis to the northwest, General Greene marched the rest of the American army northeast, towards Irwin's and Boyd's ferries and away from Williams and Cornwallis.

---

[24] Showman, ed., "General Greene to General Washington, 9 February, 1781," *The Papers of General Nathanael Greene*, Vol. 7, 267-269

Cornwallis picked up the trail of the American light corps on the first day of the march. They appeared to be headed to Dix's Ferry, (modern day Danville, Virginia) some twenty miles west of General Greene's true destination.

With Cornwallis now on his trail, Colonel Williams hastened his march northward. Every mile of road that Colonel Williams drew Cornwallis down provided General Greene with more time to reach the Dan River. The danger for the American light troops, however, was that every step also took them further away from the support of General Greene's army. By February 13th, Colonel Williams decided it was time to re-direct his march towards Irwin's Ferry. At almost the same moment, General Cornwallis discovered the American ruse and re-directed his march eastward as well.[25] Both forces raced towards the road that General Greene was on. Colonel Williams, who was further north than Cornwallis, managed to position his light corps between Cornwallis and Greene. The race to the Dan was now a sprint.

With General Cornwallis pressing the American light corps, it was crucial that Colonel Williams and his men remain vigilant. They halted only when the British did, and even then, they got little rest. Lieutenant Colonel Henry Lee, who commanded the rear guard of the light corps, recalled in his memoirs that

> *The duty, severe in the day, became more so at night; for numerous patrols and strong pickets were necessarily furnished by the light troops, not only for*

---

[25] Henry Lee, *The Revolutionary War Memoirs of General Henry Lee*, (New York: De Capo Press, 1998), 243-44 (Originally published in 1812).

> *their own safety, but to prevent the enemy from placing himself by a circuitous march, between Williams and Greene. Such a maneuver would have been fatal to the American army; and, to render it impossible, half of the troops were alternately appointed every night to duty: so that each man, during the retreat, was entitled to but six hours repose in forty-eight.*[26]

Such hard duty took a toll on the men and horses, yet, the American light troops marched on. At one point it appeared that their efforts to screen Greene's main body had failed when the van of the light corps spotted numerous campfires off in the distance. With Cornwallis still pressing their rear, the light corps feared that they had caught up to General Greene. If this were true, then all of their effort and sacrifice to provide General Greene with time to escape had been wasted. As they approached the campfires the exhausted light troops resigned themselves to one last doomed engagement against a vastly superior enemy.[27] Lieutenant Colonel Lee recalled that

> *No pen can describe the heart-rendering feelings of our brave and wearied troops.... Our dauntless corps were convinced that the crisis had now arrived when its self sacrifice could alone give a chance of escape of the main body. With one voice was announced the noble resolution to turn on the foe, and by dint of*

---

[26] Ibid., 238
[27] Ibid., 245

desperate courage, so to cripple him as to force a discontinuance of pursuit.[28]

However, to the great relief of the light troops, it was discovered that Greene's troops had left the campsite hours earlier and that local militia had maintained the fires for the benefit of the light corps.[29] Unfortunately for Colonel Williams and his tired men, the close proximity of General Cornwallis prevented the American light troops from enjoying the warmth of the campfires. Colonel Williams did find the time to write to General Greene, however, and express his anxiety about the slow progress of Greene's main body of troops:

I was exceedingly concern'd to hear...that you were yet 25 miles from the ferry. My Dear General at Sun Down the Enemy were only 22 miles from you and may be in motion now or will most probably [be] by 3 oClock in the morning.... Rely on it, my Dear Sir, it is possible for you to be overtaken before you can cross the Dan even if you had 20 boats.... I conclude you march'd as far today as you could and if your Army can make but Eleven miles in a Day you will not be able to pass the ferry in less than two Days more. In less time than that we will be driven in to your Camp or I must risqué the Troops I've the Honor to command and in doing so I risqué every thing.... The Gentlemen of Cavalry assure me their Horses want refreshment exceedingly and our Infantry are so excessively fatigu'd that I'm confident

---
[28] Ibid.
[29] Ibid.

> *I lose men every Day. We have been all this Day almost in presence of the Enemy but have sustain'd no loss but of Sick and Strollers.*[30]

Despite Colonel Williams's pessimism, the Americans marched on. Lieutenant Colonel Lee recalled that

> *About midnight our troops were put in motion, in consequence of the enemy's advance on our pickets, which the British general had been induced to order, from knowing that he was within forty miles of the Dan, and that all his hopes depended on the exertions of the following day. Animated with the prospect of soon terminating their present labors, the light troops resumed their march with alacrity. The roads continued deep and broken, and were rendered worse by being incrusted with frost: nevertheless, the march was pushed with great expedition.*[31]

General Cornwallis described his pursuit in similar terms:

> *Nothing could exceed the patience and alacrity of the officers and soldiers under every species of hardship and fatigue, in endeavouring to overtake* [the Americans]: *But our intelligence upon this occasion was exceedingly defective; which, with heavy rains, bad roads, and the passage of many deep creeks, and bridges destroyed by the enemy's light troops, rendered all our exertions vain.*[32]

---

[30] Showman, ed., "Col. Otho Williams to Gen. Greene, 13 February 1781," *The Papers of General Nathanael Greene,* Vol. 7, 285-286
[31] Lee, 246
[32] Tarleton, "Cornwallis to Lord Germain 17 March, 1781," 264

Good news finally reached the American light corps on February 14th in the form of a series of messages from General Greene informing Colonel Williams of the army's arrival at the Dan River. Greene wrote at 2:00 p.m. that, *"The greater part of our wagons are over and the troops are crossing,"* and at 5:30 p.m. Greene announced, *"The stage is clear."*[33]

The good news inspired the light troops to march with renewed vigor and they reached the ferry crossings hours ahead of the British. General Greene greeted Colonel Williams at the riverbank and crossed to the north side with him. Lieutenant Colonel Lee arrived with his Legion soon after and proudly recalled in his memoirs that he was the last to cross the Dan River.[34] The American army had achieved its goal, it had crossed the Dan River intact. It remained to be seen whether they had escaped General Cornwallis's wrath or only postponed it.

Virginia Comes to Greene's Aid

Governor Jefferson, in Richmond, first learned of General Greene's flight to the Dan River on February 15th, the day after Greene's army crossed the river. He was surprised by the turn of events in the Carolinas and immediately instructed the counties of Washington, Montgomery, Botetourt, Henry and Pittsylvania to turn out their militia:

---

[33] Showman, ed., "Col. Otho Williams to Gen. Greene, 14 February 1781," *The Papers of General Nathanael Greene,* Vol. 7, 287
[34] Lee, 247

> *I have just received intelligence from Genl. Greene that Lord Cornwallis, maddened by his losses at the Cowpens and Georgetown, has burnt his own Waggons to enable himself to move with facility, and is pressing forward towards the Virginia line, Genl. Greene being obliged to retire before him with an inferior force. The necessity of saving Genl. Green's Army and in doing that the probability of environing and destroying the Army of the enemy induce me to press to you in the most earnest terms...to collect [a portion] of your Militia, and send them forward well armed and accoutered under proper Officers to repair to the orders of Genl. Greene wherever he shall be.*[35]

Jefferson estimated that the five counties should provide over 1,000 men for General Greene but confessed his concern to General Steuben about the lack of arms for them.

Luckily for General Greene, General Cornwallis ended his pursuit at the Dan River. He spent two days gathering forage and provisions for his exhausted and hungry army and then headed south to Hillsborough, North Carolina.

This turn of events, combined with General Greene's expectation of a flood of militia reinforcements from the surrounding and western counties of Virginia, prompted a newly confident General Greene to follow Cornwallis back into North Carolina on February 22nd. Although the actual arrival of militia reinforcements took much longer than

---

[35] Boyd, ed., "Governor Jefferson to the County Lieutenants of Washington and Certain Other Counties, 15 February, 1781,", *The Papers of Thomas Jefferson* Vol. 4, 613

expected, over 2,000 Virginia and North Carolina militia as well as General Steuben's continental levies from Virginia, joined General Greene's army in the weeks following his crossing of the Dan.[36] Greene would use these men to finally confront General Cornwallis at Guilford Courthouse in mid-March, a battle that had important consequences for Virginia.

Stalemate in Portsmouth

The day before General Greene re-crossed the Dan River and marched south, General Benedict Arnold met with over 400 inhabitants of Princess Anne County at Kemp's Landing to administer an oath of allegiance to England and convince the loyal Virginians to become more involved in suppressing the American rebellion.[37] Captain Ewald observed the meeting and bitterly noted that those present, "*gladly swallowed the oath*" after assurances were given of their protection, but few stepped forward to join the fight against the rebels.[38] Ewald actually challenged a wealthy loyalist, "*one of the most distinguished and richest residents of this area*," to raise a battalion of troops for the defense of Princess Anne County.[39] The gentleman explained to Ewald that he had to first be certain that the British would honor their pledge to stay. "*You have already been in this area twice. General Leslie gave me the same assurances in the past autumn, and*

---

[36] Showman, ed.,"General Greene to Samuel Huntington, 16 March, 1781," *The Papers of Nathanael Greene*, Vol. 7, 433
[37] Ewald, 286
[38] Ibid.
[39] Ibid.

where is he now?" asked the loyal Virginia.[40] Captain Ewald was disgusted by this comment and exclaimed

> *How can you be called friends of the King if you won't venture anything for the right cause? Look at your Opposition Party:* [the American rebels] *they abandon wife, child, house, and home, and let us lay waste to everything. They fight without shoes and clothing with all passion, suffer hunger, and gladly endure all hardships of war. But you loyalists won't do anything! You only want to be protected, to live in peace in your houses. We are supposed to break our bones for you, in place of yours, to accomplish your purpose. We attempt everything, and sacrifice our own blood for your assumed cause.*[41]

Later, after he had calmed down and returned to Portsmouth with General Arnold, Ewald realized that

> *This man, who did not want to be a soldier, would have been a fool if he had acted as I had advised him. For he possessed a fortune in property...and had for a wife one of the most charming blondes that I have ever seen in all my life!*[42]

Luckily for General Arnold, his inability to attract greater loyalist support did not lead to any military reverses on the field against the numerically superior rebels. In fact, the remainder of February saw little activity between the two

---

[40] Ibid.
[41] Ibid.
[42] Ibid., 287

sides. General Muhlenberg revealed the main reason for his restrained actions in a letter to General Greene on February 24th:

> *I must acknowledge it is derogatory to the honour of the state to suffer such a handful of men* [under Arnold] *to retain possession* [of Portsmouth for] *so long; but what...is to be done? They are strongly fortified; I have near two thousand men, but among the whole about three hundred bayonets and two brass six pound* [cannon]. *With such a military apparatus, we cannot think of attacking the works by regular approaches, and all my hopes at present are, that I shall be able to coop up Arnold so close that he will be obliged to make an attempt to dislodge us.*[43]

Of course, the problem with Muhlenberg's plan was that Arnold was content to stay behind his fortifications. So in March, Muhlenberg's troops became more active, probing Arnold's outposts and pickets.

General Steuben, in Richmond, contributed to the heightened American activity by ordering General Muhlenberg to detach 800 militia (who were posted in Suffolk) to Great Bridge to reinforce General Isaac Gregory and his force of 700 North Carolinians.[44] Colonel Josiah Parker, who had been sent with 300 militia to probe the enemy at Great Bridge prior to Steuben's orders, added to Gregory's force.

---

[43] Muhlenberg, "General Muhlenberg to General Greene, 24 February, 1781," *The Life of Major-General Peter Muhlenberg*, 389-90
[44] Friar, 43

General Steuben's rationale for these movements was the imminent arrival of a French naval force with General LaFayette and American reinforcements. Steuben worried that General Arnold would attempt to escape southward, into North Carolina, upon the fleet's arrival, so the troop movements were a precaution to block such an attempt.

A curious incident occurred upon Colonel Parker's arrival at Great Bridge. A party of his men attacked and sank a British gunboat heading back to Portsmouth from Great Bridge. Among the items captured were the papers of Captain Stevenson of the Queens Rangers, and among these papers were two letters curiously addressed to General Isaac Gregory. The letters suggested the existence of a plot by Gregory to surrender his troops to Arnold:

> G.G.
> *Your well-formed plan of delivering those people now under your command into the hands of the British General at Portsmouth gives me much pleasure. Your next* [letter] *I hope will mention the place of ambuscade, and the manner you wish to fall into my hands.*[45]

Colonel Parker was stunned. Writing to General Muhlenberg the same day the letters were discovered, Parker declared that the, "*contents embarrassed me amazingly* [largely because] *General Gregory had furnished the guards for the night.*[46] [The General] *was present when I examined the papers,*" continued Parker, "*and declares himself innocent*

---

[45] Muhlenberg, "Colonel Parker to General Muhlenberg, 2 March, 1781," *The Life of Major-General Peter Muhlenberg*, 394
[46] Ibid.

of any correspondence."[47] Although General Gregory was regarded as a devoted patriot, so was General Arnold before his treason at West Point. With his trust in Gregory shaken, Colonel Parker quietly ordered his own guard detachments out to insure the safety of the camp. General Gregory, eager to clear his name, welcomed his arrest two days later. In his absence, Colonel Parker assumed command of the rebel forces outside of Great Bridge.

Although General Gregory remained under suspicion for weeks, it appears he was innocent of any plot to surrender his troops, for according to Lieutenant Colonel Simcoe, Captain Stevenson's letters were fictitious, *"written by way of amusement, and of passing the time."*[48] Simcoe noted that his officers at Great Bridge were at first amused at the trouble the letters had caused Gregory, but when they learned that he had been placed under arrest, *"Capt. Stevenson's humanity was alarmed,"* and he wrote to Colonel Parker to explain the origin of the letters and clear General Gregory of any wrongdoing.[49] The damage to Gregory's reputation had already been done, however, and he did not return to command.

Raid on Hampton

While General Gregory's personal drama played out south of Portsmouth, General Arnold, -- unconcerned about rumors of the French navy heading for Virginia to cut off his link with the sea -- sent a large detachment of the 80th Regiment, as well as a few jagers and cavalry, all under Lieutenant Colonel

---

[47] Ibid., 393
[48] Simcoe, 181
[49] Ibid.

Dundas, across Hampton Roads on the evening of March 6th to surprise a body of militia that was reportedly in Hampton.

Widely conflicting accounts of what happened present a confused picture of the evening. According to Lieutenant Colonel Simcoe, who accompanied the detachment, they initially failed to find any militia at Hampton and settled for burning some supplies and large canoes. On their way back to their boats, however, the British encountered a party of 200 militia, "*drawn up on a plain,* [with] *a wet ditch in front.*"[50] Simcoe, who commanded the cavalry with Dundas, received permission to charge the enemy with 26 horsemen and he boldly did so. He speculated after the engagement that his small numbers actually emboldened the militia, who held their fire until the cavalry was within 30 yards, and then blasted Simcoe's horsemen with a volley. Simcoe recalled that, "*this checked us, and gave them time to* [reload] *and give us a second salute, but not with the same effect.*"[51] A number of riders where unhorsed and some were hit by the gunfire, but enough remained mounted to break through the militia line and, reinforced by Dundas and the infantry (who followed on the heels of the cavalry at a jog) the British fell upon the militia with bayonets and swords, dispersing the rebels. Simcoe estimated that the enemy lost 60 men (killed, wounded, and captured), to only a handful of losses for Dundas's troops.[52]

An account of the engagement in the *Virginia Gazette* claimed that only 40 militia confronted the British and that they killed a British officer and two others and captured "five

---

[50] Simcoe, 177
[51] Simcoe, 177
[52] Ibid., 177-78

or six prisoners." The paper added that only a handful of the militia were lost.[53] Whatever the real numbers were, this engagement marked the end of Arnold's activity north of the James River.

Skirmish Near Kemp's Landing

Across the river, reports that a large reinforcement of troops had arrived south of Great Bridge (the 800 troops from Suffolk plus Colonel Parker's 300 men), coupled with General Muhlenberg's advance towards Portsmouth with his large force of militia, prompted General Arnold to re-direct his attention to Portsmouth. Arnold's concern for the security of his outpost at Great Bridge grew when communication between the fort and Portsmouth was severed. The notorious Major Weeks was responsible, having crossed a swamp to place his corps between Great Bridge and Portsmouth.[54]

In response to this development, Captain Ewald was ordered on March 10th, to march into the area and lie in ambush of Major Weeks. Ewald had with him his jagers along with 100 additional soldiers and all of the cavalry of the Queen's Rangers. He recalled that it was a very dark, but still night. Around 2 a.m. gunfire erupted in the direction of Kemp's Landing and Ewald led his detachment there. They had marched about two miles when his advance troops informed him that people were approaching his front:

---

[53] Boyd, ed., *The Papers of Thomas Jefferson,* Vol. 4, 294
  Note: Refers to Dixon & Hunter, 10 March, 1781 *Virginia Gazette*
[54] Ewald, 287

> *Hereupon I commanded, 'March! March! Lower bayonets!' whereupon a 'Who's there?' was heard, and the enemy fired a small volley. But at that instant, when I thought of fighting hand to hand with him, he scattered into the woods.*[55]

From the prisoners Ewald captured he learned that he had just engaged the rearguard of Major Weeks. Apparently the major was in the process of attacking the British outpost at Kemp's Landing when Ewald made contact with the rebel rearguard and forced Weeks to break off his attack.[56]

Portsmouth Alarmed

The threat to Great Bridge from the large rebel force south of the Elizabeth River proved illusionary, and the next few days were rather quiet around Portsmouth and its outposts. The alarm was sounded again in Portsmouth on March 17th, when a series of reports announcing the impending arrival of a large French fleet reached Arnold. Captain Ewald recalled that in response to this news

> *General Arnold, who had constantly beaten the French and Americans at table, lost his head and wanted to make up all at once for what had been neglected up to now. We now worked hastily to make this post impregnable, although the entire place consisted of miserable works of only six to eight feet on the average....*[57]

---

[55] Ibid., 288
[56] Ibid.
[57] Ibid.

Ewald continued:

> *General Arnold, the former American Hannibal, now stayed on horseback day and night, galloped constantly from the fortified windmill up to the blockhouse on the left and back, and had a dam constructed across Mill Point Creek to create a flood in front of the right.*[58]

The English warships that were still with Arnold, namely, the 44 gun *Charon*, 28 gun *Guadaloupe*, 20 gun *Fowey*, several privateers and a fire ship, were brought closer to Portsmouth, both for their own protection and that of the town. They anchored off of Mill Point and waited. Ewald, who was posted on the picket line at Scott's Creek guarding the road to Suffolk, remembered that, *"No one wanted to venture out of his hole to reconnoiter the enemy, and so we lived in anxiety for twenty-four hours."*[59]

LaFayette Arrives

General Arnold and his men were right to be anxious, for the force that the Americans and French were sending to reinforce the Virginia militia (and ultimately attack Portsmouth) was substantial. It included a powerful French fleet to wrestle control of Hampton Roads from the British, and 1,200 of General Washington's best troops, light infantry from New England and New York, under the young French volunteer, the Marquis de LaFayette. The marquis had come to America in 1777 as a volunteer, enamored by America's

---
[58] Ibid.
[59] Ibid., 289

cause, and, despite his youth, quickly won the confidence of General Washington. By 1781, General LaFayette commanded the American light infantry corps and in February, General Washington ordered LaFayette and his corps southward to Virginia. They reached Annapolis, Maryland on March 10th, but proceeded no further. The presence of British warships in the Chesapeake made it too dangerous to transport LaFayette's corps by ship to Virginia; the light infantry corps waited in Annapolis while General LaFayette, with a small escort, eluded the British and sailed to Virginia in a small, swift, ship. He reached Yorktown on March 14th and after a stop in Williamsburg, crossed the James River and arrived at General Muhlenberg's camp at Sleepy Hole, on the Nansemond River, on March 19th.

LaFayette was disappointed to learn that the French navy had yet to arrive (not aware that it had been turned back by a powerful British fleet off the Virginia capes). He was even more disappointed to discover the severe shortage of ammunition among the Virginians. LaFayette reported that, "*No men had a Sufficiency* [off ammunition] *and Many Had None at All.*"[60] Unwilling to move all of Muhlenberg's poorly supplied force closer to Portsmouth, LaFayette settled for accompanying a detachment of riflemen and militia forward to reconnoiter Arnold's works.

---

[60] Stanley J. Idzerda, ed., "General LaFayette to General Weedon, 20 March, 1781," *LaFayette in the Age of the American Revolution*, Vol. 3, (Cornell University Press, 1980,) 406

Scott's Creek

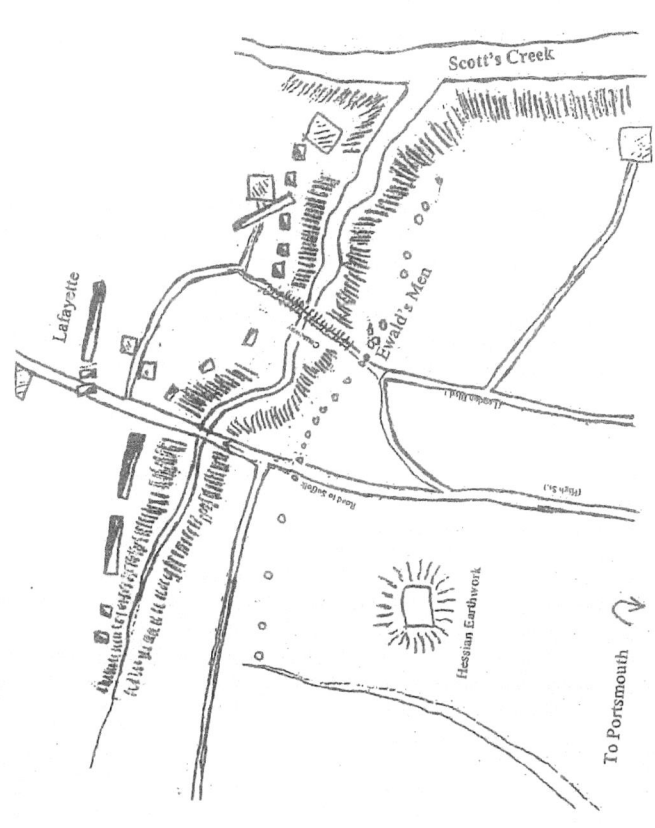

Skirmish at Scott's Creek

It had been a tense night for Captain Ewald's jagers on the picket line at Scott's Creek, made more so by the claim from a captured local inhabitant that 5,000 men under General LaFayette were marching towards Portsmouth.[61] As a precaution, the German jager commander sent a small party down the road towards Suffolk to hide in ambush and give an early warning if indeed the captive's claims were true. Ewald apparently was not too concerned, however, for he rode into town to report to General Arnold and accepted an invitation to dine with him. While he was changing for dinner, Ewald heard gunfire in the direction of Scott's Creek. He recalled in his diary that

> *I had hardly dressed when I heard several rifle shots, and shortly afterward many shots in succession. I rushed toward my picket, and called to Lieutenant Bickell to send me a noncommissioned officer and sixteen jagers, in order to double the picket and to impede the enemy's passage over the causeway.*[62]

When Ewald reached Scott's Creek he was shocked to find his picket troops gone and the entire opposite bank occupied by enemy riflemen who commenced to fire upon him. Ewald recalled

> *I found no picket, and was full of despair over the misbehavior of the noncommissioned officer of the picket. I dashed into the wood, where a short*

---
[61] Ewald, 289
[62] Ibid., 290

> *distance away I came across the* [missing] *jagers posted behind trees. With sword in hand I drove them toward the causeway again, where they fought like heroes in spite of the most frightful fire.*[63]

Reinforced by another detachment of 16 men, half of which deployed along the creek while the remainder defended the causeway with Ewald, they braced themselves for a rebel assault over the causeway. Captain Ewald recalled that

> *During this time the* [rebel] *riflemen suddenly withdrew, and* [the enemy] *advanced in closed battalions against the causeway, but not a shot was fired. Despite all the efforts of their officers, however, they came no further than the entrance of the causeway, gave fire, and withdrew again. Fresh troops advanced each time, but they fared no better.*[64]

Ewald's men kept up a hot and accurate fire, effectively blocking the causeway and bridge over Scott's Creek. In the midst of the fight, Captain Ewald was struck by a musket ball just below the knee. He recounted

> *I sat down and asked these eight brave men, of whom three already were wounded, not to leave their post, since the enemy could not come further as long as they stood firm.*[65]

---

[63] Ibid.
[64] Ibid.
[65] Ibid., 290

Lieutenant Bickell relieved Ewald, who was sent to the rear on a horse where he met 50 men heading towards the creek to reinforce the picket. When he neared the earthworks of Portsmouth he met General Arnold, who expressed his sorrow for Ewald's injury and asked whether the enemy would take the post at Scott's Creek. Captain Ewald angrily remembered

> *The question annoyed me, for he could see it all for himself. I said, 'No! As long as one jager lives, no damned American will come across the causeway!'*[66]

Ewald's pledge proved true, the Virginians never crossed the causeway and disengaged soon after Ewald was wounded.

The engagement, which LaFayette described as trifling in his report to General Washington, was certainly more significant to Captain Ewald and cost each side a handful of men. Ewald's picket detachment, including the ambush party that was overrun by LaFayette's advance, was mauled, but the survivors took pride with their commander for holding back the rebels. Ewald recorded in his diary that

> *I rejoiced over the magnificent behavior of my brave jagers, who with all éclat had thus distinguished themselves before the eyes of the English. For surely one jager had fought against thirty Americans today.*[67]

---

[66] Ibid., 291
[67] Ewald, 291

British Reinforcements Arrive

On the same day of the skirmish at Scott's Creek, General George Weedon, who had marched to Williamsburg a week earlier with militia troops from northern Virginia, wrote to Governor Jefferson with news that an unidentified naval squadron had arrived in Chesapeake Bay.[68] Weedon speculated that the ships were part of the long expected French fleet, but the following day, Commodore James Barron, in Hampton, informed the governor that the fleet was British.[69] British Vice-Admiral Marriott Arbuthnot, with twelve powerful warships including the 98 gun *H.M.S. London*, had prevailed in an engagement off the Virginia capes on March 16th, against an equally powerful French naval squadron under the command of the Chevalier Destouches.

For nearly two hours the two fleets blasted each other with broadsides, inflicting extensive damage and a number of injuries, but sinking no ships. It was actually the British who broke off the engagement, but in doing so, they sailed back into Chesapeake Bay while the French fleet headed back to Newport, Rhode Island to refit.

The news grew worse for the Virginians on March 26th when the British naval presence in Lynnhaven Bay more than doubled with the arrival of numerous transport ships. Captain Richard Barron counted over thirty vessels and upon word of this, General Steuben concluded what Virginia's authorities feared, that the transports were loaded with British

---

[68] Boyd, ed., "General Weedon to Governor Jefferson, 20 March, 1781," *The Papers of Thomas Jefferson*, Vol. 5, 185-86

[69] Boyd, ed., "James Barron to Governor Jefferson, 21 March, 1781," *The Papers of Thomas Jefferson*, Vol. 5, 187

reinforcements for Portsmouth.[70] These new troops, nearly 2500 strong, were commanded by General William Phillips, an experienced British commander who had been captured at Saratoga in 1777 and "held" in Virginia until his exchange in 1781. The arrival of General Phillips and his men altered General LaFayette's plans. He explained to General Washington that

> *The Return of the British fleet with vessels that Must Be transports from New York is a Circumstance which destroys Every Prospect of an operation Against Arnold. The Number of men is Not what I am afraid of* [as] *the French and Continental troops joined with the Militia must be Equal to a pretty Serious Siege, But Since the British fleet Have Returned and think themselves Safe in this Bay, I entertain very little Hopes of Seeing the French flag in Hampton Road.*[71]

With his hopes for a coordinated allied attack upon General Arnold dashed, General LaFayette headed back to Annapolis and proceeded to return to New York with his troops. General Washington, however, had other plans for LaFayette and his men.

---

[70] Boyd, ed., "Richard Barron to Governor Jefferson, 26 March, 1781," *The Papers of Thomas Jefferson*, Vol. 5, 238

[71] Idzerda, ed., "General LaFayette to General Washington, 26 March, 1781," *LaFayette in the Age of the American Revolution*, Vol. 3, 417

Chapter Nine

"The Militia Behaved with a Spirit and Resolution which would have done Honour to Veterans."

April – May 1781

Not all of the British ships that arrived in Virginia in late March remained in Portsmouth and Hampton Roads. A squadron of armed vessels, mostly privateers like the *Trimer* and *Surprise,* (which mounted between 18 to 24 guns each) sailed up Chesapeake Bay to the Potomac River.[1] They were joined by at least one British warship, the 16 gun sloop *H.M.S. Savage.* The squadron's main objective was to obstruct General LaFayette and his light infantry corps from crossing the Potomac River and marching south.[2] They also sought to raid the shoreline of both Virginia and Maryland and force Virginia's leaders to divert more attention to the Potomac. To accomplish this, the squadron dispersed at the mouth of the Potomac River. A few ships remained in the lower section of

---

[1] Boyd, ed. "Lindsay Opie and James Ball to Governor Jefferson, 12 April, 1781," *The Papers of Thomas Jefferson*, Vol. 5, 424 and
Palmer, ed., "Capt. W. Thomas to Thomas Symonds, 20 March, 1781," *Calendar of State Papers*, Vol. 1, 583

[2] Palmer, ed., "Capt. W. Thomas to Thomas Symonds, 20 March, 1781," *Calendar of State Papers*, Vol. 1, 583

the river near the Chesapeake and raided Northumberland County in Virginia and St. Mary's County in Maryland, while the remainder of the squadron sailed up the Potomac River towards Alexandria.

By April 1st, the *Trimer, Surprise*, and another unidentified sloop (probably the *Savage*) were anchored off Cedar Point, Maryland, about 40 miles up the Potomac from the Chesapeake.[3] Just beyond Cedar Point, the river curved to the west and the wind, which blew from the west, made it difficult for the ships to sail any further upriver, so they dropped anchor and sent a lone tender to the *Trimer,* with a crew of 21, ahead around Mathias Point to reconnoiter upriver. The tender likely overcame the wind by using its oars until the river turned north again (at Stafford County). From there the tender used its sails and the tide and made good progress upriver all the way to Fairfax County.

Raid on Alexandria

Early in the morning of April 2nd the British tender arrived off Alexandria and attempted to seize a merchant ship loaded with tobacco. Peter Wagner of Fairfax County recounted what happened:

> *A small Vessel came up to Alexandria and attempted to cut out of the Harbour a Baltimore Vessel lying there loaded with Tobacco. They boarded the vessel and had confined the men but being discovered by another Vessel in the Harbour the Town was alarmed which prevented the Enemy from carrying off the Vessel they had boarded.*[4]

---

[3] Boyd, ed., "Henry Lee Sr. to Governor Jefferson, 9 April, 1781," *The Papers of Thomas Jefferson,* Vol. 5, 393-94

[4] Boyd, ed.," Peter Wagner to Governor Jefferson, 3 April, 1781," *The Papers of Thomas Jefferson,* Vol. 5, 335-36

Potomac River

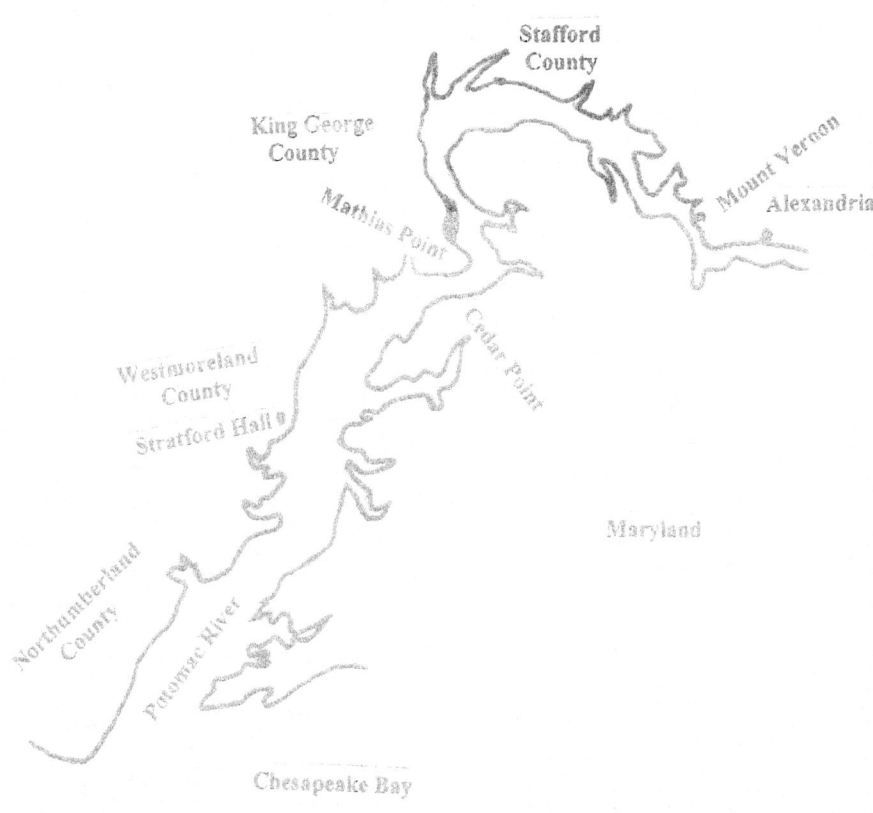

The privateers scrambled to return to their tender and escape downriver. They were pursued by two armed schooners that overtook them near Boyd's Hole in King George County.[5] In desperation, the privateers steered for the south shore of the Potomac. Colonel Henry Lee Sr., the County Lieutenant of Prince William County (and father of Light Horse Harry Lee) reported that

> *As soon as the Schooner found she Must be taken the Men took to their boats and landed on the Virginia Side of the River. Sixteen of them were taken by the Inhabitants, eight of whom were sent to Fredericksburg from whence I hear they are sent to Winchester. The others were sent up in the Vessels that Pursued them to Alexandria and are Confined in that Goal.*[6]

One of the prisoners informed Lee of their intentions had they escaped Alexandria undetected with the captured tobacco ship:

> *If the Enemy had Succeeded at Alexandria they intended; one of the Prisoners say, to have burnt Genl. Washingtons Houses, Plundered Colo. Mason and myself and endeavoured to have made me a Prisoner.*[7]

Had the tender managed to flee just a few more miles downriver, past Mathias Point and the large bend in the river, they may have reached the protection of the *Trimer* and *Surprise*. Unaware, or perhaps unable to assist the tender due to the strong westerly wind that prevented the fleet from sailing around Mathias Point, the privateers at Cedar Point spent much of April 2nd seizing tobacco from the warehouses

---

[5] Boyd, ed., "Henry Lee Sr. to Governor Jefferson, 9 April, 1781," *The Papers of Thomas Jefferson,* Vol. 5, 393-94
[6] Ibid.
[7] Ibid.

along the Maryland shore. At some point in the day, probably at ebb tide, the fleet weighed anchor and moved downriver, stopping at Cole's Point in Westmoreland County to raid the property of Robert Carter and "seize" thirty of his slaves.[8]

Cedar Point and Hooes Ferry

By April 3rd the British raiders had dropped even further downriver to St. George's Island, near the mouth of the St. Mary's River in Maryland, some thirty miles southeast of Cedar Point.[9] Richard Barnes of Maryland warned Maryland's Governor, Thomas Sims Lee, of their presence.

> *The Enemy have plundered many since I last wrote to you and are now on St. Georges Island. That party that are there have, as I have been informed, four Sloops & four or five Barges. There has been several Brushes with them and the Militia in which we have had one Man wounded.*[10]

The bulk of the privateer fleet returned upriver to Cedar Point on April 5th and turned its attention to the Virginia shore. Gerrard Hooes operated a ferry crossing in King George County, opposite from Cedar Point, and it became the next target of the raiders. John Skinker, the County Lieutenant of King George County, reported to Governor Jefferson that on the evening of April 5th,

---

[8] Ibid.
[9] J. Hall Pleasants, ed., "Richard Barnes to Thomas Sims Lee, 3 April, 1781", *Maryland Archives*, Vol. 47, (Maryland Historical Society, 1930), 159
[10] Ibid.

> *Three large Schooners and some smaller Vessels of the Enemy* [anchored] *opposite Hoes Ferry.... About 8 o' clock at night* [a party] *landed at Mr. Garrard Hoes, plundered his House and what they could not carry away they utterly distroyd. They also took off 4 of his Negroes and set fire to his House.*[11]

Fortunately for Mr. Hooes, the commander of the British landing party allowed him to extinguish the fire before it did too much damage to his home.[12]

The British fleet continued a little further upriver, plundering other homes along the Virginia shore. Robert Washington of Choptank Creek, a relative of General Washington, lost four slaves and nearly all of his furniture, which was pillaged and destroyed by a party of privateers.[13]

Maryland was not spared the privateers wrath; raiding parties landed across the Potomac where they plundered and torched buildings indiscriminately. Daniel Jenifer was in Port Tobacco during one raid and informed Maryland's governor that,

> *On Thursday evening* [April 5th] *two arm'd Schooners with a Cutter and some Barges came above Cedar point. Landed some of their Men at Mrs. Youngs Ferry, and plundered her of her most valuable Effects*[14]

The privateers stole money, clothing, furniture, livestock, and tobacco and destroyed much of what they could not take with

---

[11] Boyd, ed., "John Skinker to Governor Jefferson, 11 April, 1781," *The Papers of Thomas Jefferson*, Vol. 5, 406
[12] Ibid.
[13] Ibid.
[14] Pleasants, ed., "Daniel Jenifer to Governor Thomas Sims Lee, 8 April, 1781," *Maryland Archives*, Vol. 47, 172-73

them. They also seized slaves and burned numerous buildings. Although a handful of local militia gathered, the poorly armed Maryland troops were powerless to stop the raiders.

Alarm Spreads in Virginia

The situation along the Virginia shore was not quite as dire as that along the Maryland shore. Although state officials in Richmond were still unaware of the severity of the crisis, county leaders in Caroline, Westmoreland, King George, Stafford, Prince William, and Fairfax, acted to defend their counties. John Skinker, of King George County, assembled 260 armed militia at Boyd's Hole to protect the nearby tobacco warehouses and repel any attempted landing of the privateers.[15] Skinker regretted that he was unable to arm more men, writing to Governor Jefferson that, *"I am really sorry to inform your Excellency that not one third of my Militia have Arms fit for service."*[16] Skinker was particularly concerned about Jefferson's earlier order to send 114 armed King George County militia to Williamsburg:

> *As the situation of the Inhabitants of Potomak is very alarming and distressing and we have near 30 Miles of County to protect from the depredation of these Pirates, I beg your Excellency and the Council would take the matter under consideration, and Countermand the order for sending 114 Men with Guns (which is impossible to spare) from this County.*[17]

---

[15] Boyd, ed., "Edmund Read to Governor Jefferson, 10 April, 1781," *The Papers of Thomas Jefferson*, Vol. 5, 399

[16] Boyd, ed., "John Skinker to Governor Jefferson, 11 April, 1781," *The Papers of Thomas Jefferson*, Vol. 5, 406

[17] Ibid.

Edmund Read, the County Lieutenant of nearby Caroline County (which was not directly threatened by the privateers), responded to reports of their presence in the Potomac by leading a detachment of volunteer cavalry eastward to Hooes Ferry:

> *I thought It my Indispenceable duty to march down to the Assistance of these People,* [with] *such of my* [volunteer horsemen] *as cood by any meens do any Cervice (tho Verry Poor) Hoping to Drive off those Plunderers with the Assistance of the Gentlemen Vollenteers of this Place.*[18]

Reports of the fleet's presence at Hooes Ferry (and their intention to sail upriver) spread northward, into Stafford, Prince William, and Fairfax counties. County Lieutenant Henry Lee Sr., reported to Governor Jefferson from Prince William County that

> *On receiving official Notice from the County Lieutenant of Stafford that the Enemy were making up the river and the Town of Dumfries with the Warehouses on Quantico Creek might be their Object and that the Inhabitants might be Secured against these Plunderers I immediately ordered all the Militia that Could be Armed to rendezvous at the Mouth of Quantico* [which amounted to] *about forty.*[19]

---

[18] Boyd, ed., "Edmund Read to Governor Jefferson, 7 April, 1781," *The Papers of Thomas Jefferson*, Vol. 5, 371

[19] Boyd, ed., "Henry Lee Sr. to Governor Jefferson, 9 April, 1781," *The Papers of Thomas Jefferson*, Vol. 5, 393-94

The disappointing militia turnout in Prince William County was due largely to the high number of county militia who were already on duty in Williamsburg. With them had gone most of the county's arms.

Skirmish at Stratford Hall

For a few days it was uncertain whether the militia in northern Virginia actually needed to be alarmed or assembled; a strong northwesterly wind continued to prevent the privateer fleet from sailing around Mathias Point. By April 9th, the fleet had actually dropped down the river again to Westmoreland County where they sent raiding parties ashore near Stratford Hall. The raiders were confronted by Colonel Richard Henry Lee and the Westmoreland County militia. Lee recalled that he was

> *With the Militia on the Shore of Potomac where we had a very warm engagement with a party of the enemy, about 90 men, who landed from two Brigs, a Schooner, and a smaller Vessel under a very heavy cannonade from the Vessels of War – the affair ended by the enemy being forced to reimbark with some haste... Their Vessels are yet near the Shore, and by a deserter...I learn that their Vessels with a ship of 20 guns now lying off, are bound up the river, as high as Alexandria to interrupt the passage of Troops across Potomac.*[20]

By the next day (April 10th) the fleet had returned upriver to Hooes Ferry. Colonel Edmund Reed was still posted there with his Caroline County volunteer cavalry and reported that

---

[20] Boyd, ed., "Richard Henry Lee to Governor Jefferson, 9 April, 1781," *The Papers of Thomas Jefferson*, Vol. 5, 394

> *This morning* [the enemy] *appeared* [off] *Mr. Hooes where I was Posted with my Dragoons and some few Militia...I followed them along shore to* [Boyd's Hole]... *The whole of the fleet amounted to two twenty-four gun ships, two Eighteen* [gun ships], *and six transports and tenders. They seem to be crouded with men.*[21]

Alexandria

A shift in the wind finally allowed the British squadron to sail upriver around Mathias Point and it passed Boyd's Hole without incident. Colonel Skinker watched them pass and reported to Governor Jefferson that the fleet consisted of, "*4 Ships none less than 20 Guns,* [plus] *two Brigs and two Tenders.*"[22]

The fleet sailed through the evening and reached Alexandria by the morning of April 11th. Robert Mitchell of Georgetown, Maryland was in Alexandria and described the town's reaction to the fleet's arrival:

> *Yesterday on my Arrival at Alexandria I found the town in much confusion occasioned by a small Fleet that appeared off the Town – say, three Ships, two Brigs and two Schooners. Two of the Ships appear to be of 18 Guns each, the other I cou'd not make out what number of Guns she mounted, but believe her to be a Frigate.*[23]

---

[21] Boyd, ed., "Edmund Read to Governor Jefferson, 10 April, 1781," *The Papers of Thomas Jefferson*, Vol. 5, 399

[22] Boyd, ed., "John Skinker to Governor Jefferson, 11 April, 1781," *The Papers of Thomas Jefferson*, Vol. 5, 406

[23] Boyd, ed., "Robert Mitchell to Governor Jefferson, 12 April, 1781," *The Papers of Thomas Jefferson*, Vol. 5, 423

Mitchell added a troubling comment:

> *The Lieutenant of the County expecting a sufficient number of Militia from the Country...to defend the Town had the colours hoisted in the Fort, but finding the Militia did not come In so fast as he had reason to expect, by the persuation of the Inhabitants the colours were taken down.*[24]

Mitchell's observation suggests that the townsfolk had decided not to fight. With so few armed militia in town and appeals for help to the authorities of Prince George County across the river in Maryland falling on deaf ears, (they had their own property to defend) it is not surprising that the townsfolk contemplated submission.

As it turned out, Alexandria was spared the trauma of a raid because the privateers never attempted to come ashore. They spent most of April 11th trying to free two vessels, (one of the large ships and one of the brigs) that were grounded in shallow water just below the town.[25]

By the next day, militia reinforcements from the surrounding countryside emboldened Alexandria's defenders and dissuaded the privateers from landing. The privateers lingered a few miles below Alexandria, directing their attention to the Maryland shore where they skirmished with the local militia and burned the plantation of Colonel Lyles (after he rejected a demand for fresh provisions for the fleet).[26]

---

[24] Ibid.
[25] Ibid.
[26] Pleasants, ed., "Joshua Beall to Governor Thomas Sim Lee," 15 April, *Maryland Archives*, Vol. 47, 188

Mount Vernon is Threatened

The next day, April 13th, an incident occurred at Mount Vernon that absolutely appalled General Washington in New York. For nearly six years, General Washington's cousin, Lund Washington, had served as the caretaker of Mount Vernon in General Washington's absence. The commander-in-chief expressed complete faith in Lund's stewardship of his property, but this trust in Lund was shaken when General Washington learned that his caretaker had entered into negotiations with the commander of the *H.M.S. Savage* over the return of a large number of runaway slaves from Mount Vernon. General LaFayette, who like Washington was greatly troubled by Lund's actions, informed Washington in late April that

> *When the Enemy Came to your House Many Negroes deserted to them. This piece of News did not affect me much as I little Value* [slavery] *– But You Cannot Conceive How Unhappy I Have Been to Hear that Mr. Lund Washington Went on Board the Enemy's vessels and Consented to give them provisions.*[27]

LaFayette speculated that as General Washington's representative, Lund's actions would, *"certainly Have a Bad effect, and Contrasts with Spirited Answers from Some Neighbours that Had their Houses Burnt Accordingly."*[28]

General Washington received LaFayette's letter on May 4th, five days after a letter from Lund arrived explaining his

---

[27] Idzerda, ed., "General LaFayette to General Washington, 23 April, 1781," *LaFayette in the Age of the American Revolution,* Vol. 4, 60-61
[28] Ibid.

actions. General Washington had already responded to his cousin with a stern reprimand:

> *I am very sorry to hear of your loss; I am a little sorry to hear of my own; but which gives me most concern, is, that you should go on board the enemys Vessels, and furnish them with refreshments. It would have been a less painful circumstance to me, to have heard, that in consequence of your non-compliance with their request, they had burnt my House, and laid the Plantation in ruins. You ought to have considered yourself as my representative, and should have reflected on the bad example of communicating with the enemy, and making a voluntary offer of refreshments to them with a view to prevent a conflagration...But to go on board their Vessels; carry them refreshments; commune with a parcel of plundering Scoundrels, and request a favor by asking the surrender of my Negroes, was exceedingly ill-judged, and 'tis to be feared, will be unhappy in its consequences, as it will be a precedent for others...Unless a stop to* [the British raids occurs], *I have little doubt of its ending in the loss of all my Negroes, and in the destruction of my Houses; but I am prepared for the event....*[29]

Although Lund Washington's letter to General Washington has not been found, an account from the Marquis de Chastellux (a Frenchman travelling in Virginia in the spring of 1781 who had occasion to discuss the incident with Lund) claimed that

---

[29] John C. Fitzgerald, ed., "George Washington to Lund Washington, 30 April, 1781," *The Writings of George Washington*, Vol. 22, 14-15

> Mr. Lund Washington, a relation of the General's and who managed all his affairs during his [long] absence with the army, informed me that an English frigate [the 16 gun H.M.S. Savage] having come up the Potomac, a party was landed who set fire to and destroyed some gentlemen's houses on the Maryland side in sight of Mount Vernon, the General's house; after which the Captain [Thomas Graves] sent a boat on shore to the General's demanding a large supply of provisions, etc. with a menace of burning it likewise in case of a refusal.[30]

The Marquis failed to mention Washington's loss of 17 slaves (who fled to the British upon their arrival). He instead noted Lund Washington's defiant reply to the British commander. Lund informed Captain Graves that

> When [General Washington] engaged in the contest he had put all to stake, and was well aware of the exposed situation of his house and property, in consequence of which he had given [Lund] orders by no means to comply with any such demands, for that he would make no unworthy compromise with the enemy, and was ready to meet the fate of his neighbors.[31]

This reply angered Captain Graves and he positioned the *Savage* closer to shore as if to bombard Mount Vernon. At the same time, the British commander invited Lund aboard his

---

[30] Marquis de Chastellux, *Travels in North America in the Years 1780, 1781, and 1782*, Vol. 2, 597
[31] Ibid.

ship to discuss matters further. Lund accepted (in hopes of regaining General Washington's slaves) and brought with him, "*a small present of poultry, of which he begged the Captain's acceptance.*"[32] Lund told the Marquis that

> *His presence* [onboard the *Savage*] *produced the best effect, he was hospitably received notwithstanding he repeated the same sentiments with the same firmness. The captain expressed his personal respect for the character of the General....*[33]

Captain Graves shrewdly assured Lund that nothing but his misunderstanding of Lund's defiant reply could have compelled him to, "*entertain the idea of taking the smallest measure offensive to so illustrious a character as the General.*"[34] In other words, Graves gave Lund a chance to reconsider his initial refusal to comply with Captain Graves's demands. This time Lund acquiesced to the British commander. The Marquis recorded that

> *Mr.* [Lund] *Washington, after spending some time in perfect harmony on board, returned* [to Mount Vernon] *and instantly dispatched sheep, hogs, and an abundant supply of other articles as a present to the English frigate.*[35]

The gesture failed to gain the return of Washington's slaves, but it did preserve General Washington's home and buildings from destruction.

---

[32] Ibid.
[33] Ibid.
[34] Ibid.
[35] Ibid.

The Privateers Depart

Across the river in Maryland, Colonel Lyles was not so lucky. A party of privateers returned to his burnt out estate in Prince George County and added insult to injury by stealing some hogs. They paid a steep price for them, however, for a body of militia challenged them and captured eleven of the raiders.[36] This marked the last significant action of the privateers; their two week expedition up the Potomac River concluded with their departure from the river the next day.

The expedition's primary objective, to delay General LaFayette's crossing of the Potomac, proved to be unnecessary as LaFayette and his light infantry corps were still a hundred miles to the north, on the banks of the Susquehanna River. The fleet's secondary objective, to spread destruction along the river, was fully achieved. The squadron met little resistance and suffered few losses but inflicted thousands of dollars of property damage and freed scores of slaves. Its presence on the Potomac also strained Virginia's militia forces along the river and reaffirmed the widespread vulnerability of Virginia to attack by water.

Two weeks had passed since the privateer fleet had entered the Potomac River and British activity in the rest of Virginia had remained relatively quiet. This was about to change, for the new British commander in Virginia, General William Phillips, was determined to lead a powerful British force up the James River to once again disrupt Virginia's supply system and war effort.

---

[36] Pleasants, ed., "Joshua Beall to Governor Thomas Sims Lee, 15 April," *Maryland Archives*, Vol. 47, 188

General Phillips Sails Upriver

On April 18th, over 2,000 British troops under General Phillips sailed out of Portsmouth and up the James River.[37] Their destination was Williamsburg, where Phillips hoped to surprise a body of militia, (estimated at between 600 to 800 strong) in the former capital.[38] General Arnold accompanied General Phillips and reported to General Clinton in New York that the British force consisted of two battalions of light infantry, parts of the 76th and 80th Regiments, all of the Queen's Rangers and Yagers as well as Arnold's small American Legion corps.[39]

The British fleet of transports and warships was outpaced by rebel express riders who spread the alarm of the British movement up both sides of the James River. Lieutenant Colonel James Innes, who had assumed command of the militia in Williamsburg upon General Thomas Nelson's prolonged illness in March, learned of the enemy's approach on the afternoon of April 18th and rushed word to Richmond, where Jefferson received it the following morning. He immediately ordered the counties surrounding Richmond and Petersburg to call out all of their militia. Those from Henrico,

---

[37] Willcox, ed., *The American Rebellion: Sir Henry Clinton's Narrative...*", 280
 Note: Thomas Jefferson claimed General Phillips had 2300 troops with him and many secondary sources put the number at 2500.

[38] Simcoe, 189 and Richard K.. Macmaster, "The Journal of Dr. Robert Honeyman," *The Virginia Magazine of History and Biography*, Vol. 79, No.4, October, 1971, 392 and Mays, ed., "Edmund Pendleton to James Madison, 30 April, 1781," *The Letters and Papers of Edmund Pendleton*, Vol. 1, 352

[39] Davies, ed., "General Arnold to General Clinton, 12 May, 1781," *Documents of the American Revolution*, Vol. 20, 142

Goochland, and Hanover were instructed to march to Richmond. Those from Powhatan, and Cumberland were to march to Manchester (directly across the James River from Richmond) and the militia of Prince George, Dinwiddie, Amelia, and Chesterfield were ordered to gather in Petersburg.[40]

Back in Williamsburg, Lieutenant Colonel Innes prepared, *"to take the most expedient measures my poor Judgment dictates for the honor and Service of the State."*[41] Over the course of April 19th, the British flotilla anchored off Burwell's Ferry (the most likely landing spot for the British if Williamsburg was indeed their destination). From his position aboard a transport ship a mile offshore, Lieutenant Colonel Simcoe noted that, *"The enemy had thrown up entrenchments to secure the landing, and these appeared to be fully manned."*[42] Whether this meant the Virginians intended to resist a British landing was to be determined the next day.

Lieutenant Colonel Simcoe and his Queen's Rangers led the British assault on Burwell's Ferry in the early afternoon of April 20th. Led by a single gunboat with a six pound cannon on its bow, longboats transported the Rangers straight for the ferry landing. About half way to shore all of the long boats swung hard right. Assisted by the wind and tide, the sailors and troops rowed furiously downriver towards a creek a mile below Burwell's Ferry. The gunboat remained off of the Ferry landing and raked the shore with cannon fire to dissuade the militia at Burwell's from leaving their entrenchments and

---

[40] Boyd, ed., "To the County Lieutenants of Henrico and Certain Other Counties, 19 April, 1781," *The Papers of Thomas Jefferson*, Vol. 5, 496
[41] Boyd, ed., "James Innes to Governor Jefferson, 19 April, 1781," *The Papers of Thomas Jefferson*, Vol. 5, 499
[42] Simcoe, 190

redeploying down river to oppose Simcoe's landing. As a result, Simcoe and his rangers landed without opposition or loss.[43]

With their entrenchments flanked and the main force of General Phillips still to come ashore, the militia at Burwell's Ferry abandoned their post and withdrew to Williamsburg, just four miles inland. Although Lieutenant Colonel Innes was undoubtedly disappointed at the lack of fight in his troops, he was much more disturbed to learn (inaccurately as it turned out) that, *"several armed vessels and 16 flat bottom Boats* [had] *proceeded up to James Town where...they have since Landed."*[44] In truth, the British force in question sailed past Jamestown to the Chickahominy River, where a portion of the troops under Lieutenant Colonel Dundas disembarked while the light infantry battalions under Lieutenant Colonel Robert Abercrombie continued up the Chickahominy River by boat towards the state naval shipyard.

Regardless of the inaccurate report about Jamestown Island, Lieutenant Colonel Innes realized that he now had two strong enemy forces on either side of him and risked becoming trapped. He reported to Governor Jefferson that

> *As soon as I found the Designs of the Enemy to circumvent me, I moved the troops to this place* [Allen's Ordinary – six miles northwest of Williamsburg] *which is the nearest position to the Town that can be taken with safety while the Enemy are masters of the water....*[45]

---

[43] Ibid., 191

[44] Boyd, ed., "James Innes to Governor Jefferson, 20 April, 1781," *The Papers of Thomas Jefferson*, Vol. 5, 506

[45] Ibid.

Innes added that, *"the Troops under my Command are extremely harassed having laid upon their arms for upwards of fifty hours during such time they have received no Sustinance."* [46]

While General Phillips and General Arnold settled into Williamsburg unopposed on April 20th, Lieutenant Colonel Simcoe led 40 cavalrymen on a dash to Yorktown to surprise a small garrison of rebel artillerists posted along the York River. Despite the need to take shelter from a fierce storm during the night (which prevented Simcoe from reaching Yorktown until morning) the small British party of horse surprised and routed the rebel garrison, some of who escaped by fleeing by boat across the York River. Simcoe spiked the abandoned cannon and rode back to Williamsburg to rejoin General Phillips.[47] A few miles west of Williamsburg, Lieutenant Colonel Ambercrombie, against no opposition, destroyed the Virginia State Navy shipyard along with the naval stores and vessels under construction on the Chickahominy River.

Disappointed that the militia had escaped up the peninsula, General Phillips marched out of Williamsburg the next day (April 22nd) and reassembled his entire force at the mouth of the Chickahominy. They re-boarded their transports and sailed upriver on April 23rd, passing Hood's Point (inexplicably unmanned by the rebels) without incident. By nightfall they reached Westover, where they anchored.

Anxiety reigned in Richmond as Virginia's leaders scrambled to organize another defense of the capital. Only a small number of the summoned militia had arrived in

---

[46] Ibid.
[47] Simcoe, 191

Richmond, General LaFayette, with approximately 900 continentals fit for duty, had only reached Alexandria (100 miles away) and Lieutenant Colonel Innes with approximately 700 militia had withdrawn across the Pamunkey River, some 25 miles northwest of Richmond. Innes explained his withdrawal to Governor Jefferson:

> *Encumbered* [with] *upwards of one hundred sick and wounded, without Hospital Stores or Surgeons, burthened too with twenty waggons loaded with public Stores* [and with troops] *almost worn down with Fatigue and Hunger...* [I crossed the Pamunkey and] *shall now have it in my Power to dispose of the Invalids, give the Troops a little Refreshment, send the Baggage and Stores off to a Place of safety, and...march up towards Richmond with the Troops light, disencumber'd and refreshed....*[48]

Upon news of the British fleet's initial movement up the James, General Peter Muhlenberg, who was encamped near Suffolk, led approximately 700 militia northward. They marched 13 miles on April 19th, from their camp at Broadwater to Wall's Bridge, (which spanned the Blackwater River). Darkness forced a halt, but upon word that the enemy fleet had anchored near Williamsburg, Muhlenberg resumed his march the next day. He halted at Cabin Point on April 20th, well above the British, and waited for General Phillips's next move. It came three days later, when the British fleet sailed past Hood's Point on its way to Westover.

---

[48] Boyd, ed., "James Innes to Governor Jefferson, 23 April, 1781," *The Papers of Thomas Jefferson*, Vol. 5, 539-540

The Virginians now realized that General Phillips was heading for either Richmond or Petersburg. General Steuben had already ordered the military supplies and provisions amassed at Petersburg, Richmond, and Chesterfield Courthouse moved westward, and Governor Jefferson had ordered local militia to assemble at each location. When the British fleet anchored off of City Point at the mouth of the Appomattox River on April 24th, and unloaded over 2,000 troops and four cannon, it was finally clear where they were headed; their destination was Petersburg.

Battle of Petersburg

The town of Petersburg lay about twelve miles up the Appomattox River from City Point and served as an important supply depot for the Virginians. General Steuben defended Petersburg with approximately 1,000 militia (Muhlenberg's 700 troops plus a few hundred local militia from Prince George, Dinwiddie, and Amelia counties). Steuben explained his decision to oppose the vastly superior enemy at Petersburg to General Greene immediately after the battle:

> *I had not more than One thousand men left to oppose the Enemies advance. In this Critical situation there were many reasons against risking a Total Defeat. The Loss of Arms was a principal one, & on the other hand to retire without some shew of Resistance would have intimidated the Inhabitants and have encouraged the Enemy to further incursions. This*

last consideration determined me to defend the place as far as our inferiority of numbers would permit. [49]

Outnumbered more than two to one, General Steuben divided the militia into three detachments. A small detachment was posted to guard the bridge (and escape route) across the Appomattox River should the Virginians fail to stop the enemy advance (as expected). Two brass 6 pound cannon covered the bridge from the heights above the north bank of the river and a detachment of infantry supported the cannon at the bridge.[50]

About half a mile to the east of the bridge on the outskirts of Petersburg were two militia battalions (about 500 men total) under Lieutenant Colonel Ralph Faulkner and Lieutenant Colonel John Slaughter. They were deployed behind a shallow, marshy creek (Lieutenant Run), their left flank anchored on the tobacco warehouses along the Appomattox River and their right anchored about 500 yards to the south on rising ground upon the estate of Mrs. Mary Bolling.[51] A half mile to their front, on the eastern edge of the village of Blandford were two additional militia battalions under Lieutenant Colonel Thomas Merriweather and Lieutenant Colonel John Dick. Approximately 300 men strong, they were positioned on a small rise behind Poor's Creek and represented the first line of defense for the Virginians.[52]

---

[49] Dennis Conrad, ed., "Steuben to Greene, 25 April, 1781," *The Papers of General Nathanael Greene*, Vol. 8, (University of North Carolina Press, 1995), 147

[50] Robert Davis, *The Revolutionary War: The Battle of Petersburg*, E. & R. Davis, 2002, 10

[51] Ibid.

[52] Campbell, Charles, ed. "Banister to Bland, 16 May, 1781" *Bland Papers*, Vol. 1, (Petersburg, VA, 1840), 68

Battle of Petersburg

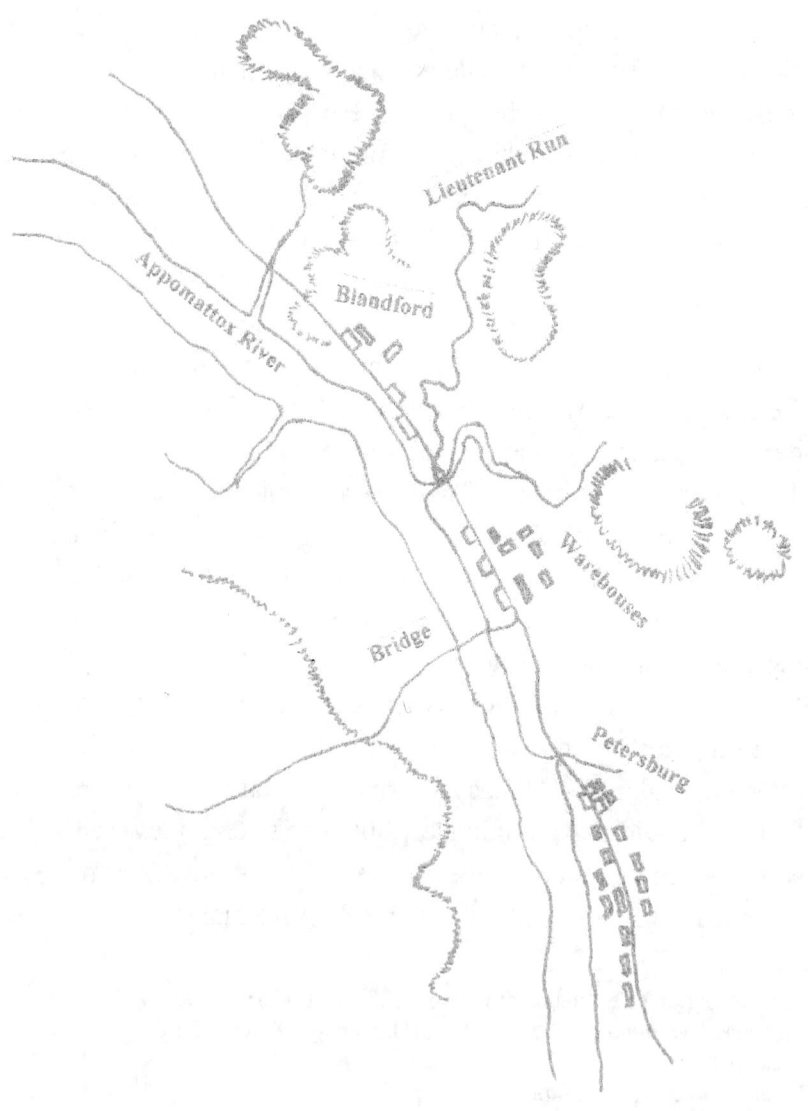

Small parties of militia were posted in advance of the first line to warn of the enemy's approach.

General Phillips and his force of over 2,000 British troops (with four 6 pound cannon) began their march from City Point to Petersburg around mid-morning on April 25th. Eleven flat bottomed boats armed with swivel guns and loaded with men and supplies advanced up the Appomattox River alongside the British column. Small militia parties posted in the neck of land between the James and Appomattox Rivers first noticed the enemy boats and fired ineffectively at them.[53] The British continued on and halted within a mile of Blandford around 2:00 p.m. to rest and refresh themselves.

General Phillips could see the militia's first line deployed beyond Poor's Creek and he realized his force significantly outnumbered the Virginians, so he formed his troops into a line of battle that extended well past the militia's right flank and ordered a frontal assault. Lieutenant Colonel Abercrombie led a battalion of light infantry and the jagers straight at the left wing of the militia line while Lieutenant Colonel Dundas struck their right with the 76th and 80th Regiments and tried to turn the rebel flank, forcing them to the river.[54]

Although they were indeed greatly outnumbered, the first militia line temporarily foiled Phillips's plan and held its ground for approximately thirty minutes. The Virginians used hedges, fences, and buildings for cover and kept up a hot fire on the British.[55] When the British boats threatened the left flank of the first militia line, Colonel Faulkner at the 2nd line rushed a company of militia to the river to confront the boats. Daniel Trabue, a Virginian soldier, recalled the incident:

---

[53] Davis, 12
[54] Ibid., 14
[55] Ibid., 16, 18

> *Colonel* [Faulkner] *called out for volunteers to go with him to take a britesh vesil that was ½ mile below and aground....The company was made up and started in 5 Menuts. We went in a run, and before we got to them they fired on us. We went on the bank oppersit the vessil within 60 or 70 yards and fired on them as fast as we could load and shoot. They fired several times at us. When Capt. Epperson saw them putting their Mach to their cannon he would cry out, "Shot!" All of us would fall Down and the cannon ball generally went over our heads. We would Jump up and fire again at the men we could see on Deck and Did actually kill the most of them....* [Suddenly] *Col.* [Faulker] *came riding as fast as he could, hollowing, "Retreat! Retreat! Retreat!" We started and when he Met us he told us their was several hundred of the enemy a surrounding us. We run a long* [way] *up the river...to our redgement.*[56]

The force of the British assault eventually overwhelmed the first line of Virginians, and they withdrew towards Petersburg before the British were able to envelope them,

    The second militia line, partially reinforced by some of the more resolute troops from the first line, made an equally determined stand on the edge of Petersburg.. Private George Connolly claimed that he fired twenty-three rounds (virtually an entire cartridge box) before wounds forced him to retire.[57] Over the span of an hour, two British charges were repelled. General Phillips finally used his cannon to break the Virginians, who withdrew towards the lone bridge across the Appomattox River.

---

[56] Lillie DuPuy VanCulin Harper, ed., *Colonial Men and Times: Containing the Journal of Col. Daniel Trabue*, 90-91
[57] Davis, 20

The British pressed the militia, but Steuben's rear guard used the town's warehouses and buildings for cover and maintained a hot fire that slowed their pursuit.[58] As the militia crossed the river, they fanned out on the other side to provide support for the beleaguered rearguard. Daniel Trabue remembered:

> *As soon as we Got over the bridge we went above and below the bridge on the edge of the water to save the Retreat over the bridge.... When the enemy Discovered our men crossing the bridge they rushed after them.... The bridge was not wide enough for the men to get over fast enough. The enemy came Rushing Down to cut off our rear...charging with their bayonets. And our men resisted and Defended themselves some little, but at last they* [captured] *about 40 or 50 of our men before our faces within 60 or 70 yards of us but they paid dear for these men. Our regiment at the bridge fired 10 or 12 times each. I fired 13 very fair shoots.... And when I fired I looked where I shot at and I could see them tilt over. And when they* [the British] *Retreated up the hill from the bridge they run, as our men would keep on fireing at their flanks so as not to hurt our men who was Just made prisoners.*[59]

The Virginians' heavy fire from the opposite riverbank, along with the removal of the bridge planks by the retreating militia, prevented the British from charging across the bridge.[60] Phillip's troops contented themselves with a few parting cannon shots at the Virginians to conclude the affair.

---

[58] Lillie DuPuy VanCulin Harper, ed., *Colonial Men and Times: Containing the Journal of Col. Daniel Trabue*, 90-91

[59] Ibid., 90

[60] Conrad, ed., "Baron Steuben to General Greene, 25 April, 1781," *The Papers of General Nathanael Greene*, Vol. 8, 148

The Battle of Petersburg ended as expected, in a British victory. Casualty reports, as is often the case, varied significantly. General LaFayette (presumably reporting militia losses received from General Steuben) informed General Greene three days after the battle that, *"our loss it is said is about 20 killed and wounded."*[61] General Muhlenberg, a participant in the fight, estimated militia losses, *"will not exceed sixty."*[62] Governor Jefferson reported a similar number to General Washington noting that, *"Our Loss was between sixty and seventy killed, wounded and taken."* Jefferson added that the enemy's losses were probably equivalent, *"As they broke twice and run like Sheep till supported by fresh Troops."*[63]

Not surprisingly, British estimates of American casualties were much higher, with General Arnold and Lieutenant Colonel Simcoe both claiming 100 militia killed and wounded. General Arnold, writing to General Clinton on behalf on a gravely ill General Phillips in early May, reported British losses at Petersburg as only one man killed and ten men wounded.[64] It's hard to believe given the stubborn resistance of the militia at Petersburg that the British suffered so few casualties, but all the British accounts of their losses at Petersburg describe them as trifling.

Although victory belonged to the British, General Steuben and General Muhlenberg were pleased that their outnumbered troops fought as well as they did.[65] General Muhlenberg, who

---

[61] Idzerda, ed., "General LaFayette to General Greene, 28 April, 1781," *LaFayette in the Age of the American Revolution*, Vol. 4, 68
[62] Muhlenberg, *The Life of Major-General Peter Muhlenberg*, 250
[63] Boyd, ed., "Thomas Jefferson to General Washington, 9 May, 1781," *The Papers of Thomas Jefferson*, Vol. 5, 623
[64] Banastre Tarleton, "General Benedict Arnold to General Henry Clinton, 12 May, 1781," *A History of the Campaigns of 1780 and 1781 in the Southern Provinces of North America*, (North Stratford, NH: Ayer Co., 1999), 335 (Originally printed in 1787)
[65] Conrad, ed., "Baron Steuben to General Greene, 25 April, 1781," *The Papers of General Nathanael Greene*, Vol. 8, 148

appears to have spent most of the battle within the militia lines east of the bridge, bragged to his brother that, *"every inch of ground to the bridge was warmly disputed...*[and that] *the militia behaved with a spirit and resolution which would have done honour to veterans."*[66] General Steuben was equally complimentary of Muhlenberg, reporting to General Greene that

> *General Muhlenberg merits my particular acknowledgements for the good disposition he made & the great Gallantry with which he executed it.*[67]

As night fell on Petersburg, General Steuben led the militia northward towards Chesterfield Courthouse, ten miles above Petersburg. General Phillips did not pursue and spent the night at Petersburg, satisfied that his army had driven the Virginians from an important rebel supply depot. The British lingered in Petersburg another day, burning some tobacco warehouses along the river (along with 4,000 hogsheads of tobacco) and a few small boats, but sparing the town from destruction.[68]

On April 27th, General Phillips marched his army across the Appomattox, dividing his force. General Arnold led the 76th and 80th Regiments, the Queen's Rangers, his own American Legion and part of the jagers towards Osborne's Landing, ten miles north of Petersburg on the James River, to challenge the remnants of the Virginia State Navy. General Phillips led the remainder of his force, which included two battalions of light infantry, the cavalry of the Queen's Rangers, and the rest of the jagers, to Chesterfield Courthouse, the muster point for Virginia's continental recruits.[69] Over 150 log huts capable of housing 2,000 recruits had been

---

[66] Muhlenberg, *The Life of Major-General Peter Muhlenberg*, 250
[67] Conrad, ed., "Steuben to Greene, 25 April, 1781," *The Papers of General Nathanael Greene*, Vol. 8, 148
[68] Tarleton, "General Arnold to General Clinton, 12 May, 1781," 335
[69] Ibid.

constructed at Chesterfield Courthouse, but when General Phillips arrived he found the encampment deserted. General Steuben had moved on to Richmond to rendezvous with General LaFayette and his continental reinforcements. Phillips contented himself with burning the huts and destroying 300 barrels of flour.[70]

Battle of Osborne Landing

While General Phillips raided Chesterfield Court House, Benedict Arnold approached Osborne's Landing to confront the bulk of Virginia's state navy. The potential firepower of the small flotilla at Osborne's Landing was impressive and included the 18 gun *Apollo*, two 16 gun ships, the *Tempest* and *Renown*, the 14 gun *Jefferson*, and several other vessels.[71] Fully manned, these ships held nearly 700 men, but desertions and the lack of new recruits meant that only 78 men were on duty.[72] Just five men crewed the *Apollo,* and only six were aboard the *Tempest*. Both ships, when fully manned, held crews of 120 each.[73]

This undermanned force, along with a few hundred Virginia militia on the northern bank of the James, confronted Arnold's force around noon on April 27th. Arnold hoped the rebel commander would realize the futility of resistance and sent a flag of truce to Captain William Lewis demanding the flotilla's surrender. Lewis spurned the demand and vowed to fight.[74]

---

[70] Ibid.
[71] Boyd, ed., "James Maxwell to Thomas Jefferson, 26 April, 1781," *The Papers of Thomas Jefferson,* Vol. 5, 557
[72] Ibid., 558
[73] Ibid., 557
[74] Hugh Rankin, *The War of the Revolution in* Virginia, (Williamsburg, VA: Virginia Independence Bicentennial Commission, 1979), 31

Arnold brought two 3 pound and two 6 pound cannon to a bluff overlooking the ships and commenced a bombardment of them. At the same time, a detachment of jaegers positioned themselves on a bluff overlooking the anchorage to sweep the rebel decks with their rifles. The rest of Arnold's force pitched in with musket fire.[75]

The Virginians fought back, but their fire was ineffective. The cannon onboard the ships could not elevate their fire high enough to reach the bluff and the Virginia militia on the opposite shore were too far away to fire effectively at Arnold's men. When a lucky British artillery shot cut an anchor cable of the *Tempest* (causing the ship to drift and expose the crew to fire from bow to stern) her skeleton crew abandoned her. This sparked panic among the other ships. Some crews scuttled their vessels, others torched their ships while the remainder simply abandoned them to Arnold. As the state navy sailors scrambled to reach the northern bank of the river, some of Arnold's men moved to seize the abandoned and damaged ships as prizes. Lieutenant Colonel Simcoe proudly described how one of his officers, Lieutenant Fitzpatrick, captured two ships:

> *The enemy had scuttled several of their ships, which were now sinking; others, boarded by the intrepid Lt. Fitzpatrick, were on fire; and although cannon and musketry from the opposite shore, kept up a smart fire on him, that active officer rowed on. He put three men on board one ship, and cut her cable, and he left...three more in another and attained himself the headmost, whose guns he immediately turned upon the enemy.*[76]

---

[75] Simcoe, 199
[76] Simcoe, 200

Although the loss of the state naval fleet was complete, most of the sailors, along with the militia posted on the north bank of the river, escaped. The bulk of Virginia's state navy was destroyed in less than an hour without the loss of a single British solider.[77]

Phillips is Foiled at Richmond

General Phillips joined Arnold at Osborne's Landing (seven miles east of Chesterfield Courthouse) a few hours after the engagement and the British troops spent the next two days repairing some of the captured vessels. On April 30th, Phillips marched north towards Richmond, halting in Manchester (a village directly across the James River from Richmond) where his troops destroyed 1,200 hogsheads of tobacco. General LaFayette, who had reached Richmond the day before with 900 continental soldiers, observed the destruction from across the river.[78] With General Steuben and most of the militia a day's march northwest of the capital and LaFayette's cannon and baggage yet to arrive in Richmond, there was little LaFayette could do except post troops on the heights of Richmond, summon General Steuben to join him with the militia, and hurry along his artillery and baggage train.

Upon observing LaFayette's troops deployed on the heights overlooking the capital and river, General Phillips, unaware of LaFayette's lack of cannon, canceled his planned attack on Richmond. LaFayette bemusedly reported to General Washington that an observer with General Phillips claimed the British general, *"flew into a Violent passion and Swore Vengeance against* [LaFayette]," as he ordered his army to

---

[77] Rankin, 31-32
[78] Idzerda, ed., "General LaFayette to General Weedon, 3 May, 1781," *LaFayette in the Age of the American Revolution*, Vol. 4, 77

march southward from Manchester to rejoin the British transport ships at City Point.[79]

General Phillips and his army boarded the transport ships on May 2nd and proceeded downriver. They sailed as far as Hog Island when General Phillips received instructions from General Cornwallis on May 7th, to rendezvous with him at Petersburg. General Phillips immediately changed course and sailed upriver to Brandon Plantation in Prince George County, where the bulk of his force disembarked and marched 25 miles to Petersburg. The British light infantry battalions and part of the Queen's Rangers continued upriver by ship to City Point and marched to Petersburg from there. By May 10th, General Phillips, who had fallen gravely ill, and his army were quartered in Petersburg, waiting for General Cornwallis and his weary force of 1,500 men to arrive from North Carolina.

---

[79] Idzerda, ed., "General LaFayette to General Washington, 4 May, 1781," *LaFayette in the Age of the American Revolution*, Vol. 4, 82

Chapter Ten

"The Enemy's Intention has been to Destroy this Army."

May – July 1781

It had been a difficult spring for Lord Cornwallis and his troops in North Carolina. Although they had prevailed over General Greene's much larger American army at Guilford Courthouse in mid-March, the British army under Cornwallis emerged from Guilford battered and exhausted. Cornwallis, with a force of 2,500 men, had pursued General Greene and his American army into North Carolina in January, but the toil of the pursuit and frequent clashes (culminating with the Battle of Guilford Courthouse) left Cornwallis with less than 1,500 effective troops by mid-March.

A few days after his victory in North Carolina, General Cornwallis marched southeastward towards Wilmington to resupply his weakened force. A British garrison held Wilmington and was sufficiently supplied to provision Cornwallis's troops. Cornwallis could also use the secure line of communication between Wilmington and Charleston to receive updates from South Carolina. When he did so, he learned that General Greene's return to South Carolina threatened British control of the province.

Despite his concern for the security of South Carolina, Lord Cornwallis gambled in April and marched his troops north towards Virginia in hopes of luring General Greene in pursuit. When Greene declined to pursue, Cornwallis continued northward, leaving the British forces posted in South Carolina to face General Greene alone. Cornwallis believed that Virginia, which had long provided a large number of men and supplies to General Greene's army, was the the key to victory in the South and he was determined to unite his force with General Phillips in Petersburg, subdue the Old Dominion, and end Virginia's support for General Greene.

LaFayette Awaits Cornwallis

While General Cornwallis and his army marched north from Wilmington, General LaFayette spent the first half of May reacting to the movements of General Phillips. When Phillips sailed down the James River in early May, LaFayette marched his force of continentals (down to 800 effectives due to illness) 15 miles east of Richmond to Bottoms Bridge in anticipation of a possible march to Fredericksburg to defend Hunter's Iron Works.[1] LaFayette speculated to General Washington that

> *Having Missed Richmond Mr. Hunter's works at Fredericksburg Must Be their Next object as they are the only support of our operations in the Southward.*[2]

LaFayette expected Phillips to sail his force into the Chesapeake Bay and then up the Potomac or Rappahannock River to strike Fredericksburg. Of course, General Phillips might also move against Williamsburg again, or return to Portsmouth, so militia detachments were sent downriver to guard against those possibilities.[3] Until General LaFayette was sure of General Phillips's destination, he remained encamped at Bottom's Bridge, ready to march in multiple directions.

---

[1] Idzerda, ed., "General LaFayette to General Greene, 3 May, 1781," *LaFayette in the Age of the American Revolution*, Vol. 4, 79

[2] Idzerda, ed., "General LaFayette to General Washington, 4 May, 1781," *LaFayette in the Age of the American Revolution*, Vol. 4, 83

[3] Ibid.

Reports that General Phillips had actually reversed direction on the James River and had returned to Petersburg prompted LaFayette to march his army to Osborne's Landing (via Richmond). LaFayette did so with a sense of foreboding for recent letters from North Carolina informed him that General Cornwallis was marching to Virginia to join General Phillips. LaFayette discussed his concern in a letter to the Chevalier de La Luzerne:

> *My situation...cannot help being a bit confining. When I look to the left, there is General Phillips with his army and absolute command of the James River. When I turn to the right, Lord Cornwallis's army is advancing as fast as it can go to devour me, and the worst of the affair is that on looking behind me I see just 900 Continental troops and some militia, sometimes more and sometimes less but never enough to not be completely thrashed by the smallest of the two armies that do me the honor of visiting.*[4]

With General Phillips (who was still gravely ill) and his force securely in Petersburg awaiting the arrival of Lord Cornwallis, General LaFayette withdrew back across the James River on May 10th, and encamped at Wilton Plantation, the estate of William Randolph, to await developments. On May 15th, General LaFayette bemoaned the situation confronting him to General George Weedon of Fredericksburg:

> *The Arrival of the Ennemy at Petersburg, their Command of the James and Appomattox River, the approach of Lord Cornwallis...Such are the Reasons which Render our Situation precarious and with the Handful of Men I have, there is No chance of*

---

[4] Idzerda, ed., "General LaFayette to the Chevalier de La Luzerne, 3 May, 1781," *LaFayette in the Age of the American Revolution*, Vol. 4, 89

Resisting the Combined Armies unless I Am Speedily and powerfully Reinforced.[5]

Just such a reinforcement of Pennsylvania continentals under General Anthony Wayne had been ordered to Virginia weeks earlier, but morale and transport problems delayed their march and it would be another month before they joined LaFayette. In the meantime, the young French commander of American forces in Virginia had to organize some sort of resistance to the soon to be reinforced and vastly superior enemy in order to maintain patriot morale in the state. The trick was to do so without risking his army, which LaFayette reported on May 18th, amounted to approximately 900 continentals, 1,200 militia, 6 artillery pieces and a handful of cavalry.[6]

Cornwallis Arrives

The arrival of General Cornwallis and his 1,500 troops in Petersburg on May 20th, swelled the number of British troops in central Virginia to nearly 5,000. Within days, additional reinforcements from New York arrived, bringing General Cornwallis's total force in Virginia (including the garrison at Portsmouth) to over 7,000 troops.[7] Circumstances had developed nicely for General Cornwallis, but there was one significant setback. A week before he reached Petersburg, General Cornwallis's friend and subordinate, General Phillips, succumbed to his illness and died. Benedict Arnold had assumed command upon the death of General Phillips, but soon after Cornwallis arrived, Arnold returned to Portsmouth and then sailed to New York.

---

[5] Idzerda, ed., "General LaFayette to General Weedon, 15 May, 1781," *LaFayette in the Age of the American Revolution*, Vol. 4, 104
[6] Idzerda, ed., "General LaFayette to General Greene, 18 May, 1781," *LaFayette in the Age of the American Revolution*, Vol. 4, 113
[7] Selby, 275

Across the James River at Wilton Plantation, General LaFayette reacted to the arrival of Cornwallis by moving his army to Richmond. On May 22nd, he candidly described the challenge before him to the Chevalier do La Luzerne:

> *We are still alive, Monsieur le Chevalier, and so far our little corps has not received the terrible visit.... The proportion of* [the enemy's] *regular infantry to ours is between four and five to one and their cavalry ten to one; there are a few Tories, with whom I hardly bother. Our militia is not very numerous on paper, and it is even less so in the field. We lack arms, we haven't a hundred riflemen, and if we are beaten, that is to say if we are caught, we shall all be routed. The militia is used to advantage in the North, but in this country there are so many roads that one's flanks are constantly exposed wherever one turns. We must maneuver, we must reconnoiter, and all that (especially without cavalry) is very difficult for us.*[8]

Four days later, General Cornwallis, who had moved his army across the James River to Westover, revealed his plan for Virginia in a letter to General Clinton in New York:

> *I shall now proceed to dislodge La Fayette from Richmond, and with my light troops destroy any magazines or stores in the neighbourhood which may have been collected either for his use or for General Greene's army.*[9]

Dislodging LaFayette from Richmond proved a simple task. The American commander had no interest in an engagement

---

[8] Idzerda, ed., "General LaFayette to the Chevalier de La Luzerne, 22 May, 1781," *LaFayette in the Age of the American Revolution*, Vol. 4, 120

[9] Tarleton, "Earl Cornwallis to Sir Henry Clinton, 26 May, 1781," 343

with Cornwallis, so when the British army broke camp from Westover on May 26th, and marched northwestward to Turkey Island Creek (about 12 miles from Richmond) LaFayette and his outnumbered army abandoned the capital and marched north, away from Cornwallis.

When the British army changed direction and swung directly north towards Bottoms Bridge, LaFayette concluded that Hunter's Foundry in Fredericksburg was Cornwallis's target. He informed Governor Jefferson on May 28th that

> *The Enemy's intention has been to destroy this army and I conjecture would have been afterwards to destroy the stores which it covers. They have now undertaken another movement and it appears they are going through the country to Fredericksburg. Their Dragoons were this morning near Hanover Court House and (unless this is a feint) I expect the Army will be there this evening.*[10]

Recognizing that he was powerless to stop Cornwallis, LaFayette added, *"We shall be upon a parallel line with the Enemy keeping the upper part of the Country."*[11]

LaFayette's goal was to hover on the British left flank to deter any westward movement of the enemy while at the same time close the gap between his army and the 1,200 Pennsylvania continentals General Anthony Wayne was leading southward from Pennsylvania. LaFayette hoped that the addition of Wayne's troops would give his outnumbered American army a better chance, slim as it might be, of success against Cornwallis when the time came to fight.

Until Wayne and his troops arrived, however, LaFayette was determined to avoid a general engagement with Cornwallis. The challenge was to do this without appearing

---

[10] Idzerda, ed., "General LaFayette to Governor Jefferson, 28 May, 1781," *LaFayette in the Age of the American Revolution*, Vol. 4, 136
[11] Ibid.

Central Virginia

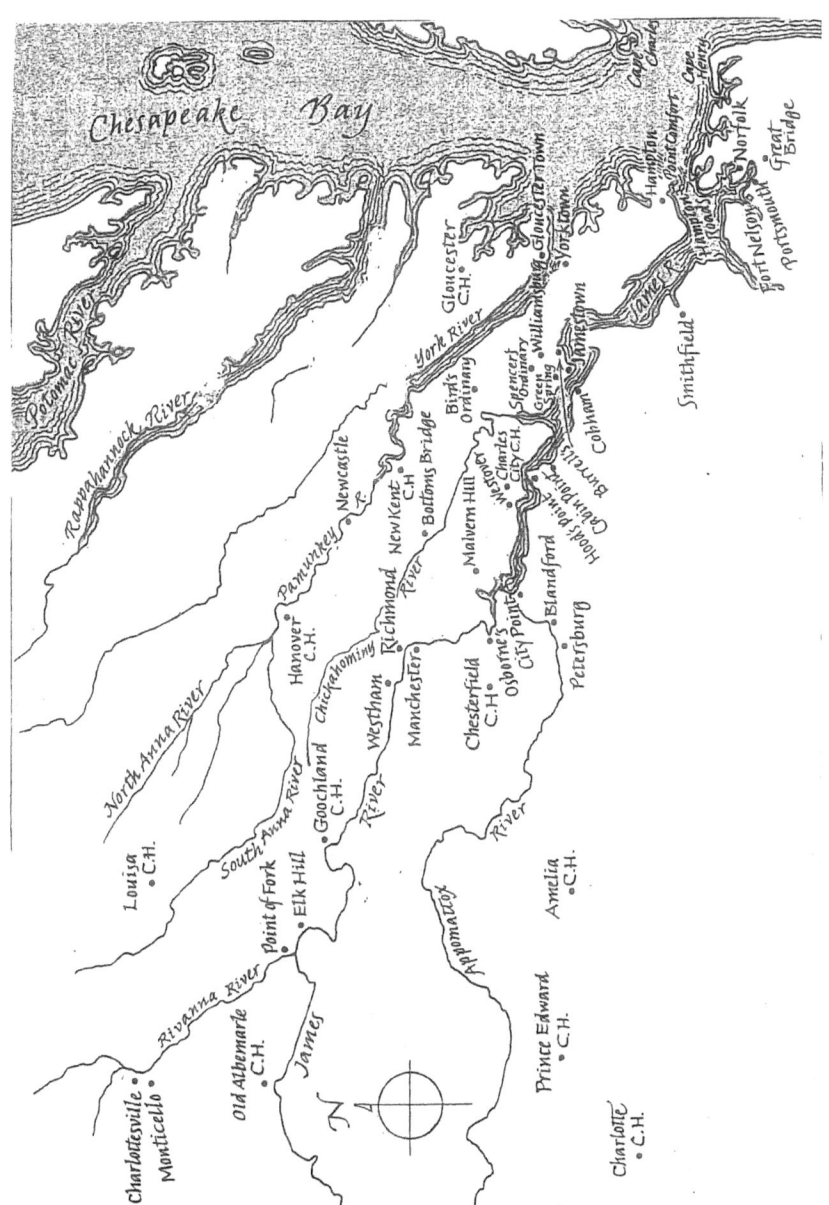

weak and ineffectual against the enemy, hence LaFayette's measured movements on a parallel track with Cornwallis. When Cornwallis marched north, as he did on May 29th and 30th to Newcastle and Hanover Courthouse, LaFayette followed suit, marching to Scotchtown and Anderson Bridge on the North Anna River. Along the way LaFayette apprised Generals Steuben, Weedon, and Wayne as well as Governor Jefferson (whose term as governor was about to end) of his movements. On May 31st, LaFayette reported to Jefferson (inaccurately it turned out) that

> *Tomorrow I form a junction with Gen. Weedon at Mattopony church and should General Waine Arrive our Inferiority will not Be quite So alarming.... Lord [Cornwallis] is going from His friends and we are going to Meet ours.*[12]

Alas, Weedon and his reinforcements never arrived. General Weedon sheepishly wrote to LaFayette to explain their absence:

> *I intended moving to-night with the small handful of men at this place, but not being able to remove the stores and disperse the tobacco...[from Fredericksburg, I] have risked your censure for the completion of this object, well knowing that a few men added to your operating force, could have but small weight in anything decisive....*[13]

LaFayette marched a few miles further northwest to Corbin's Bridge on June 2nd and encamped along the Po River.

Although General Cornwallis ordered some of his cavalry and light troops across the North Anna River in early June, his

---

[12] Idzerda, ed., "General LaFayette to Governor Jefferson, 31 May, 1781," *LaFayette in the Age of the American Revolution*, Vol. 4, 149

[13] Idzerda, ed., "General LaFayette to General Weedon, 1 June, 1781," *LaFayette in the Age of the American Revolution*, Vol. 4, 158

focus swung westward, away from Fredericksburg and LaFayette, on June 2nd. Lieutenant Colonel Banastre Tarleton claimed years later in his recollections of the American campaign that when Cornwallis learned that the Virginia General Assembly and Governor Jefferson had gathered in Charlottesville, and that Baron Von Steuben with a detachment of continental levies guarded important military stores at the Point of Fork on the James River, Cornwallis decided to end his march to Fredericksburg and instead, send two detachments westward to strike Charlottesville and Point of Fork.[14] General Cornwallis explained his rationale for ending his march to Fredericksburg to General Clinton:

> *By pushing my light troops over the North Anna, I [threatened both] Fredericksburgh, and... [LaFayette's] junction with General Wayne, who was then marching through Maryland. From what I could learn of the present state of Hunter's iron manufactory, it did not appear of so much importance as the stores on the other side of the country, and it was impossible to prevent the junction between the Marquis and Wayne: I therefore took advantage of the Marquis's passing the Rappahannock, and detached Lieutenant-Colonel Simcoe and Tarleton to disturb the assembly then sitting in Charlottesville, and to destroy the stores there, at Old Albemarle court house, and the Point of Fork.*[15]

Cornwallis sent Lieutenant-Colonel Simcoe and Lieutenant-Colonel Tarleton, with their detachments, westward ahead of the army on June 2nd, and trailed behind them with the rest of his troops.

---

[14] Tarleton, 295
[15] Tarleton, "Earl Cornwallis to Sir Henry Clinton, 30 June, 1781," 348-49

It took a couple of days for General LaFayette to realize Cornwallis's sudden shift in strategy. He had continued to march north, across the Rapidan River into Culpeper County, hoping to unite with General Wayne's reinforcements at any moment. The Pennsylvanians were still a week away, however, and when LaFayette finally learned that Cornwallis had diverted his army westward to threaten Virginia's political leaders and the important military stores stockpiled at Point of Fork, he adjusted his own march route southwestward, sending word to General Wayne to catch up to him as quickly as possible.

LaFayette still recognized that his army was too weak to directly challenge General Cornwallis, but he wanted to position it so that when he was finally reinforced by General Wayne, he might be able to defend some of the military stores in central Virginia. Unfortunately, it was too late to protect the state legislators in Charlottesville or the military stores at Point of Fork; Tarleton and Simcoe had already struck those places.

Tarleton's Raid on Charlottesville

On June 3rd, Lieutenant Colonel Banastre Tarleton, with 180 Legion dragoons and 70 mounted infantry of the 23rd Regiment dashed westward across Hanover and Louisa counties towards the Virginia assembly in Charlottesville.[16] The rapid pace and heat of the day forced Tarleton to halt at mid-day to, *"refresh his men and horses,"* but they soon returned to their saddles where they remained for the rest of the afternoon and most of the evening.[17] They rested again near Louisa Courthouse at 11 p.m., but were back on the road by 2 a.m., determined to surprise Governor Jefferson and the Virginia General Assembly in Charlottesville.

---

[16] Tarleton, 295-96
[17] Ibid., 296

Fortunately for the Virginians, Tarleton's force was observed by 26 year old Jack Jouett a few miles east of Louisa Courthouse at the Cuckoo Tavern. Jouett quickly deduced Tarleton's destination and slipped away, riding approximately 40 miles over back roads and country paths to warn Governor Jefferson and the legislators of Tarleton's approach.[18] Jouett rode first to Jefferson's home at Monticello, which sat upon a 850 foot high mountain overlooking Charlottesville. Staying with Jefferson and his family were Archibald Cary and Benjamin Harrison, Speakers of the House of Delegates and State Senate, as well as Thomas Nelson, Jr., Jefferson's soon to be successor as governor.

The entire household was roused from their beds at dawn by Jouett, whose face was streaked with scratches and blood from the numerous branches and briars he encountered on his ride to Monticello.[19] Governor Jefferson received Jouett's news calmly and insisted that there was time for breakfast.[20] While Jefferson and his family and guests took breakfast, Jouett rode to Charlottesville to warn the town and the rest of the Assembly.

Going door to door to spread the alarm, Jouett was initially met with skepticism and disbelief.[21] Most legislators assumed that Charlottesville was beyond Cornwallis's reach. Jouett's earnestness soon convinced them that they were in danger and they reluctantly voted to adjourn and reconvene the Assembly in a week on the other side of the Blue Ridge Mountains in Staunton.[22] Most then hurriedly packed their belongings and fled westward over the mountains. House Speaker Benjamin Harrison recalled that the bulk of the legislators, "*had not left*

---

[18] Kranish, 275-76
[19] Ibid., 278
[20] Ibid., 280
[21] Ibid.
[22] *Journal of the House of Delegates*, 4 June, 1781, (Richmond, 1828), 10

town an hour before [Tarleton] *entered,"* and credited Jouett (without naming him) for the assembly's escape:[23]

> *Had it not been for the extraordinary exertions and kindness of a young gentleman who discovered* [Tarleton's] *intentions and got round* [his force] *in the night, not one man of those in town would have escaped; as it was, so incredulous were some of us, that it was with much difficulty* [that the Assembly] *could be prevailed on to adjourn.*[24]

Not all of the legislators made it out of town before Tarleton arrived; a handful, including Daniel Boone, tarried too long and were seized. Many more would have been captured had Tarleton not stopped outside of Charlottesville to destroy a small wagon train of continental supplies heading to the Carolinas. Another stop at Dr. Thomas Walker's plantation at Castle Hill (a few miles from Charlottesville) also cost Tarleton precious time. Tarleton seized some of Dr. Walker's guests, including a South Carolina delegate to the Continental Congress and two members of the Virginia House of Delegates, and continued on to Charlottesville.

Tarleton's advance guard of dragoons was met on the outskirts of Charlottesville by approximately 100 local militia who guarded the ford across the Rivanna River. Tarleton recalled that he ordered an immediate attack and, *"the cavalry charged through the water with very little loss and routed the detachment posted at that place."*[25] The bulk of Tarleton's force rushed into town, *"to continue the confusion of the Americans, and to apprehend, if possible, the governor and assembly."*[26]

---

[23] Jones, "Benjamin Harrison to Joseph Jones," *Letters of Joseph Jones of VA:1777-87*, (Washington: Dept. of State, 1889), 82

[24] Ibid.

[25] Tarleton, 296

[26] Ibid., 297

Unsure of Jefferson's location, Tarleton sent a separate detachment to Monticello under Captain Kenneth MacLeod to search for the governor. Jefferson, who had lingered at his home after his guests and family had fled, observed Tarleton's arrival in Charlottesville through a spyglass and realized it was time to leave.

As MacLeod and his men made their way up the winding road to Monticello, Jefferson fled his estate in the opposite direction on horseback, *"plunging into the woods of the adjoining mountain."*[27] He escaped unnoticed by the British by mere minutes. While MacLeod and his men searched the mansion and grounds, Jefferson continued through the woods until he came to the road that his wife and children had fled on and soon caught up with their carriage. They all continued on to John Coles's estate at Enniscorthy.[28] Fortunately for Jefferson, Captain MacLeod obeyed Tarleton's instructions to spare Monticello of any damage and Jefferson's estate escaped unscathed from the British intruders.

Thwarted in his goal of capturing Governor Jefferson as well as key members of Virginia's legislature, Tarleton had to settle for dispersing the Virginia Assembly (which disrupted Virginia's war efforts) and destroying, *"a great quantity of stores,"* including (claimed Tarleton) nearly 400 barrels of gunpowder and 1000 new muskets that were abandoned by the routed Virginians.[29] Tarleton was also pleased to "liberate" twenty British soldiers from General Burgoyne's captured army at Saratoga.[30] They had somehow remained in the area after the bulk of the convention prisoners were sent to Winchester and when they learned of Tarleton's presence in Charlottesville, they reported to the British commander. Tarleton speculated that many more prisoners would have

---

[27] Kranish, 283
[28] Ibid., 284
[29] Tarleton, 297
[30] Ibid.

joined him if he had remained in Charlottesville beyond the one night he spent there.[31] Alas, his instructions were to join Lieutenant Colonel Simcoe at Point of Fork, so he departed on the afternoon of June 5th and headed east.

Raid on Point of Fork

At almost the same moment that Tarleton left Charlottesville, Lieutenant-Colonel John Simcoe was securing a large cache of military stores that his troops had seized from General Steuben at Point of Fork, 25 miles southeast of Charlottesville. This supply depot, located at the juncture of the Rivanna and Fluvanna rivers (which came together to form the James River) was an important staging area for Virginia troops and supplies bound for General Greene's army in South Carolina.

General Cornwallis wanted to disrupt the flow of reinforcements and supplies to General Greene so he sent Lieutenant Colonel Simcoe to raid Point of Fork on the same day that he ordered Tarleton to strike Charlottesville. Simcoe's force included his own Queen's Rangers (reduced to 200 worn down infantry and 100 cavalry) along with a battalion of the 71st Regiment, detachments of jaeger and loyalist riflemen, and one 3 pound cannon and crew.[32] Simcoe's force, which was mostly on foot, conducted several long marches of 25 to 30 miles a day through Hanover and Goochland County to reach Point of Fork by June 4th. Simcoe recalled that, *"The incessant marches of the Rangers...had so worn out their shoes, that...it appeared that near fifty men were absolutely barefooted."*[33]

Encamped at Point of Fork and unaware of Simcoe's approach were approximately 550 continental levies (new

---

[31] Ibid.
[32] Simcoe, 212
[33] Ibid.

recruits) and over 300 recently arrived militia.[34] Steuben had planned to send the continental troops southward to reinforce General Nathanael Greene in South Carolina, but a shortage of clothing delayed their departure.

General Steuben first learned of the approach of the enemy in the predawn hours of June 4th. Two enemy detachments (one inaccurately reported to be 1,000 strong) were heading west towards Point of Fork.[35] Realizing that the Rivanna River was fordable in several places upriver and that his position on the point was thus vulnerable to attack from these detachments, Steuben ordered the troops and military stores at Point of Fork removed to the southern bank of the deeper and wider Fluvanna River. A picquet of fifty men remained on the point of land between the two rivers and a small party of dragoons was sent up the road from the point about two miles to reconoitre.[36] These dragoons, as well as one of Steuben's mounted aide-de-camps who had returned to the point at mid-morning to recall the picquet, were promptly captured by Simcoe's advance guard. Informed by the captives that most of the military stores and troops had already been removed across the river, Simcoe pressed forward to investigate. He recalled:

> *The cavalry immediately advanced, and the enemy being plainly seen on the opposite side, nothing remained but to stop some boats, which were putting off from the extreme point; this Capt. Shank effected, and took about thirty people who were on the banks, from which the embarkation had proceeded.*[37]

---

[34] Idzerda, ed., "General Steuben to General LaFayette, 3 and 5 June, 1781," *LaFayette in the Age of the American Revolution*, Vol. 4, 166 and 170

[35] Idzerda, ed., "General Steuben to General LaFayette, 5 June, 1781," *LaFayette in the Age of the American Revolution*, Vol. 4, 170

[36] Simcoe, 216

[37] Ibid., 217

With the bulk of his troops and supplies safely across the Fluvanna (James) River, General Steuben faced a tough decision. Should he hold his position and try to repulse the enemy when they attempted to cross the river, or should he withdraw to the south, taking what supplies he could carry but leaving the rest behind. For the moment, Steuben held his ground. Across the river, Lieutenant-Colonel Simcoe took measures to convince the general to withdraw.

Aware that his detachment was outnumbered by Steuben's force, Lieutenant-Colonel Simcoe engaged in deception to convince the Prussian commander to withdraw from the river. Simcoe recalled:

> *Every method was now taken to persuade the enemy, that* [his detachment] *was Earl Cornwallis's army, that they might leave the opposite shore, which was covered with arms and stores: Capt. Hutchinson with the 71st regiment, (clothed in red,) was directed to advance as near to the banks of the Fluvanna as he could...the baggage and women halted among the woods, on the summit of the hill, and, in that position, made the appearance of a numerous corps: the three-pounder was carried down, the artillery men being positively ordered to fire but one shot and.... The troops occupied the heights which covered the neck of the point, and their numbers were concealed in the wood.*[38]

General Steuben (who was deployed with the bulk of his troops atop a ridge overlooking the river) was undoubtedly discouraged to learn that a single cannon shot from the enemy had scattered a 50 man detachment posted below the ridge at the boat landing. He noted that it was only through, *"much*

---

[38] Simcoe, 217-18

persuasion and many threats" that the rattled Virginians returned to their post.[39]

As night fell, Lieutenant-Colonel Simcoe developed his own concern, admitting that he was

> *Apprehensive lest Baron Steuben, having secured his stores of which were of great value, over a broad and unfordable river, and being in possession of all the boats, should repass his troops in the night, higher up the river, and fall on him, so that, if the British troops should be beaten, they would have no retreat, being shut up between two rivers* [the Fluvanna and Rivanna]. [40]

Simcoe confessed further that he would have withdrawn his force from Point of Fork had his troops not been so fatigued from the long march there. Instead, he kept his troops on alert and hoped that his earlier deception would prevent Steuben from launching an attack. Simcoe's efforts apparently did more than that, for around midnight, his men heard the sounds of Steuben's boats being destroyed across the river.[41] General Steuben had decided to withdraw under cover of darkness, abandoning a vast amount of military stores that included:

> *Two thousand five hundred stand of arms, a large quantity of gunpowder, case shot, &ct., several casks of saltpeter, sulphur, and brimstone, and upwards of sixty hogsheads of rum and brandy, several chests of carpenters' tools, and upwards of four hundred intrenching tools, with casks of flints, sail cloth and wagons....*[42]

---

[39] Kapp, 442
[40] Simcoe, 219
[41] Ibid., 220
[42] Ibid.

A variety of artillery pieces were also abandoned, "*all French pieces and in excellent order*," noted Simcoe.[43]

As General Steuben fled south with his troops towards the Staunton River to escape the reach of Simcoe, Lieutenant-Colonel Tarleton and General Cornwallis (who had trailed behind Simcoe with the main army) converged on Goochland County. They united just a few miles downriver from Point of Fork at Thomas Jefferson's Elk Hill Plantation. Cornwallis rested his army and used Jefferson's house as his headquarters. He did nothing to stop his troops from plundering the estate as well as neighboring properties and Elk Hill was soon reduced to, "*an absolute waste.*"[44]

While General Cornwallis and his 5,000 man army enjoyed the offerings of Jefferson's property, General LaFayette cautiously marched southwestward from the Rapidan River through Orange and Louisa counties. General Anthony Wayne had still not joined LaFayette but the Pennsylvanians were only a few days behind and finally caught up with LaFayette at Boswell's Tavern near the South Anna River on June 10th. General Wayne's 800 continental reinforcements emboldened LaFayette to move even closer to Cornwallis. On June 13th, the young French commander informed General Steuben that, "*we Have Again got Between the Ennemy and our* [remaining] *Stores.*"[45] LaFayette ordered Steuben to proceed northward with the continental levies to reinforce him. General Greene would have to wait.

At Elk Hill, Cornwallis learned that the bulk of the remaining American military stores in the area had been moved further west, out of reach. Concluding on June 13th, that there was little else to accomplish west of Richmond, General Cornwallis headed east towards the capital. It was

---

[43] Ibid.
[44] Kranish, 292
[45] Idzerda, ed., "General Lafayette to General Steuben, 13 June, 1781," *LaFayette in the Age of the American Revolution*, Vol. 4, 179

time to see if any instructions from General Clinton had arrived from New York.

LaFayette trailed cautiously behind, encouraged by the addition of hundreds of riflemen under General William Campbell. On the same day that Cornwallis entered Richmond, LaFayette wrote a candid letter to his friend, the Chevalier de La Luzerne. In it he subtly criticized General Wayne and not so subtly criticized General Steuben:

> *As yet...[Cornwallis] has not succeeded in bringing us into an action. For a long time we had Tarleton entering our camp two hours after it was abandoned. There was not a shot fired, and the junction with the Pennsylvanians was made. I expected that the junction would be made sooner. I expected they would be more numerous. I expected that 500 regular troops and a corps of militia attacked by 400 men, 200 of whom were armed with swords, would prevent their crossing an impassable river.*[46]

LaFayette continued with a description of his own actions:

> *After having slipped rather fortunately between the enemy army and our stores, we made a junction with a few riflemen. Lord Cornwallis seemed not to like these hilly terrains and withdrew towards Richmond. We make it seem we are pursuing him, and my riflemen, their faces smeared with charcoal, make the woods resound with their yells; I have made them an army of devils and have given them plenary absolution. What regular troops I have are very good but few in number.*[47]

---

[46] Idzerda, ed., "General LaFayette to the Chevalier de La Luzerne, 16 June, 1781," *LaFayette in the Age of the American Revolution*, Vol. 4, 186

[47] Ibid.

LaFayette's effective continentals now numbered approximately 1,600 men from New England and Pennsylvania. General Wayne commanded these troops, which LaFayette described as his first line. LaFayette's second line was comprised of Virginia militia, whose numbers fluctuated greatly but averaged between 1,500 to 2,000 troops. Virginia's new governor, Thomas Nelson Jr. of Yorktown, commanded these troops. Another Virginian general, Peter Muhlenberg, was placed in charge of the riflemen and a detachment of light infantry. General George Weedon commanded a small party of militia in Fredericksburg and General Steuben led his force of 500 or so continental recruits north to reinforce LaFayette. Altogether, LaFayette commanded approximately 4,500 troops and although this approached the number Cornwallis had, the caliber and experience of Cornwallis's troops far surpassed that of LaFayette's men, so the French general remained cautious in his "pursuit".[48]

General Cornwallis stayed in Richmond for just a few days and then marched east to Bottom's Bridge, then New Kent Courthouse, and ultimately Williamsburg, which he entered on June 25th. Lieutenant-Colonel Tarleton commanded the rear guard of the army and trailed the column, but Lieutenant-Colonel Simcoe and his detachment broke from the column on June 22nd, at Bottom's Bridge and marched a few miles north towards Newcastle to screen the army and draw LaFayette's attention in that direction. The next day, June 23rd, Simcoe was ordered to march along the Chickahominy River and destroy whatever boats were discovered. He was also instructed to spend a day or two collecting cattle for the army in Williamsburg.[49]

---

[48] Idzerda, ed., "General,LaFayette to the Chevalier de La Luzerne, 16 June, 1781," and "General LaFayette to General Washington, 18 June, 1781," *LaFayette in the Age of the American Revolution*, Vol. 4 186 and 195

[49] Simcoe, 225

Battle of Spencer's Ordinary

On the same day that General Cornwallis's army reached Williamsburg, (June 25th) Lieutenant Colonel Simcoe halted 20 miles away at Cooper's Mills. Simcoe was anxious about the whereabouts of LaFayette's army for, *"he had not the smallest information of the enemy's movements, whom he knew to be active and enterprising."*[50] With Cornwallis and the main British army a day's march away, Simcoe worried that his detachment was vulnerable to a sudden strike by LaFayette's much larger force. If LaFayette managed to catch Simcoe's detachment before Simcoe closed the gap with Cornwallis, it was unlikely help from Williamsburg could arrive in time to prevent disaster.

Simcoe's concern prompted him to resume his march towards Williamsburg at 2 a.m.; he sent his infantry (200 Queen's Rangers and detachments of jager and loyalist riflemen) with his lone cannon down the Williamsburg road under Major Armstrong ahead of his cavalry (100 strong) and cattle. Simcoe ordered Major Armstrong to proceed as far as Spencer's Ordinary (about fourteen miles from Cooper's Mills and only six miles northwest of Williamsburg) and wait there for the cavalry and cattle to catch up. Lieutenant-Colonel Simcoe and his cavalry remained at Coopers Mills with the cattle drivers (North Carolina Loyalist Militia) and waited for enough light to move the cattle that had been collected. They proceeded towards Spencer's Ordinary around 3 a.m.

Simcoe's infantry, which reached Spencer's Ordinary ahead of the cavalry, was resting in platoons along the road when the cavalry and cattle arrived a few hours after dawn. An impatient Captain Johann Ewald (who had recovered from his wound at Scott's Creek and had rejoined his jager company) requested permission to resume the march to Williamsburg

---

[50] Ibid., 226

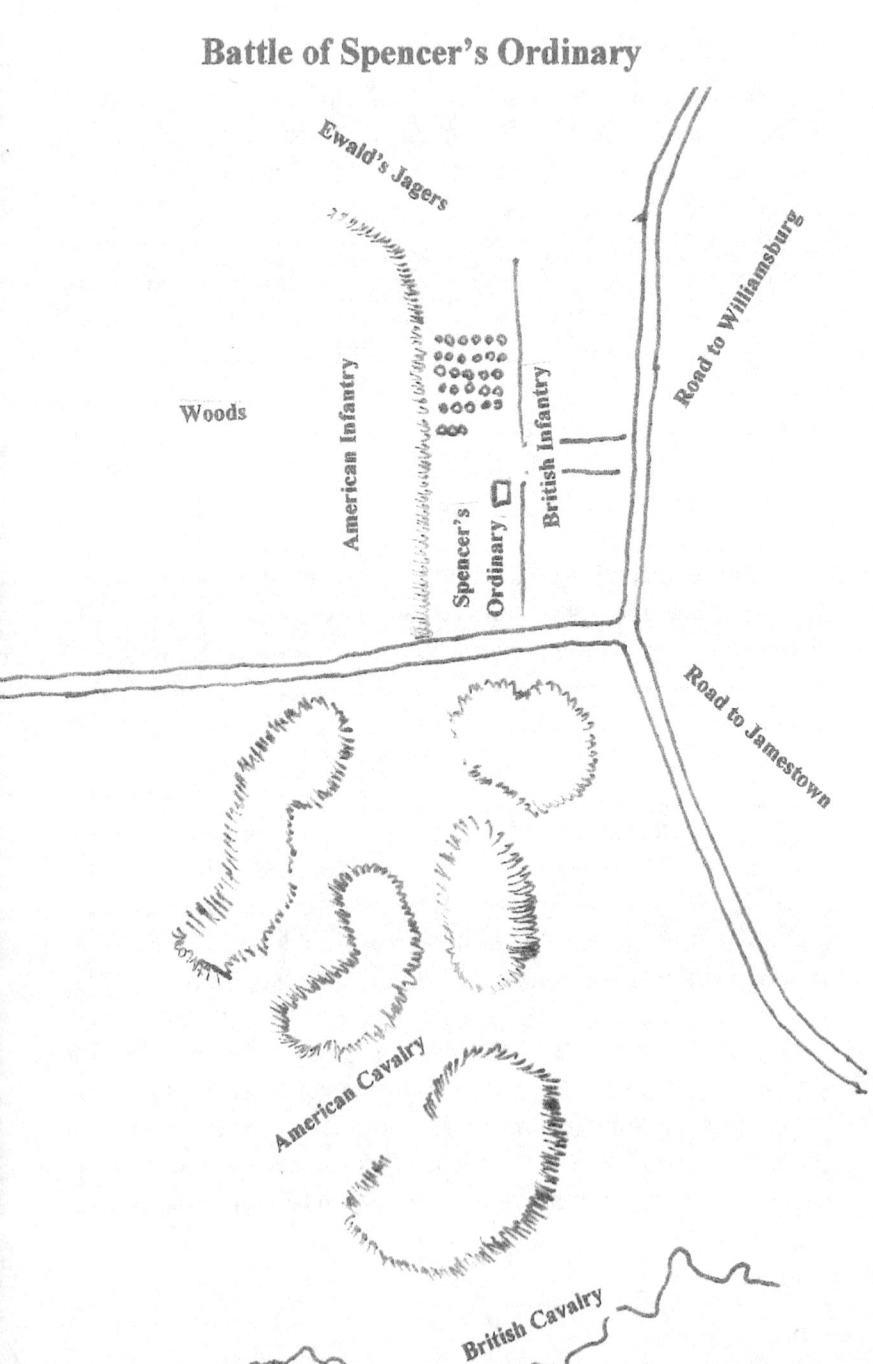

to avoid the oppressive mid-day heat of Virginia, but Lieutenant-Colonel Simcoe decided to rest his cavalry and collect more cattle before his entire detachment proceeded on to Williamsburg.[51] While a party of loyalists collected more cattle in the neighborhood of Spencer's Ordinary, Simcoe's cavalry dismounted to feed and water their horses at a nearby farm. The infantry remained along the road and finished breakfast.

Unbeknownst to Simcoe, a large American detachment under Colonel Richard Butler of Pennsylvania had marched all night in pursuit. Butler's force included a regiment of Pennsylvania continentals and two contingents of Virginia riflemen. These foot soldiers trailed behind 50 dragoons under Major William McPherson who, *"having taken up fifty light infantry behind fifty dragoons, overtook Simcoe, and regardless of numbers made an immediate charge,"* soon after Simcoe's cavalry halted.[52] Major McPherson's double mounted horsemen surprised Simcoe's scattered foragers and a chase ensued as the startled foragers scurried back towards Simcoe's dismounted cavalry, abandoning the new cattle they had just collected. A lone trumpeter posted between Simcoe's foragers and his cavalry alerted Simcoe's horsemen of the enemy's approach, calling out, *"draw your swords Rangers, the rebels are coming!"*[53] The young trumpeter drew the charging American dragoons away from his dismounted comrades in an effort to give them time to remount their horses. The ploy worked so well that the charging Americans exposed their left flank to Simcoe's horsemen. Simcoe proudly recalled that his cavalry commander, Captain Shank, *"led* [his horsemen] *to the charge on the enemy's flank, which was somewhat exposed…*[and] *broke them entirely."*[54] The

---

[51] Ewald, 308
[52] Simcoe, 228
[53] Simcoe, 228
[54] Ibid.

American cavalry commander was unhorsed in the melee and forced to hide in a nearby swamp until the fight concluded. His dragoons were scattered in all directions. Fortunately for the Americans, their infantry arrived in time to take up the fight.

At the first sound of gunfire, Lieutenant-Colonel Simcoe raced from Spencer's Ordinary, where he was meeting with Major Armstrong and the infantry, towards his cavalry to investigate the situation. Realizing that a strong enemy force was upon him, Simcoe ordered the baggage wagons and cattle to proceed immediately to Williamsburg. He also sent an express to General Cornwallis, six miles away, with news of the American attack.[55]

Simcoe witnessed his cavalry repulse the American horsemen, but in their pursuit of the vanquished Americans, Simcoe's cavalrymen rode into the fire of American riflemen deployed in a thick wood. Simcoe's startled horsemen disengaged and withdrew out of range of the Americans where Simcoe joined them.[56]

While Lieutenant-Colonel Simcoe worked to reorganize his cavalry, Captain Ewald took charge of the infantry and prepared to attack the large American force of riflemen and continental troops that had just deployed in the woods. Simcoe's infantry formed for battle in the ploughed fields and orchard of Spencer's Ordinary, extending a battle line (with gaps between companies) from the road eastward to an orchard. Captain Ewald's jagers held the right flank of this line, which due to the gaps in it extended beyond the American left flank. Ewald immediately saw an opportunity to exploit this situation and ordered his jagers to circle around the Americans to attack them from the side and rear while the rest of Simcoe's infantry held the enemy's attention with a

---

[55] Ibid.
[56] Ibid.

direct frontal assault.[57] Ewald personally led this assault and recalled that

> *I called to Lieutenant Bickell to...fall upon the enemy's left flank and rear with all the jagers. At that instant, I jumped off my horse and placed myself in front of the center of the grenadiers and light infantry company. I asked them not to fire a shot, but to attack with the bayonet...The enemy, who had moved forward, was taken aback by our advance.* [They] *waited for us up to forty paces, fired a volley, killed two thirds of the grenadiers, and withdrew...We came among them and engaged them hand to hand. The enemy now came under rifle fire from the jagers on his flank and rear, and hurried to escape. We captured a French officer, a captain of riflemen, and twenty-two men, partly from the so-called Wild Irish Riflemen, and partly from the light infantry.*[58]

As Ewald and the bulk of Simcoe's infantry advanced directly at the Americans, they were suddenly flanked on their left by a detachment of rebels from across the road. This force, which was separated from the rest of the American line by the fenced road, wheeled left in an attempt to blast the left flank of Simcoe's advancing infantry. To do this though, the Americans had to scale two high, sturdy, fences that bordered both sides of the road, and as they climbed over them they became disordered. It was at this moment that Simcoe struck with his cavalry, leading his horsemen in a charge against the rear of the disordered American detachment. Lieutenant-Colonel Simcoe recalled that

---

[57] Ewald, 309
[58] Ibid.

[The rebels] *did not observe the cavalry, which while they were in this disorder, lost not the moment, but...charged them up the road, and upon its left, entirely broke and totally dispersed them.*[59]

While Lieutenant-Colonel Simcoe neutralized this American threat to Ewald's left flank, the bold German officer continued forward, pushing the American infantry back into the woods. He recalled that

After I had advanced several hundred paces into the wood, I halted and reformed the remainder of the three ranger companies, which did not number sixty men. We fell in on a footpath which ran through a thick brushwood.[60]

Lieutenant Bicknell suddenly appeared in the woods and asked Ewald for permission to sound the call to reassemble his jagers, many of who were scattered throughout the woods in pursuit of fleeing rebels. Ewald did not want to reveal his position to the Americans and denied the request, which turned out to be a very fortunate decision for about a minute later Ewald learned of a large American reinforcement approaching. The bold German officer recalled that

I went several paces ahead on the path and suddenly ran into people. I could not help myself and cried, "Fire! Fire!" The rangers fired, and a running fire broke out from the enemy's side for several minutes. Then it was quiet again. I now observed that it was time to fall back and signaled to the jagers and rangers.[61]

With his baggage and cattle safely en route to Williamsburg, Lieutenant-Colonel Simcoe disengaged his troops and resumed his march towards Williamsburg. As he had sent all

---

[59] Simcoe, 32
[60] Ewald, 309
[61] Ibid.

of the baggage towards Williamsburg at the start of the engagement, there were no wagons available to transport the wounded, so Simcoe left them behind at Spencer's Ordinary under a flag of truce. About two miles into his march, Simcoe met General Cornwallis with a large reinforcement and together they returned to Spencer's Ordinary where they happily discovered that their wounded had not been captured; the Americans had also withdrawn, taking their casualties but leaving the British behind.

Both sides claimed victory in the engagement. General LaFayette reported losses of 9 killed, 14 wounded, 1 captured and 13 missing to Congress and estimated Simcoe's losses at 60 killed and 100 wounded.[62] He also highlighted the boldness of Major McPherson's cavalry and the effectiveness of the riflemen in a separate letter to Thomas Nelson of Yorktown.[63]

General Cornwallis estimated his losses in killed and wounded at 33 and reported to General Clinton that nearly the same number of Americans were captured. He offered no estimate of American killed and wounded aside from the observation that it was considerable.[64] Lieutenant-Colonel Simcoe was more specific, reporting losses of 11 killed and 25 wounded in his journal.[65] Captain Ewald put the number of British killed and wounded at over 60 and speculated that the Americans suffered far more.[66]

Simcoe accompanied General Cornwallis back to Williamsburg, which was occupied by the British for over a week. The Americans spent that time encamped at Tyree's Plantation, a few miles southeast of New Kent Court House.

---

[62] Idzerda, ed., Note 2, *LaFayette in the Age of the American Revolution*, Vol. 4, 217

[63] Idzerda, ed., "General LaFayette to Thomas Nelson, 28 June, 1781," *LaFayette in the Age of the American Revolution*, Vol. 4, 217-18

[64] Tarleton, "General Cornwallis to General Clinton, 30 June, 1781", 350

[65] Simcoe, 234

[66] Ewald, 312

In late June, General Cornwallis received new instructions from General Clinton in New York. The British commander-in-chief was concerned about a possible French-American offensive against New York. Eager to concentrate his forces to repulse the expected attack, Clinton instructed Cornwallis to establish a defensive post in a healthy location in Virginia (he suggested Williamsburg or Yorktown), retain the troops needed to defend the post, and send the remainder of his force to New York via transport ships.[67] Cornwallis's view that Virginia was the key to success in the South was thus dismissed by General Clinton.

A frustrated General Cornwallis replied to Clinton on June 30th, insisting that, *"until Virginia was to a degree [subjugated] we could not reduce N. Carolina or have any certain hold of the back country of S. Carolina...."*[68] Cornwallis added that the departure of a significant portion of his troops to New York would leave him too weak to adequately defend Yorktown (which Clinton's wanted to utilize as a port for the navy). Cornwallis further questioned, (prophetically) *"whether it is worthwhile to hold a sickly defensive post* [like Portsmouth] *in this bay which will always be exposed to a sudden French attack..."*[69] General Cornwallis clearly did not agree with his commander's decision to limit activities in Virginia to a defensive nature, yet, as he wrote to General Clinton he also made preparations to cross the James River and march to Portsmouth to rendezvous with the British navy and comply with Clinton's instructions.

---

[67] Davies, ed. "General Clinton to General Cornwallis, 11 June, 1781," 157-58

[68] Davies, ed., "General Cornwallis to General Clinton, 30 June, 1781," 166

[69] Ibid.

Battle of Green Spring

On July 4th, General Cornwallis led his army out of Williamsburg and marched to Jamestown to cross the James River. His destination was Portsmouth. Before he crossed the river, however, Cornwallis tried to lure General LaFayette into one last engagement. Sending the Queen's Rangers across the James River with the army's baggage on July 6th, Cornwallis hid the rest of his troops along the northern shore of the river. Picquets were placed on the road to Green Spring, a plantation two miles northeast of the river crossing. Cornwallis wanted to convince LaFayette that only his rearguard remained on the north side of the river in hopes that the young French general would rashly attack. He instructed his pickets to draw the Americans towards Jamestown and a trap.

LaFayette's advance guard, which numbered around 500 troops under General Anthony Wayne, cautiously marched towards Jamestown and halted at Green Spring at 2 p.m. Wayne's force consisted of Major McPherson's 50 continental dragoons (augmented by a handful of gentlemen volunteers under Lieutenant-Colonel John Mercer), a detachment of militia riflemen under Major Richard Call, (about 150 strong) a 60 man light infantry detachment under Major William Galvan, the 1st Pennsylvania Regiment under Colonel Walter Stewart, (250 strong) and one six pound cannon.[70]

Conflicting reports on the number of enemy troops that had actually crossed the James River concerned General LaFayette. He had no desire to risk his army in a general engagement against Cornwallis. Instead, the young French commander hoped only to strike the British rearguard as it covered Cornwallis's retreat across the river. Conflicting

---

[70] Jared Sparks, ed. "General Wayne to General Washington, 8 July, 1781," *Correspondence of the American Revolution Being Letters of Eminent Men to George Washington*, (Boston: Little, Brown, and Co., 1853), 348

Battle of Green Spring

intelligence caused LaFayette to order the rest of his continental troops (who had remained at Norrell's Mills and Chickahominy Church, eight miles in the rear) forward to Green Spring as a precaution. Three light infantry battalions and two Pennsylvania regiments hurried to Green Spring in the early afternoon. The Virginia continentals and militia remained further back at Byrd's Ordinary, twelve miles away.

After an hour's pause at Green Spring with General Wayne's advance guard, General LaFayette, uncertain of the situation before him but determined to strike at Cornwallis in some way, ordered Wayne forward. Led by a small party of volunteer horsemen under Lieutenant-Colonel Mercer and Major Call's riflemen, (who fanned out in skirmish order and slowly advanced along both sides of the road to Jamestown) General Wayne's force cautiously crossed a causeway over a marsh and continued on through the open fields of Green Spring Plantation.

About half a mile into the march the road entered a long stretch of woods. Waiting in the woods were small parties of British skirmishers with orders to strongly resist the rebel advance. General Cornwallis believed that such a show of resistance would convince the Americans that they were indeed confronting the British rearguard and thus, the rebels would push on into the trap that Cornwallis had set. He explained his thinking to General Clinton after the battle:

> *Concluding that the enemy would not bring a considerable force within our reach, unless they supposed that nothing was left but a rear guard, I took every means to convince them of my weakness, and suffered my pickets to be insulted and driven back.*[71]

---

[71] Tarleton, "Earl Cornwallis to Sir Henry Clinton, July 8, 1781," 400

Cornwallis's picquet (largely selected from the 76th and 80th Regiments) waged a spirited two hour skirmish in the woods against the American riflemen, grudgingly yielding ground under the "galling" and steady fire of the rebel riflemen. An officer of the 76th Regiment recalled that the rebels

> *First began by attacking a small picquet consisting of 20 Highlanders of the 76th, commanded by Lieut. Balvaird of the 80th, who being early wounded, Lieut. Alston of the same regiment, who was accidently there, took the command of the picquet, he was also wounded. Lieut. Wemys, who was acting as adjutant to the 76th, being sent on a message to the picquet, seeing Alston wounded, dismounted and gave him his horse, drew his sword, and took command of the picquet. He had hardly had two minutes when he was wounded, and though half of the men were by this time killed or wounded the rest of the brave Highlanders kept their ground...till ordered in by Lord Cornwallis, but not before they had expended about 50 rounds each man.* [72]

The British picquet (whose determined resistance and lack of reinforcement suggested to General Wayne that his riflemen were indeed engaged with the rearguard of Cornwallis's army) eventually withdrew from the woods. They hurried across an open field and re-deployed amongst some farm buildings and fences facing the American advance.

Lieutenant Colonel Mercer, who in the middle of the fight in the woods was called away from his horsemen on the road and ordered to command the American riflemen on the right flank, joined them at the edge of John Harris's farm. He recalled that

---

[72] *Caledonian Mercury*, 10 October, 1781, "Extract of a letter from an officer in the 76th regiment dated on board the Lord Mulgrave transport, Hampton Road, Virginia, July 23, 1781," 3

> *I found the Riflemen advanc'd near the edge of the wood* [400 yards southwest of the road] *& firing at long shot on the sentinels of a Pickett paraded before a small clapboard house.*[73]

Riflemen on General Wayne's left flank under Major Call and Major McPherson, positioned themselves similarly in the woods at the edge of a field and fired at British pickets positioned at William Wilkinson's farm. McPherson could not see the main British force, deployed in two lines about half a mile to the southeast, but Mercer noticed them. He recalled that

> *The horse of Tarleton were form'd, at the respectable distance of four or five hundred yards; their left flank was protected by a skirt of woods, in front of which was form'd a Pickett of 100 or 150 men, beyond this on the right of Tarleton, & across the main road & in front of the church appeared, indistinctly, the main body of the British army.*[74]

Thousands of British troops stood in two lines on the opposite side of John Harris's farm field and across the road to Jamestown, waiting to join the battle. Lieutenant-Colonel Thomas Dundas commanded the left wing of Cornwallis's first line, which included the 43rd, 76th, and 80th Regiments with two 6 pound cannon and Tarleton's Legion. The right wing of the line consisted of two battalions of light infantry under Lieutenant-Colonel John Yorke. The Brigade of Guards, 23rd and 33rd Regiments and the Prince Hereditaire Hessian Regiment made up a second line (which would not be needed).

---

[73] Gillard Hunt, ed., "Colonel John Francis Mercer," *Eyewitness Accounts of the American Revolution: Fragments of Revolutionary History*, (NY Times & Arno Press, Reprint, 1971), 48

[74] Ibid., 47-48

LaFayette had indeed fallen into a trap. What was worse, at least for him, was that he discovered the trap while his men skirmished with the enemy pickets in the woods, but it was now too late to stop the engagement. Soon after General Wayne had advanced down the causeway towards Jamestown, LaFayette had gone to the river's edge southwest of Green Spring to view the ferry crossing at Jamestown. What he saw on both sides of the river convinced him that Cornwallis had not yet crossed the James River with his main force.

LaFayette dashed back to Green Spring to recall General Wayne, but it was too late, Wayne's advance guard had reached the other end of the woods. All that LaFayette could do was order his last two light infantry battalions (which had just arrived at Green Spring) to prepare to cover the inevitable American retreat and then ride forward to join General Wayne. A battalion of light infantry under Major John Wyllys and the 2nd and 3rd Pennsylvania Regiments had already gone ahead to reinforce Wayne.

While LaFayette and the reinforcements hurried to join the battle, Lieutenant-Colonel Mercer and the riflemen on the American right flank concentrated on driving the British pickets from John Harris's clapboard house and farm. Mercer described what happened:

> *The* [enemy] *Picket was speedily driven* [from the house] *with loss, & possession gain'd of the house. To support them & regain the house,* [a second British detachment] *advanc'd with spirit, but they were unable to stand the deadly fire of the Riflemen, and were driven back with...loss.... The Riflemen embolden'd by this success, were with difficulty restrain'd from advancing...and a number of them crowded into the house and began to fire to the left on the main body of the British army now plainly discover'd at a distance of about 300 yards.*[75]

---

[75] Ibid., 48

Lieutenant-Colonel Mercer noted that the rifle fire from the house drew the attention of British artillerists who

> *Open'd 3 pieces of artillery on us, at from three to four hundred yards. Almost at the first discharge my horse received a cannon ball in his body, which carried away my stirrups & bruis'd my foot...the shot passing through the clapboard house alarming the Riflemen within so much that they fled instantly with great trepidation; by this time I had mounted another horse, but it was impossible to rally those who had fled or stop those advanced into the field, who dispers'd in great confusion.*[76]

When a report reached General Wayne (who had halted with the remainder of the advance guard still unaware of Cornwallis's trap) that a lone British cannon was struggling to withdraw on the American right, Major Galvan requested permission to seize it. Wayne acquiesced and Galvan reported that

> *I moved* [with approximately 60 troops] *towards the place where the* [cannon reportedly was]: *we soon came up with several parties of the riflemen from which I could learn nothing of the pretended retreating field piece...I kept moving forward and met Col. Mercer whose horse had been killed and who, wounded himself, had the gallantry to guide my little column till we came in full sight of the British line.*

Undoubtedly taken aback by the number of enemy troops to his front, Galvan noticed that the enemy line extended as far as he could see to his right [Cornwallis's left] but that the end of Cornwallis's right flank was obscured by woods. Wrongly

---

[76] Ibid., 49

assuming that it did not extend very far beyond the woods, Major Galvan decided to attempt to turn Cornwallis's right flank. He recalled that

> *I therefore wheeled to the left and soon came to a large open field, where I perceived them drawn up and stretching out of my sight with a field piece opposite to me which had already begun to play.*
> *In this critical situation, a retreat, when so far from the American line and only within 300 yards of the British was excessively dangerous.*[77]

Expecting to be reinforced at any moment by Major Wyllys's light infantry battalion, Galvan chose to fight. He moved his men (under heavy fire) across the front of the British line to a skirt of wood on his left, then wheeled right to face the enemy and commenced a, *"smart, running fire,"* just 60 yards from the foe.[78] Galvan, unaware that Major Wyllys's battalion had become heavily engaged on Galvan's right against the advancing British line, declared that his men fought the whole British line alone for 15 minutes before they were nearly enveloped and forced to retire.[79] Other witnesses remember a shorter stand, but whatever the length of time, Galvan's fight was a bold display of determination and bravery.

On their way to the rear, Major Galvan and his men encountered General Wayne, now fully aware of Cornwallis's trap. The two detachments from the 2nd and 3rd Pennsylvania Regiments had arrived in time to support the 1st Pennsylvanians (who had not yet engaged in the fight) and General Wayne, whose flanks and front were being pressed,

---

[77] "Major William Galvan to Richard Peters, 8 July, 1781," *Gazette of the American Friends of LaFayette*, Vol. 1, No. 1, (February, 1942), 3 (Henceforth referred to as Galvan)

[78] Ibid.

[79] Ibid.

boldly ordered his vastly outnumbered troops to form into line of battle and advance. In a letter to General Washington after the engagement, Wayne justified his decision to attack the vastly superior enemy:

> *It was determined among a choice of difficulties, to advance and charge them. This was done with such vivacity as to produce the desired effect, that is, checking them in their advance, and diverting them from their [attempted encirclement].*[80]

Lieutenant William Feltman of the 1st Pennsylvania Regiment described the advance:

> *We...displayed to the right and left, the 3rd battalion on our right, and the 2nd on our left, being then formed, [we] brought on a general engagement, our advance [was] regular at a charge till we got within eighty yards of their whole army, they being regularly formed, standing one yard distance from each other...We advanced under a heavy fire of grape-shot at which distance we opened our musketry.*[81]

Ensign Ebenezer Denny, who was also in the center of General Wayne's line with the 1st Pennsylvania Regiment, was thrust in charge of his company after his captain was wounded and candidly described the experience in his journal.

> *Young and inexperienced, exhausted with hunger and fatigue, had like to have disgraced myself – had eat nothing all day but a few blackberries – was faint,*

---

[80] Sparks, ed. "General Wayne to General Washington, 8 July, 1781," *Correspondence of the American Revolution Being Letters of Eminent Men to George Washington*, 348

[81] Peter Decher, ed., *Journal of Lt. William Feltman of the First Pennsylvania Regiment, 1781-1782*, (Samen, NH: Ayer Co, 1969), 7

> *and with difficulty kept my place; once or twice was about to throw away my arms (a very heavy espontoon)....* [82]

Although his memory of the engagement likely lasted a lifetime, Denny recalled that

> *We could not have been engaged longer than about three or four minutes, but at a distance of sixty yards only.* [83]

All who participated or witnessed the engagement noted the intensity of those few minutes when Wayne advanced. British Lieutenant-Colonel Banastre Tarleton actually complimented the American continentals for their gallantry:

> *The conflict in this quarter was severe and well contested. The artillery and infantry of each army...were for some minutes warmly engaged not fifty yards asunder...on the left of the British, the action was for some time gallantly maintained by the continental infantry.* [84]

Major Galvan, who managed to redeploy his detachment on the left of the Pennsylvania line and join Wayne's advance, recalled that the American line advanced about thirty yards, which prompted the British to halt their advance and pour, "*an immense fire upon us.*"[85] Wayne's bold advance had momentarily frozen Cornwallis's troops, but the Pennsylvanians soon halted too. Major Galvan noted that

---

[82] Ebenezer Denny, *Military Journal of Major Ebenezer Denny*, (Philadelphia: J.B. Lippincott & Co., 1859), 37

[83] Ibid.

[84] Tarleton, 354

[85] Galvin, 4

> *Our stop encouraged the British and, tho' our fire was as brisk as could be expected from so small a line, they began to move rapidly upon us and the right of the Pennsylvanians to give way, the left followed, and the enemy making a devil of a noise of firing and huzzaing (tho' by the by they did not push on very fast) all on our side became a scene of confusion.*[86]

General Wayne, realizing that his unexpected advance had achieved all that it could achieve, ordered a retreat. He explained to General Washington that, *"being employed by numbers,* [vastly greater than his and with] *many brave and worthy officers and soldiers killed or wounded, we found it expedient to fall back half a mile to Green Spring Farm."*[87]

Luckily for the Americans, the lateness of the day prevented a strong pursuit from Cornwallis, a decision that apparently did not sit well with some of Cornwallis's subordinates. A Pennsylvania newspaper printed an excerpt of a letter from an American officer that claimed

> *The British officers we are informed, are much displeased at* [the outcome of the battle] *and acknowledge they were outgeneraled; otherwise they must have cut to pieces our small detachment, aided as they were by 500 horse, and a considerable body of their infantry mounted.*[88]

The American officer went on to defend General Wayne's bold decision to attack:

---

[86] Ibid.
[87] Sparks, ed. "General Wayne to General Washington, 8 July, 1781," *Correspondence of the American Revolution Being Letters of Eminent Men to George Washington,* 348
[88] *Pennsylvania Packet,* 21 July, 1781, "Extract of a letter from an officer of rank, July 11, 1781,"

> *We could not possibly have extricated ourselves from the difficulties we were in, but by the manouvre we adopted, which although it may have the appearance of temerity to those unacquainted with circumstances, yet was founded upon the truest military principles: And was one of those necessary, though daring measures, which seldom fail of producing the desired effect, that is, confusing the enemy and opening a way to retreat in sight of a much superior army.*[89]

Although the Battle of Green Spring was a British victory, American losses, (which were roughly double the 70 men Cornwallis lost) could have been far worse.[90] In that sense, the Green Spring was a missed opportunity for the British.

---

[89] Ibid.
[90] Henry P. Johnson, *The Yorktown Campaign and the Surrender of Cornwallis:* 1781, (Eastern National, 1997), 190 (Originally printed in 1881)

Chapter Eleven

"Should a Naval Superiority Come, Great Advantage Might Be obtained in this Quarter."

July – September 1781

In the days following the Battle of Green Spring, General Cornwallis completed his movement across the James River, informed General Clinton in New York that the troops Clinton requested from Virginia would soon depart from Portsmouth (most would not) and ordered Lieutenant Colonel Tarleton to raid Prince Edward Courthouse and New London (in Bedford County) far to the west. Tarleton was instructed to, "*do everything in your power to destroy the supplies destined for the rebel army.*"[1] This included, "*all public stores of corn and provisions.*"[2] Cornwallis added:

> *If there should be a quantity of provisions or corn collected at a private house, I would have you destroy it, even [if] there should be no proof of its being intended for the public service, leaving enough for the support of the family, as there is the greatest reason to apprehend that such provisions will be ultimately appropriated by the enemy to the use of General Greene's army....*[3]

Across the James River, General LaFayette misinterpreted reports of British troop movements westward (Tarleton) to

---

[1] Tarleton, "General Cornwallis to Tarleton, 8 July, 1781," 402
[2] Ibid.
[3] Ibid., 402-03

mean that Cornwallis was heading back to the Carolinas. Further reports correctly indicated that only part of the British army had marched towards Petersburg, the rest headed south towards Portsmouth. Unsure what General Cornwallis was up to, LaFayette split his army. General Wayne led approximately 500 Pennsylvanian and 400 Virginian continentals across the James River, then northwest to Goode's Bridge in Amelia County to be in position to strike Tarleton on his return or follow Tarleton southward if his destination was the Carolinas.[4]

While Wayne camped at Goode's Bridge, Tarleton completed a two week, 400 mile circuit of south-central Virginia and returned to Portsmouth without incident, upset that, *"the stores destroyed...were not in quantity or value equivalent to the damage sustained in the skirmishes on the route, and the loss of men and horses by the excessive heat of the climate."*[5]

General LaFayette and the rest of the American army in Virginia (the light infantry corps and militia) spent most of July a few miles below Richmond at Malvern Hill, waiting for Cornwallis's intentions to become clear. LaFayette's encampment sat on the north side of the James River and was described by the general as, *"the Most Airy and Healthy place this side of the Mountains."*[6] Across the river and far to the south, outside of Portsmouth, Colonel Josiah Parker commanded a detachment of militia but his numbers were too small to challenge Cornwallis in Portsmouth.

General Clinton in New York was not pleased to learn of Cornwallis's move to Portsmouth. He informed his subordinate in mid-July that

---

[4] Idzerda, ed., "General LaFayette to General Washington, 20 July, 1781" *LaFayette in the Age of the American Revolution*, Vol. 4, 256
[5] Tarleton, 358
[6] Idzerda, ed., "General LaFayette to General Washington, 20 July, 1781" *LaFayette in the Age of the American Revolution*, Vol. 4, 256

> *I had flattered myself* [that]...*you would, at least, have waited for a line from me...before you finally determined upon so serious and mortifying a move, as the re-passing James River and retiring with your army to Portsmouth.*[7]

General Clinton and the British navy wanted Cornwallis to establish a secure, deep water port for the navy around Hampton or Yorktown. Clinton planned to send a large expedition up the Chesapeake Bay in the fall and desired a staging area other than Portsmouth to launch it from. Additionally, the British navy desired a safe location for part of its fleet to spend the winter. Portsmouth was deemed too sickly and confined for such a post, Clinton preferred Old Point Comfort near Hampton or Yorktown, which sat on the York River and looked out onto Chesapeake Bay. Clinton left the choice of sites to Cornwallis and instructed him to retain whatever troops necessary to properly defend the post.[8] To comply with General Clinton's wishes, General Cornwallis retained the troops that were about to embark for New York and made preparations to abandon Portsmouth.

James Armistead

General LaFayette received detailed reports of Cornwallis's decisions from James Armistead, a Virginian slave and American spy who had "run away" to the British in early July. He soon found service as one of General Cornwallis's servants and used his position to gather intelligence for General LaFayette. General LaFayette referred to Armistead in a letter to General Washington on July 31st:

---

[7] Tarleton, "General Clinton to General Cornwallis, 15 July, 1781," 404-05
[8] Tarleton, "General Clinton to General Cornwallis, 11 July, 1781," 404

> [My] *Servant to Lord Cornwallis writes on the 26th of July at Portsmouth, and Says His Master* [Cornwallis], *Tarleton, and Simcoe are still in town But Expect to Move. The Greatest Part of the Army is Embarked....*[9]

LaFayette added that General Cornwallis is, "*so shy of His papers that My Honest friend Says he Cannot get at them...But as a Servant* [he] *Has opportunities to Hear....*"[10]

At great personal risk, James Armistead listened closely to General Cornwallis's discussions and observed the activities of the British army in order to provide General LaFayette with a steady flow of intelligence. Unfortunately, some of Armistead's information confirmed LaFayette's mistaken belief that Cornwallis was going to send part of his force out of Virginia. LaFayette assumed that the destination of the departing British troops was New York, but the possibility that they might instead sail up the Chesapeake or the Potomac River could not be ignored. As a result, LaFayette remained cautious and held his army in place until more definitive intelligence could be obtained. He explained his caution to General Wayne, who was still encamped at Goode's Bridge:

> *Should the Ennemy Remain in this State we must not Give them the Credit of Having out Maneuvred us By a feint Embarkation. Should they* [sail] *up Pottowmack You Are Not farther from...that River than we are Here – and In Case a large Detachment is Made to New York which I think will Become a Matter of Necessity you are on Your way to Carolina.* [In addition to] *these Reasons, I* [also] *Hate Giving the troops Unnecessary fatigues.*[11]

---

[9] Idzerda, ed., "General LaFayette to General Washington, 31 July, 1781" *LaFayette in the Age of the American Revolution*, Vol. 4, 290-91

[10] Ibid.

[11] Idzerda, ed., "General LaFayette to General Wayne, 23 July, 1781," *LaFayette in the Age of the American Revolution*, Vol. 4, 274

LaFayette's uncertainty about General Cornwallis's intentions eased in early August when reports reached him that Cornwallis had landed troops near Yorktown. In response, LaFayette ordered General Wayne to march eastward, closer to the army; but the young commander still held doubts about Cornwallis's intentions:

> *From the Moment the Ennemy Embarked I was Certain New York would Be the object, and a part of Lord Cornwallis's Army would attempt Going to Carolina. At the time they went up the Bay and when Every Intelligence Seemed to Ascertain their Going to Baltimore I Still thought that* [the] *fleet would tack about and push for New York. Their landing at York Has Yet Appeared to me a feint to draw me to the Northward and if possible very low down* [so] *that His lordship Might Push for Carolina.*[12]

Although his army was still divided, LaFayette's two detachments were now within supporting distance of each other. Both encamped on the north side of the James River, LaFayette near Newcastle on the Pamunkey River and Wayne near Bottoms Bridge on the Chickahominy River.

LaFayette acknowledged the British activity around Yorktown and Gloucester Point, but still believed there was a high probability that at least some of Cornwallis's troops were destined for New York.[13] He expressed his continued concern at being out maneuvered by Cornwallis to General Washington:

---

[12] Idzerda, ed., "General LaFayette to General Wayne, 4 August, 1781," *LaFayette in the Age of the American Revolution*, Vol. 4, 294

[13] Idzerda, ed., "General LaFayette to General Washington, 6 August, 1781," *LaFayette in the Age of the American Revolution*, Vol. 4, 299

Southeastern Virginia

> *We shall act agreeably to Circumstances But Avoid drawing ourselves into a false Movement which for want of Cavalry and Command of the Rivers would give the Ennemy the Advantage of us. His Lordship plays So well that no Blunder Can Be Hoped from Him to Recover a Bad Step of ours.*[14]

LaFayette also casually noted Cornwallis's vulnerability at Yorktown, declaring, *"Should a [French] fleet Come in at this Moment our Affairs would take a very Happy turn."*[15]

Yorktown and Gloucester Point

While the bulk of Cornwallis's force unloaded the transports ships and prepared encampments at Yorktown and across the York River at Gloucester Point, British light parties scoured the surrounding countryside in search of rebels and provisions. Captain Johann Ewald of the Jagers led one such party about ten miles inland from Gloucester Point to Abingdon Church where he discovered hundreds of cattle that the locals had gathered to keep them out of British hands. Ewald recalled that

> *I felt sorry for these poor people and wished that they had escaped from me, but the army was nearby. I had to obey the orders and let the cattle be driven off* [to the army].[16]

Ewald continued on to Gloucester Courthouse and routed a militia patrol, capturing two of them. Several other skirmishes with local militia occurred over the course of the month near Sewell's Ordinary and Abingdon Church. One such affair on August 18th, involved Ewald's old nemesis from Princess Ann County, Major Amos Weeks.

---

[14] Ibid.
[15] Ibid.
[16] Ewald, "2 August, 1781," 322

Informed by a local slave that Major Weeks, with a large party of militia, was in Gloucester County, Ewald informed Lieutenant Colonel Simcoe and together they led 50 horsemen and 200 infantry to attack their old foe.[17] Ewald recalled that

> *One English mile from the enemy position [Simcoe] ran into an enemy patrol of two men, who ran back. But the colonel, and I with most of the men who could run swiftly, arrived at the same time as the patrol in the camp of the enemy, who had no time to get their arms and tried to save themselves. I tried to create still greater confusion by continuous haphazard firing, and we became masters of the whole enemy camp. We took one lieutenant and twenty-two men prisoner, captured forty-three horses and all the baggage....*[18]

Lieutenant Colonel Simcoe recorded in his journal (no doubt with a mixture of disappointment and satisfaction) that his men stormed Weeks's camp and burst into the house in which he was staying, but the rebel commander escaped with his men in, *"great confusion into the woods, leaving their dinner behind them."*[19]

LaFayette Holds His Force Together

While General Cornwallis secured his position at Yorktown and Gloucester, General LaFayette struggled to properly supply his troops and prevent the Pennsylvanians and Virginians from killing each other. A Virginian soldier actually did mortally wound a Pennsylvanian officer whom he found in bed with his wife. The Virginian was duly executed, no doubt increasing tensions between the two sides.

---

[17] Ewald, "18 August, 1781, 323
[18] Ibid., 323-24
[19] Simcoe, 249

Letters from General Wayne in early August described a detachment that was largely shoeless and in rags, struggling to march over, "*sharp pebbles & thro burning sands.*"[20] Under such conditions it was not surprising that Wayne's troops and officers seized every opportunity to relieve their suffering. One such opportunity appeared in late July when Wayne discovered a stash of nearly 200 pair of shoes. Unfortunately, the shoes belonged to Virginia. General Wayne explained to LaFayette that

> *The situation* [the shoes] *were found in, & the danger of being* [stolen] *or destroyed, added to the distressed Condition our people were in for want of shoes & Overalls (more than three fourths being totally destitute of the first article, & too many bare legged – rather too high up for a modest eye to view --) as well on the presumption that* [the shoes] *were the property of the United States, Induced me to* [seize them].[21]

Wayne professed surprise that the shoes belonged to Virginia and grudgingly agreed to return them, if necessary, but he warned that if he did, "*173 Veterans must inevitably be rendered unfit for service for want of these essential articles.*"[22] Wayne spitefully added that his shoeless troops would have to be removed from duty until shoes and overalls arrived from Pennsylvania. Furthermore, threatened Wayne, he would be forced to write to General Irvine in Pennsylvania and instruct him not to send any more Pennsylvania troops to Virginia unless they were properly clothed from the start with

---

[20] Idzerda, ed., "General Wayne to General LaFayette, 9 August, 1781," *LaFayette in the Age of the American Revolution*, Vol. 4, 308
[21] Ibid., 307
[22] Ibid.

everything they needed.[23] The implication was clear. If Virginia was not willing to "share" badly needed supplies with the Pennsylvanians, Wayne was going to remove his ill-supplied troops from the field.

The resentment felt by Wayne and his men towards Virginia troubled LaFayette and he wrote to General Washington on August 11th, about his concern:

> *The Pennsylvanians and Virginians Have Never Agreed but at the Present time, it is worse than Ever. I Receive Every day Complaints. Some from the [Governor] I Have Been obliged to take Notice of.... Gal. Waine thinks He and His people Have not Been well used. In a Word, I perceive the Seeds of a future Dispute Between States – and Every Day the troops Remain Here adds to the Danger.*[24]

LaFayette informed Washington that due to the mounting tension in his ranks he had decided to send Wayne's Pennsylvanians to General Greene in South Carolina as soon as 500 continentals arrived from Maryland.[25] In the meantime, LaFayette's troops remained encamped in King William and New Kent County and Wayne's troops remained at Bottom's Bridge.

While he waited for Cornwallis to reveal his intentions, LaFayette penned a letter to General Henry Knox that recapped the events of the summer and described the recent activity at Yorktown and Gloucester Point:

---

[23] Ibid.
[24] Idzerda, ed., "General LaFayette to General Washington, 11 August, 1781," *LaFayette in the Age of the American Revolution*, Vol. 4, 312
[25] Ibid.

> *Lord Cornwallis Having not Succeeded in land journeys Has Undertaken a Water Voyage. I thought first the Man was Going to New York – then to Pottowmack or Baltimore – But on a Sudden He Entered York River and is at York and Gloster out of our Reach, Refreshing our troops and Meditating Mischief. York is on High Ground Surrounded with Creeks and Morasses Accessible By one Single Avenue – There to My Surprise He does not fortify. Gloster is a Neck of land Projecting into the River and Very useful to the defense of Shipping – There My lord is fortifying....* [26]

LaFayette included yet another observation on the opportunity that existed for the allies should the French navy suddenly appear in the Chesapeake Bay.

A week later, General LaFayette updated Washington on Cornwallis's activities in Yorktown, reporting that

> *I have Got Some Intelligence By the Way of this Servant I Have once Mentioned* [James Armistead]. *A Very Sensible fellow Was With Him and from Him as Well as Deserters I Hear that they Begin fortifying at York.* [27]

Although the situation in Virginia appeared to be stalemated in August, a bold decision by General Washington soon changed everything.

---

[26] Idzerda, ed., "General LaFayette to Henry Knox, 18 August, 1781," *LaFayette in the Age of the American Revolution*, Vol. 4, 332

[27] Idzerda, ed., "General LaFayette to General Washington, 25 August, 1781," *LaFayette in the Age of the American Revolution*, Vol. 4, 357

General Washington

In New York, General Washington had come to the disappointing realization in mid-August that his long desired joint operation with the French to recapture New York from the British was not going to occur in 1781. The failure of the northern states to meet their recruitment quotas, combined with the decision of French Admiral de Grasse to sail his powerful West Indies fleet to the Chesapeake Bay instead of New York, forced Washington to adjust his plans. Fortunately, Washington had anticipated this possibility and had hinted to General LaFayette that he might soon send troops southward to help expel the British from the southern states.[28] On August 14th, General Washington resolved to do this very thing, recording in his diary that

> *I was obliged...to give up all idea of attacking New York; & instead thereof to remove the French Troops & a detachment from the American Army to the Head of Elk to be transported to Virginia for the purpose of cooperating with* [de Grasse] *against the Troops in that State.*[29]

General Washington wrote to LaFayette the next day to inform him of Admiral de Grasse's intentions to sail to the Chesapeake. Washington instructed LaFayette to position his army, "*as will best enable you to prevent* [the enemy's]

---

[28] Idzerda, ed., "General Washington to General LaFayette, 30 July, 1781," *LaFayette in the Age of the American Revolution*, Vol. 4, 288

[29] Donald Jackson, ed. "August 14, 1781," *The Diaries of George Washington*, Vol. 3, 409

sudden retreat thro North Carolina," and told LaFayette to expect reinforcements from New York.[30]

General LaFayette received Washington's instructions on August 21st, and immediately wrote to Governor Nelson to request that 600 militia be called out for service on the south side of the James River. General Wayne was ordered to march to Westover and prepare to cross the river, but LaFayette's detachment remained near West Point 25 miles up the York River from Yorktown.

LaFayette informed Washington that the troops presently in Virginia fit for service consisted of 400 Virginia continentals, 600 Pennsylvania continentals, 850 continental light infantry, 120 dragoons, and 3,000 militia.[31] LaFayette also expected 500 Maryland continentals to arrive at any moment. As for supplies and provisions, LaFayette lamented that

> *There is Such a Confusion in affairs in this part of the World that Immense Difficulties are found for a proper formation of Magazines.... We Have No Cloathing of any Sort – no Heavy Artillery in order. Some Arms will Be wanting – Some Horse Accoutrements – and Great deal of Ammunition.*[32]

LaFayette urged General Washington to come to Virginia himself, unaware that the American commander-in-chief had already begun the march south to oblige LaFayette.

---

[30] Idzerda, ed., "General Washington to General LaFayette, 15 August, 1781," *LaFayette in the Age of the American Revolution*, Vol. 4, 330

[31] Idzerda, ed., "General LaFayette to General Washington, 21 August, 1781," *LaFayette in the Age of the American Revolution*, Vol. 4, 338

[32] Ibid.

Washington – Rochambeau March

General Washington faced a daunting challenge in moving a portion of the American army and all of the French army from New York to Virginia, a journey of over 400 miles. The logistical challenges of suddenly moving thousands of troops hundreds of miles as quickly as possible were compounded by communication challenges that saw Washington and LaFayette receive messages from each other that were usually a week old and often older. This meant that General Washington usually had to make decisions based on outdated information.

Unsure whether Cornwallis would still be in Virginia when he and General Rochambeau arrived, Washington pushed forward, asking Count de Grasse in a letter on August 17th to send all of his frigates and transport ships to the Elk River at the head of Chesapeake Bay in order to meet the allied troops and hasten their movement southward.[33] Washington proceeded on faith that Admiral de Grasse would first secure control of the bay and then send the requested transport ships up the bay to the Elk River.

Leaving troops in New York under General William Heath to defend West Point and the New York Highlands, Washington led a detachment of approximately 2,500 continentals across the Hudson River and southward through New Jersey. Three thousand French troops marched south as well.[34] Fortunately for the allies, the heavy French siege guns and ordinance were transported by a French naval squadron out of Rhode Island.

---

[33] Fitzpatrick, ed. "General Washington to Comte de Grasse, 17 August, 1781," *The Writings of George Washington*, Vol. 23, 10-11
[34] John D. Grainger, *The Battle of Yorktown, 1781: A Reassessment*, 63

Efforts to deceive General Clinton into believing that New York City was Washington's target were initially successful. General Clinton reported in a letter to Lord George Germain in the British Ministry in early September that Washington had, *"crossed the* [Hudson] *River and by the position he took seemed to threaten Staten Island."*[35] By September 7th, however, reports that Washington and Rochambeau had crossed the Delaware River convinced Clinton that Virginia was Washington's real target.[36] By then, a large portion of Washington and Rochambeau's troops had boarded transport ships at Head of Elk, Maryland to sail down the Chesapeake and join General LaFayette in Virginia. The transports were protected by Admiral de Grasse's powerful French fleet, which had arrived in Chesapeake Bay on August 30th.

Three days after his arrival, Admiral de Grasse landed 3,250 French troops on Jamestown Island and two days after that, on September 5th, de Grasse sailed with his fleet out of the Chesapeake to confront a British fleet led by Admiral Thomas Graves.[37] The ensuing Battle of the Capes was a pivotal engagement in the Yorktown campaign; control of the Chesapeake Bay would largely determine the outcome of the confrontation that was brewing at Yorktown.

While the bulk of their troops and supplies sailed down the Chesapeake Bay, General Washington and General Rochambeau continued south by land with the army's cavalry, empty wagons, and cattle, unaware of the major naval engagement off the coast of Virginia. Washington reached Virginia on September 9th, and stopped with Rochambeau for four nights at his home, Mount Vernon. Six years had passed since Washington had last been home and although Mrs.

---

[35] K.G. Davies, ed. "General Sir Henry Clinton to Lord George Germain, 7 September, 1781," *Documents of the American Revolution: 1770-1783*, Vol. 20, 222

[36] Ibid.

[37] Idzerda, ed., " Comte de Grasse to General LaFayette, 30 August, 1781," *LaFayette in the Age of the American Revolution*, Vol. 4, 374

Washington had joined the general at every winter encampment, few soldiers had been in the field as long as the command-in-chief.

General Washington first learned of Admiral de Grasse's departure from the Chesapeake on the day he resumed his march south (September 13th). Stunned and anxious for the safety of his troops, as well as the French fleet, Washington dispatched orders to halt the troop transports until it was deemed safe for them to continue down the bay.[38]

Washington quickened his pace south and arrived in Williamsburg on September 14th, where he was greeted by an exuberant General LaFayette. LaFayette had reunited his separated detachments in Williamsburg a week earlier and then impatiently waited for Washington to arrive. General Washington was relieved to learn from LaFayette that the French navy had successfully engaged the British navy off the capes of Virginia on September 5th, and had returned to the Chesapeake to continue its blockade and protect the allied transport ships. Washington sent word for the transports to resume their journey down the bay and then began planning the next step of this daring operation, to besiege General Cornwallis at Yorktown and Gloucester Point.

---

[38] Fitzpatrick, ed., "General Washington to Thomas Sims Lee, 15 September, 1781," *The Writings of George Washington*, Vol. 23, 115

Chapter Twelve

"A Few Weeks Exertions and the Enemy is Expelled from Our State Forever."

September – October 1781

In Yorktown and Gloucester Point, General Cornwallis and his 7,000 man army (of which only 5,500 were listed as fit for duty) prepared themselves for the upcoming military siege.[1] A shortage of entrenching tools and the hot Virginia summer had hampered British construction of fortifications in August. The earthworks at Gloucester Point received much more attention than the fortifications at Yorktown, which were entirely inadequate when the French navy sailed into the Chesapeake on August 30th.

Admiral de Grasse's arrival triggered a new sense of urgency in the British camp and hundreds of men, both soldiers and runaway slaves who were promised their freedom by the British, worked feverishly to construct earthworks and redoubts at Yorktown. The terrain around the town offered some assistance to Cornwallis. The York River, which curved westward at Yorktown, shielded the town from the north and east. The threat of a French assault by sea existed, but British warships, fireships, and sunken transports (to obstruct the French) as well as artillery along the bluffs and across the river at Gloucester Point, defended Yorktown from a naval attack. A strong redoubt manned by the Royal Welch

---

[1] Jerome A. Greene, *The Guns of Independence: The Siege of Yorktown, 1781*, (California: Savas Beatie, 2005), 33

Fusiliers of the 23rd Regiment guarded the Williamsburg road that ran along the shore northwest of Yorktown. To the west of the town was a creek and swampy morass that made any approach from that direction extremely difficult. As a result, General Cornwallis concluded that the allied attack on Yorktown would come from the south and he concentrated his defensive efforts accordingly.

Not all of Cornwallis's thoughts were defensive in nature, however. A series of reconnaissance patrols directed at the allied forces gathering at Williamsburg caused Cornwallis to seriously consider an attack in mid-September. Seemingly unconcerned with the 3,250 French troops that landed in Virginia at the beginning of September, Cornwallis resolved to strike Williamsburg at dawn on September 27th.[2]

The arrival of two letters from General Clinton in New York just hours before the assault, however, (written on September 2nd and 6th respectively) caused Cornwallis to cancel the attack. In his first letter, General Clinton assured Cornwallis that, *"I shall either endeavor to reinforce the army under your command by all the means within the compass of my power, or make every possible diversion in Your Lordship's favor."*[3] Clinton's second letter announced to Cornwallis that

> *I think the best way to relieve you is to join you as soon as possible with all the force that can be spared from hence, which is about 4000 men. They are already embarked, and will proceed the instant I receive information from the Admiral that we may venture.... By accounts from Europe we have every reason to expect Admiral Digby hourly on the coast.*[4]

---

[2] Ibid., 32

[3] Wilcox, ed., "Extract of a letter from Sir Henry Clinton to Earl Cornwallis, 2 September, 1781," *The American Crisis*, 563

[4] Ibid., "Extract of a letter from Sir Henry Clinton to Earl Cornwallis, 6 September, 1781," *The American Crisis*, 564

Assured by General Clinton that help was on the way, Cornwallis resolved to dig in and wait for the promised relief. Cornwallis replied to Clinton and explained his decision:

> *If I had no hopes of relief, I would rather risk an action than defend my half-finished works. But, as you say Admiral Digby is hourly expected and promise every exertion to assist me, I do not think myself justifiable in putting the fate of the war on so desperate an attempt. My provisions will last at least six weeks from this day....*[5]

Cornwallis added a dire warning at the end of his letter.

> *If you cannot relieve me very soon, you must be prepared to hear the worst.*[6]

The very next day, (September 18th) General Rochambeau's French troops from New York stepped off their transports near Jamestown and proceeded to Williamsburg. They were joined two days later by General Washington's troops. Across the York River in Gloucester County, General George Weedon's 1,500 Virginia militia, who had kept an uneasy surveillance upon the British force at Gloucester Point, was reinforced by a legion of French cavalry and infantry under Armand de Lauzun.[7] In just a matter of weeks the allied presence in Virginia had swelled to nearly 18,000 men fit for duty.[8]

On the morning of September 28th, this enormous force marched to the outskirts of Yorktown and spent the night under arms. The baggage and camp equipment were still a day away, so the Americans, including General Washington

---

[5] Wilcox, ed., "Extract of Cornwallis to Clinton, 16-17 September, 1781," *The American Crisis,* 571

[6] Ibid.

[7] Greene, 74-75

[8] Ibid., 79

and his aides, slept under the stars.[9] The last great battle of the Revolutionary War was about to begin.

Siege of Yorktown

American and French troops moved closer to Yorktown on September 29th. They formed a rough semi-circle around the British fortifications and blocked all land access to and from the town. General Cornwallis appeared unconcerned by the allied presence. He was confident that his men, behind their earthworks, could defend Yorktown until the British navy ended the French blockade and relieved him.

To prevent the French fleet from sailing up the York River to shell Yorktown, Cornwallis scuttled a number of transport ships and prepared a few fire ships. Three of these fire ships were unsuccessfully sent amongst a portion of the French fleet a week before Washington and Rochambeau arrived at Yorktown, and the possibility of a second attack kept Admiral de Grasse and his fleet at a safe distance.[10] General Cornwallis also erected several outworks a half a mile in front of his main fortifications to hamper the approach of the Americans and French.. These redoubts were the allies' first target.

General Washington and his officers spent September 29th reconnoitering the British outworks. Skirmishes between Virginia riflemen and German jaegers took place but were of little consequence.[11] The allies awoke the next morning to a pleasant surprise. Upon receipt of a new message from General Clinton, Cornwallis abandoned most of his outworks under cover of darkness, withdrawing the defenders to the main works at Yorktown. Clinton's message, dated

---

[9] Henry Commager & Richard Morris, eds., "Journal of Colonel Jonathon Trumbull," *The Spirit of 'Seventy-Six: The Story of the American Revolution as Told by Participants*, (NY: Castle Books, 1967), 1127
[10] Ewald, 328
[11] Fitzpatrick, ed., "General Orders 27 September, 1781," *The Writings of George Washington*, Vol. 23, 148   and   Tarleton, 373

September 24th, informed Cornwallis that a Council of War in New York had

> *Unanimously determined that above 5000 men shall be embarked on board the King's ships, and the joint exertions of the fleet and army shall be made in a few days to relieve you. There is every reason to hope we shall start from hence the 5th of October.*[12]

In response to the news that a relief force would soon embark from New York, General Cornwallis decided to spare his troops in all but two of the vulnerable outworks from needless sacrifice and reposition them in the main fortifications at Yorktown and Gloucester Point. The allies promptly occupied the abandoned outworks and converted them into their own fortifications.

The next few days were relatively uneventful as both armies concentrated on preparations for the siege. General Washington was careful to rotate the duties of the troops so no single unit was overworked or overextended. While some units rested in camp, others worked on the earthworks and constructed implements of siege warfare (gabions and fascines). The allied camps and work parties were protected by large covering parties that defended against a sudden enemy attack.[13]

Across the York River in Gloucester County, a Virginia militia force of 1,500 men, with 600 French troops, had a different mission. They were ordered to, "*be exceedingly watchfull upon the Motions of the Enemy...and prevent, as much as possible, without risquing too much, the Enemy's gaining Provisions or Supplies from the Country....*"[14] This

---

[12] Wilcox, ed., "Extract of minutes of a council of war held at New York, 24 September, 1781," *The American Crisis*, 574

[13] Fitzpatrick, ed., "General Orders, 30 September, 1781," *The Writings of George Washington*, Vol. 23, 154-155

[14] Ibid., "General Washington to General Weedon, , 23 September, 1781," *The Writings of George Washington*, Vol. 23, 130

meant that the allied troops at Gloucester, under the command of General George Weedon did not have to press or besiege the British, they simply had to stay alert and challenge them if they advanced out of their fortifications.

Concern about the effectiveness of his militia caused General Weedon to post his men ten miles north of Gloucester Point.[15] General Armand Lauzun, the commander of the French troops with Weedon was incredulous at Weedon's "caution" and urged the militia general to move closer to the enemy to curtail their foraging. Weedon worried that this would expose his inexperienced militiamen to a sudden attack, so he chose to remain at a safe distance. Lauzun questioned Weedon's bravery, and the two men developed a strong dislike for each other. On October 1st, the arrival of eight hundred French reinforcements under General Choisy resolved the matter. Choisy outranked Weedon and led the reinforced allied detachment closer to Gloucester Point.

Battle of the Hook

The Battle of the Hook (also known as the Battle of Gloucester Point) began on the morning of October 2nd, when a party of General Weedon's mounted militia stumbled upon the rear guard of a large British foraging party a few miles from the British earthworks at Gloucester Point.[16] The British force, commanded by Lieutenant Colonel Banastre Tarleton, was in the midst of a profitable morning of foraging when the militia horsemen spotted them and raced back to report their activity. The Virginia horsemen soon met the Duke de Lauzun with a detachment of French hussars (cavalry) in advance of the allied troops marching towards Gloucester Point. Lauzun recalled with a hint of criticism that

---

[15] Harry M. Ward, *Duty, Honor, or Country: General George Weedon and the American Revolution.* (Philadelphia: American Philosophical Society, 1979), 216-217
[16] Tarleton, 376

> *Just as we reached the Gloucester plain some Virginia State Dragoons came up in great fright and told us that they had seen the English dragoons out and that for fear of accident they had hurried to us at full speed without stopping to see anything more.*[17]

Lauzun led his cavalry forward to investigate and encountered

> *A very pretty woman at the door of a little farm house on the high road; I went up to her and questioned her; she told me that Colonel Tarleton had left her house a moment before; that he was very eager to shake hands with the French Duke. I assured her that I had come on purpose to gratify him....*[18]

Lieutenant Colonel Tarleton was aware of Lauzun's approach; a rearguard patrol had reported his presence. As the French cavalry drew closer, "*a column of dust...became visible.*"[19] Lauzun remembered that he had not yet gone, "*a hundred steps*" from the little farm house when

> *I heard pistol shots from my advance guard. I hurried forward at full speed to find a piece of ground where I could find a line of battle. As I arrived I saw the English cavalry in force three times my own.*[20]

Tarleton's wagons, loaded with forage and escorted by the bulk of his detachment, were already on their way back to Gloucester Point when Lauzun appeared on the field. Tarleton ordered the wagons to continue on but

---

[17] "Narrative of the Duke de Lauzun," *The Magazine of American History*, Vol. 6, (1881), 52

[18] Ibid.

[19] Tarleton, 376

[20] "Narrative of the Duke de Lauzun," *The Magazine of American History*, Vol. 6, (1881), 52

> *Part of the legion* [cavalry]...*the 17th* [Light Dragoons] *and Simcoe's dragoons, were ordered to face about in the wood, whilst Lieutenant-Colonel Tarleton... reconnoitered the enemy,"* [with a troop of horse].[21]

It was probably these cavalry detachments, located on the edge of the wood, that Lauzun saw in the distance when he first arrived on the field. Positioned between the British cavalry and Lauzun was Tarleton with his single troop of horsemen, reconnoitering the situation. Lauzun charged forward to engage Tarleton and recalled that

> *Tarleton saw me and rode towards me with pistol raised. We were about to fight single handed between the two troops when his horse was thrown by one of his own dragoons pursued by one of my lancers. I rode up to him to capture him; a troop of English dragoons rode in between us and covered his retreat, he left his horse with me.*[22]

Tarleton recounted that while he and Lauzun clashed

> *The whole of the English rear guard set out full speed from its distant situation, and arrived in such disorder, that its charge was unable to make an impression on the Duke of Lauzun's hussars....*[23]

Tarleton remounted and ordered a withdrawal, pursued by Lauzun and his horsemen. Musket fire from 40 British infantry posted in a thicket, *"restrained"* Lauzun, who halted his charge.[24] This allowed Tarleton to rally his cavalry,

---

[21] Tarleton, 376-377
[22] "Narrative of the Duke de Lauzun," *The Magazine of American History*, Vol. 6, (1881), 52
[23] Tarleton, 377
[24] Ibid.

reverse direction, and once again charge upon Lauzun. Tarleton recalled that

> *A disposition was instantly made to charge the front of the hussars with one hundred and fifty dragoons, whilst a detachment wheeled upon their flank: No shock, however, took place between the two bodies of cavalry; the French hussars retired behind their infantry and a numerous militia who had arrived at the edge of the plain.*[25]

The "numerous militia" that Tarleton observed were approximately 160 Virginians under Lieutenant Colonel James Mercer. They arrived on the scene just in time to see the French horsemen repulsed. Mercer recalled that his men *"were at first somewhat startled to find the French horse retreating so rapidly…"*[26] The Virginians quickly recovered their nerve and deployed to meet the oncoming British. Mercer proudly recalled:

> [My men formed] *with great celerity & good order, & commenced firing, one half on the cavalry on the right, & the other half on the infantry advancing rapidly thro' the wood. The horse of the enemy had approach'd within 250 yards & the infantry were not at more than 150 yards distance when the firing began. No regular troops cou'd behave with more zeal & alacrity than this corps of Militia; their spirits had been rais'd by running them up, and being hurried into action without time to reflect on their danger, they discovered as much gallantry & order as any regular corps that I ever saw in action. Fortunately Tarleton did not like the reception prepared for him & at a critical moment*

---

[25] Ibid., 377-378
[26] Hunt, ed., "Colonel John Francis Mercer," *Eyewitness Accounts of the American Revolution: Fragments of Revolutionary History*, 58

> sounded a retreat, when not 100 cartridges remain'd unexpended in the regiment....[27]

Each of the three sides involved in the engagement suffered losses. Lieutenant Colonel Mercer reported 2 killed and 11 wounded from his force of Virginia militia. Lauzun reported 3 killed and 16 wounded, while Tarleton claimed that only one of his officers was killed and a dozen soldiers were wounded.[28]

The significance of the Battle of the Hook did not lie in the losses inflicted, however, but rather, it marked the last time the British ventured out of their Gloucester Point earthworks in any significant force.

Opening the Trenches

Across the river, Washington applauded the outcome of the engagement and prepared to open the first parallel (siege trench). He informed Edward Rutledge of South Carolina:

> *We have been hitherto employed in constructing some necessary advanced Works, in preparing fascines, Gabions etc. and bringing our heavy Artillery and Stores from the landing place on James River. This last has been carried on slowly till within a few days past, when our Waggons arrived from the Northward. The Engineers now think we have a sufficient stock to commence serious operations, and we open Trenches this Evening.*[29]

On the evening of October 6th, General Washington's army crept forward under cover of darkness to dig the first parallel about six hundred yards from the British works.

---

[27] Ibid., 59
[28] Greene, 147
[29] Fitzpatrick, ed., "General Washington to Edward Rutledge, 6 October, 1781," *The Writings of George Washington*, Vol. 23, 186

Lieutenant Colonel Richard Butler of Pennsylvania described the process:

> *The first parallel and other works being laid out by the engineer; a body of troops* [were] *ordered...to break ground and form works, the materials being got ready and brought previously to the spot.*[30]

Sergeant Joseph Plum Martin of Connecticut recalled that General Washington ceremoniously started the trench with a pick ax:

> *The troops of the line were there ready with entrenching tools and began to entrench, after General Washington had struck a few blows with a pickax, a mere ceremony....The ground was sandy and soft, and the men employed that night* [were not idle], *so that by daylight they had covered themselves from danger from the enemy's shot ....*[31]

Surgeon James Thacher observed the opening of the parallel and recalled:

> *This business was conducted with great silence and secrecy, and we were favored by Providence with a night of extreme darkness, and were not discovered before day-light. The working party carried on their shoulders fascines and intrenching tools, while a large part of the detachment was armed with the implements of death. Horses, drawing cannon and ordinance, and wagons loaded with bags filled with sand for constructing breastworks, flowed in the rear.*[32]

---

[30] Commager and Morris, "Journal of Colonel Richard Butler, 6 October, 1781," 1229

[31] Joseph Plum Martin, *Private Yankee Doodle*, (Eastern Acorn Press, 1962), 232   (Originally published in 1830)

[32] James Thacher, *Military Journal of the American Revolution*, Gansevoort, NY: Corner House Historical Publications, 1998, 281-282 (Originally published in 1862)

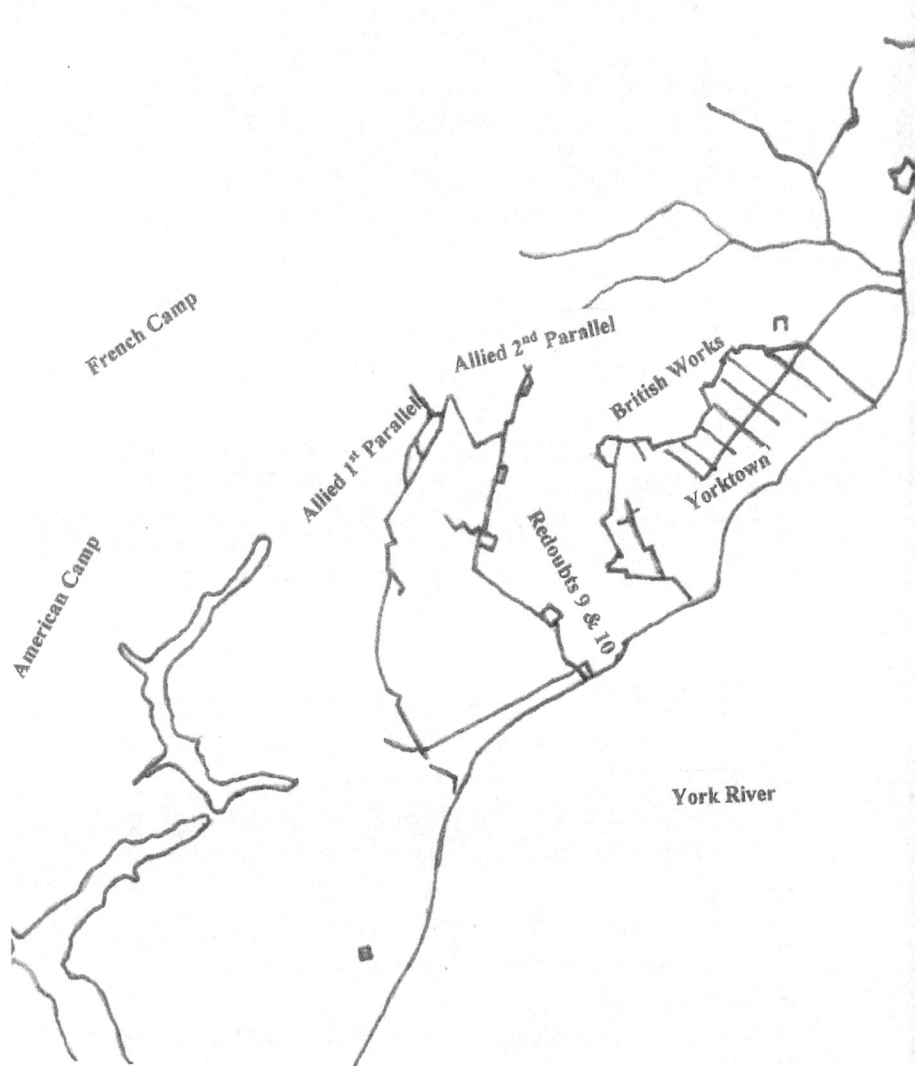

The British discovered the new allied works at sunrise and unleashed an intense artillery barrage. Over the course of the next two days, American and French work parties labored to improve the fortifications and construct battery positions for their cannon, all under a steady, but ineffective, British bombardment.

The allied work parties were not the only ones exposed to British artillery fire, covering parties rotated into the allied line as well to defend against British sorties. During one such rotation, Lieutenant Colonel Alexander Hamilton ordered his light infantrymen to stand upon the parapet of the trench in broad daylight and perform the entire manual of arms in view of the enemy. The British were apparently astonished at such a brash display of recklessness and held their fire, much to the relief of Hamilton's troops, many who undoubtedly did not appreciate that their commander had, *"wantonly exposed the lives of his men,"* to the British.[33]

Allied Bombardment Begins

The allies completed construction of their first artillery batteries on October 9th, and responded to the British bombardment with one of their own. The French were first to fire, directing cannon, howitzer, and mortar shot and shell at an isolated redoubt on the right flank of the British works and on British ships in the river.[34] General Washington reportedly commenced the American bombardment two hours later, touching off an 18 pound cannon whose solid shot smashed through a building with British officers inside, killing one instantly and tearing the leg off another.[35] The rest of the American grand battery (made up of two 24 pound cannon, twelve 18 pound cannon, two howitzers and four mortars)

---

[33] Wm. H. Egle, ed., "Diary of Captain James Duncan of Colonel Moses Hazen's Regiment in the Yorktown Campaign, 1781," *Pennsylvania Archives*, 2nd Series, Vol. 15, (1890), 749
[34] Greene, 190
[35] Ibid., 191

followed suit and pounded two redoubts on the British left.[36] Over the next two days, additional allied batteries joined the bombardment, and soon over fifty artillery pieces hurled their deadly ordinance into Yorktown.[37] American Captain James Duncan described the allied bombardment of Yorktown from his perspective in the first parallel:

> *The whole night was nothing but one continual roar of cannon, mixed with the bursting of shells and rumbling of houses torn to pieces. As soon as the day approached the enemy withdrew their pieces from their embrazures and retired under cover of their works, and now commenced a still more dreadful cannonade from all our batteries without scarcely any intermission for the whole day.*[38]

Captain Johann Ewald described the impact from inside the British works:

> *Since yesterday the besiegers have fired bombshells incessantly.... The greater part of the town lies in ashes, and two [of our] batteries have already been completely dismantled.*[39]

Stephan Popp, another German soldier, noted:

> *The heavy fire forced us to throw our tents in the ditches.... We could find no refuge in or out of town. The people fled to the waterside and hid in hastily contrived shelters on the banks, but many of them were killed by bursting bombs.*[40]

---

[36] Ibid.
[37] Selby, 306
[38] Egle, ed., "Diary of Captain James Duncan..." *Pennsylvania Archives*, 2nd Series, Vol. 15, 751
[39] Ewald, 334
[40] Nell Moore Lee, *Patriot Above Profit: A Portrait of Thomas Nelson Jr., Who Supported the American Revolution With His Purse and Sword*, (Nashville, TN: Rutledge Hill Press, 1988), 471

Lieutenant Bartholomew James, a British naval officer detached from his ship to serve on an artillery battery in the British works at Yorktown, described the suffering those trapped in Yorktown experienced during the allied bombardment:

> *Upwards of a thousand shells were thrown into the works on this night* [October 11] *and every spot became alike dangerous. The noise and thundering of the cannon, the distressing cries of the wounded, and the lamentable sufferings of the inhabitants, whose dwellings were chiefly in flames, added to the restless fatigues of the duty, must inevitably fill every mind with pity and compassion who are possessed of any feelings for their fellow creatures.*[41]

In a letter to the Governor of Maryland, General Washington provided a more tactical assessment of the siege's impact on the British works:

> *Our Shells have done considerable damage to the Town, and our fire from the Cannon have been so heavy and well directed against the embrasures* [openings in the British works which their cannon fire through] *that they have been obliged, during the day, to withdraw their Cannon and place them behind their* [earthworks].[42]

Lieutenant Colonel St. George Tucker observed the allied bombardment from his post with the Virginia militia and made a similar observation about its effectiveness.

---

[41] John K. Laughton, ed., *The Journal of Rear-Admiral Bartholomew James*, (1896), 122

[42] Fitzpatrick,ed., "General Washington to Governor Thomas Sims Lee, 12 October, 1781," *The Writings of George Washington*, Vol. 23, 210

> *A number of shells have been thrown into the Enemy's Works, & the shot so well directed in general that many of the Embrasures of the Enemy's are wholly rendered incapable of offensive Operations – there are but two Cannon now to be seen in their Embrasures.*[43]

With the situation growing desperate, General Cornwallis updated General Clinton in New York and warned that

> *Nothing by a direct move to York River – which includes a successful naval action – can save me.* [44]

Cornwallis added that since the enemy had commenced their bombardment, *"without intermission with forty pieces of cannon (mostly heavy) and sixteen mortars.... We have lost about seventy men, and many of our works are considerably damaged."*[45] The besieged British commander at Yorktown closed his letter with a dire assertion:

> *With such works on disadvantageous ground, against so powerful an attack, we cannot hope to make a long resistance.*[46]

---

[43] Edward M. Riley, ed., "St. George Tucker's Journal of the Siege of Yorktown, 1781, *The William and Mary Quarterly*, Vol. 5, No. 3, (July 1948), 10 October, 1781 Entry, 386

[44] Wilcox, ed., "Copy of a letter from Earl Cornwallis to Sir Henry Clinton, 11 October, 1781," *The American Crisis*, 581

[45] Ibid.

[46] Ibid.

Second Parallel : The Allied Noose Tightens

Baffled by what he viewed as Cornwallis's, *"passive beyond conception"* response to the siege, Washington moved to open a second parallel closer to Yorktown.[47] He hoped to compel Cornwallis to capitulate before a British relief force arrived from New York. On the evening of October 11th, allied troops crept closer to Yorktown and constructed a new parallel within 300 yards of the British works.[48] Lieutenant William Feltman of Pennsylvania recounted that

> *Just at dusk we advanced within gun-shot of the enemy, then began our work. In one hour's time we had ourselves completely covered, so we disregarded their cannonading; they discharged a number of pieces at our party, but they had but little effect and only wounded one of our men.*[49]

Lieutenant Feltman and his fellow soldiers were actually more endangered from errant allied cannon fire than fire from the British lines:

> *We were in the center of two fires, from the enemy and our own, but the latter was very dangerous; we had two men killed and one badly wounded from the French batteries, also a number of shells burst in the air above our heads, which was very dangerous to us. We dug the ditch three and a half feet deep and seven feet in width.*[50]

---

[47] Fitzpatrick, ed., "General Washington to Governor Thomas Sims Lee, 12 October, 1781," *The Writings of George Washington*, Vol. 23, 210

[48] Fitzpatrick, ed., "General Washington to the President of Congress, 12 October, 1781," *The Writings of George Washington*, Vol. 23, 213

[49] Decher, ed., *Journal of Lt. William Feltman of the First Pennsylvania Regiment, 1781-1782*, 19

[50] Ibid

Militiaman Daniel Trabue described the enormous mortar shells that the allies lobbed towards the British, some of which burst prematurely over the allied lines:

> *The shells were made of pot metal like a jug 1-2 inch thick, without a handle, & with a big mouth. They were filled with powder, and other combustibles in such a manner that the blaze came out of the mouth, and keeps on burning until it gets to the body where the powder is, then it bursts and the pieces fly every way, and wound & kill whoever it hits.*[51]

Trabue added that the rapid rate of allied artillery fire, which he described as one, "*every minute and sometimes 10 or 15 at the same time,*" wreaked havoc on the enemy:[52]

> *There were so many* [shells] *flying and falling in* [their] *Fort that we had no Doubt but that we were paying them well for their mischief to us.*[53]

Dr. James Thacher also acknowledged the intense allied bombardment, but added that the British responded with a bombardment of their own:

> *From the 10th to the 15th, a tremendous and incessant firing from the American and French batteries is kept up, and the enemy return the fire, but with little effect.... We have now made further approaches to the town, by throwing up a second parallel line, and batteries within about three hundred yards; this was effected in the night, and at day-light the enemy roused to the greatest exertions; the engines of war have raged with redoubled fury and destruction on*

---

[51] Lillie DuPuy VanCulin Harper, ed., *Colonial Men and Times: Containing the Journal of Col. Daniel Trabue,* 112
[52] Ibid.
[53] Ibid.

> both sides, no cessation day or night...The siege is daily becoming more and more formidable and alarming, and his lordship must view his situation as extremely critical, if not desperate.[54]

A French observer also noted the increased intensity of the siege upon the opening of the second parallel and speculated that General Cornwallis had been hording his ammunition in anticipation of the allied advance:

> The day was spent in cannonading and firing bombs at each other in such profusion that we did one another much damage. The enemy seemed to have been saving up their ammunition for the second parallel. It was of very small caliber and very effective, being fired at short range. That night we had six men killed and twenty-eight wounded.[55]

The accuracy of allied gunfire, particularly from the French guns, also played a significant role in suppressing British firepower. Naval Lieutenant Bartholemew James commanded a detachment of 36 sailors who were posted in the hornwork section of the British earthworks, just 300 yards from the French line and batteries. He recalled that

> In fifty-two minutes after my arrival in the hornwork the enemy silenced the three left guns by closing the embrasures, shortly after which they dismounted a twelve pounder, knocked off the muzzles of two eighteens, and for the last hour and a half left me with one eighteen-pounder with a part of its muzzle

---

[54] Thacher, 283-284
[55] Howard Rice and Anne Brown, "Clermont, Crevecoeur Journal, " *The American Campaigns of Rochambeau's Army,* Vol. 1, (Princeton, NJ: Princeton University Press, 1972), 59

> *also shot away, which I kept up a fire till it was also rendered useless.*[56]

As he neared the end of his eight hour shift in the hornwork, Lieutenant James was nearly killed by a shell that burst nearby and gave him a contusion on his face and leg. He was lucky, the losses among his detachment were devastating:

> *During my stay in the works [I] had nine men killed, twenty-seven wounded, eight of which died [since] they were removed, and most of the wounded had lost an arm or leg, and some both. In short, myself and the midshipman, both wounded were the only two returned out of thirty-six, having stood a close cannonade with the enemy for eight hours, who had ninety-seven pieces of heavy cannon playing on us all that time.*[57]

While British casualties rose steadily due to the allied shelling (as well as rampant illness that raged among the confined troops) allied casualties were rather low in comparison. In the two weeks that had passed since their arrival at Yorktown, the allies had suffered 118 casualties. The French lost 9 killed and 67 wounded and the Americans 14 killed and 30 wounded.[58]

Despite the death and destruction that was inflicted by the constant barrage of artillery, Dr. Thacher found the aerial display over the battlefield fascinating:

---

[56] John K. Laughton, ed., *The Journal of Rear-Admiral Bartholomew James*, (1896), 124

[57] Ibid.

[58] "Return of Killed and Wounded..." *The Pennsylvania Gazette and Weekly Advertiser*, No. 2681, 31 October, 1781, 2

> *Being in the trenches every other night and day, I have a fine opportunity of witnessing the sublime and stupendous scene which is continually exhibiting. The bomb-shells from the besiegers and the besieged are incessantly crossing each other's path in the air. They are clearly visible in the form of a black ball in the day, but in the night, they appear like a fiery meteor with a blazing tail, most beautifully brilliant, ascending majestically from the mortar to a certain altitude, and gradually descending to the spot where they are destined to execute their work of destruction.... When a shell falls, it whirls round, burrows and excavates the earth to a considerable extent, and bursting, makes dreadful havoc around. I have more than once witnessed fragments of the mangled bodies and limbs of the British soldiers thrown into the air by the bursting of our shells....[59]*

Completion of the American section of the second parallel was obstructed by the presence of two British redoubts in advance of the left section of Cornwallis's main line. These outworks, situated near the river about 300 yards in front of the main British works, protected Cornwallis's left flank and prevented the Americans from extending their 2nd parallel to the river. As a result, General Washington determined that the British outworks had to be taken and directed his artillery batteries be pound the two redoubts in preparation for an assault.

Storming Redoubts 9 and 10

In the early evening of October 14th, two 400 man detachments, one American and the other French, moved against the British outposts, known today as Redoubts 9 and 10. The Americans, led by Colonel Alexander Hamilton,

---

[59] Thacher, 284

attacked Redoubt 10, which sat on the edge of a bluff overlooking the York River and was defended by approximately 70 British soldiers.[60] The French, under Colonel de Deux-Ponts, assaulted Redoubt 9, which sat about 225 yards southwest of Redoubt 10. This post was larger and was defended by over 120 German and British soldiers.[61] Both redoubts were protected by earthen walls, a ditch and palisade, and extensive abatis, all of which the allies had to overcome before they reached the enemy.

The American and French detachments approached the redoubts around 7:00 p.m. with unloaded muskets to prevent an accidental discharge. Their bayonets would decide the struggle. Captain Stephen Olney, who commanded a company of Rhode Island light infantry in General LaFayette's division, participated in the assault and recalled that

> *The column marched in silence, with guns unloaded, and in good order. Many, no doubt, thinking, that less than one quarter of a mile would finish the journey of life with them. On the march I had a chance to whisper to several of my men (whom I doubted) and told them that I had full confidence that they would act the part of brave soldiers....*[62]

Captain Olney continued:

> *The column...moved on, six or eight pioneers* [sappers and miners] *in front, as many of the forlorn hope next, then Colonel Gimatt with five or six volunteers by his side then my platoon, being the front of the column....*[63]

---

[60] Nell Moore Lee, 476
[61] Ibid.
[62] Mrs. Williams, ed., "Life of Captain Stephen Olney of Rhode Island," *Biography of Revolutionary Heroes*, (1839), 276
[63] Ibid.

Sergeant Joseph Plum Martin of Connecticut, who was one of the sappers in the front of the column, recalled that

> *We...moved silently on toward the redoubt we were to attack, with unloaded muskets. Just as we arrived at the abatis, the enemy discovered us and directly opened a sharp fire upon us.... Our people began to cry, "The fort's our own!" and "Rush on boys!" The Sappers and Miners soon cleared a passage for the infantry, who entered it rapidly.... While passing,* [through the abatis] *a man at my side received a ball in his head and fell under my feet, crying out bitterly. While crossing the trench, the enemy threw hand grenades into it. As I mounted the breastwork, I met an old associate hitching himself down into the trench. I knew him by the light of the enemy's musketry, it was so vivid.*[64]

Captain Olney recorded a similar account of the attack:

> *When we came near the front of the abatis, the enemy fired a full body of musketry. At this, our men broke silence and huzzaed; and as the order for silence seemed broken by every one, I huzzaed with all my power, saying, "see how frightened they are, they fire into the air!"*[65]

Struggling through the dense abatis, then into the ditch and over the palisade and parapet, Captain Olney and the Americans engaged in desperate hand to hand combat. Olney recalled that when he ascended the parapet he called out in a calm tone, *"Captain Olney's company form here!"*[66] This

---

[64] Martin, 235-236

[65] Mrs. Williams, ed., "Life of Captain Stephen Olney of Rhode Island," *Biography of Revolutionary Heroes,* (1839), 276

[66] Ibid., 277

attracted the enemy's notice, who pushed, *"not less than six or eight bayonets at me."*[67] Olney continued:

> *I parried as well as I could with my espontoon, but they broke off the blade part, and their bayonets slid along the handle of my espontoon and scaled my fingers; one bayonet pierced my thigh, another stabbed me in the abdomen just above the hip bone. One fellow fired at me, and I thought the ball took effect in my arm; by the light of the gun I made a thrust with the remains of my espontoon in order to injure the sight of his eyes; but as it happened, I only made a hard stroke to his forehead.*[68]

With Americans pouring into the redoubt from all directions, British resistance collapsed. Many fled out the rear of the redoubt in hopes of escaping to the main British works 300 yards away. A majority made it out, but some were cut off and captured by an American detachment that had circled around in anticipation of just such a move. Those few remaining British troops still in the redoubt pleaded for mercy and surrendered. About a quarter of the 70 man British garrison of Redoubt 10 were killed, wounded or captured. American casualties were higher, with 8 killed and 36 wounded.[69]

Two hundred yards to the left, the French were still engaged in a bloody struggle for Redoubt 9. A French participant recounted that

> *The enemy discovered the column early and opened a very lively musket fire upon it. We found their abatis in far better condition than we had anticipated, since*

---

[67] Ibid.
[68] Ibid.
[69] Greene, 251 and "Return of Killed and Wounded…" *The Pennsylvania Gazette and Weekly Advertiser*, No. 2681, 31 October, 1781, 2

> *much of our artillery had been battering the redoubt for several days. Ignoring the enemy fire and slashing those that resisted with their axes, our pioneers had opened passages for us....*[70]

Initially unable to penetrate the redoubt's thick abatis, the French suffered a significant number of casualties before they finally broke through. Pouring over the parapet and into the redoubt, a scene of mass confusion and brutality ensued. One of the attacking French regiments wore blue coats instead of the traditional white coats of the French army. In the chaos of the night battle, it was difficult to distinguish between the blue coats of the German defenders and those of the French troops. As a result, a number of French soldiers were cut down by their own men within the redoubt.[71]

Although it took longer and cost more men, Redoubt 9 fell to the French at the loss of approximately 80 soldiers killed and wounded. German and British losses at Redoubt 9 were estimated at between 55 to 65 troops killed, wounded and / or captured.[72] The remainder fled back to the main works, hazarding fire from their comrades who mistook them for the enemy.

The capture of these two outposts allowed the Americans to complete the second parallel. Allied work parties immediately followed the assault and worked feverishly to incorporate the captured redoubts into the second parallel. By daybreak they had succeeded, and the noose tightened once again around the British in Yorktown.

---

[70] Howard Rice and Anne Brown, "Verger Journal" *The American Campaigns of Rochambeau's Army*, Vol. 1, 142

[71] Greene, 251

[72] Ibid., 252

Cornwallis Responds

General Cornwallis responded to the loss of his outposts with a furious bombardment of the allied lines. Lieutenant William Feltman of Pennsylvania noted that *"the enemy threw a number of shells this day and wounded a great number of men, especially militia."*[73] Feltman had little sympathy for the wounded militia:

> *Several were wounded this day in their sleep, such is the carelessness of those stupid wretches who are not acquainted with the life of a soldier.*[74]

In addition to the intensified bombardment of the allied lines, General Cornwallis also sent his first sortie against the allies. In the early morning hours of October 16th, Lieutenant Colonel Robert Abercrombie led 350 soldiers into the French and American trenches.[75] They overwhelmed two artillery batteries and spiked a number of cannon before withdrawing in the face of a French counterattack. The assault, although brave, was largely ineffectual as most of the spiked cannon were repaired and put back in service by that afternoon.

Once the batteries of the second parallel became operational, the allies poured deadly shot and shell upon the British from point blank range. Dr. James Thacher noted:

> *Not less than one hundred pieces of heavy ordinance have been in continual operation during the last twenty-four hours. The whole peninsula trembles under the incessant thunderings of our infernal machines; we have leveled some of their works in*

---

[73] Decher, ed., *Journal of Lt. William Feltman of the First Pennsylvania Regiment, 1781-1782*, 20
[74] Ibid.
[75] Tarleton, 386

> *ruins and silenced their guns; they have almost ceased firing.*[76]

With his ordinance and provisions nearly exhausted, and his force reduced by death, injury, and illness, General Cornwallis made one last attempt to forestall disaster. During the evening of October 16th, he ferried part of his army across the river to Gloucester Point. He hoped to assemble all those who could march on the north side of the river and break through the allied line at Gloucester. His plan was foiled when a violent storm scattered many of his boats. It was now impossible to complete the movement before daylight, so Cornwallis cancelled the attempt and recalled the troops to Yorktown.

Captain Johann Ewald grimly assessed the British situation on October 17th:

> *All the batteries were dismuntled, the works destroyed, munitions and provisions wanting, the wounded and sick lying helpless without medicine, and the army melted away from 7,000 to 3,200, among whom not a thousand men could be called healthy....*[77]

In a bitter letter to General Clinton written days after the siege, Cornwallis described a similar situation on October 17th:

> *Our works...were going to ruin. And, not having been able to strengthen them by abatis nor in any other manner than by a slight fraising (which the enemy's artillery were demolishing wherever they fired),* [I determined that the works] *in many parts were very assailable...and that by the continuance of the same fire for a few hours longer they would be in*

---

[76] Thacher, 286
[77] Ewald, 336

> such a state as to render it desperate, with our numbers, to attempt to maintain them. We at that time could not fire a single gun: only one eight-inch and little more than one hundred cohorn shells remained. A diversion by the French ships of war that lay at the mouth of York River was to be expected. Our numbers had been diminished by the enemy's fire, but particularly by sickness; and the strength and spirits of those in the works were much exhausted by the fatigue of constant watching and unremitting duty.[78]

With no British relief force in sight, there was only one thing left for Cornwallis to do, surrender. He rationalized his decision to General Clinton a few days after the siege:

> Under all these circumstances I thought it would have been wanton and inhuman to the last degree to sacrifice the lives of this small body of gallant soldiers – who had ever behaved with so much fidelity and courage – by exposing them to an assault which, from the numbers and precautions of the enemy, could not fail to succeed. I therefore proposed to capitulate.[79]

At 10:00 a.m. on October 17, 1781, General Cornwallis ordered a British drummer to beat a parley upon the parapet of the British earthworks. Alongside the drummer stood a British officer with a white handkerchief. The American gunners opposite the scene could not hear the drummer over the noise of the shelling, but they recognized the meaning of a white flag and ceased their bombardment. A flurry of messages passed between the lines, followed by two days of

---

[78] Wilcox, ed., "Extract of a letter from Earl Cornwallis to Sir Henry Clinton, 20 October, 1781," *The American Crisis*, 585-586
[79] Ibid., 586

negotiations that resulted in the capitulation of General Cornwallis and his army on October 19th.

Nearly 7,100 British and German soldiers surrendered at Yorktown. This number swelled to 8,100 when the captured British sailors and camp followers were included.[80] The three week siege inflicted nearly 500 casualties (156 killed and 326 wounded) on Cornwallis's force.[81] The French reported 60 of their troops killed and 194 wounded. The Americans only lost 28 men killed and 107 wounded.[82]

General Washington granted similar terms of surrender to Cornwallis that were granted to the Americans when they surrendered at Charleston in 1780. This meant that most of the British prisoners were not paroled, but held as prisoners of war until they could be exchanged for American prisoners.[83] The British and German prisoners were marched to Winchester under militia escort. General Cornwallis and a few of his fellow officers avoided this humiliation. They were granted their parole and allowed to return to New York unescorted.

Just days after the victory at Yorktown, General George Washington returned north with most of the American continental troops to rejoin the rest of the American army outside of New York. Part of the French army remained in Virginia for the winter, much to the pleasure of many Virginians who enjoyed their company and most particularly, their commerce.

---

[80] Greene, 308
[81] Ibid., 307
[82] Ibid.
[83] Greene, 307

Although General Washington's decisive victory at Yorktown significantly weakened Britain's will to continue the war, peace negotiations dragged on for over a year before a final agreement was reached that recognized American independence. During this time, bloodshed continued on the frontier, in the South, and around New York, but the engagements were small and inconsequential to the overall conflict.

Finally, in 1783, Britain, France, and America agreed to the Treaty of Paris. The bloody eight year war was finally over. It was a war that many Virginians felt in the homes and communities, and through their suffering and sacrifice, Virginians played an enormous role in gaining independence for America.

Bibliography

Anderson, D. R. ed., "The Letters of Colonel William Woodford, Colonel Robert Howe, and General Charles Lee to Edmund Pendleton," *Richmond College Historical Papers*, June, 1915.

Ballagh, James C., ed., *The Letters of Richard Henry Lee,* Vol. 1, NY: Macmillan Co., 1911.

Boyd, Julian P. ed., *The Papers of Thomas Jefferson,* Vol. 1-6 Princeton, NJ: Princeton University Press, 1950-51.

Brock, R.A. ed., "Orderly Book of the Company of Captain George Stubblefield, 5th Virginia Regiment: From March 3,1776 to July 10, 1776, Inclusive," *Virginia Historical Society Collections,* New Series 6, 1887.

Brock, R.A. ed., "Papers Military and Political, 1775-1778 of George Gilmer, M.D. of Pen Park, Albemarle Co., VA," *Miscellaneous Papers 1672-1865 Now First Printed from the Manuscripts in the Virginia Historical Society,* Richmond, VA, 1937.

Buchanan, John. *The Road to Guilford Courthouse: The American Revolution in the Carolinas.* NY: John Wiley & Sons, Inc., 1997.

Campbell, Charles, ed., *The Bland Papers: Being a Selection from the Manuscripts of Colonel Theodorick Bland Jr. of Prince George County, Virginia,* Vol. 1. Petersburg: Edmund & Julian Ruffin, 1840.

Campbell, Charles, ed. *The Orderly Book of that Portion of the American Army Stationed at or near Williamsburg 6th Regiment...from March 18, 1776 to August 28, 1776*. Richmond, 1860.

Cecere, Michael. *Captain Thomas Posey and the 7th Virginia Regiment*. Westminster, MD: Heritage Books, 2006.

Cecere, Michael. *Great Things Are Expected from the Virginians: Virginia in the American Revolution*. Westminster, MD: Heritage Books, 2008.

Cecere, Michael. *Wedded to My Sword: The Revolutionary War Service of Light Horse Harry Lee*. Westminster, MD: Heritage Books, 2012.

Chase, Philander D. ed., *The Papers of George Washington, Revolutionary War Series,* Vol. 1-5, Charlottesville, VA: University Press of Virginia, 1985-93.

Clark, William, ed., *Naval Documents of the American Revolution*, Vol. 1-5. Washington, D.C., 1964.

Commager, Henry Steele. *Documents of American History*. New York: Appleton-Century-Crofts, 1963.

Conrad, Dennis ed., *The Papers of General Nathanael Greene*, Vol. 8, Chapel Hill: University of North Carolina Press, 1995.

Danske Dandridge, Danske. *Historic Shepherdstown*. Charlottesville, VA: Michie Co., 1910.

Davies, K. G., ed., *Documents of the American Revolution,* Colonial Series, Vol. 12-20 Irish University Press. 1976-79.

Davis, Robert. *The Revolutionary War: The Battle of Petersburg*. E. & R. Davis, 2002.

De Chastellux, Marquis. *Travels in North America in the Years 1780, 1781, and 1782, Volume 2*. The New York Times and Arno Press, 1968.

Decher, Peter. ed., *Journal of Lt. William Feltman of the First Pennsylvania Regiment, 1781-1782*. Samen, NH: Ayer Co, 1969.

Dean, Nadia. *A Demand of Blood: The Cherokee War of 1776*, Cherokee, North Carolina: Valley River Press, 2012.

Denny, Ebenezer. *Military Journal of Major Ebenezer Denny*, Philadelphia: J.B. Lippinscott & Co., 1859.

Dixon, Max. *The Wataugans: First "free and independent community on the continent…"* Johnson City, TN: Overmountain Press, 1976.

Dorman, John. ed., *Virginia Revolutionary Pension Applications*, Vol. 12. Washington, D.C.: 1965.

Ewald, Captain Johann. *Diary of the American War: A Hessian Journal*. New Haven: Yale Univ. Press, 1979. Translated & edited by Joseph Tustin.

Fitzpatrick, John C. *The Writings of George Washington from the Original Manuscripts, 1745-1799*. Washington: U.S. Govt. Printing Office, 1931.

Force, Peter. ed., *American Archives: 5th Series*. Vol. 1-3 Washington D.C.: U.S. Congress, 1848-1853.

Ford, Worthington C., et al eds., *Journals of the Continental Congress*, Vol. 1-27, U.S. Government Print Office, 1904-37.

Friar, Robert. *The Militia are Coming in from all Quarters: The Revolution in Virginia's Lower Counties.*

Grainger, John D. *The Battle of Yorktown, 1781: A Reassessment.* Boydell Press, 2005.

Greene, Jerome A. *The Guns of Independence: The Siege of Yorktown, 1781.* California: Savas Beatie, 2005.

Hamilton, Stanislaus M., ed. *Letters to Washington & Accompanying Papers*, Vol. 5. Boston & New York: Houghton Mifflin, Co., 1902.

Hammon, Neal O., and Richard Taylor, *Virginia's Western War: 1775-1786.* Stackpole Books, 2002.

Harper, Lillie DuPuy VanCulin, ed., *Colonial Men and Times: Containing the Journal of Col. Daniel Trabue.* Innes & Sons : Philadelphia, PA, 1916.

Hartley, Cecil B., *The Life and Times of Colonel Daniel Boone...to which is added Colonel Boone's Autobiography Complete, as dictated to John Filson, and published in 1784*, Philadelphia : G. G. Evans Publisher, 1860.

Henings, William W., *The Statutes at Large Being a Collection of all the Laws of Virginia,* Vols. 5-9. Richmond: J. & G. Cochran, 1821

Hume, Ivor Noel. *1775: Another Part of the Field.*
    New York: Alfred A. Knopf, 1966.

Hunt, Gillard ed., *Eyewitness Accounts of the American Revolution: Fragments of Revolutionary History.* NY Times & Arno Press, Reprint, 1971.

Idzerda, Stanley J., ed., *Lafayette in the Age of the American Revolution: Selected Letters and Papers*, Vol. 1-3, Cornell University Press, 1980.

James, Alton James, ed., *George Rogers Clark Papers: 1771-1781*, Virginia Series, Vol. 3, Illinois State Historical Library : Springfield, Illinois, 1912.

Jackson, Donald, ed. *The Diaries of George Washington*, Vol. 3, Charlottesville: University Press of Virginia, 1978.

Johnson, Henry P. *The Yorktown Campaign and the Surrender of Cornwallis:* 1781. Eastern National, 1997. Originally printed in 1881.

Jones, Joseph. *Letters of Joseph Jones of VA:1777-87.* Washington: Dept. of State, 1889.

Journal of Continental Congress.
    (Accessed via the Library of Congress website at www.loc.gov)

Journal of the House of Delegates,1828, Richmond, Virginia State Library.

Journal of the House of Delegates, 1835-36, Doc. No. 43, Richmond, 1835, Virginia State Library.

Kapp, Friedrich. *The Life of Frederick William von Steuben.* NY: Corner House Historical Publications, 1999. (Originally published in 1859).

Kennedy, John Pendleton, ed., *Journal of the House of Burgesses*: 1773-1776, Richmond: VA, 1905.

Kranish, Michael. *Flight from Monticello: Thomas Jefferson at War.* Oxford University Press, 2010.

Laughton, John K. ed., *The Journal of Rear-Admiral Bartholomew James*, 1896.

Lee, Charles. *The Lee Papers, Vol. 1.* Collections of the New York Historical Society, 1871.

Lee, Henry. *The Revolutionary War Memoirs of General Henry Lee.* New York: Da Capo Press, 1998. Originally Published in 1812.

Lee, Nell Moore. *Patriot Above Profit: A Portrait of Thomas Nelson Jr., Who Supported the American Revolution With His Purse and Sword.* Nashville, TN: Rutledge Hill Press, 1988.

Lengel, Edward ed., *The Papers of George Washington,* Vol. 20, Charlottesville: University of Virginia Press, 2010.

Marshall, John, *The Life of George Washington,* Vol. 2. Fredericksburg, VA: The Citizens Guild of Washington's Boyhood Home, 1926.

Martin, Joseph Plum. *Private Yankee Doodle.* Eastern Acorn Press, 1962.

Mays, David John, ed., *The Letters and Papers of Edmund Pendleton*, Vol. 1. Charlottesville: University Press of Virginia, 1967.

McILwaine, H. R. ed., *Journals of the Council of the State of Virginia, Vol. 1*. Richmond, 1931.

Moore, Frank. *Diary of the American Revolution, from Newspapers and Original Documents*. 2 vols. New York: Charles Schibner, 1860. Reprint. New York: New York Times & Arno Press, 1969.

Morgan, William J., ed. *Naval Documents of the American Revolution*, Vol. 5, Washington D.C.: 1970.

Muhlenberg, Henry A. *The Life of Major-General Peter Muhlenberg*. Philadelphia: Cary and Hart, 1849.

Palmer, William ed., *Calendar of Virginia State Papers*, Vol. 1. 1875.

Pleasants, J. Hall. Ed., *Maryland Archives*, Vol. 47. Maryland Historical Society, 1930.

Posey, John Thornton. *General Thomas Posey: Son of the American Revolution*. East Lansing: Michigan State Univ. Press, 1992.

Powell, Robert. *Biographical Sketch of Col. Levin Powell, 1737-1810: Including his Correspondence during the Revolutionary War*. Alexandria, Virginia: G.H. Ramey & Son, 1877.

Rankin, Hugh F. *The War of the Revolution in Virginia*. Williamsburg, VA: Virginia Independence Bicentennial Commission, 1979.

Rice, Howard C. and Anne S. K. Brown, translated and edited. *The American Campaigns of Rochambeau's Army:* 1780-1783. Princeton, NJ: Princeton University Press, 1972. (Two Volumes)

Rutland, Robert A. ed., *The Papers of George Mason, Vol. 1.* University of North Carolina Press, 1970.

Ryan, Dennis P. *A Salute to Courage: The American Revolution as Seen Through Wartime Writings of Officers of the Continental Army and Navy.* NY: Columbia University Press, 1979.

Saffell, W.T.R. *Records of the Revolutionary War, 3rd ed.* Baltimore: Charles Saffell, 1894.

Sanchez-Saavedra, E.M. *A Guide to Virginia Military Organizations in the American Revolution, 1774-1787.* Westminster, MD: Willow Bend Books, 1978.

Scribner, Robert L., and Brent Tarter ed., (comps). *Revolutionary Virginia: The Road to Independence,* Vol. 1-7. Charlottesville: University Press of Virginia, 1973-1978.

Selby, John. *The Revolution in Virginia: 1775-1783.* Colonial Williamsburg Foundation, 1988.

Showman, Richard K. *The Papers of General Nathanael Greene.* Vol. 7, Chapel Hill: University of North Carolina Press, 1994.

Simcoe, Lt. Col. John. *Simcoe's Military Journal: A History of the Operations of a Partisan Corps Called the Queen's Rangers, Commanded by Lieut. Col. J. G. Simcoe, During the War of Revolution.* New York: New York Times and Arno Press, 1968.

Smith, Paul H. ed., *Letters of Delegates to Congress: 1774-1789*. Washington, D.C.: Library of Congress, 1976.

Sparks, Jared ed. "General Wayne to General Washington, 8 July,1781," *Correspondence of the American Revolution Being Letters of Eminent Men to George Washington*. Boston: Little, Brown, and Co.,1853.

Stedman, C. *The History of the Origin, Progress, and Termination of the American War, Volume 1 & 2*. London, 1794.

Stille, Charles. *Major-General Anthony Wayne and the Pennsylvania Line in the Continental Army*. Port Washington, NY: Kenniket Press, Inc., 1968. First published in 1893.

Tarleton, Banastre. *A History of the Campaigns of 1780 and 1781 in the Southern Provinces of North America*. North Stratford, NH: Ayer Co., Reprinted, 1999 Originally printed in 1787.

Thacher, James. *A Military Journal during the American Revolutionary War*. Hartford: CT, S. Andrus and Son, 1854. Reprint, New York: Arno Press, 1969.

Thwaites, Reuben Gold and Louise Phelps Kellogg, eds. *Frontier Defense on the Upper Ohio, 1777-1778*, Madison: Wisconsin Historical Society, 1912.

Ward, Harry M. *Duty, Honor, or Country: General George Weedon and the American Revolution*. Philadelphia: American Philosophical Society 1979.

Willcox, William B. ed., *The American Rebellion: Sir Henry Clinton's Narrative of His Campaigns, 1775-1782*, New Haven: Yale University Press, 1954.

Williams, Mrs. ed., "Life of Captain Stephen Olney of Rhode Island," *Biography of Revolutionary Heroes,* 1839.

Journals & Articles

Brown, William Dodd. "Dangerous Situation, Delayed Response: Col. John Bowman and the Kentucky Expedition of 1777," *The Register of the Kentucky Historical* Society, Vol. 97 No. 2 (Spring 1999).

Egle, Wm. H. ed., "Diary of Captain James Duncan of Colonel Moses Hazen's Regiment in the Yorktown Campaign, 1781," *Pennsylvania Archives,* 2nd Series, Vol. 15, (1890).

Elmer, Ebenezer. "The Journal of Ebenezer Elmer," *The Pennsylvania Magazine of History and Biography.* Vol. 35 Philadelphia: Historical Society of Pennsylvania, (1911).

"Expedition to Portsmouth," *The William and Mary Quarterly,* 2nd Series, Vol. 12, No. 3, (July 1932).

Fuss, Norm. "Billy Flora at the Battle of Great Bridge," *Journal of the American Revolution.* 14 October, 2014. (Online at www.allthingsliberty.com)

"Invoice of Stores found at Kemp's by the 42d or Royal Highland Regiment, May 17, 1779," *The William And Mary Quarterly,* 2nd Series, Vol. 12, No. 3 (July, 1930),

Lafferty, Maude Ward. "Destruction of Ruddle's and Martin's Forts in the Revolutionary War," *The Register of the Kentucky Historical Society,* Vol. 54, No. 189. (October, 1956).

"Major General Mathew to General Sir Henry Clinton, 16 May, 1779," *William and Mary Quarterly*, 2nd Series, Vol. 12, No. 3, (July 1932).

"Major William Galvan to Richard Peters, 8 July, 1781," *Gazette of the American Friends of LaFayette*, Vol. 1, No. 1, (February, 1942).

Macmaster, Richard K. "The Journal of Dr. Robert Honeyman," *The Virginia Magazine of History and Biography*, Vol. 79, No.4,(October, 1971).

McMichael, James. "The Diary of Lt. James McMichael of the Pennsylvania Line, 1776-1778," *The Pennsylvania Magazine of History and Biography*. Vol. 16, no. 2, (1892).

"Narrative of the Duke de Lauzun," *The Magazine of American History*, Vol. 6, (1881).

Riley, Edward M. ed., "St. George Tucker's Journal of the Siege of Yorktown, 1781, *The William and Mary Quarterly*, Vol. 5, No. 3, (July 1948),

Seymour, William. "Journal of the Southern Expedition, 1780-1783", *The Pennsylvania Magazine of History And* Biography, Vol. 7. (1883).

"Sir George Collier to General Sir Henry Clinton, May 16, 1779," *The William and Mary Quarterly*, 2nd Series, Vol. 12, No. 3 (July, 1930).

"Virginia Legislative Papers...Reports of Colonels Christian and Lewis During the Cherokee Expedition, 1776," *The Virginia Magazine of History and Biography*, Vol. 17, No. 1,(Jan. 1909).

Williams, Samuel C., "Col. Joseph Williams' Battalion in Christian's Campaign," *Tennessee Historical Magazine*, Vol. 9, No. 2, (July, 1925).

Newspapers

Caledonian Mercury, 10 October, 1781.

Connecticut Journal, 15 February, 1781.

Dixon and Hunter, *Virginia Gazette,* 28 October, 1775.

Dixon and Hunter, *Virginia Gazette*, 15 June, 1776.

Dixon and Hunter, *Virginia Gazette*, 3 August, 1776.

Dixon and Hunter, *Virginia Gazette*, 17 August, 1776

Dixon and Nicolson, *Virginia Gazette*, 26 February , 1779

Dixon and Nicolson, *Virginia Gazette*, 5 March, 1779.

Dixon and Nicolson, *Virginia Gazette*, 12 March, 1779.

Dixon and Nicolson, *Virginia Gazette,* 19 March, 1779

Dixon and Nicolson, *Virginia Gazette*, 24 April, 1779.

Dixon and Nicolson, *Virginia Gazette*, 15 May 1779

Dixon and Nicolson, *Virginia Gazette*, 22 May 1779,

Dixon and Nicolson, *Virginia Gazette*, 29 May, 1779

Dixon and Nicolson, *Virginia Gazette*, 26 June, 1779.

Dixon and Nicolson, *Virginia Gazette*, 31 July, 1779,

Dixon and Nicolson, *Virginia Gazette*, 25 September, 1779.

New York Gazette and Weekly Mercury, February 5, 1781

New York Royal Gazette, 3 February, 1781

New York Royal Gazette, 7 February, 1781

Pennsylvania Gazette and Weekly Advertiser, "Return of Killed and Wounded…" No. 2681, 31 October, 1781,

Pennsylvania Packet, 21 July, 1781.

Pinkney, *Virginia Gazette*, 26 October, 1775

Pinkney, *Virginia Gazette,* 2 November, 1775

Purdie, *Virginia Gazette, Supplement*, 30 June, 1775

Purdie, *Virginia Gazette,* 14 July, 1775

Purdie, *Virginia Gazette,* 4 August, 1775

Purdie, *Virginia Gazette*, 1 March, 1776

Purdie *Virginia Gazette,* 8 March, 1776

Purdie, *Virginia Gazette*, 26 April,

Purdie, *Virginia Gazette*, 12 July, 1776

Purdie, *Virginia Gazette*, 9 August, 1776

Royal Georgia Gazette, 8 March, 1781

Unpublished Sources

"Embarkation Return for the Following Corps, 11 December, 1780, New York," *Sir Henry Clinton Papers*, Vol. 113, item 15, University of Michigan, William L. Clements Library.

Goodwin, Mary. *Clothing and Accoutrements of the Officers and Soldiers of the Virginia Forces: 1775-1780*. 1962

Orderly Book of the Company of Captain George Stubblefield, Fifth Virginia Regiment From March 3 to July 10, 1776. Accessed via www.revwar75.com

Posey, Thomas. "*A Short Biography of the Life of Governor Thomas Posey*," Thomas Posey Papers. Indiana Historical Society Library, Indianapolis, IN.

Posey, Thomas. "Thomas Posey's Revolutionary War Journal," *Thomas Posey Papers*. Indiana Historical Society Library, Indianapolis, IN

Index

1st Continental Dragoon Regiment, 154
8th Regiment of Foot, 162
14th Regiment of Foot, 10, 15-16, 33, 45, 49, 57, 61, 67, 70
17th Light Dragoon Regiment, 168
33rd Regiment of Foot, 339
42nd Highland Regiment, 142, 155
43rd Regiment of Foot, 339
71st Regiment of Foot, 320
76th Regiment of Foot, 338
80th Endinburgh Royal Volunteers Regiment, 180, 184, 201, 203, 211, 224, 225, 226, 261, 289, 297, 301, 338, 339

A

Abercrombie, Lt. Col. Robert, 291, 297, 388
Abington Church, 353
Albemarle County, VA, 4, 7
Alexandria, VA, 78, 153, 274, 276, 281, 282, 283
Allen, Lt., 16, 291
Alston, Lt., 338
Althouse, Capt. John, 181, 186, 201, 203, 211
Amelia County, VA, 290, 294, 348
Amphitrite HMS, 180
Anderson Bridge, 314
Andre' Maj. John, 179
Andrew Doria, (ship) 101-102
Annapolis, MD, 266, 272
Apollo, (ship), 302
Armand, Lt. Col. Charles, 236, 365, 368
Armistead, James, 193, 349-350, 357
Armstrong, Major, 327, 330
Arnold, Gen. Benedict, 178-182,
  expedition to Virginia, 184, 186, 188-189, 193-196, 199-205
  attacks Richmond, 206, 208, 210-218,
  returns to Portsmouth, 219, 221-227, 229-231

occupies Portsmouth, 233-234, 236, 238-240, 246-247, 257-261, 263-266, 268, 270, 272,
sails up James River, 289, 292, 300-301,
attacks Osborne's Landing, 302, 303-304,
departs for NY, 310
Arundel, Capt. Dohickey, 106
Augusta County, VA, 135
Augusta County Militia, 196

B

Bailey, Lt. 137
Balvaird, Lt., 338
Barnes, Richard, 277
Barron, Capt. James, 77, 101, 182
  Commodore, 271
Barron, Capt. Richard, 102, 271
Batut, Lt. John, 56, 64, 67
Bedford County, VA, 347
Bellew, Capt. Henry, 76, 80-82
Betsy (ship), 10
Bickell, Lt., 243, 245, 268, 270, 331
Bird, Capt. Henry, 162-164
Blackburn, Thomas, 61
Bland, Col. Theordorick, 64, 154, 223, 295
Blandford, VA, 295, 297
Blonde HMS, 168
Bolling, Mary, 295
Bonetta HMS, 180
Boone, Capt. Daniel, 118-119, 124-127, 318
Boone, Rebecca, 125
Boone, Squire, 127
Boonesborough, KY, 114, 117-120, 124, 163
  siege of, 125-129
Boston, MA, 6, 10, 11, 17, 39, 45, 79, 101, 335
Botetourt County Militia, 255
Bottom's Bridge, VA, 308
Bowman, Capt. Joseph, 136-137
Bowman, Col. John, 120, 127, 162
Brandon Plantation, 305
Brandywine
  battle of, 108, 152, 159, 229
Brent, William, 108
Brigade of Guards, 168, 339

British Legion, 249
Buford, Capt. Abraham,
  23-24, 26
Burgoyne, Gen. John, 319
Burwell, Nathanael, 194
Burwell's Ferry, 30, 92,
  193, 194, 195, 196, 290,
  291
Butler, Lt. Col. Richard,
  329, 373
Byrd, William, 202

C

Cabin Point, VA, 171-172,
  227, 235-236, 293
Cahokia, IL, 133
Call, Maj. Richard, 246,
  335, 337, 339
Camden,
  battle of, 166, 177
Campbell, Gen. William,
  325
Caroline County, VA, 8,
  90, 279-281
Cary, Colonel, 24
Cary, Archibald, 317
Cedar Point, MD, 274,
  276-277
Charles City Courthouse,
  raid on, 219-221

Charleston, SC, 166, 186,
  307, 391
Charlottesville, VA, 152,
  173, 197, 315, 316, 317,
  318, 319, 320
Charon HMS, 180, 184,
  189, 191, 265
Chasellux, Marquis de,
  285, 286
Cherokee Expedition of
  1776, 114-118
Cherokee Indians, 109,
  110, 112-117
Chesterfield Courthouse,
  197, 234, 294, 301, 304
Chief Black Fish, 119, 124
Chief Cornstalk, 123
Chief Pluggy, 117
Chillicothe, OH, 124, 162,
  164
Choisy, Marquis de, 368
Christian, Col. William,
  114-116
City Point, VA, 294, 297,
  306
Clark, Col. George Rogers
  Clark, 119-120, 127,
  129-140, 162, 164, 165,
  222
Clinton, Gen. Henry, 87,
  142, 148, 154-156, 158,

160, 167-170, 177-178, 180-182, 193, 202, 212, 214, 216, 223, 225-226, 289, 300-301, 311, 315, 325, 333-334, 337, 347-349, 361, 364-366, 378, 389-390
Cocke, Col. James, 200, 201
Coles, John, 319
Collier, Commodore Sir George, 142, 144, 145, 146, 155, 156, 157, 158, 160, 165
Connolly, Dr. John, 78
Connolly, George, 298
Continental Congress, 90, 93
Corbin's Bridge, VA, 314
Cornwallis, (ship), 193, 201
Cornwallis, Gen. Charles, 146, 167, 169, 170, 174, 175, 177, 234,
  race to the Dan, 249, 250, 251, 252, 253, 254, 255, 256
  in Virginia, 305, 307-312, 314-317, 320, 322, 324-327, 330, 333-335, 337-342, 344-350,
  at Yorktown, 351, 353-354, 356-357, 360, 362-367, 378-379, 381, 383, 388-391
Cowpens,
  battle of, 234, 247, 249, 256
Cuckoo Tavern, 317
Culpeper County, VA, 316
Culpeper Minutemen, 23-24, 28, 31, 42-43, 50, 62, 66
Cumberland County, VA, 7, 152,
Cumberland County Militia, 290

D

Daingerfield, Col. William, 96-98
Dartmouth, Lord, 2, 5-6, 11, 14, 16-17, 21, 25-26, 35, 37, 40-41, 47, 55, 57-58, 67-69, 72-73, 75, 82, 84
Delight HMS, 168
Denny, Ebenezer, 343-344
DePeyster, Maj. Arent, 163
Destouches, Chevalier, 271
Detroit, MI, 124, 126, 129-130, 133, 163-164

Dick, Lt. Col. John, 295
Digby, Admiral Robert, 364-365
Dinwiddie County, VA, 290, 294
Dragging Canoe, 110, 113, 116
Dumfries, VA, 88, 280
Duncan, Capt. James, 375, 376
Dundas, Lt. Col. Thomas, 180, 203, 226, 262, 291, 297, 339
Dunmore (ship), 104-105
Dunmore, Earl of John Murray, 1-2, 4-7, 10-11, 14-17, 19, 21, 25-33, 35-41, 43, 45, 109, 120-121, 123, 140, 142, 144
 battle of Great Bridge, 46- 48, 50, 52-59, 61, 65-69
 Norfolk abandoned and burned, 70, 72- 75, 77-85
at Tucker's Point 86, 87, 88-90, 93,
at Gwynn's Island, 94, 96-106, 108,
Dunmore's Ethiopian Regiment, 41
Dunmore's Proclamation, 38

E

Eilbeck, (ship) 14, 32, 79
Elk Hill Plantation, 324
Epperson, Capt., 298
Ewald, Capt. Johann, 180, 194-195, 201-205, 217, 219, 221, 223,
 skirmish at Warwick, 186-188
 attacks Richmond, 208-213
 ambush at Hood's Point, 224-226,
 battle of Mackie's Mill, 230-231
 occupies Portsmouth, 238-242, 244, 246-247, 257-258, 263-265,
 wounded at Scott's Creek, 268,-270
 at Spencer's Ordinary, 327, 329- 333
 at Yorktown, 353, 354, 366, 376, 389

F

Fairfax County, VA, 96, 274, 279-280

Faulkner, Lt. Col. Ralph, 295, 297-298
Feltman, Lt. William, 343, 379, 388
Ferguson, Maj. Patrick, 169, 175, 177
Fincastle County, VA, 114
Fitzpatrick, Lt., 303
Flora, Billy, 59
Fordyce, Capt. Charles, 61, 63-64, 67
Forsyth, Major Robert, 151, 153
Fort Henry, 121-122
Fort Nelson, 144, 146-147, 155, 158, 161
Fort Pitt, 120, 122, 132, 135
Fort Randolph, 120, 123
Fort Ticonderoga, 178
Fort Watuaga, 109-110, 113
Fowey, HMS, 2, 4-5, 10, 96, 102, 180, 265
Fredericksburg, VA, 62, 153, 236, 276, 308-309, 312, 314-315, 326
French and Indian War, 7-8

G

Galvan, Maj. William, 335, 341-342, 344
Gates, Gen. Horatio, 166, 171, 177, 181
Gayton, Commodore George, 169
Georgetown, KY, 117
Georgetown, MD, 282
Georgetown, SC, 117, 256, 282
Germain, Lord George, 88, 100, 101-102, 105, 142, 144-146, 156-157, 168-169, 254, 361
Germantown
  battle of, 108, 152, 159, 229
Gilmer, Lt. George, 7
Gloucester County, VA, 23, 54, 94, 96, 365, 367
Gloucester Courthouse, VA, 99
Gloucester Point, 351, 353-354, 356, 362-363, 368-369, 372, 389
  battle of, 368-372
Goochland County, VA, 4, 290, 320, 324
Goode's Bridge, 348, 350

Gosport, VA, 45, 84, 146, 147, 158
Grasse, Admiral de, 358, 360, 361,-363, 366
Graves, Capt. Thomas, 286-287, 361
Great Bridge, VA, 35-36, 43, 45-46, 48, 50, 54-55 72-73, 77, 86, 145, 147, 154, 168, 170, 174, 229, 238-241, 247, 259-261, 263-264
battle of, 59-70,
Green, Lt. 31
Green Spring
   battle of, 335-347
Greene, Gen. Nathanael, 151, 153, 166, 183, 215, 222, 234, 246, 249, 250, 251, 252, 253, 254, 255, 256, 257, 259, 294, 295, 299, 300, 301, 307, 308, 310, 311, 320, 321, 324, 347, 356, 363, 365, 372, 375, 386, 387, 391
Gregory, Gen. Isaac, 247, 259, 260, 261
Guadaloupe HMS, 265
Guilford Courthouse
   battle of 249, 257, 307

Gwynn's Island,
   battle of, 94-108

H

Halifax County, VA, 250
Halifax, Nova Scotia, 101
Hamilton, Lt. Col.
   Alexander, 375, 383
Hamilton, Lt. Gov. Henry, 124, 126, 129-130 133-139
Hamond, Capt. Andrew, 94, 96- 99, 101-106
Hampton, VA, 11-12, 14, 30, 35, 77, 102, 150-151, 158-159, 191, 271, 349
   battle of, 1775, 19-28
   raided 1780, 169-179
   raided 1781, 184-186,
   skirmish at, 261-262
Hanover County, VA, 8, 316, 320
Hanover County Militia, 290
Hanover Courthouse, VA, 312, 314
Harlem Heights, NY, 159
Harris, John, 338-340
Harrison, Benjamin, 204-205, 317-318
Harrod, Major, 193

Harrodsburg, KY, 114, 117-118, 120, 127
Hawk, (pilot boat), 25
Hawthorne, Capt., 184-185
Head of Elk, MD, 358, 361
Heath, Gen. William, 360
Helm, Capt. Leonard, 134
Henrico County, VA, 204, 289, 290
Henry County Militia, 255
Henry, Patrick, 1, 8, 89-91, 114, 116, 130, 136, 148, 150, 168
Hessian Regiment von Bose, 168
Hillsborough, NC, 256
Hog Island, 189, 305
Holland, 141
Holland, Lt., 220
Holt, John, 14
Hood's Point, ambush, 222-226
Hooes Ferry, VA, 277, 280, 281
Hooes, Gerrard, 277
Hope HMS, 180, 193, 201
House of Burgesses, 2
Howard, Lt. Col. John, 249
Howe, Col. Robert, 73-76, 80, 82-86
Howe, Gen. William, 17, 39-40, 45-46, 101, 108
Huntington, Samuel, 174
Hutchings, Col., 37-38
Hunter's Iron Works, 308

I

Innis, Lt. Col. James, 193, 194
Irvine, Gen. William, 355
Isle of Wight County, VA, 226
Isle of Wight Militia, 229

J

James, Lt. Bartholomew, 184, 186, 190, 377, 382
James City County Militia, 4
Jamestown Island, 30, 35, 92, 102, 195, 199, 226, 291, 335, 337, 339, 340, 361, 365
Jefferson (ship), 302
Jefferson, Thomas, 23, 31, 41, 164, 168-169, 171-174, 182-183, 189, 193-194, 196-197, 199, 204-205, 211, 213- 216, 218, 222, 227, 232, 235, 255-256, 263, 271-274, 276-

283, 289-291, 293-294, 300, 302, 312, 314-317, 319, 324
Jenifer, Daniel, 278
Jouett, Jack, 317

K

Kaskaskia, IL, 130, 132, 134-136
Kelly, Sergeant, 219-220
Kemp's Landing, VA battle of, 35-38
Kenton, Simon, 119
King Fisher, HMS, 31-32, 70, 79
King George County, VA, 4, 276, 277, 279
King William County, VA, 356
Kings Mill, VA, 193-194
Knox, Gen. Henry, 356-357

L

LaFayette, Gen Marquis de, 260, 265-266, 268, 270, 272-273, 284, 288, 293, 300, 302, 304-305, 308- 312, 314-316, 321, 324-327, 333, 335, 337, 340, 342, 347-351, 353-362, 384
Lauzun, Gen. Armand, 368-370
Lawson, Col. Robert, 36, 37, 148, 151-152, 171, General, 234-236
Lee, Gen. Charles, 91-93, 99-101
Lee, Gov. Thomas Sims, 277-278, 288, 377
Lee, "Light Horse Harry", 249, 276
Lee Sr., Henry, 276, 280
Lee, Richard Henry, 79, 93, 281
Lee, Thomas Ludwell, 53
Lee's Legion, 249, 251-52, 254-255
Leslie, Capt. Samual, 15-17, 35-37, 45, 56-59
Leslie, General Alexander, 167-170, 172-175, 177, 257
Leslie, Lt. Peter, 66
Lewis, Gen. Andrew, 90, 99-101, 103, 106, 115-116
Lewis, Capt. William, 302
Lexington and Concord, 1
Liberty (ship), 77, 101, 182

Lincoln, Gen. Benjamin, 142
Liverpool, HMS, 76, 79, 80, 81, 87
London, HMS, 271
London Bridge, VA, 243, 244
Louisa County, VA, 316-317, 324
Louisa County Militia, 4
Loyal American Regiment, 181
Luzerne, Chevalier de la, 309, 311, 325-326
Lyles, Col., 283, 288
Lyne, Capt., 21-22, 27

M

Mackie's Mill battle of, 229-231
MacLeod, Capt. Kenneth, 319
Magdalen, HMS, 1, 4
Malvern Hill, VA, 348
Manchester, VA, 213, 290, 304-305
Marshall, Lt. John, 62, 159
Marshall, Maj. Thomas, 151, 158-159
Martin, Joseph Plum, 373, 385
Mason, Capt. Samuel, 121
Mason, George, 121, 135, 137-138, 276
Mathew, Gen. Edward, 142, 147-148, 154-155, 157-158, 160, 165
Mathias Point, VA, 274, 276, 281, 282
Matthews, Maj. Thomas, 145, 146-147, 158, 161
Mattopony Church, 314
McClellan's Station, 114
McPherson, Maj. William, 329, 333, 335, 339
Mercer, Hugh, 99,
Mercer, Lt. Col. James, 335, 337- 341, 371-372
Mercury, HMS, 10
Merriweather, Lt. Col. Thomas, 295
Mingo Indians, 117, 129
Mitchell, Richard, 282-283
Montgomery County Militia, 255
Monticello Plantation, 189, 317, 319
Morgan, Gen. Daniel, 94, 97, 99, 101-105, 107, 234, 249-250
Morris, Joseph, 366, 373

Mounmouth,
 battle of, 108, 152
Mount Vernon, 284, 286, 287, 361
Muhlenberg, Gen. Peter, 171-172, 235-236, 246-247, 259-260, 266, 293-294, 300-301
Murray, Capt., 223

N

Nansemond County Militia, 190-191, 229
Nelson, Capt. Hugh, 159
Nelson Jr., Gen. Thomas, 151, 159, 168, 171-172, 182-183, 193, 195-197, 215, 218, 232, 236, 289, 317, 326, 333, 359, 376
New Kent County, VA, 215, 327, 333, 356
New Kent County Militia, 4
New London, VA, 347
New York Highlands, 360
Newcastle, VA, 314, 326, 351
Newport News, VA, 168-169, 184, 186, 189, 192
Newtown, VA, 16

Nicholas, Capt. George, 21-22, 24, 26, 48
Norfolk, VA, 7, 10, 14-16, 19, 28-30, 32-35, 39, 41, 43, 45-46, 52-54, 57, 59, 68-70, 73-74, 76, 79, 90, 94, 100, 103, 144, 154, 229, 236-239,
 burned, 80-86,
Northumberland County, VA, 274
Northwest Landing, 244

O

Old Albemarle Courthouse, 315
Old Point Comfort, VA, 349
Olney, Capt. Stephen, 384-385, 402
Orange County, VA, 324
Osborne's Landing, VA 301, 309
 battle of, 302-305
Otter, HMS, 5-6, 10-12, 26, 32, 57, 61, 63, 70, 74, 75, 79-80, 96, 144
Oxford (ship), 101, 189

P

Page, John, 23-25, 31, 32, 37-38, 41, 54
Parker, Col. Josiah, 99, 171-172, 229-230, 236, 259-61, 263, 348
Patriot (ship), 102, 376
Patton, William, 128
Pendleton, Edmund, 30-31, 43, 47-48, 51-52, 55-56, 60, 62, 67-69, 75-76, 86, 90, 152, 175,
Petersburg, VA, 167, 169-170, 178, 196-197, 204, 215, 222, 289, 305, 308-310, 348
battle of, 294-301
Phillips, Gen. William, 272, 288-289, 291-294, 297-298, 300-302, 304-305, 308-310
Piqua, OH, 164, 165
Pittsylvania County Militia, 255
Point of Fork, 315-316, 320-324
Point Pleasant, 109, 120, 123
Popp, Stephen, 376
Port Tobacco, MD, 278
Portsmouth, VA, 10, 43, 45, 86, 140, 143-147, 150, 152, 154-156, 158, 168-170, 172- 175, 182, 185, 221, 227, 229, 231-233, 236, 238-240, 246-247, 257-261, 263-266, 268, 270, 272-273, 289, 308, 310, 334-335, 347-350
Posey, Capt. Thomas, 96-98, 105-107
Powhatan County, VA, 247, 290
Prince Edward Courthous, 347
Prince George County, 305
Prince George Courthouse, 222
Prince William County, VA, 276, 280, 281
Princess Anne County, VA, 15, 28, 34-35, 41, 149, 154, 182, 229, 236-240, 257, 353
Princeton,
battle of, 108, 152, 159, 229
Pungo Church, 244

Q

Queen's Own Loyal Virginia Regiment, 40

R

Race to the Dan, 247-255
Rainbow HMS, 142, 144, 145
Raisonable HMS, 142, 144
Raleigh Tavern, 91
Randolph, William, 309
Reed, Edmund, 281
Renown, (ship) 302
Richmond, VA, 8, 10, 17, 162, 167, 169-170, 173, 178, 182-183, 193-194, 196-197, 199, 203-205, 222, 233, 235, 255, 259, 279, 289, 292-294, 302, 305, 308-309, 311, 317, 324-326, 348
  raided by Arnold,, 206-217
Robinson Jr., Col. Beverly, 181, 203, 211, 224-225
Rochambeau, General, 360-361, 365-366, 381, 387
Rockbridge County, VA, 196
Rockingham County, VA, 196
Roebuck, HMS, 86, 96, 97, 104
Romulus HMS, 168, 247
Russia, 141
Rutledge, Edward, 372, 376

S

Saratoga,
  battle of, 108, 173, 177, 179, 272, 319
Savage HMS, 273, 274, 284, 286, 287
Scotchtown, 314
Scott, Charles,
  Capt., 7
  Lt. Col. 43, 46-48, 50-52, 54- 56
  Gen., 152-154
Scott's Creek,
  skirmish at, 268-270
Sewell's Ordinary, 353
Shank, Capt., 242-243, 321, 329
Shawnee Indians, 90, 109, 117-121, 123-127, 129, 162, 164-165
Shelby, Capt. Evan, 114
Shelby, Capt. James, 112

Shenandoah County, VA, 196
Shepherdstown, VA, 394
Shippen, Peggy, 202
Simcoe, Lt. Col. John, 180, 199-203, 205-206, 208-212, 217, 219-224, 226, 229-231, 240-241, 244, 246-247, 261-262, 289-290, 292, 300, 303, 315-316, 320-324, 326-327, 329-333, 350, 354, 370
Skinker, John, 277-279, 282
Slaughter, Lt. Col. John, 295
Sleepy Hole, VA, 236, 266
Smith, Capt. William Baily, 120
Smithfield, VA, 148, 150-153, 171-172, 227, 229, 236
Spain, 141
Spotswood, Maj. Thomas, 45, 60- 62, 65-66
Spotsylvania County, VA, 4
Sprowles, Andrew, 45, 84
Squire, Capt. Matthew, 5, 11-12, 14-15, 19, 22-23, 35, 74-75, 80, 127

St. Augustine, FL, 10, 108
St. Mary's County, MD, 274, 277
St.. George's Island, MD, 277
Stafford County, VA, 4, 53, 108, 274, 279-280
Steuben, Gen. Friedrich von, 183, 193, 197, 204, 213, 215, 222, 227, 229, 232-236, 256-257, 259-260, 271, 294-295, 299, 300-302, 304, 314-315, 320-326
Stevens, Col. Edward, 50-51, 66
Stewart, Col. Walter, 335
Stratford Hall Plantation, 281, 300, 401
Suffolk, VA, 43, 46, 86, 88, 147-150, 152-153, 170, 174, 190, 236, 259, 263, 265, 268, 293
Surprise (ship), 273-274, 276
Surry County, VA, 226
Swift HMS, 193
Sycamore Shoals, TN, 110, 113
Symonds, Commodore Thomas, 180, 273

T

Tarleton, Lt. Col. Banastre, 249, 254, 300-301, 311, 315-320, 324-326, 333, 339, 344, 347-350, 366, 368-372
Tatham, Williams, 193
Tempest (ship), 302, 304
Thacher, Dr. James, 373, 380,-383, 388-389
Tibbs, Lt., 47
Trabue, Daniel, 128, 297-299, 380
Travis, Lt. Edward, 60-61
Treaty of Hard Labour, 109
Treaty of Lochaber, 109
Trenton, battle of 108, 152, 159, 177, 229
Trimer (ship, 273, 274, 276
Tuckahoe Plantation, 213
Turkey Island Creek, 312

V

Valley Forge, PA, 152, 183
Vincennes, IN, 133-137, 139, 162, 222
Virginia Committee of Safety, 28-29, 31-33, 48, 51, 53-54, 70, 75-77, 88, 90

Virginia Conventions
3rd, 10
4th, 51, 53, 77, 86
5th, 94
Virginia Continental Regiments,
1st Regiment, 88-90
2nd Regiment, 21, 23, 28, 43, 88, 90
3rd Regiment, 88
4th Regiment, 88, 229
5th Regiment, 88, 92
6th Regiment, 88
7th Regiment, 88, 92
8th Regiment, 88
Virginia State Navy, destroyed, 303-304
Volunteers of Ireland, 142

W

Wagner, Peter, 274
Walker, Dr. Thomas, 318
Waller's Grove, 7
Warwick, VA, 186, 188-189
Washington County Militia, 255
Washington, Gen. George, 79, 92, 96, 108, 142, 144, 149, 152-154, 157, 160-161, 165, 249, 265,

270, 272, 278, 287, 300, 304-305, 308, 318, 326, 335, 343, 345, 348-351, 356-362,
  incident at Mount Vernon, 284-286
  marches south, 360-362
  at Yorktown, 365, 366-367, 372-373, 375, 377, 379, 383, 391-392
Washington, Lund, 284-286
Washington, Martha, 361-362
Washington, Robert, 278
Wayne, Gen. Anthony, 310, 312-316, 324-326, 335, 348, 350-351, 355-356, 359
  at Battle of Green Spring, 337-345,
Weedon, Gen. George, 171-173, 236, 266, 271, 305, 309-310, 314, 326, 365, 367-368
Weeks, Maj. Amos, 239-247, 263-264, 353-354
Wemys, Lt., 338
West Point, NY, 144, 179, 261,
West Point, VA, 359-360

Westham Foundry, 211, 213, 215-216
Westmoreland County, VA, 277, 279, 281
Westover Plantation, 202-205, 214, 217-219, 221, 292-293, 311-312, 359
William & Mary, College Company, 159
Williams, Col. Otho, 250-255
Williamsburg, VA, 1, 2, 4, 7-8, 12, 23, 28, 30, 32, 39, 45-46, 48, 50-51, 53, 55, 70, 77, 86-88, 91-92, 97, 99, 101-103, 105, 107, 140, 151-154, 159, 161, 169, 193, 196, 236, 266, 271, 279, 281, 289-293, 302, 308, 326-327, 329-330, 332-335, 362, 364-365
Williamsburg Independent Militia Company, 4
Willis, Major, 227, 236
Wilmington, NC, 307-308
Wilton Plantation, 183, 197, 309, 311
Winchester, VA, 154, 276, 319, 391

Wolf Hills, VA, 110, 114
Woodford, Col. William, 8, 30, 32-33, 41-42, 73-76, 84, 86, 88, 90,
  at Battle of Hampton, 23-29
at Battle of Great Bridge, 43-69
Wray, Jacob, 182
Wright, Lt., 25, 27

Y

Yorke, Lt. Col. John, 339
Yorktown, VA, 4-5, 10, 92, 100, 151, 182, 266, 292, 326, 333-334, 346, 349, 351, 353-354, 356-357, 359-363, 365
Yorktown, Siege of, 366-392

www.ingramcontent.com/pod-product-compliance
Lightning Source LLC
Chambersburg PA
CBHW050831230426
43667CB00012B/1952